ROMANTICISM AND THE PAINFUL PLEASURES OF MODERN LIFE

Writers of the Romantic period were fascinated by experiences of pain and misery, and explored the ability to derive pleasure, and produce creative energy, out of suffering and submission. These interests were closely connected to the failure of the industrial and democratic revolutions to fulfill their promise of increased economic and political power for everyone. Writers as different as Frances Burney, William Hazlitt, John Keats, and Lord Byron both challenged and came to terms with the injustices of modern life through their representations of willing submission. Andrea K. Henderson teases out these configurations and analyzes the many ways in which ideas of mastery and subjection shaped Romantic artistic forms, from literature and art to architecture and garden design. This provocative and ambitious study ranges widely through early nineteenth-century culture to reveal the underlying power relations that shaped Romanticism.

ANDREA K. HENDERSON is Associate Professor of English at the University of California, Irvine.

CAMBRIDGE STUDIES IN ROMANTICISM

This series aims to foster the best new work in one of the most challenging fields within English literary studies. From the early 1780s to the early 1830s a formidable array of talented men and women took to literary composition, not just in poetry, which some of them famously transformed, but in many modes of writing. The expansion of publishing created new opportunities for writers, and the political stakes of what they wrote were raised again by what Wordsworth called those "great national events" that were "almost daily taking place": the French Revolution, the Napoleonic and American wars, urbanization, industrialization, religious revival, an expanded empire abroad and the reform movement at home. This was an enormous ambition, even when it pretended otherwise. The relations between science, philosophy, religion, and literature were reworked in texts such as *Frankenstein* and *Biographia Literaria*; gender relations in *Vindication of the Rights of Woman* and *Don Juan*; journalism by Cobbett and Hazlitt; poetic form, content, and style by the Lake School and the Cockney School. Outside Shakespeare studies, probably no body of writing has produced such a wealth of comment or done so much to shape the responses of modern criticism. This indeed is the period that saw the emergence of those notions of "literature" and of literary history, especially national literary history, on which modern scholarship in English has been founded.

The categories produced by Romanticism have also been challenged by recent historicist arguments. The task of the series is to engage both with a challenging corpus of Romantic writings and with the changing field of criticism they have helped to shape. As with other literary series published by Cambridge, this one will represent the work of both younger and more established scholars, on either side of the Atlantic and elsewhere.

For a complete list of titles published see end of book.

ROMANTICISM AND THE PAINFUL PLEASURES OF MODERN LIFE

ANDREA K. HENDERSON

CAMBRIDGE
UNIVERSITY PRESS

CAMBRIDGE UNIVERSITY PRESS
Cambridge, New York, Melbourne, Madrid, Cape Town,
Singapore, São Paulo, Delhi, Mexico City

Cambridge University Press
The Edinburgh Building, Cambridge CB2 8RU, UK

Published in the United States of America by Cambridge University Press, New York

www.cambridge.org
Information on this title: www.cambridge.org/9780521884020

First published 2008
First paperback edition 2011

A catalogue record for this publication is available from the British Library

ISBN 978-0-521-88402-0 Hardback
ISBN 978-0-521-17544-9 Paperback

For Michael and Clara

Contents

List of illustrations

Acknowledgments

Marjorie Levinson, Carla Mazzio, Adela Pinch, Michael Schoenfeldt, Rei Terada, Yopie Prins, Marlon Ross, Lisa Freeman, and Kerry Larson all provided vital commentary and encouragement throughout the drafting of this book. I owe its completion to their example, their criticism, and their friendship.

This project got its start during my time at the Michigan Society of Fellows, under the headship of James Boyd White; I am grateful to the Society and to the University of Michigan English department for their support in the early phases of the book's preparation. The Humanities Center at the University of California, Irvine provided support at the end of the process. Alan Bewell, Marshall Brown, Jerry Hogle, Geri Friedman, Laura Mandell, Anne Mellor, Mark Schoenfield, Teresa Goddu, Jay Grossman, George Bornstein, Stuart Curran, Jay Clayton, and Valerie Traub read portions of the manuscript and have been unflaggingly helpful and generous interlocutors. Hugh Roberts, Jerry Christensen, Jayne Lewis, Richard Kroll, Ann Van Sant, Victoria Silver, and Jim Steintrager all offered valuable advice at the final, and most difficult, stages of composition, as did my readers at Cambridge and my editors, Jim Chandler and Linda Bree.

Michael Szalay, who patiently read draft after draft, helped me to reconceive the book in crucial ways. Its final form owes much to him. It is he and Clara Szalay, along with Glenn, Dorothy, and Teri Henderson, who have kept me going through the rough spots.

Two sections of Chapter 2 originally appeared elsewhere in somewhat different form: one as "Commerce and Masochistic Desire in the 1790s: Frances Burney's *Camilla*" (*Eighteenth-Century Studies* 31:1) and the other as "Burney's *The Wanderer* and Early-Nineteenth-Century Commodity Fetishism" (*Nineteenth-Century Literature* 57:1). A portion of Chapter 3 appeared as "Passion and Fashion in Joanna Baillie's 'Introductory Discourse,'" in *PMLA* 112:2. I am grateful to those publishers for allowing me to reprint modified versions of that material here.

Introduction: Submitting to liberty

> She burnt, she lov'd the tyranny.
> – John Keats, "Lamia", (1820)[1]

In 1933 Mario Praz argued that the literature of the nineteenth century was characterized by a fascination with "the mysterious bond between pleasure and suffering." Indeed, *The Romantic Agony* treats the peculiar "erotic sensibility" of nineteenth-century literature as its most salient feature. Seventy years later, the canon of British Romantic literature looks rather different, but the "sexual idiosyncrasies" Praz described still figure prominently in it.[2] Not only do critics speak of a masochistic impulse in the lives and works of figures such as Samuel Taylor Coleridge and John Keats,[3] but many of the protagonists of the literature of the period seem to enjoy submission and suffering. Thus in William Hazlitt's *Liber Amoris* (1823), H asks his adored S, "How can I escape from you, when every new occasion, even your cruelty and scorn, brings out some new charm. Nay, your rejection of me, by the way in which you do it, is only a new link added to my chain."[4] Charlotte Smith, in her *Elegiac Sonnets* (1784), writes an ode in which the speaker "woo[s]" Despair by promising him "a willing victim, / Who seeks thine iron sway – and calls thee kind!"[5] The desire of these

---

[1] John Keats, "Lamia," in Keats, *Complete Poems*, ed. Jack Stillinger (Cambridge, Mass.: Harvard University Press, 1978), 353; Part II, l. 81.
[2] Mario Praz, *The Romantic Agony*, 2nd edn, trans. Angus Davidson (Oxford: Oxford University Press, 1970), xxi, xv, xv.
[3] W. Jackson Bate describes Coleridge's tendency, throughout his life, toward "apologetic self-abasement" (*Coleridge* [Cambridge, Mass.: Harvard University Press, 1987], 2), and Richard Holmes, Coleridge's most recent biographer, speaks of "masochistic displacement" as typical of Coleridge (*Coleridge: Darker Reflections, 1804–1834* [New York: Pantheon, 1998], 40). Lionel Trilling remarks that "Keats's mind was profoundly engaged by the paradox of the literary genre of tragedy, which must always puzzle us because it seems to propose to the self a gratification in regarding its own extinction" (*Freud and the Crisis of Our Culture* [Boston: Beacon Press, 1955], 25).
[4] William Hazlitt, *Liber Amoris or The New Pygmalion*, intro. Michael Neve (London: Hogarth Press, 1985), 12–13.
[5] Charlotte Smith, "Ode to Despair," from Smith's novel *Emmeline* (1788), and reprinted in *Elegiac Sonnets* (*The Poems of Charlotte Smith*, ed. Stuart Curran [Oxford: Oxford University Press, 1993], 79). The logic

heroes and heroines of Romantic literature would seem to be precisely for the painful nonsatisfaction of desire: they are attracted most to those people who keep them in suspense, dominate them, and even humiliate them. Their lovers are *belles dames sans merci* and "Barbarous, unfeeling, unpitying" men whom they nevertheless not only find irresistible but actively idealize.[6]

Praz's study, which is largely descriptive, takes for granted the attractions of such "perversities."[7] Viewed historically, however, Praz's thesis raises a pressing question: how is it that a body of literature renowned for its articulation of new ideologies of equality could also be characterized by a fascination with willing submission? Why is it that a canonical touchstone such as William Wordsworth's "Preface" to the *Lyrical Ballads* (1802), which opens with an argument for the dignity of the common man, goes on to speak so longingly of the value of "real and substantial action and *suffering*"?[8] What attracted writers devoted to the idea of social progress and even revolution to representations of suspense and delay? Why should poets and novelists who highly valued artistic originality and social change also be drawn to medieval literary forms and the fixed hierarchies they embodied?

This book will show that it was precisely the failed advent of modernity – with its promise of increased economic and political power for everyone – that gave rise to these ambivalences and apparent contradictions. I argue that the Romantic agony turns on the aesthetic management of what one historian has called the "revolutions in rising frustrations."[9] On the one hand, industrialization made power and comfort in the form of commodities more available than ever before. On the other, the necessary limitations of personal means relative to such large-scale production taught that living in

of the poem is that despair is at least less painful than hope, but the poem's *frisson* arises from the speaker's active courtship of what she acknowledges as a "fatal power."

[6] The first phrase is of course a reference to Keats's poem; the second is from Mary Hays's *The Memoirs of Emma Courtney*, ed. Eleanor Ty (Oxford: Oxford University Press, 1996), 126.

[7] The word is Frank Kermode's, from his foreword to *The Romantic Agony*. He sums up Praz's work as a study of "the perversities of pleasure and pain" (Praz, *Romantic Agony*, v).

[8] William Wordsworth, "Preface," in Wordsworth, *Lyrical Ballads*, ed. R. L. Brett and A. R. Jones (New York: Methuen, 1963), 256, emphasis mine. While Wordsworth's primary concern is to distinguish the merely imitative passions of the poet from the lived experience of the subjects he treats, it is nevertheless striking that he so readily assumes that suffering – not only a painful but also a passive state – can be linked to "freedom and power" (256). In Wordsworth's poetics the suffering of another is the object of the poet's envy, the object of his desire. His aim is to "bring his feelings near to those of the persons whose feelings he describes" (256), and even to question the feasibility of this project would be to give way to "unmanly despair" (257).

[9] Colin Campbell, *The Romantic Ethic and the Spirit of Modern Consumerism* (Oxford: Basil Blackwell, 1987), 38. Further references will be given parenthetically in the text.

an economy of abundance meant learning how *not* to have all that advertisers, merchants, and trendsetters proclaimed was essential for happiness. Rather than urge an ascetic renunciation of the allure of consumer culture, much of the writing of the early nineteenth century imagines a roundabout way to appreciate the pleasures this culture promised to all, but would fail to deliver to most: it showed that one could enjoy the idealization of objects of desire even while suffering from their unattainability or their ephemerality. Indeed, it showed that one could indulge in such idealization even while conscious of the essential mundanity of its object. Just as merchants urged consumers to titillate themselves with the thought of what they could not have, so many Romantic-era writers taught that wanting was its own reward, and should persist in spite of disappointment.

The attitude of these writers to consumerism proper was often ambivalent and sometimes even hostile; their aim was not to support the consumer economy but simply to provide affective paradigms that were appropriate to their times. Thus, for example, even though Joanna Baillie explicitly argues against the overvaluation of consumer goods, she unselfconsciously develops a theory of desire that makes use of current assumptions regarding consumer habits.[10] In the chapters that follow, each of the writers I examine engages the relation between desire and consumption in her or his own way: while Keats celebrates the pains of consumption, Lord Byron mocks his aristocratic contemporaries for their readiness to submit to the "rack of pleasures."[11] But in the writings of both, the dangers of desire are not only treated as a fact of life but are used as an opportunity for self-discovery and self-expression. In essence, much Romantic-era writing aestheticizes one of the primary contradictions of industrial culture, recasting it in the form of a thrilling, if also painful, private psychodrama. It turns imaginative idealization in the face of personal dissatisfaction into something interesting and compelling.

This response to the consumer revolution served other ends as well. For the complications surrounding economic power in a burgeoning industrial society were recapitulated at the theoretical level, in the domain of political ideology. Talk of reform and the rights of individuals, inspired by the French example, was marked by the same tension between promise and performance. From the writings of Jean-Jacques Rousseau to those of Hazlitt

---

[10] See Chapter 3.
[11] For a discussion of Keatsian consumption, see Chapter 5; Byron's phrase is from *Don Juan*, Canto XIV: "high life is oft a dreary void, / A rack of pleasures, where we must invent / A something wherewithal to be annoy'd" (Jerome McGann, ed., *Byron* [Oxford: Oxford University Press, 1986], 813, ll. 625–7).

and later John Stuart Mill, liberal political theory would turn on the difficulty of providing for personal power and freedom – the rights of man – in collective forms of organization. It comes as little surprise that conservative writers, who feared that legal restraint might prove inadequate to the task of controlling the ambitions of Jacobinical individuals, espoused an ideology of self-imposed limitation on personal power; thus John Bowles argued that preventing luxury would make the English "orderly, tractable, and easily governed. Having such powerful restraints within, they will require fewer restraints from without."[12] But even radical writers argued that self-restraint was essential to effective government – they eliminated real kings only to internalize their function: "Emperor and King are but the lord lieutenants of conquered Souls – secondaries and vicegerents who govern not with their own right but with power delegated to them by our Avarice and appetites! Let us exert over our own hearts a virtuous despotism, and lead our own Passions in triumph, and then we shall want neither Monarch nor General."[13] Even when not framed in religious terms, reformist political theory at the turn of the century suggested that effective democratic governance could only be founded on the individual's willing internal renunciation of personal satisfaction in the name of ostensibly universal ideals. Thus for Hazlitt individuals were capable of altruism by virtue of their capacity to regard the future wellbeing of others as formally interchangeable with their own future wellbeing. In this way submission of the self to an internalized vision of the public welfare could serve as the purest form of power and liberty. Here again the aesthetic of pleasurable renunciation is brought into play: the characters of early nineteenth-century literature learn to enjoy and even exult in the internalization of conflict, and they learn to make self-subordination an occasion for personal development. At the same time, fictions of submission provided readers an opportunity to think through the costs and benefits of power hierarchies more generally.

By casting this frustrated, submissive desire in erotic terms, Romantic-era literature rendered the pleasure-in-pain aesthetic it espoused, if not "reasonable," at least comprehensible. There was, after all, literary precedent for the idea of suffering from love and even taking pleasure in that suffering. "Romantic," as I use the term in this book, is to be understood as a period

[12] John Bowles, *Thoughts on the Late General Election. As Demonstrative of the Progress of Jacobinism*, 2nd edn (London: 6. Woodfall, 1802), 33.
[13] S. T. Coleridge, *Six Lectures on Revealed Religion*, in *The Collected Works of Samuel Taylor Coleridge*, 16 vols., vol. I, ed. Lewis Patton and Peter Mann (Princeton: Princeton University Press, 1971), 228–9.

designation only, a name for the literature produced between the 1790s and the 1830s. But this study does suggest that the association of late eighteenth- and early nineteenth-century literature with the chivalrous eroticism of medieval romance is not simply a tired convention. For the name "Romantic" speaks not just to the continuities of literary history but also to the fact that much of the literature of the turn of the century effected the reinstatement of traditional social hierarchy as private erotic fantasy. Romantic-era literature turned a nostalgic eye to a set of literary conventions that rendered self-sacrifice and self-abasement significant, and used them to give meaning to the frustrations of desire that characterized so much of late eighteenth- and early nineteenth-century social life. Medieval romance provided a highly suitable template for representing and rendering aesthetic the affective challenges of modern society. Flamboyantly anachronistic, "Romantic" desire makes a spectacle, at once beautiful and absurd, of the deferral of the promises of modernization, promises posed by the enchanted world of consumerism and the discourses of political reform. During the twentieth century, much of the debate surrounding Romanticism centered on whether Romantic-era writers were culpably self-indulgent or laudably self-transcendent.[14] I would argue that "Romanticism" is precisely a technique for making self-sacrifice feel like self-indulgence.

Indeed, these fictions of self-sacrifice were so compelling that they often fared better in the early nineteenth-century art and literature market than the optimistic fictions of mastery that set themselves in deliberate competition with them. The latter, which embodied the promises of a modern political economy in a more or less straightforward fashion, were governed by an aesthetic logic of control and unlimited consumption, and rendered the fantasy of direct self-gratification in an ostensibly rational and reliable form. Thus the picturesque of the 1790s and its later, urban incarnation in the gardenesque deliberately set their face against the suspenseful, sublime pleasures of self-abnegation. But as we will see, even those writers who most strenuously supported fictions of mastery typically found themselves waging a losing battle: thus Baillie's play on the dangers of submissive eroticism met with a popular success never rivaled by her pendant piece on the virtues of the masterful and reliable pleasures of "picturesque" eroticism.

So popular were these accounts of eroticized submission that they can be found in all varieties of Romantic-era writing, whether by highbrow or popular authors, fiction or nonfiction writers, novelists or poets, women

---

[14] For examples of the former, consider the work of Irving Babbit and T. E. Hulme; for examples of the latter, Herbert Read, M. H. Abrams, and Harold Bloom.

or men. Letitia Elizabeth Landon explores the dynamics of erotic suffering with as much care as Keats; Caroline Lamb is as fascinated by the link between political and sexual submission as is Byron. Moreover, these concerns influenced all the major artistic modes of the period: they are at work not only in literature but also in painting, landscaping, and architecture. Thinkers as different as dramatist and dramatic theorist Baillie, essayist Charles Lamb, and painter John Constable explored the attractions of painful desire in both explicit and subtle ways. Some Romantic artists, as we will see, take desire and its relationship to political and economic ideologies and practices as their explicit subject. Thus, for instance, Baillie develops a theory of human desire that takes the popular fascination with consumer goods as its starting point, and Hazlitt has the narrator of his *Liber Amoris* delight in the radical political implications of his willing submission to a lower-class woman. But the political and economic bearings of submissive desire are just as often left implicit; Keats describes the exquisite pains of melancholy using metaphors of consumption rather than discussing the paradoxes of modern consumption practices outright.

Indeed, as we will see, the problem of the management of desire is not only of historical interest but is intimately bound up with the aesthetics of Romanticism itself. Techniques for managing desire played a central role in shaping the formal features of Romantic art, so that conceptions of art and desire became mutually sustaining. Thus Edmund Burke's sublime and Uvedale Price's picturesque both, in their different ways, understand aesthetic attractiveness in terms of a power struggle between the subject and his or her object of (aesthetic) desire. Similarly, in his late poetry Coleridge embraces allegory, which he regards as an artificial and disjunctive representational mode, as the best vehicle for describing the pains of suspenseful, unsatisfied desire. This book is an exploration of the political and economic origins and repercussions of the Romantic fascination with individual desire, but it is also a study of the varied and striking aesthetic forms to which this fascination gave rise.

I DEFINITIONS AND DISCRIMINATIONS

As frequently as suspenseful, idealizing, and self-abnegating desire appears in Romantic literature, it is not treated in a systematic way or referred to by a single name. Frances Burney calls it "perverseness of spirit," Keats, "perplexed delight"; for Byron it is the "rack of pleasures," while for Hazlitt it is simply "love."[15] It is important, then, to begin with an account of the typical features of this form of desire. First, it invokes the paradox of pleasure in pain; Romantic-era fictions of eroticized power relations not only presume the high cost of pleasure but also take for granted that the keenest pleasures are allied to pain.[16] This is not to say, however, that any and all pain is considered valuable. Pain becomes meaningful in the context of desire: it is the pain of unsatisfied desire that brings pleasure. This pain arises not simply from the absence of straightforward satisfaction but from the frustration and humiliation attendant upon nongratification. It is therefore felt most keenly in cases where gratification should have been possible. Although idealized by their adorers, Romantic-era objects of desire are usually, according to conventional standards, attainable: thus the protagonist of *Liber Amoris* longs for a girl who works as his servant, and the aristocratic hero of *The Wanderer* (1814) pines for a woman who appears to have neither money nor family connections. Like a commodity behind a pane of glass, the Romantic object of desire simultaneously makes a display of its availability and of its separateness. The mortification of finding oneself unable to possess it is a pain peculiar to a culture of abundance, a culture in which disappointment is common largely because expectations are high.

In many Romantic writings the humiliation attendant upon the failure to attain the object of desire is further heightened by suspense. The capacity of deferral to inflame desire is of course a common theme in love literature generally, but Romantic-era writers often take deferral to an extreme, so that it produces not only feelings of impatience but intense anxiety. As we will see, this anxiety and suspense are central to Romantic-era representations of love: lovers as different as the main couple in Burney's novel of manners *Camilla* (1796) and Baillie's love-tragedy *Count Basil* (1798) experience desire as indistinguishable from anxiety and suspense.[17]

---

[15] Frances Burney, in *Camilla*, in which she describes the perverseness of spirit that grafts desire on what is denied (*Camilla*, ed. Edward and Lillian Bloom [New York: Oxford University Press, 1983], 7); John Keats, in "Lamia," in which the central couple experience "unperplex'd delight" for only a short time (*Poems*, 349); Byron, in an account of the perversities of "high life" in *Don Juan* (*Byron* 813); William Hazlitt, in *Liber Amoris*, where the self-abasing character of the protagonist's affection is presented as the sign of his sincere devotion.

[16] This paradox is of course central to the classic psychoanalytic concept of masochism; thus Jean Laplanche describes "the pleasure of unpleasure," a situation in which, as Freud explains, "physical pain and feelings of distress" cease to be signals of danger and become "ends in themselves" (Jean Laplanche, *Life and Death in Psychoanalysis*, trans. Jeffrey Mehlman [Baltimore: Johns Hopkins University Press, 1976], 103; Sigmund Freud, "The Economic Problem in Masochism," in *General Psychological Theory*, ed. Philip Rieff [New York: Macmillan, 1963], 190). The eroticized submission that fascinated Romantic-era artists focuses on emotional rather than physical pain.

[17] It is worth noting that suspense is also crucial in the novels of Sacher-Masoch: Gilles Deleuze contrasts the "quantitative reiteration" typical of de Sade's work with the "qualitative suspense" found in

The deferral of gratification is both the result of and the enabling condition for the lover's idealization of the object of desire. In Romantic-era writing desired people are often described in terms at once inflated and abstract: these "ideal objects" are perfect, one-of-a-kind, even divine, and allied with or represented as angels, fairies, goddesses or gods, and allegorical abstractions. At the same time, these women and men are also represented as something less than divine: in more or less realistic narratives, secondary characters remark on their imperfections; in fantastic narratives, there is something grossly sensual or even evil in the immortal, powerful, and beautiful beloved – the fairy is a snake from the waist down. This doubleness serves to highlight the fact that the idealization of the beloved is a deliberate, imaginative act on the part of the lover. The Romantic-era lover understands his or her frustration as an act of willing subordination to an ideal. This idealization of the beloved makes consummation impractical if not impossible. It also stimulates an ever-increasing self-abasement in the lover: as H tells S in *Liber Amoris*, since she is "divine," he is her "creature," her "slave."[18] To the true lover, maintaining the ideal status of the beloved is more important than ameliorating his or her own self-conception; indeed, the lover typically revels in the nonrequital of affection precisely because it can be read as further proof of the superiority of the beloved. Thus Burney's Camilla, painfully in love with Edgar Mandelbert, finds herself "honouring even his coldness" towards her.[19]

Given the importance of idealization in Romantic-era representations of desire, it is not surprising that imagination should also figure largely in those representations. Not only is much Romantic-era writing preoccupied with imagination *per se* but it also selfconsciously explores the relation between desire and that other product of imagination which is art.[20] Within their

---

Sacher-Masoch (Gilles Deleuze, "Coldness and Cruelty," in Deleuze, *Masochism* [New York: Zone Books, 1989], 134).

[18] Hazlitt, *Liber Amoris*, 8.   [19] Burney, *Camilla*, 542.

[20] Interestingly, late nineteenth-century sexologist R. von Krafft-Ebing noted the importance of imagination for the masochists he studied, arguing that "the whole thing chiefly belongs to the realm of imagination" (*Psychopathia Sexualis*, trans. F. J. Rebman from the 12th German edn [New York: Physicians and Surgeons Book Company, 1926], 144). Krafft-Ebing argues that the "main root" of masochism is "the tendency of sexually hyperaesthetic natures to assimilate all impressions coming from the beloved person" (208) – a form of hypersensitivity that in the late eighteenth century would simply have been termed "sensibility." Of course, the psychoanalytic term itself has its roots in the aesthetic; Krafft-Ebing, who derived it from the name Sacher-Masoch, called that writer "the poet of Masochism" (132). Although his sense of disgust at the phenomenon often leads Krafft-Ebing to describe masochism as "unaesthetic," his awareness that it has its own aesthetic logic often reveals itself, as when he argues that "the 'poetry' of the symbolic act of subjection is not reached" in female masochism because quotidian exertions of male power are concerned with "solid advantages" rather than "display" (196). For Krafft-Ebing, and for most of his psychoanalytic

works Romantic-era writers often analogize the beloved and the art object, likening adored people to figures from romances, masques, poems, paintings, and statues. This analogy provides an opportunity for writers to comment upon the proper posture of both writer and reader before the artwork. Often, indeed, writers and readers are represented in Romantic-era writing as literally enthralled by art, an art perceived not as a craft but as a quasi-divine power, one that masters not only its consumer but also its producer. Thus Smith opens her *Elegiac Sonnets* with an ambivalent poem of thanks, in which the gift of the "partial Muse" is accompanied by pain: poetry is beautiful but it also "point[s] every pang" in the poet's melancholy heart.[21] Similarly, the speaker of Percy Bysshe Shelley's "Ode to the West Wind" asks to be lifted and borne along by that "Spirit fierce" so as to produce a tone "Sweet though in sadness."[22] For all their idealizations, these are works that never forget the cost to the self of idealizing or submitting to another.

The logic of desire I have described here, with its emphasis on the painful, anxious deferral of gratification and the abasement of the self in the service of imaginative idealization, has, of course, important historical and literary precedents. As noted already, early nineteenth-century art draws on a rich literary tradition, from the romances of the seventeenth century back through Renaissance and medieval texts that celebrated an ideal

---

successors, "true" masochism is symbolic or representative; it is the world of power relations reproduced as poetry or drama. Deleuze notes that scenes in Sacher-Masoch's work replicate works of art or duplicate themselves in mirrors, and that the despotic lover is likened to statues and paintings (Deleuze, "Coldness and Cruelty," 33). These points of similarity between the late nineteenth-century paradigm of masochism and early nineteenth-century Romantic art speak both to the influence of Romanticism and to the common social pressures to which they were responding.

Working from a different angle, recent accounts of masochism by literary critics have often linked its "shattering of the human subject" to the experience of art generally (Leo Bersani, *The Freudian Body* [New York: Columbia University Press, 1986], 107). Thus Bersani ponders what it would mean to "speak of the esthetic as a perpetuation and elaboration of masochistic sexual tensions" (107), and Linda Williams considers the implications of reading in the manner of erotogenic masochism, in which one "offer[s] up oneself as a slave to the text" ("Reading and Submission: Feminine Masochism and Feminist Criticism," *New Formations* 7 [1989], 10). Paul Mann suggests that it is not the reader *per se* but the critic who is masochistic, her or his work being always derivative: "Whatever semblance of mastery one manages to project, and whatever critical distance one arrogates to oneself, writing entails orders of submission that cannot be reduced to operational, ideological, or linguistic protocols alone. The Something else to which one's discourse is always subjected, and which one seeks to control through myriad proxies, is in the end the master that can never be mastered" (*Masocriticism* (Albany: SUNY Press, 1999), 24). For Mann, the only solution to this impasse is to embrace "masocriticism": to write essays that deliberately unravel in an effort to bring about the death of criticism itself.

[21] Smith, *Elegiac Sonnets*, 13.

[22] Percy Bysshe Shelley, *Shelley's Poetry and Prose*, ed. Donald Reiman and Sharon Powers (New York: Norton, 1977), 223.

of service and self-sacrifice. There are, however, important distinctions – both formal and substantial – to be drawn between those older practices and Romantic-era representations of desire. Medieval mysticism, for instance, shares with early nineteenth-century fictions of submission a reliance on the conjunction of pleasure and pain. Thus the female mystics described so vividly by Caroline Walker Bynum deliberately heightened their own experience of the body – in forms both painful and pleasurable – as a way of consolidating their connection with the incarnate Christ.[23] They were thereby able to make the association of the female with the fleshly a source of spiritual authority. But whereas the pain they suffered was a form of *imitatio Christi*, the self-imposed suffering of Romantic heroes and heroines, as we will see, typically does not aim at an imitation of its idealized object but uses self-abasement as a way of articulating the individuality of the desiring subject. For the Romantic-era protagonist, moreover, it is the power and not the pathos of the object of desire that makes it compelling.

Medieval asceticism, too, provides a model for Romantic-era fictions of submission, though asceticism differs from them in fundamental ways. Unlike the Romantic lover, the ascetic aims to control or expunge desire rather than inflate it: "asceticism makes explicit its violence against desire *and* satisfaction. This violence extends beyond the *desire* to take in the *desirable* as well."[24] For this reason, as Karmen MacKendrick notes, "asceticism, of all the counterpleasures, is most spectacularly ill-suited to consumer culture," whereas, as we shall see, the eroticized submission of the Romantic era tends to mimic that culture.[25] The pains of asceticism, furthermore, are also usually self-inflicted, and the response to those pains is different for the ascetic and the Romantic:

Though it often produces vivid images – one need only think of St. Teresa, virgin and sculptural inspiration – asceticism is not essentially imagistic in Masoch's frozen sense. That is, it does not set up and recur to scenes by moving from real to phantastic. Though certain ascetic *behaviors* are fetishistically repeated, they are repeated on the same plane, as acts. The ascetic is closer to Sade's proud sovereign, who embraces even his own pain without bending, than to Masoch's submissive protagonist, who demands to be humiliated and delights in flinching before the whip – even though humility is a constant quest for the religious ascetic.[26]

[23] See Caroline Walker Bynum, *Holy Feast and Holy Fast: The Religious Significance of Food to Medieval Women* (Berkeley: University of California Press, 1987) and *Fragmentation and Redemption: Essays on Gender and the Human Body in Medieval Religion* (New York: Zone Books, 1992), especially chapters 4, 5, and 6.
[24] Karmen MacKendrick, *Counterpleasures* (Albany: SUNY Press, 1999), 78.   [25] *Ibid.*, 71.
[26] *Ibid.*, 74.

Like Leopold von Sacher-Masoch's protagonists, the British Romantic-era sufferer makes a display, not of his or her capacity to endure privation, but of his or her sensitivity to suffering. Moreover, the Romantic protagonist, even more than Sacher-Masoch's Severin, suffers primarily in fantasy, anxiously reiterating the power of the beloved to give pain. Indeed, fantasy and imagination figure so largely in British Romantic-era accounts of suffering that they often sustain their pathos without making reference to physical suffering at all, and sometimes even without making reference to material reality; thus Coleridge laments the "silent strife" that mars the "dream of life"[27] even as he rehearses it again and again.

It is perhaps courtly love literature, with its representations of self-abasement and suffering before an idealized beloved, that provides the best likeness to the fictions of erotic submission one finds in nineteenth-century literature. As Mark Miller notes, in both medieval courtly love literature and the writings of Sacher-Masoch "the routine pains of romantic love . . . have been elaborated, formalized, and radicalized into something like allegory."[28] Indeed, as we will see, the problems of agency and autonomy that Miller argues animate medieval courtly poetry are, like the allegorical form in which they are explored, central to Romantic accounts of erotic submission as well. Nevertheless, and as the term "courtly" suggests, the medieval phenomenon must be understood in terms of its specific social context; while the propriety of the term "courtly love" itself has been much and heatedly debated, one can, as Janina Traxler argues, at least "talk of lyric conventions of love poetry intended for a sophisticated audience at court," conventions that include

natural attraction for the beloved, a belief that the lover is unworthy of the beloved, and a tendency for the characterization of this love to rise above mere carnality to something more spiritual . . . such love is typically expressed in vocabulary which idealizes the beloved, often using religious terminology to portray the beloved as a deity and the lover as supplicant, or using feudal terminology to portray the beloved as *seigneur* and the lover as serf or prisoner.[29]

In the Romantic period these older forms for expressing love were reinterpreted for use in a very different social world. This reinterpretation,

[27] S. T. Coleridge, from the poem "Phantom or Fact?," in *Poetical Works*, ed. E. H. Coleridge (Oxford: Oxford University Press, 1988), 484.

[28] Mark Miller, *Philosophical Chaucer: Love, Sex, and Agency in the Canterbury Tales* (Cambridge: Cambridge University Press, 2004), 154.

[29] Janina Traxler, "Courtly and Uncourtly Love in the *Prose Tristan*," in Donald Maddox and Sara Sturm-Maddox, eds., *Literary Aspects of Courtly Culture* (Cambridge: D. S. Brewer, 1994), 161, 162.

however, necessarily involved a change, for both the spiritual and the practical meanings of courtly convention were rooted in the specifics of medieval life. Denis de Rougemont argues in his classic study *Love in the Western World* that the "Tristan Myth," which he regards as "typical of the relations between man and woman in ... the courtly society, saturated with chivalry, of the twelfth and thirteenth centuries" was not only popularized and bourgeoisified at the turn of the nineteenth century, but also took on a new character: "the *claim to passion* put forward by the romantics . . . becomes a vague yearning after affluent surroundings and exotic adventures."[30] For de Rougemont, those elements of the Tristan story that had signaled a longing for spiritual transcendence were now used simply to signify the intensity of passions that were essentially mundane; in the Romantic period painful erotic yearnings were keyed not to transcendental but to worldly desires. More recent commentators, who regard medieval erotic practices somewhat more cynically than de Rougemont, have shown that the conventions of courtly love can themselves be understood in terms of practical, worldly advantages; those advantages, however, were of a very different nature from those that arguably gave Romantic-era art its quotidian bearings. The latter was clearly not an outlet for the tensions of an enclosed life at court, a means for social advancement via attachment to a noble woman, or a reflection upon and reaction to the reformulation of matrimonial codes.[31] I will argue that outside the medieval context, painful, idealizing passion was no longer a means towards either religious transformation or courtly advancement but a way of wanting that was fostered by modern developments in the marketplace and the political arena. Nineteenth-century writers were themselves often self-conscious regarding the worldly and artificial nature of self-abasing desire. Thus Landon writes a homage to a woman in a portrait that takes as its subject the impossibility of unselfconscious adoration in the nineteenth century:

> If thou hadst lived in that old haunted time,
> When sovereign Beauty was a thing sublime . . .
> Then had this picture been a chronicle
> Of whose contents might only poets tell,
> What king had worn thy chains, what heroes sigh'd

---

[30] Denis de Rougemont, *Love in the Western World* (Princeton: Princeton University Press, 1983), 19, 233.

[31] These are the major historical-causal explanations of the development of courtly love. For a discussion of these accounts and the significance of the term generally, see Catherine Bates, *The Rhetoric of Courtship in Elizabethan Language and Literature* (Cambridge: Cambridge University Press, 1992), 16–19.

What thousands nameless, hopeless, for thee died.
But thou art of the Present – there is nought
About thee for the dreaming minstrel's thought,
Save vague imagination, which still lives
Upon the charmed light all beauty gives . . .
The poet hath no part in it, his dream
Would too much idleness of flattery seem;
And to that lovely picture only pays
The wordless homage of a lingering gaze.[32]

This increase of self-consciousness serves only to heighten admiration and dejection, to multiply paradoxes as the poet – who addresses the woman in her painted form rather than the woman herself – laments the impossibility of producing a straightforward poetic tribute.

If Romantic-era fictions of eroticized submission were sometimes less spiritual than courtly love purported to be, they were nevertheless more idealizing and imaginative than the erotic flagellation practices that might otherwise seem to provide their contemporary objective correlative. The pleasures of flagellation had long been described as mechanical in nature, and were understood to have their foundation in the body, not the mind. Johann Meibom's 1639 treatise *On the Use of Flogging in Venereal Affairs* is typical in that it represents flogging as an antidote to impotence and explains the effectiveness of such therapy in purely anatomical terms. For most of the eighteenth century, this conception of flogging was still standard; a 1761 reprint of the treatise is prefaced by a letter to Meibom's son in which a physician named Thomas Bartholin writes that "I have determined, as well as your father, Meibomius, has, that by flogging of the loins, and heating the reins, the matter of the seed is either quickened or increased."[33] Meibom's first concern is in fact to convince the reader that erotic flagellation exists at all: the bulk of his treatise is taken up with anecdotes of flagellation, the veracity of which he rather anxiously asserts. Eighteenth-century fictions of erotic flagellation, in similar fashion, typically begin by offering proofs of its existence, often through the device of having a knowing practitioner persuade an incredulous friend of its popularity. Thus in *Exhibition of Female Flagellants* (186?), Flirtilla teaches Clarissa – surely a mockery of Samuel Richardson's paragon of virtue – that flagellation is delightful in spite of its painfulness,

[32] Letitia Elizabeth Landon, *Selected Writings*, ed. Jerome McGann and Daniel Riess (Peterborough: Broadview Press, 1997), 135–6.
[33] Johann Meibom, *On the Use of Flogging in Venereal Affairs* (1639) (Chester: Import Publishing, 1961), 27.

and that women enjoy the practice as much as men.[34] Of course, this impulse to begin with explanation cannot be taken straightforwardly as a sign of the rarity of the practice, but it does suggest that in the eighteenth century the notion that physical pain could be used to promote sexual pleasure was not commonplace.

In the latter part of the century, however, flagellation literature began to proliferate, and paradigms used to describe and explain erotic flagellation came to reflect a growing interest in the psychological as well as the physiological complexities of the pleasure-in-pain paradox.[35] Pain itself became an important object of study, and scientists explored its capacity to link body and mind while revitalizing both. Roselyne Rey argues in *The History of Pain* that medical men such as Cabanis worked toward developing a "psycho-physiology of pain" and that they gave it a positive role in the life of vital systems: "with the work of Cabanis, as with that of Hufeland in Germany, one really comes to understand how applying the concept of energy to a physiological idea could be interpreted in a romantic way. It is only insofar as pain awakens or stimulates weak or dormant vital forces that one may refer to the usefulness of pain."[36] Rey notes in an aside that this notion gives us insight into the work of de Sade:

In de Sade's universe, its violence and cruelty claimed to be based on the laws of Nature itself and its characters acquired their energy and pleasure from contact with pain, though it was usually by inflicting it rather than submitting to it themselves. Without doubt, this sadistic world was conceived at a time when the love of life and the exultation of sensibility often adopted an explosive dimension to an extent summarised by the concept that it is pain "which gives new strength to the principle of life."[37]

As Rey herself suggests, this conception of life and the body helps us to understand the interest in undergoing suffering even more than the desire to inflict it on others.

---

[34] Flirtilla avoids explaining the workings of this pleasure – perhaps because the standard physiological explanation was grounded in the male body – and assimilates it instead to the common practice of the corporal punishment of children (Anon., *Exhibition of Female Flagellants*, vols. I and II of *Library Illustrative of Social Progress*, 7 vols., collected by Henry Thomas Buckle [London: Printed for G. Peacock, 186?]).

[35] Indeed, one could argue that the late nineteenth-century medical psychologization of sexual experience, what Arnold Davidson calls "the emergence of sexuality," had its roots in developments that began in the late eighteenth century ("Sex and the Emergence of Sexuality," in Davidson, *The Emergence of Sexuality: Historical Epistemology and the Formation of Concepts* [Cambridge, Mass.: Harvard University Press, 2001] 30–65).

[36] Roselyne Rey, *The History of Pain*, trans. Louise Elliott Wallace, J. A. Cadden, and S. W. Cadden (Cambridge, Mass.: Harvard University Press, 1998), 114, 115. [37] *Ibid.*, 130.

British pornographic literature of the latter half of the eighteenth century similarly registers a shift toward a psycho-physiological account of the pleasures of flagellation. John Cleland's mid-century *Memoirs of a Woman of Pleasure* (1748), for example, is not unusual in including a flagellation scene in which the focus is largely, but no longer entirely, on physical stimulation. Fanny voices the traditional view that this "strange fancy" generally attacks old men who are "obliged to have recourse to this experiment, for quickening the circulation of their sluggish juices."[38] Given this preconception, she cannot entirely account for such a fancy in her customer Mr. Barvile since he is a healthy young man. As John Atkins remarks, in *Memoirs* one can see the first signs of a shift from understanding flagellation as a mechanical practice to understanding it as merely one part of that more complicated set of desires and behaviors we are used to calling masochism: "Flagellation was assuming a new role. From being a stimulant it was becoming a practice in its own right. De Sade was ten years old at the time."[39] In a work of the 1770s, *Madame Birchini's Dance*, the heroine, in curing a man of impotence, confidently reassures him in good traditional fashion that "A Rod's the best invigorator."[40] She also uses the model of schoolboy chastisement to familiarize her proceedings to the man, who upon first seeing a rod in her hand makes clear that he "'by no means lik'd the fun.'" But Birchini's instructions that the man "'must act a Child; / And I your Step-mamma will be,'" which at first seem merely to provide a pretext for her actions, prove to be something more: the pretense of domination and submission begins to yield its own pleasure, and the man spends most of the latter part of the poem crying out ecstatically for his "Momma's" mercy. As Birchini says, "'These little tricks enrich the treat.'"[41] By the end of the eighteenth and the beginning of the nineteenth century, the English flagellation brothel was at its peak of popularity,[42] but, more importantly, the "little tricks" had come to take on a real importance of their own. By that point it was clear that some people could find pleasure in being dominated even without physical stimulation. In the late nineteenth century, when representations of eroticized suffering formed one of the most important classes of a

[38] John Cleland, *Memoirs of a Woman of Pleasure*, ed. Peter Sabor (Oxford: Oxford University Press, 1986), 143.
[39] John Atkins, *Sex in Literature*, 4 vols., Vol. IV (New York: Riverrun Press, 1982), 144.
[40] Anon., *Madame Birchini's Dance*, 9th edn, vol. V of *Library Illustrative of Social Progress*, 16.
[41] Ibid., 15, 14, 16.
[42] See John Noyes, *The Mastery of Submission: Inventions of Masochism* (Ithaca: Cornell University Press, 1997), 86.

proliferating pornographic literature,[43] Richard von Krafft-Ebing would find it necessary finally and definitively to distinguish what he called "masochism" from mere "passive flagellation," which he, like Fanny Hill, describes as a mechanical technique "used by weakened debauchees to help their diminished power."[44] Like the phenomenon Krafft-Ebing calls "true" masochism, the agony found in the late nineteenth-century novels of Leopold von Sacher-Masoch and in the less overtly sexual works of early nineteenth-century British writers had its foundation in the mind and emotions rather than the body. In many a Romantic-era poem or novel, "ideal objects" and demon lovers would inflict immaterial pains that were subtle in their workings but devastating in their effects.

II

The road of excess leads to the palace of wisdom.
– William Blake, *The Marriage of Heaven
and Hell* (*c.* 1790)[45]

To understand the history of suspenseful, self-abasing desire in nineteenth-century England, we must first understand the contemporary function of the concept of desire itself. Terry Eagleton argues that in the nineteenth century "the determinant role and regular repetition of appetite in bourgeois society" gave rise to "a dramatic theoretical shift: the construction of desire as a thing in itself, a momentous metaphysical event or self-identical force, as against some earlier social order in which desire is still too narrowly particularistic, too intimately bound up with local or

[43] For a discussion of the place of flagellation in Victorian pornography, see Stephen Marcus, *The Other Victorians* (New York: Basic Books, 1964). Marcus notes that the growth of the pornography industry itself would seem to signal an increase in the "deflection" of sexual impulses, what he calls "part of the price we pay for social advancement" (262). Michel Foucault would later argue that this deflection could be related to new technologies of power (*History of Sexuality.* 3 vols., vol. I, trans. Robert Hurley [New York: Vintage Books, 1980]). As we will see, one could argue further that eroticized submission, as a highly aestheticized, theatrical, and self-conscious form of desire, is ideally suited to the modern world of deflected desires. The frequency of the appearance of submission in pornography would therefore be a sign not only of its interest for modern readers but also of its structural affinities with pornography itself.
[44] Krafft-Ebing, *Psychopathia*, 141. It should be noted that passive flagellation was not simply replaced by the more emotionally complicated practice that Krafft-Ebing calls masochism. The strictly physiological pleasures of flagellation continued to be explored in the Victorian period, the widespread prevalence of such practices as pedagogical corporal punishment helping to ensure this continuance.
[45] William Blake, *The Marriage of Heaven and Hell* (1790) (Oxford: Oxford University Press, 1975), xviii.

traditional obligation, to be reified in quite this way."[46] One thinks here of Blake's poetry, where desire is elevated to the level of an independent force or a mode of cognition in its own right, where the creative energy of lust and rage is embodied in the mythical figure of Orc. Eagleton links the change in the conception of desire to a newly "perceived *infinity* of desire in a social order where the only end of accumulation is to accumulate afresh, [and where] desire comes to seem independent of any particular ends, or at least as grotesquely disproportionate to them."[47] Desire as we now understand it, as a thing in itself, a mark of healthy subjectivity, and an illimitable fund of energy, is an historical artifact, as is our expectation that desire will always outstrip satisfaction.

Studies in consumerism suggest that this conception of desire was already taking shape in the eighteenth century, and that it reflected the exigencies not of capitalist accumulation but of the formation of a "consumer society."[48] For although both contemporary observers and more modern critics of capitalism have tended to focus their attention on production, it is clear that the success of industrial capitalism in Britain relied not only on the growth of production but also on the growth of home demand.[49] And indeed, eighteenth-century England saw fundamental changes in consumption habits. In the pre-industrial economy members of the middle and lower classes tended to hoard their surplus income or use it to pay for help with their labor (*Romantic Ethic*, 18). From the eighteenth century on, that attitude toward expenditure gradually changed, not only among the middling classes, but even lower down the social scale. As early as the 1730s, a decline in the price of food and a rise in wages permitted many working people to participate in fashionable public pleasures and purchase a greater volume and variety of goods.[50] Even the humblest households made use of newly fashionable commodities, sometimes at the

---

[46] Terry Eagleton, *The Ideology of the Aesthetic* (Oxford: Basil Blackwell, 1990), 159.   [47] *Ibid.*

[48] Such recent studies include Neil McKendrick, John Brewer, and J. H. Plumb, eds., *The Birth of a Consumer Society: The Commercialization of Eighteenth-Century England* (Bloomington: Indiana University Press, 1982); Campbell, *Romantic Ethic*; Grant McCracken, *Culture and Consumption: New Approaches to the Symbolic Character of Consumer Goods and Activities* (Bloomington: Indiana University Press, 1988); G. J. Barker-Benfield, *The Culture of Sensibility* (Chicago: University of Chicago Press, 1992); and John Brewer and Roy Porter eds., *Consumption and the World of Goods* (New York: Routledge, 1993).

[49] Until fairly recently, consumerism has been viewed as suspicious not only in itself but also as a subject of scholarly inquiry; as John Brewer and Roy Porter point out, "this distaste for the fruits of capitalism may be regarded as an honourable tradition of idealist dissenting radicalism; alternatively one may see it as displaced Puritanism, latter-day Luddism, elitist snobbery or pseudo-aristocratic prejudice" (*World of Goods*, 3).

[50] Peter Borsay, *The English Urban Renaissance: Culture and Society in the Provincial Town, 1660–1770* (Oxford: Clarendon Press, 1989), 303.

cost of neglecting what some considered more basic needs. By 1825 William Cobbett would complain of the ubiquity, even in the provinces, of refined consumption habits. Families now had "two or three nick-nacks to eat instead of a piece of bacon and a pudding."[51] While surely influenced by a desire to exhibit a refined taste, the preference among the poor for luxury foods such as sugar and tea, even when more nutritious food was available, might also have reflected a wish to enter a realm in which desire outstripped need.[52] What Neil McKendrick calls the consumer revolution was permanently to change the relationship between needs and wants.[53] Indeed, it was during the eighteenth century that the verb "to want," which had traditionally been used only negatively to signal absence or lack, first came to be used positively to express desire, its primary modern usage.

Changing consumption patterns went hand in hand with the development of new, recognizably modern, conceptions of the market. Joyce Appleby speaks of late seventeenth-century writers who, "responding to the obvious, if uneven economic growth, began to speculate upon the dynamic effect of increased demand. The word 'markets' in their pamphlets subtly changed from a reference to the point of sales to the more elusive concept of expandable spending."[54] The traditional emphasis on fair trade rather than free trade reflected the older conception of the market: it was believed that, because consumption levels were finite, excessive sales by one merchant or set of merchants would necessarily be attended by losses to other merchants. This understanding, "the very old economic assumption that demand curves are inelastic, and that competitive pricing will not increase sales sufficiently to maintain profit margins,"[55] came to seem increasingly untenable over the course of the eighteenth century. Legal structures, including sumptuary laws, had supported this older form of localized trade, but by the beginning of the eighteenth century those structures had largely disappeared and the system they supported gradually lost ground over the course of the century.[56] By the century's end retailers,

[51] William Cobbett, *Rural Rides*, ed. E. W. Martin (London: Macdonald, 1958), 222.
[52] Carole Shammas, *The Pre-Industrial Consumer in England and America* (Oxford: Clarendon Press, 1990), 146.
[53] McKendrick, et al. *Birth of a Consumer Society*.
[54] Joyce Appleby, "Ideology and Theory: The Tension between Political and Economic Liberalism in Seventeenth-Century England," *The American Historical Review* 81:3 (June 1976), 500–1.
[55] David Alexander, *Retailing in England during the Industrial Revolution* (London: Athlone Press, 1970), 161.
[56] See James Carrier, *Gifts and Commodities: Exchange and Western Capitalism since 1700* (New York: Routledge, 1995), 74.

especially in London, had developed an arsenal of new techniques for actively stimulating consumer demand.

The expression of consumerist desire was further encouraged by the new role of consumer goods in the establishment of personal identity. G. J. Barker-Benfield describes the way changed environments brought with them new notions of individuality:

> People painted and papered their better-lit and heated rooms into which domestic space was increasingly divided, therein creating orderly spaces to display as well as store their chinaware, books . . . their children's toys, and their fashionable clothing in walnut or mahogany furniture . . . Here, behind hardwood "doors embellished with brass locks," they dressed themselves, read, and wrote letters in newly private "closets," sitting on more comfortable chairs, activities and spaces historians see as the generators of individualism. Self-conception could be literalized and more carefully shaped in reference to mirrors. (*Sensibility*, 100)

The broadened range of commercially available objects, and the increasingly specialized and particularized spaces in which people lived, became the foundation of new kinds of individualism and the emblems of new forms of personal value. Barker-Benfield considers the extension and democratization of opportunities for self-fashioning through consumerism critical to eighteenth-century culture, a culture obsessed with self-improvement (83). The display of one's taste as a consumer became a primary mode of self-expression. It is therefore not surprising that goods themselves came to be valued not just as the visible proof of wealth but also as particular objects, things that are themselves "individualized." Thus, for instance, while family portraits at the beginning of the eighteenth century represented standard interiors whose only function was to symbolize wealth, by the end of the century they tended to serve as accurate catalogues of personal possessions.[57] Whereas only ownership matters when objects are intended to communicate wealth, when objects are used to establish individuality even desire that does not eventuate in ownership is meaningful. That is, desire itself, even when it did not lead to possession, was socially significant as a sign of taste. It makes sense then that such mundane activities as shopping might become more meaningful and apparently more pleasurable than they previously had been. Merchants both benefited from and helped to produce a new culture of shopping, one in which the act of buying came to be perceived less as a necessary task than

---

[57] See Charles Saumarez Smith, *Eighteenth-Century Decoration: Design and the Domestic Interior in England* (New York: Abrams, 1993).

as a form of recreation. Luxury shops were themselves luxuriously furnished, manufacturers such as Wedgwood hosted exclusive assemblies for the introduction of new products, and market streets and squares came to function like outdoor assemblies, redesigned so as to give an impression of orderly, classical elegance.[58]

Historians of eighteenth-century England have thus argued that desire itself came to be cultivated as a badge of individuality. It was, moreover, directed not only toward specific objects – whether attainable or not – but also toward purely speculative ones. By the early eighteenth century the finance capitalism that had developed in the late seventeenth century had changed concepts of wealth, property, and personality. J. G. A. Pocock points out that in speculative finance capitalism "property – the material foundation of both personality and government – has ceased to be real and has become not merely mobile but imaginary."[59] As he persuasively argues, "the century that followed the Financial Revolution witnessed the rise in Western thought . . . of an ideology and a perception of history which depicted political society and social personality as founded upon commerce: upon the exchange of forms of mobile property and upon modes of consciousness suited to a world of moving objects."[60] Not only new forms of speculation but even the simple fact of the gradually rising importance of money contributed to this abstraction of value – Donald Meyer speaks of the "infinitely transformative power" of money, which, as it renders all things equivalent, renders character itself speculative, flexible, and negotiable.[61] The practice of speculation transformed not just the objects but also the ideology of desire: as desire and fulfillment came to stand in an increasingly tenuous and distant relation to one another, desiring came to seem an end in itself, a meaningful imaginative exercise.

By the early nineteenth century, this exercise of the imagination was understood by contemporaries to be commonplace, especially among members of the growing middle class. Colin Campbell argues that the daydreaming so important to Romantic culture "helps to make desiring itself a pleasurable activity" (*Romantic Ethic*, 86), but insofar as it flirts with nongratification, such reverie has the potential to be painful as well as pleasurable. Thus many Romantic-era poems and novels warn that the deliberate cultivation of desire is often attended by frustration. Campbell notes

---

[58] On the construction of the new streets and squares, see Borsay, *Urban Renaissance*, 60, *passim*.
[59] J. G. A. Pocock, *Virtue, Commerce, and History* (Cambridge: Cambridge University Press, 1985), 112.
[60] *Ibid.*, 109.
[61] Donald Meyer, *Sex and Power: The Rise of Women in America, Russia, Sweden, and Italy* (Middletown, Conn.: Wesleyan University Press, 1987), 254.

with respect to the economic growth beginning in the eighteenth century that the "revolution in rising expectations, since it is linked to a new tendency for expectations to consistently exceed realization, has been redubbed 'the revolution in rising frustrations'" (38). In a similar vein, John O'Neill remarks that modern consumers must learn to live with "economic tension"; they must recognize that most of their desires will never be satisfied.[62] The cultivation of desire made that desire passionate in both senses of the word; it was suffused with emotion and it was a form of suffering.

In both fictional and autobiographical works, writers of the late eighteenth and early nineteenth centuries suggested that even when one had the financial means to enter the luxury economy, the act of desiring itself often remained emotionally complicated. In his *Confessions* (1781–8) Rousseau describes the struggle with desire in personal terms:

Countless times, during my apprenticeship and since, I have gone out with the idea of buying some dainty. As I come to the pastry-cook's I catch sight of the women behind the counter and can already imagine them laughing amongst themselves and making fun of the greedy youngster. Then I pass a fruiterer's, and look at the ripe pears out of the corner of my eye; the scent of them tempts me. But two or three young people over there are looking at me . . . I am frightened by everything and discover obstacles everywhere. As my discomfort grows my desire increases. But in the end I go home like an idiot, consumed by longing and with money enough in my pocket to satisfy it, but not having dared to buy anything.[63]

Rousseau's paranoid anxieties are eccentric, to be sure, but his hesitancy over making a purchase, his almost sexual modesty about shopping, would later be echoed by British Romantic-era writers as different as Jane Austen and Charles Lamb. In "Old China" Lamb dramatizes the ironies of abundance in the form of a dialogue between Elia and his cousin Bridget, who complains, "I wish the good old times would come again . . . when we were not quite so rich . . . A purchase is but a purchase, now that you have money enough and to spare. Formerly it used to be a triumph . . . A thing was worth buying then, when we felt the money that we paid for it."[64] In an interesting turn on Rousseau, Bridget adds that in the good old times, when they had to "squeez[e] out our shillings

[62] John O'Neill, "The Productive Body: An Essay on the Work of Consumption," *Queen's Quarterly* 85 (Summer 1978), 225.

[63] *The Confessions of Jean-Jacques Rousseau* (1781), trans. and ed. J. M. Cohen (London: Penguin, 1953), 45.

[64] Charles Lamb, "Old China," in Lamb, *Elia and the Last Essays of Elia*, ed. Jonathan Bate (Oxford: Oxford University Press, 1987), 282.

a-piece" for seats in the gallery, their "pleasure was the better for a little shame."[65] Like the young Jean-Jacques, Bridget finds that shamefulness enhances desire.

Just as desires, like consumer goods, took on a new social importance as indicators of character, so, too, did the often painful feelings that accompanied them. Indeed, during the late eighteenth century feelings themselves came to be valued as possessions. Writers on sensibility, since their philosophy arose out of a faith in the morality of spontaneous sentiment, celebrated feelings and those who were susceptible to them. At the same time, they recognized that the pleasure of experiencing powerful feelings usually came at a price, both economic and emotional. Campbell points out that the feelings associated with sensibility were often described as a "luxury": "luxury of tears," "luxurious woe," "luxurious pity" (*Romantic Ethic*, 141). As Campbell's examples of tears, woe, and pity suggest, however, the luxurious and glamorous feelings of sensibility were almost invariably painful. Ann Van Sant notes that "sensibility is regularly and explicitly associated with pain in psychological contexts. [Hugh] Blair's use is typical. Although he insists that the pleasures of sensibility more than make up for its pains, that pleasure itself has pain as its foundation."[66] The pleasure-in-pain of sensibility often had, moreover, an erotic character: Scottish moralist David Fordyce argued that the enjoyments of the benevolent man

are more numerous, or, if less numerous, yet more intense than those of bad Men . . . It is true, his friendly *Sympathy* with others subjects him to some Pains which the hard-hearted Wretch does not feel; yet to give a loose to it is a kind of agreeable Discharge. It is such a Sorrow as he loves to indulge; a sort of pleasing Anguish, that sweetly melts the Mind, and terminates in a Self-approving Joy.[67]

Such feelings of "pleasing Anguish" are an indulgence, and provide an "agreeable Discharge." The eighteenth-century ideology of sensibility, because it focused on sympathy with rather than desire for another, located pain not in frustration but in communion. Nevertheless, because it made anguished feelings themselves objects of desire, it effectively added another loop to the knot that bound together desire, pleasure, and pain.

---

[65] *Ibid.*, 284.
[66] Ann Jessie Van Sant, *Eighteenth-Century Sensibility and the Novel* (Cambridge: Cambridge University Press, 1993), 52. Van Sant argues further that sensibility had much in common with contemporary physiological experimentation, and that both relied on the infliction of pain to provoke a response. See Chapter 3, "Gazing on Suffering: the Provocation of Response."
[67] David Fordyce, *The Elements of Moral Philosophy* (London: Dodsley, 1754), 263–4.

The desirability of painful feelings was further enhanced by the disciplinary function inherent in sensibility. Many a traditional eighteenth-century moralist complained of the contemporary "passion for pleasure" – the excess of feeling and desire often associated with sensibility – but even the votaries of sensibility themselves strove continually to refine its excesses and prove its genuineness by emphasizing its austere side. For although well-suited to serve the burgeoning market, sensibility was at the same time designed to control and direct the desires it sponsored. Thus the relentless concern with refinement, delicacy, and taste: "the evident fact of women's appetite for consumer pleasures had always gone hand in hand with attempts to control it. This is the perspective from which one must view the culture of sensibility's insistence on a tasteful relationship with the goods and services supplied by 'bourgeois consumerism'" (*Sensibility*, 205). The encouragement of feelings and desires went hand in hand with an impulse to channel and control them. True taste required discrimination, and although this was an ostensibly natural capacity, in practice it was typically deliberately cultivated.

Because of the value placed on sensitive, discriminating desire and feeling, upper- and middle-class men and women of the late eighteenth century considered it a mark of distinction to be capable of intense, focused desire on a single, extraordinary object. At the turn of the century, this attitude was further supported by new techniques in retailing. As we will see in Chapter 1, the practices of window display, fixed-pricing, and open-ticketing encouraged a conception of the commodity as aloof and autonomous, possessed of an unknown, and therefore unlimited, potential to gratify. Writers as different as Mary Robinson and Keats comment on the fact that consumers were learning to idealize the objects of their desire, and developing new pleasure in sustaining that desire. Writers contemplated the possibility that the consumer might find it most satisfying to remain in a speculative posture, money in hand; the goal of the consumer was no longer simply to buy, but to shop. In Romantic-era literature desire no longer aims at acquisition and accumulation, or even the profitable returns of investment, as it had in early eighteenth-century texts such as *Robinson Crusoe* (1719). Instead, the consumer develops obsessive attachments to idealized objects of desire that are imagined to be capable of providing infinite satisfaction even as they withhold that satisfaction.[68] Thus one finds in many texts of this period representations of desire that involve a sustained – sometimes even paralyzed – focus on a single idealized

---

[68] The modern association of masochism and fetishism – the cliché of the leather-clad woman with the whip – could in fact be argued to have its roots in nineteenth-century consumerism.

object. Varieties of this form of engagement can be found throughout Romantic-era writing, from Coleridge's constancy to an ideal object to Shelley's idealization of the unattainable beloved in *Epipsychidion* (1821). Even that champion of reason Mary Wollstonecraft took it as a given that "solitude and reflection" were valuable because they gave "to wishes the force of passions, and . . . enable[d] the imagination to enlarge the object, and make it the most desirable."[69] In the writings I treat in this book, suspenseful, idealizing desire, however disastrous or unfulfilling, is represented as the most virtuous kind. Beloved persons are idealized in much the same way that commodities are, but in this period to be like a commodity is to resist immediate consumption. Such persons please by virtue of their capacity to keep their lover in a pleasurable but anxious and even painful state of suspense.

This passionate, idealizing, and disciplined mode of desire is not only represented within Romantic-era art but is embedded in the very aesthetic categories through which that art was produced. This is most obviously true in the case of the aesthetic of the sublime. The usefulness of the sublime as a model of heightened but restrained desire was already clear early in the eighteenth century. As Barker-Benfield argues,

> the conscious target of *The Spectator* was the uncontrolled experience of pleasure. The authors confronted what they saw as a new historical situation in which many people . . . were pursuing pleasure for its own sake and doing so "transiently," skipping from one source of pleasure to the next. They and their fellow moralists recognized what a twentieth-century historian terms the old "hierarchically structured" system for distributing consumption . . . was breaking down, to be replaced by "consumer sovereignty". . . In order to shape such consumer appetite, *The Spectator* claimed that it controlled special keys to unlock still higher degrees of pleasure . . . [This included] taking delight in descriptions that aroused "terror and grief"; or in descriptions of "dangers that are past" . . . [or] "the apprehension of what is great or unlimited." (*Sensibility*, 62)

The sublime experience could in fact be described as one of thwarted consumption. Of course, the sublime has been variously defined both by its original analysts and by modern commentators, and in the Kantian formulation at least the displeasure of having one's imaginative faculty overwhelmed is compensated by the pleasure of feeling the true power of one's cognitive faculties. For Kant, the experience of the sublime merely provides an opportunity for the self-aggrandizing experience of reasoning subjectivity. But the version of the sublime rooted in English empiricism

[69] Mary Wollstonecraft, *Vindication of the Rights of Woman* (1792) (New York: Penguin, 1975), 149.

and schematized by Burke is one in which the power of the sublime object is
not necessarily recuperated for use by the subject; in much eighteenth- and
nineteenth-century British art the sublime object is defined first and foremost by the threat it poses, and it is in the experience of that imagined
threat, and not the subsequent recognition that the threat is only imagined,
that the pleasure of the sublime lies.[70] In this account the dynamic of the
sublime involves a powerful attraction to a single object, an attraction
that is nevertheless suspended, with subject and object held apart indefinitely. The sublime experience is thus one of intense, sustained feeling,
but it is also an experience of pleasure in pain, of being compelled by an
object perceived as so powerful that the object's very presence threatens
the subjectivity of the perceiver. This "modern affect," as Thomas
Weiskel calls it,[71] has been defined by some theorists precisely in terms of
its paradoxical combination of pleasure and pain; thus Jean-François
Lyotard speaks of the "pleasure of a displeasure" in the sublime experience.[72]

Weiskel suggests that the psychological precursor to the modern
construction and experience of the sublime was a boredom that "increased
... astonishingly during the eighteenth century."[73] One might venture that

---

[70] The psychoanalytic framing of some of the best modern critiques of the sublime has tended to go
hand in hand with a preference for the Kantian formulation – with its emphasis on resolution
and ultimate empowerment – and an assumption that both the sublime itself and the person who
experiences it must be masculine. Thus, for instance, Thomas Weiskel resolves the "ability to
hurt" that Edmund Burke attributes to the sublime into castration anxiety, which leads him in
turn to an understanding of the sublime as a recapitulation of the Oedipus complex, the goal of
which is a "positive resolution" that can serve as "the basis of culture itself" (*The Romantic
Sublime* [Baltimore: Johns Hopkins University Press, 1976], 93–4). Even in Weiskel's discussion
of Burke, then, it is not suspension in the sublime moment but the resolution following it that is
accented. As Neil Hertz notes, Weiskel's rather anxious sequel to this argument, in which he
invokes a pre-Oedipal moment of attachment to the mother, cannot dislodge the Oedipal telos of
his schema taken as a whole. Hertz argues that this tendency to replace "difficulty" with "absolute
blockage" or full confrontation is the result of a wish for a "confirmation of the unitary status of
the self" ("The Notion of Blockage in the Literature of the Sublime," in Hertz, *The End of the
Line: Essays on Psychoanalysis and the Sublime* [New York: Columbia University Press, 1985], 53).
Given the masculinist quality of the confrontational character of the sublime as "blockage," it is interesting that it should be feminist critics of the sublime who not only remind us of the possibility of
female involvement in the sublime, but also highlight the moment of suspense and self-dissolution
rather than the resolution that might follow. Thus Barbara Freeman opens her study of the "feminine
sublime" by arguing that "unlike the masculinist sublime that seeks to master, appropriate, or colonize
the other, I propose that the politics of the feminine sublime involves taking up a position of respect
in response to an incalculable otherness," and she reminds us that the sublime practiced by writers
such as Keats and Coleridge was very different from the Wordsworthian sublime, and that the
former "depends upon the self's awareness of its own absence" (Barbara Claire Freeman, *The
Feminine Sublime: Gender and Excess in Women's Fiction* [Berkeley: University of California Press,
1995], 11, 8).   [71] Weiskel, *Romantic Sublime*, 13.
[72] Jean-François Lyotard, *The Differend: Phrases in Dispute*, trans. Georges Van Den Abbeele (Minneapolis: University of Minnesota Press, 1988), 165.
[73] Weiskel, *Romantic Sublime*, 97.

such boredom was the result not of a convergence of individual pathologies but of the new prosperity of eighteenth-century England. Indeed, Frances Ferguson shows that the popularity of the sublime can be related to a new demand for novelty,[74] a demand that, as we shall see in Chapter 2, has its roots not only in abstract aesthetic considerations but also in commercial developments. But while in theory the novelty of the sublime object should allow us, in Burke's terms, to use it to "enlarge our stock" of mental images,[75] the very nature of the sublime gives rise to what Ferguson calls "distribution problems."[76] That is, the demand for sublime experiences necessarily exceeds the supply, and the very fashionableness of sublime experience renders it familiar, thereby destroying its appeal. The sublime therefore represents an effort to escape the contradiction embedded in the fashionable taste for novelty, even while it reduplicates it. Thus not only the sublime object but even the sublime experience is the more desirable for being less available; the desire for the experience of thwarted consumption must itself sometimes be thwarted.

It is not only in its intensity, idealization, and novelty that the sublime shows its links to the painful forms of desire sponsored by eighteenth-century commerce. The sublime generated by obscurity and indeterminacy thrives not just on the uncommonness and inaccessibility of the object but also on its power to provide purely speculative pleasures. Barbara Freeman notes the importance of speculation in Burke's account of the sublime, and remarks on the Janus-faced quality of that speculation: while "theoretical" speculation implies lofty disinterestedness, financial speculation involves quite the opposite. Freeman argues that the Burkean sublime itself is similarly Janus-faced: it poses as disinterested aesthetic appreciation while it functions in fact as "a strategy of appropriation."[77] I would argue that the appeal of the sublime object lies precisely in its resistance to appropriation, but as we have seen, in the late eighteenth century even distanced, non-appropriative appreciation can function as a consumer pleasure – indeed, as one of the most fashionable and sophisticated consumer pleasures available.

For late eighteenth- and early nineteenth-century thinkers, then, desire in excess of the possibilities for gratification often seemed to be the very best kind, and for a number of reasons. On the one hand, it ensured support for

---

[74] Frances Ferguson, *Solitude and the Sublime: Romanticism and the Aesthetics of Individuation* (New York: Routledge, 1992), 46.

[75] This phrase arises in the context of a general discussion of the pleasure of producing new mental images. See Edmund Burke, *A Philosophical Enquiry into the Origin of Our Ideas of the Sublime and Beautiful* (London: Rivington, 1812), 18.

[76] Ferguson, *Solitide and the Sublime*, 46.   [77] Freeman, *Feminine Sublime*, 41, 3.

the consumer economy, for it primed consumers to take advantage of any surplus income with which they might find themselves. On the other hand and at the same time, it gave consumers practice in speculation, and allowed them, even in the absence of adequate means, to refine and display their taste. But even more importantly, such desire had the virtue of appearing to be uncalculating and disinterested. It provided an opportunity for an expression of self at the same time that it afforded protection from moral injunctions against selfishness and self-indulgence. Desiring without hope of gratification was regarded by contemporaries as the sign of a willingness to dream and to risk; it seemed to set its practitioner apart from the mundane world of getting and spending. By the end of the eighteenth century, writers and other artists were not only keen to represent this desire but also linked it to artistic production itself: they argued that intense, idealizing desire was the sign of a generous, sympathetic, and, above all, imaginative nature.

III

Romanticism, in order that it may be free to dream, becomes a literary...
liberalism, or rule of *laissez-faire*.
  – F. L. Lucas, "La Princesse Lointaine: or the Nature of
Romanticism"[78]

During the Romantic period, the issue of the management of desire was of course complicated by political hopes, anxieties, and conflicts. Arguments for the liberation of desire – desire not only for economic but also for political power – elicited passionate counter-arguments for the necessity of restraint. The result was a situation in which the possibilities for the fulfillment of political longings seemed at once boundless and arbitrarily restricted – Wordsworth's bliss at being alive in that dawn combined with Pittite repression. The political situation thus reduplicated the structure we have seen at work in the economic domain. During the 1790s in particular, but throughout the Romantic period, radical aspirations, from William Godwin's belief in the perfectability of humanity to Shelley's hopes for a democratic England, were productive of "revolutions in rising frustrations" that extended beyond the strictly economic. Indeed, the two were directly linked, for the French example made clear that a primary political concern of the common man was the amelioration of his economic state. The expectations raised in the economic domain by industrialization

---

[78] Robert Gleckner and Gerald Enscoe, eds., *Romanticism: Points of View*, 2nd edn. (Detroit: Wayne State University Press, 1975), 131.

thus found their political complement in the burgeoning language of the rights of man and woman.

These expectations could not, however, be immediately met. Indeed, in the political domain "revolutions in rising frustrations" sprang not only from disenchantment with the practice of politics but also from contradictions inherent in contemporary radical political theory. In the eighteenth century liberal political economists had typically imagined that the growth of the free market economy would of itself tend to equalize power, including, ultimately, political power. John Millar argued that the free market, by propagating sentiments of personal independence, would be an engine for social change: "the prerogatives of the monarch and of the ancient nobility will be gradually undermined . . . the privileges of the people will be extended in the same proportion, and . . . power, the usual attendant of wealth, will be in some measure diffused over all members of the community."[79] In fact, however, the extraordinary productivity of industrial capitalism created power that seemed to be in excess of all known mechanisms of "diffusion." Political theorist Sheldon Wolin opens his commentary on Alexis de Tocqueville by describing what he calls the paradox of modern power: "Tocqueville singled out 'powerlessness' as the striking characteristic of the politics of the times. Yet those times might also be described as notable for the abundance and variety of powers rather than their scarcity."[80] Wolin goes on to argue that "modern power," the product of scientific and technological advances, industrialization, and urban population growth, demanded a political organization that would allow for its inherent tendency to increase:

Where contract theory was mostly concerned to find a formula for limiting political power and thereby reassuring the citizenry and insuring their obedience, the system of modern power wanted more than mere compliance of consent from its "citizens." It aimed, first, to enlist their skills and their energy, then, second, to adapt them to the new enterprise of developing power, not constraining it.

The "system of modern power" made early modern conceptions of constitutionalism – which typically emphasized the importance of setting limits to the exercise of power – obsolete.[81] But as this power increased, the individuals enlisted in its production often felt, as de Tocqueville did, helpless in

---

[79] John Millar, *The Origin of the Distinction of Ranks* (1771) in *John Millar of Glasgow*, ed. W. C. Lehmann (Cambridge: Cambridge University Press, 1960), 292.
[80] Sheldon Wolin, *Tocqueville between Two Worlds* (Princeton: Princeton University Press, 2001), 13.
[81] *Ibid.*, 19.

the face of it. Just as economic abundance brought with it an ideology in which desire outpaced possession, so the increase of human power generally tended to leave particular persons feeling more than ever that they were at the mercy of large social forces – whether they believed those forces to be embodied in the government, industry, capital, or the "mob."

Economic and political theorists from Adam Smith to Mill struggled to reconcile the power of the individual – in the form of liberties and rights – with the power of the collective. Despite the disadvantages Wolin notes above, throughout the eighteenth and early nineteenth centuries consent theory provided one of the most popular theoretical models for reconciling these two interests.[82] Thus Hazlitt, in his essay "What is the People?" uses the notion of consent to democratize the traditional – and satisfyingly holistic – metaphor of the body politic; he writes that the People "is the hand, heart, and head of the community, acting to one purpose, and with a mutual and thorough consent."[83] Despite its rhetorical advantages, however, the logic of consent theory, even when propounded by its advocates, tended to run into paradox, as in the following passage from Rousseau's *The Social Contract* (1762):

Hence, in order that the social pact shall not be an empty formula, it is tacitly implied in that commitment – which alone can give force to all others – that

[82] While consent theory focused on protecting the rights of individuals, the Enlightenment notion of sympathy delineated mechanisms intended to ensure that even empowered individuals would seek the public good. In a world where men acted as free economic agents, seeking to maximize their own advantage, sympathy was to serve as a sort of affective glue to bind society together. The practical shortcomings of relying on sympathy to resolve conflicts and inequities were, however, already apparent to eighteenth-century thinkers. Like many of her contemporaries, Hannah More, who celebrates sensibility, nevertheless worries over the ways it can become a mask for selfishness: "the graceful drapery Pity wears . . . may be counterfeit" ("Sensibility: An Epistle," in Roger Lonsdale, ed., *Eighteenth-Century Women Poets* [Oxford: Oxford University Press, 1990], 328, ll. 34–8). Recent commentators take their critique further still, arguing that the cultivation of sympathy is in fact sadomasochistic: "The reproduction of sentiment calls forth images of femininity, sympathy, and virtuous moral feeling. But the reproduction of sentiment also relies upon a visual power structure gendered male, and a sympathetic spectator whose 'sentiments' are sadomasochistic" (Laura Hinton, *The Perverse Gaze of Sympathy: Sadomasochistic Sentiments from "Clarissa" to "Rescue 911"* [Albany: SUNY Press, 1999], 2). The sympathetic spectator both masochistically identifies with the suffering object of his gaze and sadistically enjoys a sense of distance from, and power over, that object. Hinton goes on to link this dynamic with the vicissitudes of individualism: "If the sadomasochistic subject is the product of a 'stifling individualism' generating overvaluation toward an object, the subject of sentiment openly revalidates 'excessive' dependency" (11–12). For Hinton, the intimacy fostered by sympathy is thus both false and pathological; the subject's fascination with the object actually serves to keep it at a distance. Under the guise of selflessness and affective vulnerability, then, sympathy allows an indulgence in sadomasochistic pleasures. Because the struggle for power must be disavowed it becomes literally perverse.

[83] William Hazlitt, *The Complete Works of William Hazlitt*, 21 vols., vol. VII, ed. P. P. Howe (London: J. M. Dent and Sons, 1930–4), 267.

whoever refuses to obey the general will shall be constrained to do so by the whole body, which means nothing other than that he shall be forced to be free; for this is the condition which, by giving each citizen to the nation, secures him against all personal dependence, it is the condition which shapes both the design and the working of the political machine, and which alone bestows justice on civil contracts – without it, such contracts would be absurd, tyrannical and liable to the grossest abuse.[84]

To be constrained by the general will is to be free.[85] For Rousseau, this paradox resembles the paradox of modern economic power, which he describes in personal and emotional terms in his *Confessions*:

I love liberty; I hate embarrassment, worry, and constraint. So long as the money lasts in my purse it assures me of independence and relieves me of the need of

[84] Jean-Jacques Rousseau, *The Social Contract*, trans. Maurice Cranston (New York: Penguin, 1968), 64.

[85] If contract theory suggests that one can be "forced to be free," it also allows for the "freedom to be forced"; after all, one can consent to one's own slavery. In his *Happy Slaves: A Critique of Consent Theory* (Chicago: University of Chicago Press, 1989), Don Herzog examines precisely this problem. Herzog argues that the notion of individual consent is necessarily a fiction, and a problematic one. Consent is typically understood to be "implied" by the individual's failure to resist the power of state institutions – in spite of the fact that such resistance is often impracticable. Even where the act of consent takes physical form, as in oath-taking, it is arguably still coercive. The fiction of consent thus demands that the individual embrace his subjection as self-chosen, almost in the manner of a masochist. Indeed, recent commentators on masochism argue that the masochist deliberately reveals this contradiction in the idea of consent by highlighting it. Kaja Silverman, in her study of male masochism, describes the masochist in just this way: "he acts out in an insistent and exaggerated way the basic conditions of cultural subjectivity, conditions that are normally disavowed; he loudly proclaims that his meaning comes to him from the Other, prostrates himself before the gaze even as he solicits it, exhibits his castration for all to see, and revels in the sacrificial basis of the social contract" (*Male Subjectivity at the Margins* [New York: Routledge, 1992], 206). In spite of her reference to the social contract, Silverman is more interested in the politics of gender relations than the structure of governments.

Others, however, have demonstrated just how pointedly political masochistic practice can be. Walter Benn Michaels, in a study of Frank Norris's *McTeague* (1899), shows that masochism is often predicated on the structures of liberal ideology: "if the masochist's desire to be owned is perverse, it is nevertheless a perversion made possible only by the bourgeois identification of the self as property. Without that, no truly modern slavery is possible, since only if you identify freedom with self-ownership can being owned by someone else seem an intrinsic abridgment of that freedom. Hence, an increased investment in the values of autonomy will naturally be accompanied by an increased insecurity about the status of that autonomy" ("The Phenomenology of Contract," in Michaels, *The Gold Standard and the Logic of Naturalism* [Berkeley: University of California Press, 1987], 124). The form of the contract is particularly amenable to masochistic subversion; Sacher-Masoch used the contract as a tool for gaining power precisely by ceding it. Over the course of his life, he drew up increasingly elaborate contracts in which he relinquished more and more power to his mistress. The result is "a liberal parody of liberal law" (Noyes, *Mastery of Submission*, 71). In the words of Gilles Deleuze, "since the law results in our enslavement, we should place enslavement first, as the dreadful object of the contract. One could even say, as a general rule, that in masochism the contract is caricatured in order to emphasize its ambiguous destination" ("Coldness and Cruelty," 92).

plotting to obtain more, a need which has always appalled me. So afraid am I to see it end that I treasure it. Money in one's possession is the instrument of liberty; money one pursues is the symbol of servitude.[86]

Rousseau's enjoyment of power and liberty as embodied in money is by no means straightforward, for he can retain his liberty only by not exercising it, just as he can retain his money only by hoarding it – that is, by refusing to allow it to serve its function. In Rousseau's social philosophy these paradoxes not only resemble the paradox of erotic suffering but are in fact grounded by it; Elizabeth Wingrove argues that Rousseau finds in sexual subjugation not merely an analogy for political relationships but a means for securing a devotion to those relationships at an emotional level. The Rousseauian citizen has a "two-fold identity vis-à-vis the state: when he participates in the articulation of the general will as a legislator, he is ruler, and when he receives its pronouncements through the execution of law, he is ruled."[87] In similar fashion, a man as husband/father is ruler, but as a lover he is ruled. Wingrove thus sees both roles, public and private, as characterized by "consensual nonconsensuality," and argues that these roles are mutually constitutive: "sexual interaction is not *like* political interaction, nor are its identities preparatory in the sense of being prior to or separate from politics; rather, his [Rousseau's] republicanism consists in the proper performance of masculinity and femininity." For Rousseau, the vicissitudes of power in sexual relations provide a somatic and affective support for the consensual nonconsensuality required for a republican political order. Desire blurs the distinction between choice and compulsion, so that the good republican is "naturally" a man of "obsessive desires, devouring passion, and sensuous agonies."[88]

If Rousseau set the stage for the Romantic-era obsession with the relation between freedom and compulsion, that obsession would reach its philosophical zenith in the early nineteenth century with F. W. G. Hegel. Even while confidently proclaiming that his own moment saw the apotheosis of personal freedom, Hegel assumed that history developed through a progression of master-slave relationships. For Hegel, self-realization required the recognition of an other. Precisely because it is not a given, identity must be violently wrested from others, in a process that highlights the value of domination and subjection. This is no Hobbesian state of nature, rough and tumble and full of conflict: the violence here aims not

---

[86] Rousseau, *Confessions*, 46.
[87] Elizabeth Wingrove, *Rousseau's Republican Romance* (Princeton: Princeton University Press, 2000), 4.
[88] *Ibid.* 6, 56–7.

simply at practical advantage but at internal transformation. Thus the violent relations one has with the other are not only intimate but even erotic. As Alexandre Kojève explains it:

> For there to be Self-Consciousness, Desire must therefore be directed toward a non-natural object, toward something that goes beyond the given reality. Now the only thing that goes beyond the given reality is Desire itself. For Desire taken as Desire – i.e., before its satisfaction – is but a revealed nothingness, and unreal emptiness . . . Therefore, Desire directed toward another Desire, taken as Desire, will create, by the negating and assimilating action that satisfies it, an I essentially different from the animal "I." This I, which "feeds" on Desires, will itself be Desire in its very being, created in and by the satisfaction of its Desire.[89]

Desire not only defines the individual but binds him or her to others, as he or she endeavors to subjugate their desire to his or her own: "the *Phenomenology* must accept a[n] irreducible premise: the existence of *several* Desires that can desire one another mutually, each of which wants to negate, to assimilate, to make its own, to subjugate, the other Desire as Desire."[90] But in Hegel's narrative the master's impulse to derive recognition through domination is only one aspect of a complicated and ever-shifting relationship. For in fact the slave enjoys certain advantages in this agon of desire:

> [Servitude] does in fact contain within itself this truth of pure negativity and being-for-itself, for it has experienced this its own essential nature. For this consciousness has been fearful, not of this or that particular thing or just at odd moments, but its whole being has been seized with dread; for it has experienced the fear of death, the absolute Lord. In that experience it has been quite unmanned, has trembled in every fibre of its being, and everything solid and stable has been shaken to its foundations. But this pure universal movement, the absolute melting-away of everything stable, is the simple, essential nature of self-consciousness, absolute negativity, *pure being-for-self*, which consequently is *implicit* in this consciousness.[91]

The slave, then, derives benefits of his own from his bondage. Not only does he see himself realized – if only fleetingly – in his labor, but his very abasement affords a kind of negative self-realization. It is this paradox that stands

[89] Alexandre Kojève, *Introduction to the Reading of Hegel: Lectures on the Phenomenology of Spirit*, assembled by Raymond Queneau, ed. Alan Bloom, trans. James Nichols, Jr. (Ithaca: Cornell University Press, 1969), 5.   [90] *Ibid.*, 40.
[91] G. W. F. Hegel, *Phenomenology of Spirit*, trans. A. V. Miller, foreword J. N. Findlay (Oxford: Oxford University Press, 1977), 117.

behind Paul Mann's remark that "The Hegelian system is masochism writ large (or masochism is shrunken Hegelianism)."[92]

The writers of early nineteenth-century England struggled with these same issues of desire, freedom, and submission. Even the most optimistic of radicals found it difficult to imagine exactly what individual liberty should look like in modern society. Whatever their intentions, the shadow of compulsion invariably falls across their writings; when least obtrusive it takes strangely insidious forms. One finds perhaps the best example of this in Godwin's *Political Justice* (1793), where a person's anarchic freedom can subsist only under the rigorously watchful eyes of his or her neighbors. While Godwin tried to overcome problems arising from conflicts of interest by underscoring the human capacity for reason, most contemporary observers agreed that the extension of personal liberty was unavoidably complicated by irrational desires. Hazlitt, although a stalwart radical, argued that power inequities sprang not just from tradition but also from the desires of individuals, desires with which he sympathized even as he regarded them as perverse: "Man is a toad-eating animal. The admiration of power in others is as common to man as the love of it in himself: the one makes him a tyrant, the other a slave."[93] Like Rousseau and Hegel, Hazlitt understood that modern man, at the best, lived under a dual dispensation, enjoying new forms of freedom even as he bore with new forms of compulsion, and like them he saw that the tension between liberty and compulsion created not just practical challenges but also emotional ones. Thus in his semi-autobiographical *Liber Amoris*, the protagonist, a political radical, tries to assuage his political disaffection by wooing a cruelly tyrannical serving girl, whose heart he softens by giving her a statue of Napoleon. H's passionate self-abasement to a social inferior becomes, ironically, his best means of keeping the spirit of liberty alive.

As eccentric as *Liber Amoris* is, it was only one of many literary works in the period to explore the erotic attractions of compulsion even while proclaiming the value of liberty. In *Don Juan* (1819–24) Lord Byron attacks

---

[92] Paul Mann, *Masocriticism* (Albany: SUNY Press, 1999), 43–4. While Hegel imagines a happy ending to this tale of subordination and self-realization, Judith Butler, in her study of the "psychic life of power," raises the question of whether contemporary Western societies are not still caught up in a series of master-slave conflicts. Butler asks "how does the subjection of desire require and institute the desire *for* subjection?" (*The Psychic Life of Power: Theories in Subjection* [Stanford: Stanford University Press, 1997], 19). Taking her cue from Louis Althusser and Foucault, she notes that if power over the subject serves to form the subject, then the subject once formed must rely on that power. The subject is thus formed in a kind of dependency; the very consolidation of subjectivity involves subjection.

[93] William Hazlitt, "Illustrations of 'The Times' Newspaper: On the Connexion between Toad-Eaters and Tyrants," in Hazlitt, *Works*, VII, 148.

"tyrants" with brilliant venom but also encourages his reader to enjoy the
sight of Juan as slave to a sultana and catering to the whims of Catherine
the Great. The principal couple in Lady Caroline Lamb's *Glenarvon*
(1816), when they are not absorbed in the cause of Irish rebellion, take
turns enslaving one another erotically: "He saw that power, ambition,
was her ruling passion, and by affecting to be ruled, he completely mastered
her." Glenarvon tells Calantha, "you shall be my slave. I will mold you as I
like; teach you to think but with my thoughts, to act but with my feelings,
you shall wait nor murmur – suffer, nor dare complain – ask, and be
rejected – and all this, I will do, and you know it."[94] Keats's Lamia, who
can imagine "unperplex'd delight" with her human lover as long as they
are alone in the wilds outside the city, "burn[s]," "lov[ing] the tyranny"
when she is forced to accede to his social concerns once they enter the
public world.[95]

　　None of these narratives provides a happy resolution to the erotic tensions it describes, but *as* narratives these works do at least allow for some
kind of closure. For many thinkers of this period, narratives of submissive
love provided a useful forum in which to think through the convergences
of desire and power that made true political equality difficult to achieve.
Such narratives had, furthermore, the virtue of simplifying the most complicated political questions of the period: the workings of hierarchy could be
represented more succinctly in an interaction between two people than in
the more crowded public domain. This benefit was felt not only by progressive writers but also by conservative ones; private passions became a privileged arena for working through the conflicts of public life. Hence many
who wrote on political matters also wrote fiction or poetry, and Jacobin
and anti-Jacobin novelists alike frequently designed their plots around
erotic relationships. For those with radical sympathies, moreover, romantic
relationships could function as an ideal instantiation of the principles of
individualism and social equality, since the lover's value demanded to be
understood entirely in personal rather than class terms.

　　These romantic fictions render the struggle for power on a small, manageable scale, and they make it concrete and personal. They represent
Wolin's "modern power" in comprehensible form. They go one better
than Smith's quasi-Providential "invisible hand," for in an age when the
power of traditional authorities was being undermined they reinvest
power in actual persons. At the outbreak of the French Revolution,

[94] Caroline Lamb, *Glenarvon*, ed. Frances Wilson (London: J. M. Dent, 1995), 193, 192.
[95] Keats, "Lamia," I, l. 327; II, l. 81.

Burke claimed that monarchs were necessary in part because the embodiment of state institutions was valuable emotionally; the rule of reason could never command the loyalty a person could command. "To make us love our country, our country ought to be lovely,"[96] and what could be lovelier than Marie Antoinette? Of course, France lost its monarchy altogether, but in England, too, the madness of the King and the prodigality of the Prince Regent undermined the prestige of the monarchy. Fictions of erotic submission embodied power once again; even as the beloved is aligned with the ideal and described in abstract terms, he or she renders power material and in that sense more comprehensible.

But the eroticized submission described by so many Romantic-era writers served an even more specific and important function: it proclaimed the capacity of the individual to internalize social conflict. The self-abnegating lover pursues not only his or her own interest but also its opposite, and so is, in that regard, the ideal citizen of a democratic order. Already during the eighteenth century, philosophers and social commentators argued that civil society relied on refined techniques of self-government, manifested in forms of civility. By the end of the eighteenth century, individuals were often represented as internalizing the codification of social norms to the point of becoming self-castigating; one is struck, for instance, by the frequency with which Burney's heroines become mentally or physically ill when they believe they have transgressed against propriety. During the Romantic period, this capacity for internal regulation took on an explicitly political significance: progressive thinkers argued that the democratic political process was not a contest whose outcome was determined by numbers but an opportunity for self-realization in which individual men were called upon to reconcile contradictions of interest. That is, reformers imagined that political conflict must be resolved not just institutionally or publicly, but also internally, within each man, as he strove to act on rational and universal grounds. It was easier, after all, to proclaim the rights of men to practice their reason than to suggest they had a right to act according to their self-interest; most reformers of the period therefore made much of the capacity of individuals to seek, not just immediate personal satisfaction, but the successful instantiation of larger ideals. These reformers argued that the individual could and should freely subordinate his or her own good to the public good. Such individuals could thus serve as both the origin of rightful power and the locus of its coherence. Hannah Arendt, in her discussion of Rousseau and Robespierre, describes the result in the French

---

[96] Edmund Burke, *Reflections on the Revolution in France* (New York: Anchor Books, 1973), 91.

case: "revolutionary man" has an "innermost conviction . . . that the value of a man may be judged by the extent to which he acts against his own interest and against his own will." "To partake in the body politic of the nation, each national must rise and remain in constant rebellion against himself."[97] One finds instances of this same internal tension in English writing. It is exemplified most magnificently in Shelley's *Prometheus Unbound* (1820), which argues that it is only by "suffer[ing] woes which Hope thinks infinite," thereby bringing the dreams of hope to fruition, that an individual can achieve true "Life, Joy, Empire and Victory" both for himself and for his society.[98] *Prometheus Unbound* not only makes self-sacrificing "internal" revolution heroic but also raises the mirroring of the collective in the mind of the individual to the level of an aesthetic principle: Prometheus serves simultaneously as an example of individual moral excellence and as an allegorical figure whose unbinding represents the political and social regeneration of all mankind. More prosaically, Hazlitt was to argue in numerous philosophical essays that in their contemplation of the future men should be able to treat the interests of others as having equal weight with their own. It was this capacity for altruism that would ground Hazlitt's hopes for a more democratic political order.

That a submissive form of subjectivity could be a training ground for the modern enfranchised subject might seem at first paradoxical. But one of the goals of nineteenth-century political reform was the replacement of the chain of hierarchical social relations with a system in which all were equally subordinated to an abstract ideal. Thus the radical George Dyer describes an ideal Britain, one that is "Ardent in freedom's sacred cause," as "Proud of her rights, and *equal laws*."[99] Wordsworth celebrates these equal laws more subtly, in the form of his analogy for the difference between poetic diction and meter: poetic diction, like a *lettre de cachet*, is "arbitrary and subject to infinite caprices upon which no calculation whatever can be made," leaving the reader "utterly at the mercy of the Poet." "[T]he distinction of rhyme and metre," on the contrary, "is regular and uniform," and "obeys certain laws, to which the Poet and Reader both willingly submit because they are certain."[100] Modern law, like meter, is acceptable because, rather than favoring one man over another, it elicits

[97] Hannah Arendt, *On Revolution* (London: Penguin Books, 1990), 79.
[98] Percy Bysshe Shelley, *Prometheus Unbound*, in *Shelley's Poetry and Prose*, 210.
[99] From "An Ode, Written by G. Dyer, Esq. On Reading Major Cartwright's Appeal, & C." (originally published in 1799) Michael Scrivener, ed., in *Poetry and Reform: Periodical Verse from the English Democratic Press 1792–1824*. (Detroit: Wayne State University Press, 1992), p. 280, emphasis mine.
[100] Wordsworth, "Preface," 254, 262.

the submission of all men.[101] Increasingly, effective politics would come to depend on the willingness of individuals who no longer took their subordination for granted to submit themselves gladly to the rigors of the law.[102]

By idealizing willing submission, self-abnegating desire could afford practice in the emotional skills essential to the ideology of reform. At the same time, however, representations of submissive desire performed a commentary on the attractions and horrors of the fixed hierarchical social structures that modern British society was ostensibly leaving behind. In a compelling account of Sacher-Masoch's writings, John Noyes argues that the novelist's "exotic sexuality" "was intended as an identification with the minority experiences of Slavic life." For Noyes, Sacher-Masoch's erotica transposes "the gross social injustices and violence in Eastern Europe in the fading days of the Hapsburg Empire" into the domain of private life.[103] I would argue that one of the reasons for Sacher-Masoch's "fascination" with social injustice was that new ideologies had made older social relations visible *as* injustice. Ostensibly obsolete hierarchical power relations were both loathsome and fascinating precisely because they seemed to have no proper place in modern life. We will see that for many British Romantic writers, submissive eroticism became a way of simultaneously reviving and challenging old hierarchies, all in the ostensibly "safe" domain of private life. Orientalist narratives were a particularly popular vehicle for thinking through the consequences of modernization: conceived as the domain of unchanging hierarchies, the East was an ideal setting for submissive fantasy. Writers as diverse as Thomas De Quincey, Coleridge, Byron, and Landon repeatedly made use of Eastern settings to investigate the place of hierarchy in a rapidly changing world.[104]

---

[101] This law, because it aims for consistency and transparency, must be thoroughly codified; to this John Noyes adds that "liberalism must define with the utmost thoroughness which expressions of innate aggresivity are permissible and which are harmful. In other words, the liberal commitment to positive aggresivity is a commitment to a thorough juridical codification of social life" (Noyes, *Mastery of Submission*, 27–8).

[102] William Keach, in *Arbitrary Power*, speaks to both the pervasiveness of pejorative uses of the phrase in the period and the complications of the willing assent to subjection: "Romanticism has conventionally been celebrated, and more recently demystified, as a cultural period especially defined by a belief in the power of the free individual subject . . . But from the perspective elaborated in . . . many of the . . . texts I have foregrounded in this book, human freedom has meaning only within a process of making history in which the arbitrariness of language and the arbitrariness of political domination are encountered inside as well as outside or beyond human agency" (*Arbitrary Power: Romanticism, Language, Politics* [Princeton: Princeton University Press, 2004], 158).

[103] Noyes, *Mastery of Submission*, 53, 8.

[104] During the late nineteenth century, accounts of social relations in the colonies similarly became peculiarly compelling. Imperial social relations seemed at once modern and ancient, and so

Altogether, then, Romantic-era fictions of eroticized submission enabled
writers to represent the vicissitudes of power in personal and concrete
terms; to delineate a mental discipline that discovered pleasure in acting
against one's own self-interest; to think through the emotional attractions
of subservience; and to comment on old hierarchies and the effects of modernization. These fictions served not one function but many: they could be
used to bolster a reformist ideology but they were also suffused with nostalgia; they promoted consumerist desire but also revealed the obstacles to the
satisfaction of that desire. They simultaneously demonstrated a fascination
with and a disdain for power, for they both celebrated it and made it appear
absurd. Scenes of submissive desire embodied an erotics of ambivalence that
perfectly suited an age of rapid social change, a time when "the whirling
motion of the revolutionary wheel" "wrenched men's understandings
almost asunder."[105] They rendered the disappointment of powerlessness –
in an age that seemed to promise power enough for everyone – into an
opportunity for the display of character. Indeed, they made powerlessness
an act of will and imagination; they made it a thing of beauty.

IV

The chapters that follow explore the varied social functions that representations of self-abnegating, suspenseful, and idealizing desire served in the late
eighteenth and early nineteenth centuries in Britain. As they do so, they
examine a wide range of art forms: poems, novels, plays, and essays, but
also engravings, paintings, landscapes, and buildings. This movement
between disparate kinds of art may sometimes seem a distraction from
the book's strictly historical argument, but the book aims not only to
account for the presence of submissive eroticism in Romantic literature
but also to register its shaping influence on Romantic aesthetics. Individual

---

enjoyed both the glamour of novelty and the appeal of nostalgia. Colonial life therefore became an
important screen for the projection of erotic fantasy: "as liberalism struggled to balance ideas of universal morality with ideas of individual freedom, rumors of violent transgressions in the colonies
aroused visions of an exciting and enticing life on the far side of liberal morality" (Noyes,
Mastery of Submission, 119). Moreover, for those who spoke from the perspective of the colonies,
masochistic practices became an important means of figuring colonial life. Noyes discusses a
variety of writings on empire, from Frantz Fanon's *Black Skin, White Masks* to Joseph Conrad's
Heart of Darkness, as studies in the way the cultural contradictions of colonialism gave rise to a compensatory masochism on the part of European men. Noyes also suggests that European men relieved
some of the psychic pressure of their situation by displacing their violence against native populations
onto a brutal female proxy. James Eli Adams studies similar phenomena in *Dandies and Desert
Saints: Styles of Victorian Manhood* (Ithaca: Cornell University Press, 1995).
[105] William Hazlitt, "On Consistency of Opinion," in *Works*, XVII, 25.

chapters therefore devote some time to tracing the varied generic and formal implications of that influence. At the same time, while the book aims to be wide-ranging in its coverage, it by no means purports to be exhaustive. The roughly chronological disposition of the chapters is designed to foreground certain developments in the erotic logic the book traces, though the chapters do not provide a lock-step historical narrative. The book examines the works of both female and male writers, and includes representations of both male and female sufferers. The works selected facilitate the exploration of the workings of desire on several levels: as it is experienced by characters within a text, as it implicitly functions for the reader, as it is discussed by the writer directly, and as it appears in autobiographical works. The aim, however, is not to reveal truths about the psychic lives of Romantic artists and their contemporaries, but to understand the ways in which the place of desire in the political economy of the turn of the century gave rise to a set of peculiarly Romantic aesthetic modes.

The book's narrative begins with a brief chapter – a sort of historical backstory – on sexuality and speculation at the moment of the birth of finance capitalism. "Finance and flagellation" argues that writers of the early eighteenth century were concerned that involvement in joint-stock companies and other commercial ventures had taught their contemporaries the pleasure of speculative desire, a form of desire that thrives on risk-taking and deferral. I focus on two engravings by William Hogarth that represent the dangers of an emergent finance capitalism – *South Sea Scheme* and *The Lottery* (both 1721) – arguing that they reflect an effort to think through the links between speculation, desire, and pain. *The Lottery* is an allegorical, Italianate image featuring the enthroned female figure of Credit, and I discuss the ways in which it represents modern man as enthralled by idealized abstractions whose erotic attractiveness can never culminate in fulfillment. In *South Sea Scheme*, on the other hand, the problems of finance capitalism are challenged by means of an attack on the allegorical mode itself, which is here understood as the *ne plus ultra* of idealizing abstraction. This engraving, which is in the realistic/emblematic style for which Hogarth is so well known, nevertheless features four allegorical figures, all of whom are being tortured. Chapter 1 explores the complicated early eighteenth-century account of the eroticism of finance capitalism, showing that figures as different as Joseph Addison's Lady Credit and Daniel Defoe's Roxana function as embodiments of the object of speculative desire. We will see that given the eighteenth-century perception of the inherent painfulness of such desire, it is not surprising that one of the figures in *South Sea Scheme* is a prostitute with twigs in hand, ready to flagellate.

During the Romantic period the significance of speculation changed as its influence came to pervade the consumer realm as well. Chapter 2, "From sadism to masochism in the novels of Frances Burney," explores the changing commercial inflections of romance at the turn of the century by means of an examination of Burney's four novels, which were produced over the course of several decades. Tracing an evolution in Burney's conceptions of social life, the chapter shows that the dynamics of desire in each novel can be linked to the political economy it describes. As I demonstrate, while Burney's early novels depict a simplified consumer world shadowed by sadism, in her late, Romantic-era novels consumption is linked to labor and desire takes a masochistic form. In *Camilla* and *The Wanderer* it is no longer simply moral prohibition or the limitations of resources that stand in the way of fulfillment. The experience of desire itself has changed: pleasure is sought not in immediate satisfaction but in a prolongation of the period of desire and an almost abject submission to the whims of the beloved. For the characters of *Camilla*, the two most important means of acquisition are shopping and gambling, and these two activities serve as the primary models for the workings of desire generally, including erotic desire: characters desire not only things but also each other either in the manner of casual shoppers or in the manner of speculators. While gambling is explicitly criticized, and the prudent example of careful shopping is kept always before our eyes, the book is clearly sympathetic to the riskiness and anxious discomfort of the gambler's desire. In her final novel, however, Burney shows that by the early nineteenth century shopping had come to resemble gambling; new marketing techniques made even shop goods appear more properly objects of speculation than of possession. In *The Wanderer* Burney fashions her incognita heroine so that she has all the charms of the Romantic-era commodity: she is remote and autonomous and possessed of a skill in metamorphosis that makes her appear to be the answer to every wish. Burney represents the self-abasing desire felt by those who meet "the wanderer" as the positive sign of their willingness to respect the unseen labor that goes into making both commodities and accomplished young women.

Chapter 3, "The aesthetics of passion: Joanna Baillie's defense of the picturesque in an age of sublimity," explores the relation of conceptions of desire to the development of Romantic aesthetics. It shows that the two major aesthetic categories of the Romantic period, the picturesque and the sublime, are founded on two dominant Romantic models of desire, one masterful and the other submissive. I argue that artists working in the picturesque mode offer an optimistic account of the relation of subjectivity to its objects, one that proposes that desire is insatiable and operates serially, focusing on one object after another in succession. We see this conception of desire at work not only in the writings of landscape theorists but also in the larger domains of art and literature. This model of masterful desire was, however, challenged by a model of submissive desire, one that harnessed desire by focusing it on a single, aloof object. This self-abnegating form of desire found its aesthetic expression in the more glamorous category of the sublime, which taught the pleasures of being fixated on and overwhelmed by a more powerful being. As I show, theorist and dramatist Joanna Baillie made explicit the rivalry between these two forms of desire and the aesthetic modes that embodied them. A proponent of the picturesque, Baillie represents the sublime/submissive model of desire in all its horrors in her play *Count Basil* (1798). With this tragedy on the passion of love she contrasted her comedy on love – *The Tryal* (1798) – in which Agnes, the sprightly heroine, actively seeks to avoid inspiring slavish devotion. But for all Agnes's charms, Baillie's contemporaries were more drawn to Count Basil's beloved Victoria, a ruthless beauty of a type that was to become increasingly attractive over the next century.

Chapter 4, "Practicing politics in the comfort of home," argues for a link between Romantic-era representations of eroticized submission and liberal democratic politics. It begins with a discussion of Hazlitt's *Liber Amoris*, a semi-autobiographical account of his humiliating affair with his landlady's daughter. As I show, the eroticism of *Liber Amoris* derives as much from political as from personal interests. I argue that for Hazlitt, the deferral of consummation serves to protect a future that in his philosophical essays he insistently characterizes as democratic and altruistic. At the same time, the power inversions with which the book plays mock the traditional social order – even as they reveal a nostalgia for it. The chapter turns next to Byron's *Don Juan*, a poem that deliberately eroticizes power in an effort to make it once again palpable and material, and not simply a matter of financial wherewithal. Byron the aristocrat is drawn to the hierarchies that these somaticized forms of power produce even as Byron the liberal sympathizer is led to identify with those who suffer the effects of those hierarchies. Lady Caroline Lamb, on the other hand, suggests in her novel *Glenarvon* that the eroticization of power, far from being an invention of Byron's, is in fact the hallmark of modern politics itself. In the world of her novel, radical politics are fueled by self-abasing desire, a fact that makes them uniquely amenable to female participation. The chapter closes by arguing that even in the more baldly pornographic literature of the period one finds similar political motives at work; pornographic self-abasement functions sometimes as a nostalgic resuscitation of old hierarchies and sometimes as a model for adapting to the rigors of the rule of modern law.

The final chapter, "Mastery and melancholy in suburbia," returns to the issue of Romantic-era aesthetics. During the 1810s and 1820s, the perceived intensification of space and time led to the development of two late Romantic aesthetic forms, the first of which presents itself as a blueprint for mastery and confident possession, and the second of which celebrates the tendency of objects of desire to *resist* possession. I begin with an exploration of the way the conditions of urban and suburban life led to the establishment of what I term a synoptic aesthetic, a taste for the sensation of completeness within a small space. I show that post-picturesque landscape designers such as Humphry Repton and John Claudius Loudon began to thwart the norms of depth perspective, insistently foregrounding the figures in their designs. As in the contemporary panorama, the consumer of the gardenesque sought to see and "have it all" within the confines of a space made full and rich. This empowering synoptic aesthetic, however, with its dependence on the intensification of space, was gradually eclipsed by a more truly modern urban aesthetic, that of the ephemeral. In domains as various as the painting of Constable and J. M. W. Turner, Daguerre's diorama, and new technologies of domestic lighting, one finds a fascination with transient objects and effects, things that could not be grasped and mastered. It was Keats, more than any other writer of the period, who struggled between these two paradigms. Attracted to the synoptic aesthetic, he filled poem after poem with cozy panoramic views and snug bowers. But his own experience of consumerism suggested above all the ephemerality of things, and in his later poetry he celebrated the beauty of fleeting objects while simultaneously mourning their transience, thereby creating a philosophy of the value of pain-in-pleasure – a paradoxical state that he terms "melancholy." The chapter then turns to a consideration of the late poetry of Coleridge, which takes the logic of Keatsian melancholy a step further. The personae of Coleridge's later poems experience nothing but sadness in the two-dimensional, fleeting world in which they find themselves. This sadness is registered formally in the frequent appearance of allegory, the representational mode that seemed, for Coleridge as for Hogarth, well suited to the exploration of the abstraction and flatness of modern life. For Coleridge, it is impossible to experience the beloved except as a two-dimensional, ephemeral image, so that the act of loving becomes nothing but a repeated ritual of mourning for the inaccessibility of the beloved. In Coleridge's hands, then, erotic self-abasement becomes a highly refined, self-conscious, and abstract exercise, suffused with intense melancholy.

Six decades ago Praz opened *The Romantic Agony* with a rumination on a poem by Shelley: "'Tis the tempestuous loveliness of terror . . .' In these lines pleasure and pain are combined in one single impression. The very objects which should induce a shudder . . . all these give rise to a new sense of beauty, a beauty imperilled and contaminated, a new thrill."[106] Praz's very language here, his repetition of the word "beauty," reminds us that for him the drive to understand Romanticism was fueled in part by his desire to understand and even vindicate the late nineteenth-century culture of aestheticism and decadence. For him, that culture defined a relatively recent past. For us, this "new thrill" is so familiar as to seem anything but new. But it is time for us to look afresh at this important part of our Romantic legacy; the writings of the Romantic period still have much to teach us about the effects of our ambivalence regarding power relations, our attraction to speculation and distant objects of desire, and our impulse to regard the psyche as the primary site for social contestation. Contemporary representations of erotic life, like late nineteenth-century ones, often privatize desire, so that submissive desire appears to be little more than a matter of personal idiosyncrasy. But our public life is still largely structured by the institutions of liberal capitalism, and it would behove us to understand better the ways those institutions have shaped both Romantic-era conceptions of desire and our own.

[106] Praz, *Romantic Agony*, 26.

CHAPTER I

Finance and flagellation

William Hogarth's *South Sea Scheme*, of 1721, is an image of vice run riot, of the moral bankruptcy of a culture devoted to gambling and speculation (figure 1). It is also a document in erotic violence. Its characters not only threaten, whip, and mutilate each other, they appear to enjoy it. The man who looks, with excitement and apprehension, at a prostitute with twigs in her hand, preparing to flagellate him, emblematizes the disturbing eroticism of early eighteenth-century finance capitalism. That new forms of commercial speculation should be associated with the breakdown of traditional social relations is unsurprising, but why should speculation be explicitly linked to eroticized violence? This brief chapter will set the stage for the chapters that follow by examining the logic that brought together speculation and sexuality in the eighteenth century. As we shall see, many eighteenth-century commentators on finance capitalism believed it was driven by an unhealthy and illicit form of desire, one that was both painful and sexual. Thus, contemporaries feared, sexuality lent its energy to speculation even as speculation promoted new forms of perverse sexuality.

To understand the conceptual relay between these two domains – one private and the other public – we must first understand the rhetoric of finance capitalism. The new economy was, from the outset, conceived in terms of gender conflict. J. G. A. Pocock claims that this conflict was a specific manifestation of a longstanding tendency in Western thought:

Now it is an evident fact in the history and sociology of inter-sexual perception that masculine minds constantly symbolize the changeable, the unpredictable and the imaginative as feminine . . . The random and the recurrent, the lunar and the cyclical, were summarized by Roman and Renaissance minds in the figure of *Fortuna*, who symbolizes . . . the contingent with which virtue – that obviously virile quality – contends.[1]

---

[1] J. G. A. Pocock, *Virtue, Commerce, and History* (Cambridge: Cambridge University Press, 1985), 99.

Figure 1. William Hogarth, *The South Sea Scheme* (1721).

As Pocock goes on to demonstrate, the symbolism to which he gestures here took on a special resonance in the decades immediately following the Financial Revolution. The vicissitudes of fortune were acutely felt in an age when speculation regularly made the rich poor and the poor rich. Increasingly, wealth was not the stable, literally grounded thing that it had been: the founding of the Bank of England, the proliferation of insurance schemes, the extension of joint-stock companies past the moment when commercial ships returned safe to harbor, the acceleration of land sales (made possible by the registration of land titles), and new means for transferring private and public debts all served to make wealth more liquid. The implications of these changes were far-reaching; Pocock argues that the unprecedented development of public credit, which was necessary to cover William III's war expenses, gave rise to a new secular conception of the future. Living by speculation and credit meant believing in progress and growth, believing in a richer tomorrow. This image of the future often seemed to be founded in nothing more substantial than desire, a deeply felt hope that Fortune's wheel was on the rise. Credit, described in contemporary political and economic tracts as a desirable but unreliable woman, thus became the modern embodiment of Fortuna.

Conservative writers feared the "hysteria" of the men of this new economy, men who lived only by the laws of "passion, fantasy and appetite."[2] They represented such men as fickle, unreliable, effeminate. These men did not merely resemble Credit, but willingly subjected themselves to her. And they found in such subjection not just anxiety, frustration, and disappointment but also excitement and pleasure. As we will see, the art of the early eighteenth century argues that the credit economy, for all the anxiety it generated, also served to shape male desire into compelling new forms. Artists such as Hogarth, Joseph Addison, and Daniel Defoe claimed that finance capitalism taught men to revel in suspense and emotional extremes, and to take new pleasure in a powerful and independent female sexuality. Thus did the gendered metaphors of political rhetoric become a potent means for understanding modern sexuality.

I

Writers across the political spectrum – not simply conservative ones – represented modern finance in terms of fraught gender relations. It was the Whiggish Addison who most famously described Credit as a beautiful, but flighty, virgin. His *Spectator* essay for March 3, 1711 explores the workings of the British economy in allegorical terms. This choice of the allegorical mode is itself significant; by means of allegory Addison is able to render speculation a spectacle, to embody ephemeral phenomena and unpredictable forces. He opens the essay with a telling pun: "In one of my late Rambles, or rather Speculations, I looked into the great Hall where the Bank is kept, and was not a little pleased to see the Directors, Secretaries, and Clerks, with all the other Members of that wealthy Corporation, ranged in their several Stations, according to the Parts they act in that just and regular Oeconomy."[3] The usually fanciful act of speculating is literalized in an act of looking. But this reassuringly concrete image of order and regularity is not sufficient to render perspicuous the workings of this institution. And so the essayist turns to the highly didactic and visual form of allegory: "I fell insensibly into a kind of Methodical Dream, which dispos'd all my Contemplations into a Vision or Allegory, or what else the reader shall please to call it" (430). Such a dream is not only methodical and clear, but also reifying. If credit is notoriously hard to understand,

---

[2] *Ibid.*, 113, 112.

[3] Joseph Addison, *Spectator* 3, in Angus Ross, ed., *Selections from the Tatler and the Spectator* (London: Penguin, 1982), 430. Further references will be given parenthetically in the text.

what better solution than to embody it, and, better still, to embody it in a woman, traditionally represented as the more fully material of the two sexes.

Of course, allegorical figures are often female, and as Pocock shows, Lady Credit had a prototype in the female figure of Fortuna. But the decision to represent Credit as a hysterical virgin was an overdetermined one and not simply the necessary result of literary convention. Indeed, critics have proposed numerous explanations for the connection between women and credit: Catherine Ingrassia argues that it is an extension of the traditional practice of "gendering feminine that which is devalued," while at the same time it reflects the relatively active role that eighteenth-century women played in the stockmarket.[4] Erin Mackie, in an exploration of the discourse surrounding the hoop petticoat, suggests that the connection between women and credit was founded on the contemporary construction of feminine subjectivity as superficial and baseless – empty as the hoop skirt – just as credit appeared to be.[5] I would argue that it was not only the perceived qualities of femininity – whether material or empty, attractive or repulsive – that made Lady Credit such a useful and ubiquitous rhetorical figure. It was also that "Lady Credit" could function as an apt object of male desire. For Addison, female sexuality serves both to naturalize or ground the credit system and to account for the feelings that system seemed to elicit in men. As a virgin, Credit is potentially sexually available to all – she is not yet exclusive property. Her throne of gold declares both her desirability and her distance; she is still independent, and men must compete for her favors. Thus, although excessively hypochondriachal, this "beautiful Virgin" (430) is patently an object of sexual desire. Her ability to turn base things to gold is described in terms of the Midas-like "Virtue in her Touch" (431).

For all her attractions, however, Credit also represents an erotic threat. To describe her distress at the sight of "hideous phantoms" (432) portending political instability, Addison quotes from Ovid's account of the death of Narcissus. In these lines Narcissus wastes away with self-longing, and the beauties that had charmed Echo gradually fade. This analogy with Narcissus functions on several levels. Since credit *is* nothing but appearance, it makes sense that Lady Credit, like Narcissus, should be concerned with nothing else. Her wellbeing consists precisely in her beauty, her reputation, so it is natural that she is fascinated by her own charms. Furthermore, because, in Ovid, Narcissus's death follows upon his recognition that the object of

---

[4] Catherine Ingrassia, *Authorship, Commerce, and Gender in Early Eighteenth-Century England* (Cambridge: Cambridge University Press, 1998), 2, 30.
[5] Erin Mackie, *Market à la Mode: Fashion, Commodity, and Gender in "The Tatler" and "The Spectator"* (Baltimore: Johns Hopkins University Press, 1997), 127.

his desire is himself, the allusion suggests the danger to Credit of *recognizing* the inherent impossibility of the consummation of her desires; that is, credit would suffer were investors to become too conscious that it functions precisely by means of postponement. But the solipsistic circularity of Credit's desire tests the limits of the serviceability of the larger allegory of Credit as desirable virgin: if Credit wants no one but herself, she cannot successfully be courted, and she cannot requite the desire of the men who invest in her. Indeed, the analogy with Narcissus suggests that Credit is not only pathologically self-centered but in love with an illusion – in love, in fact, with nothing: "[Narcissus] dreams / Upon a love that's bodiless: now he / believes that what is but a shade must be / a body."[6] Worse still, because the lines Addison quotes are followed in *The Metamorphoses* by an account of Echo's suffering at the sight of Narcissus's decay, Mr. Spectator's own role as a witness, "lamenting this sudden Desolation" (433), puts him (and any other investor) in the feminized and secondary position of (an) Echo. By these lights Mr. Spectator's empowering silence among others and his status as a disinterested viewer are transvalued: it now appears that the worldly man-about-town, in his relation to credit, might in fact be helplessly infatuated, *unable* to speak for himself, his identity reduced to a mere reflex of market prosperity.

The serviceability of the female figure of Credit is, moreover, further complicated by longstanding anxieties regarding the feminine and representation. According to the dictates of neoclassical decorum, at its best allegory functions as a visual or pictorial form, and one that is characterized by stasis rather than narrative action.[7] In another of his *Spectator* essays, Addison remarks that "It is certain *Homer* and *Virgil* are full of imaginary Persons, who are very beautiful in Poetry when they are just shown, without being engaged in any Series of Action."[8] It seems that Addison designs his dream-vision to accord with this ideal – to provide a clear image in the manner of Ripa's emblems. For most Augustan writers, however, the ideal of emblematic stability was not easily achieved in practice, and the failure to achieve it was often signaled by the presence of unruly feminine figures. In fact, female allegorical figures showed a disturbing tendency to become both mobile and monstrous; in Theresa Kelley's words, "For Locke and his intellectual descendants . . . allegory dramatizes the potential risks and anomalies of representation by blowing them up into monstrous, and at times

---

[6] *The Metamorphoses of Ovid*, trans. Allen Mandelbaum (New York: Harcourt Brace, 1993), 94.
[7] See Theresa Kelley, *Reinventing Allegory* (Cambridge: Cambridge University Press, 1997), 77.
[8] Addison, *Spectator* 357, in *The Spectator*, ed. Donald Bond, 5 vols. (Oxford: Clarendon Press, 1965), III, 337.

monstrously feminine, figures that look very much like all-too-concrete universals."[9]

While Lady Credit's actions in Addison's essay are largely limited to becoming ill and reviving again, the concrete nature of her sexuality has a disturbing effect on her function as a stable sign. Indeed, the most striking feature of Addison's allegory is that it gradually works to confuse tenor and vehicle, abstraction and image. Sexual pleasure does not simply serve as a sign for material satisfaction – the two become indistinguishable. Thus the vision ends in a manner reminiscent of a wet dream: "the Lady revived, the Bags swelled to their former Bulk, the Piles of Faggots and Heaps of Paper changed into Pyramids of Guineas: And for my own Part I was so transported with Joy, that I awaked, tho', I must confess, I would fain have fallen asleep again to have closed my Vision, if I could have done it" (433). The subtle sexual suggestiveness here, which reveals how fully intertwined sex and credit have become, has little explanatory or didactic value. That is, by the end of the essay sex is no longer merely a means for explaining the workings of credit but seems instead to be an aspect of it. The project of grounding the new economy in the body for the sake of clarity here gives way to bodily pleasure itself. There is little felt need to seek argumentative closure to this dream vision since sexual closure has been achieved. Addison is able to find enjoyment, not only in the thought of national prosperity, but in the very vicissitudes of the credit system, which are themselves exciting. Ultimately, then, the feminine instability to which the allegorical mode seemed prone, though distressing to neoclassical writers generally and to Addison in particular, nevertheless proved to have certain attractions.

Hogarth's 1721 engraving *The Lottery* (figure 2) further develops the relationship between credit, allegory, and sexuality. *The Lottery* shows the influence of Hogarth's study at Vanderbank's academy: the figures are inspired by Italianate allegory, the composition reminiscent of Raphael's *School of Athens* and *Disputa*. Like Addison's verbal allegory, this allegorical image serves to methodize and clarify what Hogarth elsewhere shows to be a chaotic phenomenon. In fact, the image is rather remarkable in its rage to order. Not only is the space divided into well-defined hierarchical levels, but the figures are so disposed that right and left mirror each other both at the level of the picture as a whole and within separate groupings. Most of these groupings are modeled on the classical motif of the judgment of Hercules: winner and loser both must choose between vice and virtue. But this

---

[9] Kelley, *Reinventing Allegory*, 75.

Figure 2. William Hogarth, *The Lottery* (1721).

consummately balanced and rational vision of the state lottery, Hogarth suggests, is as much a sham as the lottery itself. The space defined by the painting is like a stage space, with curtains at the margins. Nor is it as stable as it appears: the apparently solid floor is giving way under the figure of the Arts. The pedestal upon which Credit sits enthroned not only has Fraud at its base but is hollow, with what Hogarth punningly calls a "trap-door" in its side. Indeed, the whole scene forms a kind of prison, as the small barred window at the left suggests. Thus the artificiality and theatricality of the lottery system come to seem of a piece with the Italianate allegorical mode itself, with its excessive abstraction. Hogarth was always fond of the riddling quality of allegory, and yet, as Jenny Uglow remarks, his "vital contribution was his ability to move easily *between* the symbolic and the realistic. In most of his work, he restricted his emblems to details."[10] In his unusual *Royalty, Episcopacy and Law* of 1724, in which human faces are entirely replaced with symbols such as coins and gavels, the inhumanity of extreme abstraction is perhaps most keenly felt. The figures, described as inhabitants of the moon, are horrifically depersonalized, floating on clouds high above the real world of individuals.

[10] See Jennifer Uglow, *Hogarth: A Life and a World* (London: Faber and Faber, 1997), 60.

Always patriotically suspicious of the conventions and values of Italian art, Hogarth questions them even in *The Lottery*, where he shows what he has learned from them. As he developed his own trademark style, Hogarth came to modify Italian technique, aided by his study of the Dutch tradition. His hybrid style allowed him to comment upon types while still representing individualized figures. He would never again seek to satirize his disordered culture by means of such an ordered image.[11] In *The Lottery* Hogarth suggests that allegory, while it might be an effective means to ground and comprehend credit, can also, in its abstraction, be disturbingly like it.

If Mr. Spectator's Lady Credit was flighty, at least there was no indication that he was. The players in *The Lottery*, on the other hand, are all creatures of passionate extremes. Like Suspense, who sits at the base of the lottery pedestal, the lottery participants not only struggle between virtue and vice but spin back and forth between the extremes of elation and despair. As in Addison's essay, the narrative of speculation never comes to a rational conclusion; its very nature is suspense. Perpetual movement – but without progress – is emblematized in the many wheels in the scene. The lottery wheel, like the windmill in the hand of Wantonness, is, unlike its analogs the spinning wheel and the geometer's circle, a sign not of perfection but of whimsy, contingency, and sudden change. Fortune also has her wheel, but she stands upon it rather than spinning it, so that it resembles a torturer's wheel (a use of the wheel that is made explicit in Hogarth's later *South Sea Scheme*).

This world of passion, instability, and suspense is not only dominated by a woman but is haunted by images of perverse female sexuality. Wantonness seems to be of ambiguous gender, with breasts and one leg exposed, and a wig of two different lengths. Worse still, Britannia is shown an image of "the Earth receiving enriching Showers drawn from her self (an Emblem of State Lottery's)." The picture recalls paintings of Danaë, but here the woman is fertilized by herself, a commentary on the apparently miraculous capacity of the credit system to generate wealth out of nothing. Apollo's presence on the platform under Lady Credit serves to make the absence of Zeus more disturbing: there is no God – and no man – at the top of this hierarchy. Although a portrait of a king hangs opposite the picture of the earth, it goes unheeded. The Earth, moreover, is clearly an analog for Britannia: Britannia's pose is the same as hers, and she looks towards the

---

[11] In *Hogarth*, 3 vols. (New Brunswick: Rutgers University Press, 1991), Ronald Paulson argues that with *The Lottery* Hogarth demonstrated that he knew "the proper mode was Italian" (74), but as Paulson also notes, Hogarth still distrusted the "Italianate, operatic, allegorical mode" (74).

halo-encircled Apollo just as the Earth looks towards the sun. Her knees, too, are spread apart, as if to show her readiness to receive wealth into her lap. This is a scene not only of suspense and emotional extremes but of female power and sexual self-sufficiency. The virginity of Addison's Lady Credit is here given a further disturbing twist: this woman might be not only self-absorbed but genuinely self-sufficient. Ingrassia notes that eighteenth-century male polemicists complained that female stockjobbers found in their activities a substitute for sexual satisfaction with men.[12] Such polemics deflect attention from an even more troubling possibility encoded in the masturbatory woman: Lady Credit herself might be unresponsive to the male stockjobber's desires.

If abstraction is part of the problem in the artificial world of *The Lottery*, in *South Sea Scheme* the reliance on abstraction in the form of credit elicits not just mild perversity but violence. Here the allegorical figures, although associated with virtue, are reduced to literality by being made the objects of brutality. Trade lies languishing, Honour is flogged, Honesty is broken on the wheel, and Fortune is dismembered. All the other figures in the print, even when they have an emblematic significance, are contemporary human types, with the exception of the ape and the devil. The print thus serves to reground abstract concepts – one thinks of Elaine Scarry's account of the power of suffering and dead bodies to substantiate ideologies that have come into question.[13] These allegorical bodies serve to make once-valued concepts "real" again, if only through their destruction. The principal figures of Honour, Honesty, and Fortune are relentlessly corporealized: they are stripped to the skin and tortured. The figure of Fortune, in particular, serves to make a grisly point: fortune has its limits, has only so much to give. The viewer is reminded that wealth is physical and literal, and that it cannot be spontaneously generated out of nothing. If Fortune's flesh is distributed to the masses, eventually only a pile of bones will be left.

While the print aims to offer the salutary lesson that abstract notions must have their literal bearings, it simultaneously accuses contemporary Londoners of being too materialistic, too literal. Their love of the abstract is, paradoxically, grossly corporeal. Like cannibals they wave their arms in the hope that the devil will pitch them a chunk of Fortune's flesh, and it seems that they take a sexual pleasure in their brutality. The ape who strips Honour of his robe wears a phallic sword, and Villainy, whose

[12] Ingrassia, *Authorship, Commerce, and Gender*, 35.
[13] See Elaine Scarry, *The Body in Pain: The Making and Unmaking of the World* (New York: Oxford University Press, 1985).

mask has fallen over his groin, not only flogs Honour but menaces him with a dagger. As in *The Lottery*, we see power reversals between the genders, but here they are more explicitly sexualized. In the background women crowd on a balcony to raffle for husbands with lottery fortunes. On the whirligig topped by a goat (itself a sign of bestial sensuality), a Scottish man finds himself the object of a homely old woman's attention, and a woman, presumably a prostitute, takes a priest by the chin while holding a bundle of sticks with which to flagellate him. This world of credit and abstraction is also a world of thrilling suspense and violent sexual pleasures.

In an essay on the political implications of the use of the figure of Lady Credit, Terry Mulcaire argues that the critical focus on the autonomous rational man of the marketplace has obscured the extent to which the female figure of Credit embodies an even more important aspect of liberal ideology: its faith in the value of "the fecundity or creative power of the imagination."[14] As we have seen, there is indeed an intimate bond between speculation and aesthetics in early eighteenth-century England. For Hogarth as for Addison, the aesthetic is not simply a means to represent contemporary speculation but a discourse whose formal qualities allow for its exploration. But Hogarth goes a step further, implying that the formal qualities of the allegorical aesthetic had much in common with speculation, and that those qualities shaped even that most intimate of social impulses, sexual desire. Living in a world dominated by finance capitalism is like living in a world of allegory. This is a society where people take perverse sexual pleasure in the reified abstractions that Kelley argues typify modern allegory.[15] Indeed, the distrust of allegory so often voiced in neoclassical writings would seem in part to be a sign precisely of its pervasiveness and attractiveness. In this culture, so fond of abstractions, personifications, emblems, and riddles, speculation and the artistic imagination drew sustenance from each other. (In fact, this was true not only at the formal but also at the practical level; David Dabydeen reminds us that "the Arts in the eighteenth century were organized as 'projects' or business ventures with subscriptions and dividend payments."[16]) And after all, as Mulcaire points out, the Spectator himself – that hero of Augustan literary culture – is as much an artificial construct as Lady Credit. Indeed, one could

[14] Terry Mulcaire, "Public Credit; Or, The Feminization of Virtue in the Marketplace," *PMLA* 114: 5 (October 1999), 1033.
[15] Kelley, *Reinventing Allegory*, 7.
[16] David Dabydeen, *Hogarth, Walpole, and Commercial Britain* (London: Hansib, 1987), 45. Dabydeen also argues that Hogarth's satiric method, "the shock effect of which derives, fundamentally, from the distorting of conventional and customary data," had its source in the "sudden inversion or disjunction of traditional norms" that the South Sea episode embodied for contemporaries (52).

argue that it is precisely the abstract nature of his being, the fact that he claims to be versed in the "theory" of various social roles without actually filling any of them, that gives him his peculiar social power. The early eighteenth-century speculator, like Mr. Spectator, enjoys life in a world dominated by the aesthetics of allegory, a world where delightful dream visions and painful material realities seem interchangeable.

II

For the fullest development of this set of connections we must turn to yet another genre: the novel. Defoe's *Roxana* (1724), written after the trauma of the South Sea Bubble, dramatizes his struggle to come to terms with the workings of a credit economy. Indeed, I would argue that it is this connection to credit that accounts for the fact that this is the only one of Defoe's novels that does not end with the triumph of its protagonist. We can begin to understand Defoe's problem with his heroine by noting that her profession, that of a high-class mistress, is not only lucrative but seems to operate outside the normal contingencies of trade. Defoe's notion of trade is generally quite elastic: theft and piracy, for instance, while not legitimate forms of trade, at least have the virtue of resembling it, of dealing in objects. Even common prostitution, while it does not involve an exchange of objects, does involve a fairly straightforward notion of payment for services. Given his relatively sympathetic attitude towards prostitution, it is not entirely easy for Defoe to pinpoint what it is in Roxana that makes her so disturbing. The problem would seem to be that Roxana, as mistress, earns so much for her services that it hardly seems that she is really "earning" at all. After all, the conventions of keeping a mistress make it quite unlike typical market transactions, for the lover's offerings are presented not as payment but as gifts, and so tend to exceed any notion of fair market exchange: "he gave me Money so fast, that he rather pour'd it in upon me, than left me room to ask it; so that, before I could spend fifty Pistoles, I had always a hundred to make it up."[17] As in Hogarth's prints, female sexuality is used to figure this almost magical generation of surplus wealth. Allusions to Danaë abound: "he pull'd out a silk Purse, which had three-score Guineas in it, and threw them into my Lap" (76); "After he had Eaten, he pour'd the Sweet-Meats into my Lap" (98); "Amy waited at the Room where they Play'd; sat up all-Night to attend them; and in the Morning, when they

---

[17] Daniel Defoe, *Roxana*, ed. David Blewett (London: Penguin, 1982), 112. Further references will be given parenthetically in the text.

broke-up, they swept the Box into her Lap" (222). Female sexuality serves as a means for understanding an accumulation of wealth that operates outside the rigors of production and trade; Roxana need only lean back and receive. In *The Rise and Fall of Stocks* (1720), Allan Ramsay links speculation to prostitution in similar terms: speculators

> Grow rich in Fancy, treat their Whore,
> Nor mind they were, or shall be poor,
> Like little *Joves* they treat the Fair,
> With Gowd frae Banks built in the Air,
> For which their *Danaes* lift the Lap,
> And compliment them with a Clap,
> Which by aft jobbing grows a Pox,
> Till Brigs of Noses fa' with Stocks[18]

Sex and speculation are fused in the pun on "jobbing": the profitable activity of the middleman is allied with the thrusting motion of sex, so that the rhythms of the body and the stockmarket become one and the same.

The image of the mistress as a sign for the corrupt pleasures of a credit economy pervaded eighteenth-century arts, appearing in everything from Bubble playing cards to popular songs.[19] But it is not simply in her role as mistress that Roxana is linked to a credit economy. Like Nell Gwyn, mistress to Charles II, Roxana takes as financial advisor Sir Robert Clayton, who invests her money at the exorbitant rate of 8.5 percent. Acquisition of this kind, like the surplus generated by gambling in the scene with Amy above, does not seem to be properly grounded in productive activity. Roxana's many links to Nell Gwyn underscore the fact that she enjoys a power that is both excessive and illicit. The further she strays from relatively straightforward contract-based relationships, such as the one she has with her landlord at the beginning of the narrative, the more troubling her activity becomes. Like so many of Defoe's protagonists, her desire for wealth and power would appear to be insatiable, but here for the first time Defoe's sympathy for this appetite gives way to anxiety. For Roxana craves not just profit but what appears to be excessive profit, and she usually manages to get what she wants. Her protracted argument with the Dutch merchant on the issue of marriage serves to distinguish her ideal economy from the proper economy of trade. As she confesses to the reader, Roxana's concerns about losing her liberty are largely a mask for

---

[18] Quoted in Dabydeen, *Hogarth*, 31.
[19] For examples see *Ibid.*, 30–2.

her fear of losing her power over her money. Even the merchant's insistence that he would let her control their joint finances will not satisfy her, and one suspects that this is because Roxana knows very well that "it is customary for the Person kept, to receive from them that keep" (183), whereas the contractual relation proposed by the merchant would pool resources without multiplying them. Roxana's intransigence on this occasion not only frustrates but astounds the good merchant, who finds her quite literally unaccountable. Her baffling behavior is not, however, entirely unprecedented; she acts precisely like Defoe's own allegorical "Lady Credit," as he describes her in an essay in his *Review*: "'Tis a strange thing to think, how absolute this Lady is; how despotickly she governs all her Actions: If you court her, you lose her, or must buy her at unreasonable Rates; and if you do, she is always jealous of you, and Suspicious."[20] Like Credit in Addison's essay, Roxana is given to vapourish panics and melancholy: when all is well she loves to look at the papers that form her wealth but when in financial distress she simply melts into tears. Defoe's concern that it might be impossible to keep this mercurial lady chaste is revealed in his *Eleven Opinions of Mr. Harley* (1711), in which the speaker ridicules the Whigs for believing that credit could be controlled:

That was their Opinion, I believe no Body will question, and this Opinion was founded purely upon the belief that this CREDIT was their Mistress, sure to them only, and that no Body could debauch her but the Bank, & c. little dreaming, that in spight of all Mr. Defoe's Allegories of a Beautiful Coy Virgin Lady, called CREDIT, his Virgin prov'd a Whore.[21]

Sandra Sherman argues that in Defoe's economic essays Lady Credit "oversteps the stereotypical bounds of emblem-book womanhood, attaining a narrativity (however one-dimensional) anchored in a personal, idiosyncratic life of the body."[22] This coming-to-life of allegory takes an even more striking form in *Roxana*, in which Lady Credit, fully formed, seems to have stepped out into the London streets. The feminization of credit, which began as a rhetorical device, a mere translation of abstract economic processes, has now become naturalized to the point that it can inflect

[20] Daniel Defoe, *Defoe's Review*, ed. Arthur Wellesley Secord, 22 vols. (New York: Columbia University Press, 1938), VI, 18.

[21] Daniel Defoe, *Eleven Opinions of Mr. Harley* (May 14, 1711), 41.

[22] Sandra Sherman, *Finance and Fictionality in the Early Eighteenth Century: Accounting for Defoe* (Cambridge: Cambridge University Press, 1996), 41.

characterization in a "realistic" novel. Abstract market forces and female sexuality have become indistinguishable.

As the connection with the allegorical figure of Lady Credit suggests, the peculiarities of Roxana's character have important aesthetic implications. Sherman argues that Defoe uses Roxana's similarity to Lady Credit to think through issues of fictionality: Roxana as representation (and willful misrepresentation) becomes caught in a life-or-death struggle with the post-Bubble "reader," Susan, who insists upon knowing the truth about her. To this I would add that the particular kind of fictionality that Roxana represents has much in common with allegory gone awry, in which the stability and transparency of the allegorical image, and its correspondence to a single determinate idea, have broken down. Indeed, characters within the novel use the word "allegory" pejoratively, taking its unreliability for granted.[23] For Addison and Hogarth, Lady Credit easily became more corporeal and/or more abstract than neoclassical decorum allowed, but the same is true of Defoe's novelistic character. Roxana is at once a too fleshly presence and an elusive idea. We hear much about her appearance, but we know that appearance has little to do with what she really "is"; she might put on the garb of a Quaker, but she is no paragon of modesty and virtue. A masterful manipulator of external signs, it sometimes seems that she is nothing but a sign, rather like the financial documents of which she is so fond but whose value is uncertain. It is precisely this uncertainty that allows her to serve as a screen for the projected desires of others: she can be all things to all men because each "reads" her exterior as a transparent sign of her interior – when we as readers know that interior is in fact disturbingly labile. She is not simply deceptive, but consistently remote and aloof; the name of "Roxana" is but one among many, and it is telling that even we as readers should call her by this theatrical sobriquet rather than her Christian name, which we do not learn until the end of the novel. Long before Susan enters the narrative, Roxana shows a tendency to keep herself hidden: she keeps the extent of her wealth a secret, seeks out sequestered lodging, stays often within doors, and keeps whole parts of her narrative unknown even to the reader: "There is a Scene which came in here, which I must cover from humane Eyes or Ears; for three Years and about a Month, *Roxana* liv'd retir'd, having been oblig'd to make an Excursion, in a Manner, and with a Person, which Duty, and private Vows, obliges her not to reveal, at least, not yet"

---

[23] Thus, for instance, Roxana's sister-in-law angrily accuses her husband of "bantering" her with "Allegories" (56), and Roxana says of a conversation that it was all "Allegory; but it was all true" (289).

(223). Roxana's retreat into a distanced, third-person account of herself suggests that this secrecy, ostensibly for the sake of another, comes naturally to her. In fact, it would seem that this aloofness constitutes an important part of Roxana's appeal, both to her lovers and to the reader. Like the Lady Credit of Addison and Hogarth, Roxana's aloofness is a sign of her power and a focal point of her desirability. Although she is a prostitute, she lives as retired a life as a wealthy virgin, difficult of access.

Roxana is particularly enigmatic regarding her experiences overseas: "But I have no-Mind to write the History of my Travels on this side of the World [southern Europe], at least, not now; it would be too full of Variety" (140). In an age increasingly enamored of novelty and variety, such a remark cannot but function as a tease: Roxana suggests that her narrative stores are so overfull that she could not even begin to open them up to the reader. That Roxana should be associated with foreign travel and exotic charms makes perfect sense given the reliance of finance capitalism on British imperialism: stock values on speculative ventures were able to rise as high as they did not only because those ventures were speculative but also because the English believed that foreign lands, like those the South Sea Company was to exploit, would provide illimitable wealth in the form of gold and other resources. In essence, imperialism was to allow the English to transcend ordinary laws of economic growth. Exotic lands – distant and mysterious as Roxana herself – served, like her, as the imagined origins of unaccountable surplus. It comes as little surprise, then, that Roxana's links to the exotic are also links to power. By means of her ownership of a Turkish slave, Roxana learns styles of self-presentation that she can use to fascinate men – including, it would seem, the King – back home. (As with her narrative, however, she is wise enough not to reveal too much: she pleases her house guests more with a French dance in Muslim dress than do two women who perform authentic Georgian and Armenian dances. It is the veneer of the exotic and not the genuinely foreign that appeals to the British audience.) Roxana's description of herself as an Amazon helps to underscore the point that this power, though ostensibly unfeminine, is in fact disturbingly female. Laura Brown argues that during the eighteenth century the figure of the Amazon served as an emblem for imperial expansion, one that masked the masculine character of territorial aggression. Through its eponymous heroine *Roxana* "brings trade and violence into a symptomatically significant proximity."[24]

---

[24] Laura Brown, *Ends of Empire: Women and Ideology in Early Eighteenth-Century English Literature* (Ithaca: Cornell University Press, 1993), 154.

I would argue, however, that the violence in the book arises not because of Roxana's connection with trade, but because of her lack of connection with it. Roxana represents, after all, not a concrete commercial relationship to the foreign, but a speculative relation to it, just as she hints that her travels to exotic lands are quite remarkable – while refusing to give us any account of them. Like Lady Credit she is secretive rather than frankly aggressive, and it is precisely this secretiveness that leads to the violence with which the novel ends. Roxana is not a mask for male aggression but simply a mask, and the violence that attaches itself to her appears to be a necessary result of her theatricality. It is thus perfectly fitting that, Amazon or not, she herself primly disavows any connection with Susan's death. Roxana is dangerous because she is a mere conglomeration of wishes and dreams, a fantasy of the foreign and the pleasures it can provide. Like Hogarth's Queen of the Lottery, she is part of an elaborate piece of theater, telling us "the dirty History of [her] Actings upon the Stage of Life" (111).

But if Roxana herself is largely passive and superficial in her relation to the world, she does not work alone to achieve her ends. Critics have long pondered over Roxana's unusual relation to her servant, Amy, who not only cares for Roxana without pay during hard times, but serves as a sexual substitute for her, and finally, it would seem, kills Roxana's daughter Susan "for" her. The depth of attachment between the two women, and their mutual identification, can, I would argue, be understood in terms of the dualism that credit enacts. After all, early finance capitalism is at once a way of doing business, a practice, and, as Pocock suggests, a mere fantasy of gain. If, taken on her own terms, Roxana functions as an allegorical figure, as enigmatic idea and its glamorous sign, together with Amy she configures a second-order allegory in which she is the glamorous enigmatic idea for which Amy is the practical sign. Throughout the novel, Amy serves as an adjudicator between Roxana and the world:

I walk'd sometimes in the *Mall* with my Woman, *Amy*; but I kept no Company, and made no Acquaintances, only made as gay a Show as I was able to do, and that upon all Occasions: I found however, the World was not altogether so unconcern'd about me, as I seem'd to be about them; and first, I understood that the Neighbours begun to be mighty inquisitive about me; as who I was? and what my Circumstances were? *Amy* was the only Person that cou'd answer their Curiosity, or give any Account of me, and she a tattling Woman, and a true Gossip, took Care to do that with all the Art that she was Mistress of. (206)

In relation to Amy, then, Roxana herself serves as an abstraction with Amy as her material sign. Thus do allegorical modes of representation proliferate around Roxana. While Roxana, beautiful and desirable, sits sequestered at home, Amy does her (often dirty) work in the world. Roxana is from the start of the narrative prone to nervous fits and despondency on the one hand, and exaggerated ambition on the other. Like Lady Credit, even when all is well she can become suddenly anxious: when she finds herself "very Rich," she says she is in fact "richer than I knew how to think of," and that "thinking of it sometimes, almost distracted me, for want of knowing how to dispose of it, and for fear of losing it all again by some Cheat or Trick" (148). While she embodies the glamorous and mercurial veneer of credit, its fantastic and ideal forms, it is left to Amy, her alter-ego, actually to take care of business. As Roxana laments in Amy's absence, "I was irresolute to the last Degree; I was, for want of *Amy*, destitute; I had lost my Right-Hand; she was my Steward, gather'd in my Rents, *I mean my Interest-Money*, and kept my Accompts, and, *in a word*, did all my Business" (366). Amy is the reality principle to Roxana's pleasure principle. Thus Roxana is more reliant on Amy than on any of her lovers. As she puts it, "to have fall'n upon *Amy*, had been to have murther'd myself" (350). Roxana's crisis at the end of the book is as much about the loss of Amy as it is about fears for Susan.

Susan is the first to recognize Amy for what she is – a mere stand-in for the wealth that is Roxana. She boldly tells Amy that "she could never make Instruments pass for Principals, and pay the Debt to the Agent, when the Obligation was all to the Original" (360). Amy's advice that Susan enjoy her new good fortune without questioning into it too closely foregrounds Amy's role as a distributor of dividends whose origins are deliberately mysterious. What Susan fails to recognize is that Roxana could never be fully and immediately available to her even though she is the source of Amy's alms: like any speculative venture, Roxana knows she functions best as an abstract fantasy. Susan's mother is in fact doubly distanced from her: Amy serves as a sign for Roxana, while "Roxana" herself is nothing but another sign for an even more elusive signified. Like the Londoners in Hogarth's *South Sea Scheme*, Susan is forced to navigate her way through a world of allegory, and her honest intentions ultimately make her a target for violence.

In her relations to Amy and Susan, Roxana's identity is defined in terms of two very different economic modes: if she is to Amy as interest is to instrument, she is to Susan as producer is to product. The model of trade for which Defoe had always been such a champion does not seem to be an option here: one must choose between the morally suspect world of finance and the unimpeachable work of production. Sharing her mother's name, Susan appears late in the narrative as another, and quite different, possible alter-ego for Roxana, one that would bind Roxana to a healthy, moral world of productive relations. That we do not even know Roxana's Christian name until we are introduced to her daughter makes clear that it is only through genuine production, in this case in the form of reproduction, that Roxana's value could have found an immediate, real grounding. In more ways than one, to attach herself to Susan would be to relinquish her mask of artifice. But Roxana remarks that "if I bred often, it would something impair me in the Great Article that supported my Interest, I mean, what he [the Prince] call'd Beauty" (143). She chooses to preserve appearances and serve her interest rather than turn her sexual exchanges into something genuinely productive, and it is this for which the novel condemns her. The pleasure the narrative initially takes in Roxana's triumphs finally gives way to a manifest discomfort, and with Susan's death the moral ambiguity of Roxana's conduct becomes the focus of the narrative.

As we saw with Addison and Hogarth, then, the vagaries of credit are not simply figured in a woman but figured in terms of female sexuality and violence. Roxana turns away from female sexuality in its benign form – motherhood – to embrace it in its perversely self-contained and illicit forms. Not only is Roxana remote and aloof, but in her partnership with Amy she finds a bond of identification more intense than any of her connections with men. In Amy's practicality, and Roxana's beauty and reticence, Defoe is able to represent and think through the two sides of modern credit – and their reliance on each other. The result is a vision not just of credit but of female sexuality, one characterized, from the male perspective, by narcissism and withdrawal. Like Britannia providing herself with enriching showers, the Roxana/Amy duo seems to provide for itself, with both women welcoming riches into their laps that far exceed their dues or their own productive capacities.

But if the narrative ultimately turns against Roxana, it is nevertheless important to note that she remains "beautiful" to the end. Like Lady Credit, her experience and her age never seem to make her less desirable. In this she shows her emblematic side: the appeal of finance capitalism, though damaged by the Bubble, continued through the eighteenth century and continues today. In *Roxana* we see how the visceral and emotional pleasures and pains of life in a credit economy colored conceptions of private as well as public life: the men who loved riding the whirligig of speculation seemed also to have a gust for a woman with a bundle of switches. Whether or not eighteenth-century women enjoyed real gains in power, the finance fictions of the day promoted a fantasy of sexual relations in which a mercurial and dominating woman exerted an irresistible attraction. Thus early eighteenth-century art argued that a nation "in Slavery to Creditors . . . bound Hand and Foot"[25] had learned to enjoy its bondage even as it disavowed such enjoyment, happy to maintain its Roxanas "like a Queen."[26]

---

[25] Daniel Defoe, *Fair Payment No Sponge: or, Some Considerations on the Unreasonableness of Refusing to Receive back Money lent on Publick Securities* (1717); quoted in Sherman, *Finance and Fictionality*, 15.
[26] Defoe, *Roxana*, 211.

CHAPTER 2

From sadism to masochism in the novels
of Frances Burney

During the years immediately following the South Sea Bubble, the English
were acutely attuned to the social and even psychological changes that the
Financial Revolution had brought in its train. At the end of the century,
speculation once again became a significant social issue, as it came to be
associated not only with economic activity but with possibilities for political
change as well. As Edmund Burke complained, the French revolutionary
project extended the spirit of stockjobbing to politics and even manners
and morality. As we will see, many of Burke's contemporaries, even those
who were not political radicals, linked this extension of the speculative
spirit to an efflorescence of painful, self-abnegating desire, and they
argued that such desire was not only the most virtuous kind, but should
be practiced by both men and women.

To understand this change we begin by examining the political economy
of the turn of the century and the literary genre that was, arguably, most
sensitive to its nuances: the novel. During the past twenty years, literary historians have revealed the extent to which socio-economic concerns shaped
the development of the novel,[1] and to trace the particulars of the relationship between economic developments and romance we cannot do better
than turn to "the chief local colorist of the Georgian retail scene,"

---

[1] Thus Michael McKeon shows that *Robinson Crusoe* effects the "naturalization of desire" while
Gulliver's Travels argues for the "containment of desire" (*The Origins of the English Novel 1600–
1740* [Baltimore: Johns Hopkins University Press, 1987], Chapters 9 and 10). Nancy Armstrong, in
Desire and Domestic Fiction, speaks of a general "economy of pleasure in which the novel has been
implicated since its inception," one that involves the harnessing of desire and pleasure in the name
of class-specific political ends (*Desire and Domestic Fiction: A Political History of the Novel* [Oxford:
Oxford University Press, 1987], 15). More recently, James Thompson has examined the role of the
novel in structuring and regulating the linked economies of the spheres of finance and romance,
and Deidre Lynch has argued that the very construction of character during the long eighteenth
century was economically motivated (Thompson, *Models of Value: Eighteenth-Century Political
Economy and the Novel* [Durham: Duke University Press, 1996]; Lynch, *The Economy of Character*
[Chicago: University of Chicago Press, 1998]). In this chapter I, too, will examine the links
between economics and desire in the novel, but I will aim more specifically to explore the varying
forms that desire took.

Frances Burney.[2] For while Burney is best known for her first novel, a work of the 1770s, she continued to write novels, at a rate of roughly one per decade, right through what has traditionally been known as the Romantic period, and she wrote always with an eye to the current state of her society. Burney's novelistic oeuvre provides a rare opportunity to cross period boundaries and trace the influence of historical change on the work of a single author.[3]

Burney, no less than Wulhan Hogarth and Daniel Defoe, was fascinated by the dangers of desire in her culture. In fact, Burney's best recent critics have overturned the traditional view of her as the quintessential novelist of propriety and gentility, arguing instead that her writing is obsessed with "violence and hostility."[4] Julia Epstein and Kristina Straub attribute this violence to Burney's feelings of oppression as a woman writer, Margaret Doody helps us better understand it in terms of Burney's personal life, and Claudia Johnson explores its political significance, but I will argue that the nature of this violence changes from one novel to the next and that this change can be related to an evolution in Burney's conception of economic life.[5] Each of Burney's novels presents a different paradigm for romantic love, and the evolution of these paradigms reveals a changing understanding of the workings of the market economy. With increasing self-consciousness, Burney uses her novels to explore the relationship between the dynamics of marketplace desire and the dynamics of romantic desire – and the violence that colored them both. In so doing she takes us on

[2] The phrase comes from Deidre Lynch's account of the early twentieth-century view of Burney's writing (*Economy of Character*, 168).

[3] In a review for the *Spectator*, a Victorian critic remarked that the popularity and praise enjoyed by Burney's first novel, *Evelina*, had "spoilt her for literature" (*Spectator* 55 [January 6, 1883], 18). While they have not generally couched their objections in such terms, until fairly recently even modern critics have tended to dismiss Burney's later works, regarding them as delicate novels of manners like *Evelina* that simply have the disadvantages of being less sprightly and exceedingly long. This dismissal has been unfortunate in its effects, for it has not only led to the neglect of novels rich in artistry and insight, but has also encouraged scholars to regard Burney as a strictly eighteenth-century figure. Although her writing career spans several decades, her topics include industrialization and the French Revolution, and she borrows from the Gothic novel and the Jacobin novel, Burney's work has rarely been studied by Romanticists, and even the recent blossoming of interest in Romantic women writers has not significantly changed this situation. But if Burney's first two novels reflect an eighteenth-century sensibility, her final two were written in the Romantic period and address specifically Romantic concerns.

[4] Julia Epstein, *The Iron Pen: Frances Burney and the Politics of Women's Writing* (Madison: University of Wisconsin Press, 1989), 5.

[5] See *ibid.*; Kristina Straub, *Divided Fictions: Fanny Burney and Feminine Strategy* (Lexington: University Press of Kentucky, 1987); Margaret Doody, *Frances Burney: The Life in the Works* (New Brunswick: Rutgers University Press, 1988); and Claudia Johnson, *Equivocal Beings: Politics, Gender, and Sentimentality in the 1790s* (Chicago: University of Chicago Press, 1995).

a journey from a sadistic world in which consumption is prohibited to a masochistic one in which the pleasures and perversities of early nineteenth-century politics and consumerism are fully developed. In this chapter we will first look briefly at Burney's early novels *Evelina* (1778) and *Cecilia* (1782), and then examine her later, Romantic-era novels, *Camilla* (1796) and *The Wanderer* (1814), in more depth.

I EVELINA

In Burney's first two novels, desire is relatively unproblematic; there is only one way of wanting, and the question is simply whether one's wants are likely to be gratified. In *Evelina* in particular, the characters' wishes meet with either opposition or favor, but the form of those wishes is never a matter of concern. The straightforward character of desire in this first novel is immediately made visible in the material realm, for economic life in *Evelina* is a strikingly uncomplicated affair: production, prices, expenditure, and debt hardly figure in the book, which is concerned almost solely with consumption and its moral regulation. This representation of the market-place is, moreover, exactly attuned to the representation of the romantic desires that come increasingly to preoccupy the heroine. It is not by chance that Evelina's "entrance into the world" of adult sexuality is coincident with and signaled by her entrance into the world of London consumerism, for growing up in *Evelina* is largely a matter of becoming sufficiently bold to entertain both material and erotic desires in the face of their potential prohibition. As we will see, however, the development of this boldness is no mean accomplishment, for prohibition in this book is the prerogative of father figures who often find positive pleasure in denying women's desires.

We begin then with an exploration of the consumer economy of the novel. Immediately upon arrival in the metropolis, Evelina is told by her hostess Mrs. Mirvan that the women of their party must all "*Londonize*" themselves.[6] They quickly set out to do so, going "*a-shopping*, as Mrs. Mirvan calls it . . . to buy silks, caps, gauzes, and so forth" (27). Urban life is defined by consumption, and relies, moreover, on the elasticity of the consumer's desire. The very structure of Evelina's sentence suggests the dynamic at work here: the abundance of goods is intended to meet with an expandable capacity for desire – shopping is the realm of "and so forth." Indeed, Evelina remarks that "'I thought I should never have

---

[6] Frances Burney, *Evelina*, ed. Edward and Lillian Bloom (Oxford: Oxford University Press, 1968), 25. All subsequent references to this novel will be to this edition and will be given parenthetically in the text.

chosen a silk, for they produced so many, I knew not which to fix upon, and they recommended them all so strongly, that I fancy they thought I only wanted persuasion to buy every thing they shewed me'" (27). Consumer London of the 1770s is the realm of boundless desire. This state of affairs, so familiar to the modern reader, should not be taken for granted; it was in fact quite novel. As David Alexander observes, the decades around 1800 witnessed a gradual shift away from "the very old economic assumption that demand curves are inelastic, and that competitive pricing will not increase sales sufficiently to maintain profit margins; or, looked at from another point of view, that the size of the retail market is fixed, and that increased sales in one shop means losses for others."[7] The traditional insistence on fair trade rather than free trade reflected this conception. But the legal structures, including sumptuary laws, that supported this older form of trade in its local networks had largely disappeared by the start of the eighteenth century.[8] The theory and the practice of the free-market economy required that desire be elastic, capable of keeping pace with or even outstripping production. Thus even as industrial methods of manufacture made more goods available to more people, desire remained unsated. The good consumer of the late eighteenth century, then, did not just own a certain number of things or things of a particular quality; he or she learned to enjoy the adventure of desire itself. The aim was no longer simply to own but to experience the pleasure of desire; the aim was to shop.

That *Evelina*'s London is a place where desires are stimulated and not simply satisfied is underscored by the fact that shopping there is considered a form of amusement; Evelina remarks that the shops she visits "are really very entertaining" (27). Seeing goods, seeing people, and seeing "sights" are all considered forms of entertainment, and a typical morning for a London tourist like Evelina consists of "*seeing sights*, auctions, curious shops, *and so forth*" (37, second emphasis mine). This mutually sustaining interplay between the practical and the pleasurable in the commercial domain was a relatively new phenomenon. Of course, the juxtaposition of market and spectacle was as old as the old town fairs, but the eighteenth century saw the rise of shops that catered to a high-class trade by presenting themselves simultaneously as places of business and as venues for genteel socializing and amusement. This development was epitomized in Wedgwood's establishment of elegant showrooms in exclusive

[7] David Alexander, *Retailing in England during the Industrial Revolution* (London: Athlone Press, 1970), 161.

[8] See James Carrier, *Gifts and Commodities: Exchange and Western Capitalism since 1700* (New York: Routledge, 1995).

neighborhoods – with exhibitions by invitation only. This conflation of sales and recreation did not transform the former alone; the late eighteenth-century entertainment industry grew alongside and formed an important part of fashionable consumerism. Thus it was not only obviously hybrid institutions like Cox's Museum, a showplace for mechanical toys, that made a pastime of consumerism. The various tourist sites that *Evelina* visits, ranging from the opera to Ranelagh, are, like the shops, places for admiring women's dresses, gawking at spectacles, buying refreshments and socializing, or complaining about entrance fees. Late eighteenth-century consumers were encouraged to shop, as one would attend the opera, without reference to what they had already "consumed." Burney's London is a place where desire comes to life as if for the first time, and it is the untamed energy of that desire that fuels the events of this lively novel.

For Burney, this world of entertaining consumerism is largely a woman's world, and one dominated by mother figures. For Evelina herself, entrance into the fashionable world and into womanhood are the same thing, and in this entrance she can be instructed only by older women. Thus it is Lady Howard, who refers to Evelina as "my daughter" (23), who procures permission from the reluctant Villars for Evelina to go to London. And it is the mother of Evelina's friend and her own so-called "adopted mother," "mamma Mirvan" (28) who introduces her to the world of London amusements. As older women and mothers, these women lend a certain respectability to the activity of consumption. But there is, in this female consumerism, a latent contradiction, a potential ideological problem: while consumption of fashionable and luxury items is economically useful, promoting domestic circulation, the development and intensification of female desire *per se* is perceived as potentially socially destabilizing. That is, the feminine capacity for limitless desire required by the expanding economy becomes dangerous when it spills over into noneconomic domains. In this we witness a slight shift from early eighteenth-century representations of the dangers of female desire. In Alexander Pope's *The Rape of the Lock* (1712), for instance, it is Belinda's role to own and prize material goods; the difficulty for Pope lies in the fact that Belinda's pride in possession gives her a sense of personal power and independence. The emphasis is on the empowering effects of ownership; we do not hear of how Belinda acquires her goods, but see her in the act of displaying her charms, both natural and artificial.[9] In *Evelina*, by contrast, once a woman's hair has

---

[9] Alexander Pope, *The Rape of the Lock, an Heroi-Comical Poem*, in *Pope: Poetical Works*, ed. Herbert Davis (Oxford: Oxford University Press, 1978), 86–109.

been dressed, once she has purchased her cloth, we generally do not hear of those things again. The women of *Evelina* take more pride and pleasure in shopping than in ownership. Thus, if the difficulty with Belinda is that her satisfaction in the possession of material things leaves her without desire for a man, the risk with Evelina is that through shopping she will learn to desire not only commodities but men as well – and this, of course, is precisely what happens.

This contradiction in the ideology of female consumerism is most fully embodied in Evelina's grandmother Madame Duval, whose appetite for consumer pleasures is matched by the relentlessness with which she pursues all her other aims. Of all the characters we meet, she is the most vocal in her appreciation of fashionable entertainments: she says of Cox's Museum that "'it's the grandest, prettiest, finest sight that ever I see, in England'" (76). At the same time, because "the toilette seems the chief business of her life" (155), she is deeply invested in the activity of shopping: "'Howard Grove is the worst! There's never no getting nothing one wants'" (151). With her French tastes and her obsession with her wig, her Lyons silk, and her looks, Madame Duval represents the *ne plus ultra* of fashionable femininity. She is also, however, the most willful woman in the book, the one who is most determined to have all her wishes satisfied, and outside the realm of consumption such willfulness appears not feminine but profoundly masculine. It is for this reason that Madame Duval appears at times to be almost manly, and Burney paints her as a comic monster of mixed gender attributes. As Doody argues, Burney uses the convention of transvestism in the theater "to explode and express the tensions involved in playing the female role in the eighteenth century. Madame Duval – vain, overdressed, highly painted, simpering, and rude – has all the traditional larger-than-life qualities of the stage dame."[10] The conflation in Madame Duval of the very feminine and the very masculine starkly reveals the contradictions embedded in late eighteenth-century consumerism: fashionable femininity, taken to its limit, becomes a kind of masculinity. Given this, it is not surprising that the heroine's relation to female consumerism is a complicated one. Evelina's ambivalence reflects an ambivalence in Burney herself; in her old age she "crossed out in her diaries and letters many allusions to dress."[11] This tension is felt throughout the book and stems from an awareness of the potential threat to femininity

---

[10] Doody, *Life*, 50. Doody notes, too, that in the image of Madame Duval that served as the frontispiece to volume II, "the wigless head of the helpless victim is almost male, in grotesque contrast to her remaining feminine draperies" (53).

[11] Straub, *Divided Fictions*, 68.

lodged within femininity itself; Madame Duval in particular functions as a constant reminder of what her granddaughter could become. Evelina must finish her female education by learning to desire, but she must also be careful not to take that learning too far.

Nor does the risk to Evelina lie solely in the fact that excessive female desire is unbecoming, for such desire often meets with fierce male retribution. The men in the book show themselves to be remarkably jealous of their prerogatives in the domain of desire, and often are clearly uncomfortable with the female desires set in motion in the marketplace. Both in the book's frame and within the book, male figures are associated with the prohibition of desire, and sometimes even respond to its expression with cruelty. Burney opens her book with a nervous dedication to "The Authors Of The Monthly And Critical Reviews," requesting their "patronage" (3). This plea for chivalric protection from the public at large helps to obscure the fact that the book is in fact a form of fashionable entertainment, even as the concern with reviewers makes the modernity and commercial import of the project obvious. The anonymous "editor's" initial plea for "MERCY," however, is immediately followed by a recognition that she is entitled to no more than the rough "Justice" available to those with the temerity to enter the market, where reviewers are already "engaged" to the public, "which will not fail to crave 'The penalty and forfeit of your bond'" (4). This disturbing Shylockian image reveals a powerful anxiety that the expression of desire, in this case the yearning to enter into fashionable literary commerce, might meet with violent retribution. This is the first time the shadow of violence crosses the page in relation to the world of fashion and commerce, but it is not the last; indeed, the author's effort to place herself under a kind of paternal protection from a world that takes pleasure in cruelty is reiterated in the heroine's struggles.

Evelina is introduced to us as a young woman who "must owe all her rational expectations to adoption and friendship" (19), and the plot of the novel revolves around her search for adequate patronage and protection. The paternal figure who initially provides that protection, Mr. Villars, strives to protect his ward from the world of fashion and consumption simply by barring her from it. Villars understands that that world is about much more than hairstyles and silks; it is a place where one develops habits of desire: "'can your Ladyship be serious in proposing to introduce her to the gaieties of a London life? Permit me to ask for what end, or what purpose? A youthful mind is seldom totally free from ambition; to curb that, is the first step to contentment, since to diminish expectation, is to increase enjoyment'" (18). For Villars, curbing desire, rather than practicing and developing it, is the surest way to promote enjoyment. Nothing is more threatening to happiness than an augmentation of desire; nothing is more productive of happiness than its diminution. Evelina, like Burney, understands from the outset that it is safest to align herself, at least in word, with the fathers in the novel, even if in deed she seeks to enter the female world of consumption. Thus, when she writes to request that she be permitted to visit London, she claims that "Lady Howard insists upon my writing! – yet I hardly know how to go on; a petition implies a want, – and have you left me one? No, indeed" (23). Evelina affects to adopt Villars's nondynamic view of desire, according to which desire is static rather than elastic. She tends to speak in such terms whenever she is at risk of offending a paternal authority. Hence, when discussing the issue of how best to approach her true father, she says to Villars, "'Again I must repeat, I know not what to *wish*: think for me, therefore, my dearest Sir'" (123). Nevertheless, as in that first petition to Villars, Evelina finds her desires unavoidably stimulated by those of the women around her: "'I cannot, for my life, resist wishing for the pleasures they offer me'" (23).

The irony of all this is that the father figures through whom Evelina seeks protection are the very persons from whom she needs protection. For it is fathers above all who not only wish to limit desire but who punish women for practicing it. Villars's quiet efforts to limit the play of desire find an aggressive, nasty counterpart in Captain Mirvan's disdain for feminine amusements and punishment of female appetite. The Captain's wife and daughter, and, to a lesser extent, Evelina herself, are all subjected to his cruelty, but it is Madame Duval, not surprisingly, who is his primary victim. Madame Duval, whose Frenchness is linked, for the Captain, to her interest in fashion and frippery, becomes the object of "jokes" intended to hurt her physically and mortify her. The scene at Cox's Museum crystallizes the feminine "crime" and masculine "punishment" logic of these jokes. When Madame Duval goes into "extacies" when listening to a concert of mechanical music, the Captain applies salts to her nose – as if she were, in true feminine style, in a swoon – causing her to scream aloud with "pain and surprise" (77). He thus mocks her femininity while making her physically suffer for her pleasure in consumerist entertainment. The most serious of the Captain's tricks, in which Madame Duval's clothes and wig are spoiled when she is "hanged" by the feet, is even rougher in its violence.

But while the world of fashions and amusements is considered a feminine one, it is not associated solely with women. Men concerned with fashion become, by virtue of that fact, feminized, and they, too, come in for their share of rough usage from conventionally masculine men. For if someone like Madame Duval is guilty of learning in the marketplace to usurp the masculine role of desiring subject, the fashionable man is guilty of revealing the fact that masculine desire is not merely natural and inevitable but can, like feminine desire, be fostered and learned. That is, the conspicuously fashionable man makes even male desire look artificial, acquired; he makes a show of a desire that should, though powerful in its effects, remain inconspicuous. The fop Mr. Lovel is accordingly treated by Captain Mirvan much like Madame Duval. Mirvan's comment that the "jem cracks" (110) at Cox's Museum are fit only for monkeys looks ahead to the mortification he will offer Lovel. At the end of the book, the Captain presents Lovel with a "twin brother," a monkey "full-dressed, and extravagantly à-la-mode!" (400). When Lovel, afraid to strike at the Captain, gives a furious blow to the monkey, it responds by fastening its teeth to one of his ears. Lovel, like Duval, is thus severely punished for his fashionableness; the Captain joyfully proclaims, "I'll warrant he won't give an hour tomorrow morning to settling what he shall put on; why his coat [spotted with blood] . . . would be a most excellent match for old Madame Furbelow's best Lyons' silk'" (403).

It is telling that this scene, unrelated to the love plot, is the last full scene in the novel, for such placement suggests the importance of this ostensibly offhand aggression. Captain Mirvan simply carries to an extreme the prohibitive, punishing masculine ethos that runs through the book as a whole. It is clear that on one level the book condemns this aggression and the social conditions that permit men to practice it. But it is also undeniable that such aggression is often intended to be a source of comic pleasure, and the climactic position of the scene with the monkey underscores the emotional significance of this pleasure. Even Evelina, sweet as she is, would seem to draw some satisfaction from these scenes of violence, which she describes in great detail, as in the account above of Madame Duval's disgraceful dirtying. It is true of course that Evelina accepts Mirvan's behavior only because she has no choice but to do so; whereas she is at least sympathetic to Villars's way of thinking, her alignment with Mirvan is apparently only superficial. As she says of Lovel, "I was really sorry for the poor man, who, though an egregious fop, had committed no offence that merited such chastisement" (401). And yet the reader can not help but notice the extent to which Mirvan's victims are Evelina's own antagonists, and both she and reader who identifies with her are naturally led to find some enjoyment in their mortification. After all, Madame Duval not only embarrasses Evelina but threatens to treat her as tyrannically as she did her mother, and Lovel is hostile to Evelina throughout the book, taking an almost erotic

pleasure in her discomfort: her vexation at his sneering speeches "both
stimulated and delighted him" (79). The plot itself, then, enacts the heroine's alignment with the father and shows the advantages of such an alignment. Evelina's social situation, as an orphan and a bastard, is more difficult
and defenseless than that of Burney's later heroines Cecilia and Camilla, yet
her trials are nowhere near as severe as theirs. *Evelina* stands alone among
Burney's novels in directing the bulk of the violence it represents not
only away from the heroine but toward her antagonists. An undercurrent
of cruelty pulses just below the surface of the glittering social world of
Evelina – witness Lord Merton's "twisting his whip with his fingers" even
while saying Lady Louisa is all sweetness (280) – yet Evelina herself,
under the protection of her author and her patrons within the book,
suffers relatively little from it.

  Evelina is thus a book that not only represents sadistic acts but also draws
the reader into a kind of identification with them. Indeed, it paints a world
structured according to a logic that is surprisingly consistent with that of de
Sade's novels. This is nowhere so apparent as in Evelina's relations to her
various father and mother figures. As Gilles Deleuze explains, in the
works of de Sade the "paternal and patriarchal theme undoubtedly pre-
dominates," and "the mother becomes the victim *par excellence*, while
the daughter is elevated to the position of incestuous accomplice."[12]
The same daughterly alignment with the power of fathers occurs here.
The very insecurity of Evelina's paternity permits the multiplication of
father figures and makes the desire to be "owned" by a father a primary
theme.[13] Furthermore, the "father" whom Evelina likes least but with
whom she spends the most time is, interestingly enough, Captain Mirvan,
who does indeed force her to act as accomplice in his abuse of her grandmother, an abuse that is, moreover, tinged with sexuality. Mirvan himself
describes the "use" he makes of Madame Duval in sexual terms: "'I hope
she's in good case,' said he, winking significantly, 'and won't flinch at
seeing service: she has laid by long enough to refit and be made tight'"
(391). Evelina wonders at Captain Mirvan's almost compulsive attraction

---

[12] Gilles Deleuze, "Coldness and Cruelty," in Deleuze, *Masochism*, trans. Jean McNeill (New York:
Zone Books, 1989), 59, 59–60.

[13] Here, too, we see a connection with the work of de Sade. For while Sacher-Masoch's fiction is
dominated by the contract (Deleuze, "Coldness and Cruelty," 21), "the sadist thinks in terms of institutionalized possession" (20), including the possession of persons and their bodies. Evelina's
confusion on the issue of "to whom I most belong" (353) points to the absolute necessity in her
world not only of possessing but also of being possessed; otherwise, one sits "like a cypher, whom
to nobody belonging, by nobody was noticed" (340).

to this woman he hates and remarks on the deep pleasure he takes in his "sport" with her.

Evelina's relationships to her various father figures are themselves fraught with sexual tension. There is little of this between Evelina and Captain Mirvan, although he does, as Kristina Straub points out, look at her like "a piece of meat, good only as long as she 'keeps.'"[14] But the relations between Evelina and her adopted father, and Evelina and her natural father, have a palpable erotic charge. The low-level eroticism of the relationship with Villars is epitomized in the striking ambiguity of the final sentence of the book – "the chaise now waits which is to conduct me to dear Berry Hill, and to the arms of the best of men" (406) – will Evelina spend her wedding night in Orville's arms or in Villars's? Indeed, the anagrammatic interchangeability of the names of father and husband is itself suggestive. But it is in Evelina's encounter with her real father, Belmont, that the Sadean quality of her relationship with paternal figures is most fully manifested. A highly emotional scene, it is also full of sexual energy: Belmont rhapsodically laments Evelina's resemblance to her mother, and even calls her by the name of the woman he seduced and abandoned.[15] He finally forces Evelina to consider what attaching herself to him would mean, asking if she is willing to "'own for thy father the destroyer of thy mother?'" To this "dreadful question" she responds by shuddering, unable to speak (385).

Evelina, then, represents a world in which women of some authority, usually mothers, are chastised by men, usually fathers, for the exercise of their desires. The sadism we see here is thus of a historically specific kind: the volatile blend of power and desire that underlies it signals a shift in the distribution of both. For the developing economy not only encouraged the infinite expansion of female desires but also prepared the way for new forms of female power, and masculine cruelty effectively serves to deny both. The sexualized quality of this exertion of male power stems in part from the fact that this violence is superimposed on heterosexual relations. But it is also a response to a contradiction within fashionable feminine desire itself: fashionable women were seeking to satisfy themselves but were also, at least ostensibly, working to make themselves more attractive

[14] Straub, *Divided Fictions*, 64.
[15] Irene Fizer argues that the scene is rife with incestuous tension: "Belmont acknowledges Evelina's threat to his patriarchal power: her body, as the site of his focalized view, may arouse his libidinal desire, rather than his legitimate interest" ("The Name of the Daughter: Identity and Incest in *Evelina*," in Patricia Yaeger and Beth Kowaleski-Wallace, eds., *Refiguring the Father: New Feminist Readings of Patriarchy* [Carbondale: Southern Illinois University Press, 1989], 92).

to men. On the surface, then, fashionable femininity was about promoting
not female desire but male desire, and the men of *Evelina* mockingly
respond with a combination of desire and an aggressive reassertion of privilege. That male hostility in *Evelina* is directed not just toward women but
toward fashionable consumerism itself (as in Mirvan's attack on Lovel)
reflects an awareness that the rise of the beautiful, cultured world of material
abundance was tied to the rise of feminine values. As G. J. Barker-Benfield
argues, the developing culture of sensibility worked for the reformation of
male manners in the name of a new "refinement" of feeling and behavior
that was associated with women on the one hand and the growth of commerce and the proliferation of sophisticated consumer goods on the other.[16]
It is thus not by chance that, as Deleuze notes with respect to de Sade,
"sadism is hostile to the aesthetic attitude."[17] In *Evelina* the fine objects
and beautiful sights of late eighteenth-century London are always potentially suspect, and Evelina herself has to walk a line between a proper feminine appreciation of consumer spectacle and a willingness to deprecate it.
She finds that mechanical toys such as those found in Cox's museum
have a certain charm, but agrees with Orville that objects of no utility are
of questionable value.

But if, on one level, the book allies Evelina (and through her, the reader)
with the prohibitive and even sadistic father, it also works gradually to
diminish that father's power. This is manifested most obviously in the
sequence of male authority figures to whom Evelina is attached. Belmont,
the cruel and sexual father, is replaced by Villars, the merely prohibitive
guardian. And before Belmont can be reinstated as Evelina's father, at the
close of the book she moves on to the protectorship of Lord Orville,
who, desexualized and relatively permissive, serves, finally, as the "good"
father. As Irene Fizer notes, in the proposal scene Evelina "becomes Lord
Orville's weeping 'infant' and 'child,' gratefully submitting to his paternal
authority, which Belmont has as yet denied her."[18] The advantage to
Evelina is that this particular figure of paternal authority is, as critics have
long noted, markedly generous and gentle.[19]

[16] G. J. Barker-Benfield, *The Culture of Sensibility* (Chicago: University of Chicago Press, 1992).
[17] Deleuze, "Coldness and Cruelty," 134.   [18] Fizer, "Identity and Incest," 98.
[19] This impulse to diminish the father's potency takes the form of a downright erasure in an illustration
for the 1779 edition, wherein a large female figure in antique dress gazes on the tomb of Belmont.
Margaret Doody argues that since within the novel the father Belmont is alive, the tomb must be
a memorial to Evelina's mother, whose identity and social status are at last properly, if posthumously,
recognized. In the light of such an interpretation, the meaning of the dedicatory poem, which has
generally been assumed to be addressed to Charles Burney, is significantly altered; Doody argues
that the poem, like the image, is a memorial to a mother figure, in this case Burney's own mother.

In *Evelina*, then, a young woman's entrance into the world of the marriage market – a place dominated by male desire – is also marked by her entrance into the world of the market more generally – a place where she learns to exercise desires of her own. It is not by accident that a trip that begins with going "a-shopping" for silks and caps should end with Evelina's desiring the man of her choice – an act tainted with guilt, especially since Lord Orville would appear to be beyond the reach of a penniless orphan. In many ways the economic and emotional worlds of *Evelina* are shaped by the perspective of a young girl. One's capacity to desire or consume is not limited by considerations of price, wherewithal, or any other internal economic constraint; the restrictions one suffers are arbitrarily imposed by prohibitive father figures. The fulfillment of one's desires therefore requires only a certain pliability, a willingness to join with one's father figures in their disdain for feminine consumerism and their punishment of those who practice it. As we will see, this daughter's-eye view of desire and of economic relations was to become progressively more complicated in the novels that followed.

II CECILIA

In *Evelina* the development of consumerist desire, exercised in the neverending round of fashionable amusements, leads to an open-ended wish for "more" that propels the heroine from orphan to lady, but the price paid for the fulfillment of that wish is never mentioned. Burney's next novel, *Cecilia*, would reformulate the question of desire in terms of appropriate expenditure. In *Cecilia* prohibition is not arbitrary and external but self-imposed in accordance with the fixed laws that govern social life; here it is the depth of one's purse and the regulations that govern price and debt relations that limit the gratification of one's desires. Thus, while some of the most memorable moments in *Evelina* are scenes of cruelty to others, *Cecilia* is full of images of self-dissolution – often of a quite literal

But the very ambiguity would seem to be significant: here we see Burney, like Evelina, try to have it both ways at once, satisfying the father while still recognizing the mother. At the same time, one could argue that the frontispiece image, offered as an illustration to a poem presumed to be addressed to Burney's father, is in fact of the father's tomb – and after all, Evelina's mother never enjoyed a full claim to the name Belmont. In this case the image would, as it were, look forward to the death of Evelina's father and even hint at the death of Burney's; in the context of the illustration, the dedicatory poem takes on the character of an elegy. It is clear that Burney loved her father deeply, but given the restrictions her desire to please him produced, especially with respect to her writing, the elegiac quality of the dedication makes emotional sense. It would seem that Burney, like Evelina, while she extravagantly praises her father, yearns for an end to his prohibitions.

kind. Indeed, one of the best-known scenes in *Cecilia* is that of the public suicide of the spendthrift Harrel when he realizes that he cannot repay his debts.

Harrel provides the book's most potent object lesson in the evils of extravagance, but the challenge of properly managing one's desires and expenditures is felt by all the novel's characters. Even the heroine herself, who has been taught to view "unbounded extravagance as the harbinger of injustice,"[20] must struggle to determine the right use of her riches. While she always shows herself averse to luxury and expense (795), she makes mistakes in her expenditure and the right uses of generosity right up to the end of the book. It is only in the novel's final pages that she is described as understanding "the error of profusion, even in charity and beneficence" (939). Indeed, if Evelina comes of age through the development of her desires, Cecilia becomes a woman by learning how and when to control her desires and her expenses. For in this novel Burney focuses not on consumption but on expenditure: she makes monetary profusion an analog for emotional profusion, and treats both as "errors." Harrel's house, a place of financial extravagance, is therefore also "the region of . . . licentiousness" (369). In a comic dialogue of miscommunications, Briggs asks Cecilia if Albany is "warm," i.e., rich, and Cecilia takes him to mean "passionate" (751) – an equation that relies on the peculiarities of contemporary jargon but that also reflects the logic of this book. This equation is in fact explored on the larger scale of the book's plot structure, for the love story that is the novel's main focus develops against the background of the story of Harrel's rise and fall. This double plot explores the analogy between financial and emotional extravagance: Harrel's love of the high life involves him in a monetary intemperance that leads to his undoing, while Mortimer and Cecilia give way to emotional excesses – excessive attachment to the beloved, and excessive attachment to the name Delvile – that fuel the love-plot conflict.

While Cecilia comes to see that good money management is a skill not easily learned, she finds that the proper control of one's desires and feelings is at least as difficult of achievement. The three major figures in the love plot – Mortimer, Cecilia, and Mrs. Delvile – are described as temperate and reasonable people, but the complications arising out of the Cecilia-Mortimer romance provoke emotional extravagance in all of them. Thus Mortimer claims early on that he has been "neither biassed by passion

[20] Frances Burney, *Cecilia*, ed. Peter Sabor and Margaret Doody (Oxford: Oxford University Press, 1988), 32. All subsequent references to this novel will be to this edition and will be given parenthetically in the text.

nor betrayed by tenderness" (571) in his effort to arrange a marriage with Cecilia, but over time his behavior becomes progressively wilder. Similarly, while we are twice informed that Cecilia's "passions were under the controul of her reason" (251), that is certainly not the case at the end of the novel, when she goes mad (a period during which Mortimer, too, feels an "excess" of despair [925]). Even Augusta Delvile ultimately confesses that she has herself been "extravagant," albeit for Mortimer's sake (821). Tellingly, her illness, itself the product of extravagant emotion, leads her to play a part parallel to Harrel's. Just as he uses threats of suicide to wrest money from Cecilia, so the intensity of Mrs. Delvile's wishes results in a physical breakdown that makes their satisfaction a matter of life and death, and Cecilia and Mortimer are forced to acquiesce to her demands.

But if even the novel's sympathetic characters are guilty of "errors of profusion," one reason is that the binary dynamic of desire and prohibition that governs the world of *Evelina* is not operative here: the issue is not simply how much one can safely hope for. In this book excesses occur at both ends of the spectrum. Thus, in the novel's first scenes, we are introduced to the obviously extravagant Belfield: "he lived an unsettled and unprofitable life . . . careless of his interest and thoughtless of the future; devoting his time to company, his income to dissipation" (12). But we also learn that appropriate behavior involves more than the avoidance or repression of the kind of extravagance Belfield embodies, for we see in Monckton an opposite kind of "extravagance": he is entirely too intent upon his own interest, too calculating. He is determined to "pursue the project he had formed" (10) of making Cecilia's person and wealth his own, and is himself aware that his conniving sometimes leads him to outrageous acts (124). From the outset, then, we are encouraged to view the characters who surround Cecilia in terms of opposed extremes. It would therefore seem that while *Evelina* operates according to a sliding scale of improvement (Belmont-not good; Villars-better; Orville-best), *Cecilia* will offer its lessons in the form of a search for a happy medium. Thus, for instance,

finding the error into which her ardour of reformation had hurried her, and that a rigid seclusion from company was productive of a lassitude as little favourable to active virtue as dissipation itself, [Cecilia] resolved to soften her plan, and by mingling amusement with benevolence, to try, at least, to approach that golden mean, which, like the philosopher's stone, always eludes our grasp, yet always invites our wishes. (131)

But this golden mean, one soon realizes, is not only difficult to approach but difficult even to define. Burney pointedly problematizes it by repeatedly presenting us with a pair of opposites and then adding to it a third term that does not in fact mediate between the first two. We see this, for instance, in the comic classification of the types of character fashionable with the *ton*. The talkative Miss Larolles, described by Mr. Gosport as a "VOLUBLE" (280), is set in opposition to Miss Leeson, who, in her unwillingness to talk, proves herself a member of the set of "SUPERCILIOUS" (280). But Mr. Gosport goes further to form a "happy Triplet" (280) by adding to these two the "INSENSIBILIST" (279) Mr. Meadows, who talks to and ignores Cecilia at intervals, and is no more pleasant a companion than the first two. More strikingly still, the opposition drawn between Cecilia's first two guardians – Harrel the spendthrift and Briggs the miser – suggests that the third guardian, Delvile, will represent some happy medium. It is with the Delvile family that Cecilia will ultimately ally herself, but they have their own distinctive set of moral shortcomings centering on their family pride – a pride that is related to but by no means reducible to family wealth. Walking a middle road in *Cecilia* means not only forging one's own path in a world of extremes but doing so in a constantly changing terrain, where the extremes to be avoided vary from one minute to the next.

As with *Evelina*, then, the ethics of desire and passion in this novel are shaped by economic concepts, but the peculiar difficulties with which these characters must struggle reflect a rather more sophisticated understanding of economic interrelations. It is not by chance that the characters understand their lives in terms of getting, spending, and debt; that proper self-management is a matter of constant negotiation; or that the notion of a middle state or mean point is so important. For the world of *Cecilia* is, through and through, the world of Adam Smith and liberal economics. *Evelina* shows an absorption in the pleasures of fashionable commerce without any sense of its costs, but *Cecilia* fills in the economic picture with extraordinary thoroughness. Here costs and profits, losses and gains, define every aspect of social life. This is a society structured by relations of debt and credit, not only at the economic level, but at every level of social interaction. Metaphors of indebtedness do not merely describe but actively structure noneconomic relations. Mrs. Delvile says that she means "'very speedily to pay that debt'" of a visit (171), and one hears of people being "in arrears" with their conversation (323), and with provocations they have received (721). Cecilia herself, although she experiences a "natural" horror to contracting a voluntary debt (189), is nevertheless not entirely averse to borrowing; in buying books "she confined not her acquisitions to the limits of her present power, but, as she was laying in a stock for future as well as immediate advantage, she was restrained by no expense" (103). This principle is understood to operate even in cases where no money at all is involved: "Pleasure given in society, like money lent in usury, returns with interest to those who dispense it" (9).[21]

Not only do debt metaphors govern both economic and noneconomic interactions, but value is understood in terms of the variability of relative price: Sir Robert Floyer looks at Cecilia "with the scrutinizing observation of a man on the point of making a bargain, who views with fault-seeking eyes the property he means to cheapen" (34). Skill in the determination of relative value is most fully manifested in the worldly characters, and most baldly in men of commerce. Briggs, who prides himself on knowing when to buy and sell, argues that finding Cecilia a husband will be difficult because "'hard times! men scarce! wars and tumults! stocks low! women chargeable!'" (96). In spite of Briggs's confidence, however, the fully accurate determination of relative value would in fact require a bird's-eye view of the general economy of social life. And because this economy is dynamic, one would need not only to understand the big picture but to understand how it changes over time. Correct behavior, like the sound evaluation of financial options, is extremely difficult in this book in part because values are constantly shifting in relation to one another. This absence of absolute values is signaled by the characters' frequent recourse to the image of balancing scales. In discussing Cecilia's value Mrs. Delvile admits that if she were poor "'every claim of interest would be overbalanced by her virtues'" (674), and Cecilia chides Mr. Gosport for leaving her for a half-hour in the company of Mr. Meadows by saying, "'you were determined to add weight to the value of your company, by making me fully sensible where the balance would preponderate'" (278).

But while in specific cases the balance may preponderate on one or the other side, one of the critical metaphors in *Cecilia*, as in liberal economics, is of a balance in equilibrium. Of course, the idea of balance had long been central to mercantilist doctrine, but equilibrium was what one wanted to avoid; the aim was to tip the balance of trade in one's own favor. With liberal economics the image of the balance was construed anew: "Earlier the balance had been judged to be in its proper state when one

---

[21] This indebtedness arguably extends even to the reader; as Catherine Gallagher argues, "the moral reader does not simply 'borrow' fictional personae; she borrows with a promise to repay with interest. Disinterested benevolence actually exacts a usuriously high level of interest" (Gallagher, *Nobody's Story: The Vanishing Acts of Women Writers in the Marketplace, 1670–1820* [Berkeley: University of California Press, 1994], 237).

scale – the one that measured the flow of payments into the country – was unambiguously low. Now the preferred state of the balance was equilibrium, preferred not for its inherent advantages but for its recognized inevitability."[22] One might upset this balance temporarily, but the system would ultimately and automatically right itself. Adam Smith's *Wealth of Nations* (1776), which offered the most coherent account of economic liberalism, built its arguments around this central concept of self-regulation. Smith shows how self-regulation works at every level of the economy, creating a balance between supply and demand, domestic and foreign wealth, the advantages of different forms of employment, and so on. As Smith writes of price,

the natural price . . . is, as it were, the central price, to which the prices of all commodities are continually gravitating. Different accidents may sometimes keep them suspended a good deal above it, and sometimes force them down even somewhat below it. But whatever may be the obstacles which hinder them from settling in this center of repose and continuance, they are constantly tending towards it.[23]

Economic systems were always in the process of finding their own balance, a state of natural equilibrium. Smith's famous image of the "invisible hand," the unseen force that coordinates the self-interested actions of individuals, is but another metaphor for this same idea. The authoritarian regulation so dear to mercantilism is now replaced by the manipulations of this ghostly hand, the power of which is entirely impersonal – "an abstract power immanent in the system" itself.[24]

This fluctuation around a point of equilibrium governs not only small-scale interactions in *Cecilia* but the narrative dynamic as a whole. That Cecilia, an heiress, should be reduced to a state of relative impoverishment at the novel's close reflects something more than the Johnsonian adage that perfect human felicity is not to be found; in a very real sense, Cecilia "pays" with her fortune to have Mortimer for a husband. This is simply the best deal that Cecilia and the Delviles can come to; as Cecilia remarks bitterly, Mortimer must "'keep his name! . . . what presumption in me, to suppose myself an equivalent for its loss!'" (515). But if this bargain elicits an occasional murmur from Cecilia (941), it seems nevertheless to represent

[22] Otto Mayr, *Authority, Liberty, and Automatic Machinery in Early Modern Europe* (Baltimore: Johns Hopkins University Press, 1986), 147.
[23] Adam Smith, *An Inquiry into the Nature and Causes of the Wealth of Nations*, 2 vols., vol. I, ed. R. H. Campbell and A. S. Skinner (Oxford: Oxford University Press, 1976), I, 75.
[24] Mayr, *Authority, Liberty*, 175.

the rightful balance of things. After all, at the book's opening the narrator tells us that Cecilia was "largely indebted to fortune," while "to nature she had yet greater obligations" (6). Throughout the book Cecilia endeavors to acquit herself of this debt through acts of generosity, and even, in the mode of finance capitalism, to pay appropriate interest: we hear more than once that she considered her affluence as "a debt contracted with the poor, and her independence, as a tie upon her liberality to pay it with interest" (55). But given her initial indebtedness, such efforts can never be sufficient. It seems finally that the loss of Cecilia's fortune is therefore inevitable. Dr. Lyster, who enjoys a moral as well as doctorly authority, speaks of how "'wonderfully is good and evil balanced'" (930), and later "'with what scrupulous exactness the good and bad is ever balanced'" (937). The modern reader is apt, like Cecilia herself, to "murmur" at all this, but the novel's resolution accurately expresses the "natural" fluctuation toward a Smithean mean that governs this world.

This operational logic is reflected even in the book's narrative format; it is fitting that this is not an epistolary but a narrated fiction, and one that includes moments of free indirect speech.[25] The narrator – an invisible eye to Smith's invisible hand – quietly and unobtrusively offers a perspective from above, an account of the subtle and continuous negotiations between characters. Unlike a letter, a narrated chapter can move rapidly between points of view – can capture, for instance, the quick shuffle of strategies, intentions, and suspicions in the late conversations of Cecilia and Mr. Monckton. No frame-story or preface, no authorial claims to be merely an editor or to have heard the story elsewhere are needed in this case, because the frame inheres in the texture of the story itself, in the voice of the omniscient narrator. The narrator's encompassing vision provides the rational and ethical framework within which the novel's events appear both meaningful and inevitable.

Of course, Burney's insistence on the moral necessity of self-regulation rings a change on classical political economy. In a liberal economic order, balance is achieved through the conflicts and negotiations of self-interested individuals; thus does private vice become public good. As Delvile half-jokingly remarks to Cecilia, "'self-denial is no longer in fashion!'" (429). But Burney requires that her sympathetic characters absorb the larger lesson about balances and mean points on the individual level, that they personally master the competing demands of social life. Thus, if the ideal liberal economic order is a self-regulating system, *Cecilia*'s principal characters

---

[25] On Burney's use of this technique, see Doody, *Life*, 124, and Epstein, *Iron Pen*, 140.

themselves function as such systems. As Catherine Gallagher argues, Cecilia's notion of morality is founded on a belief in the value of "objectivity"; Cecilia aims at the achievement of "a vantage point so comprehensive that it would include even herself, a site outside time and space."[26] Gallagher notes the resemblance between this desire for an "objective" view of the self and the division of the self into both subject and object of judgment that Smith describes as necessary to the assessment of one's morality. The ethical imperative to strive for a distanced, comprehensive view of social life is the necessary counterpart, in the domain of morality, of the new belief in the impersonality and self-regulating qualities of the economy. All ends for the best in both the economic and moral domains, but this truth is visible only from the perspective of the objective spectator of modern life.

That these characters personalize social conflict and try to resolve it at the level of the individual is most clearly manifested in the fact that they all, at some point, fall ill. These characters' illnesses, moreover, not only reflect emotional distress but also provide a means for its relief. Cecilia and the Delviles, in the manner of the self-regulating machines of the period, need to "let off steam" in order to return to a state of healthy equilibrium (one is reminded, too, of a caricature that Epstein attributes to Burney's cousin which represents Burney herself as a sort of steam machine for writing.)[27] Under extreme emotional pressure, Cecilia "burst into tears, which happily relieved her mind from the conflict with which it was labouring, and which, not thus effected, might have ended more fatally" (847). When she does go mad, it is because that physical release mechanism is no longer properly triggered by the build-up of internal pressure: "every pulse was throbbing, every vein seemed bursting" (899). The physical distress suffered by the sympathetic characters, moreover, not only mirrors emotional excess and provides for its relief but causes a suffering that serves to compensate for, to pay for, that excess. Overweening

---

[26] Gallagher, *Nobody's Story*, 236. Gallagher argues that Burney represents this aim as unhealthy and associates it with death. Linking it to Cecilia's efforts to acquit herself of her debts, Gallagher claims that this striving for universal subjectivity involves Cecilia in a vicious cycle wherein the repayment of debt simply leads to greater indebtedness, and the effort to become a "universal subject" ends in madness. But the narrator insists on the rightness of Cecilia's full "payment" for her advantages, and the narrative structure itself, as discussed above, signals an investment in the ideal of a comprehensive view.

[27] For a discussion of the relation between self-regulating mechanisms in liberal thought and the technology of self-regulating machines, especially the steam engine, see Mayr, *Authority*, Part II: "Liberal Systems." Julia Epstein suggests that the drawing of Burney as a machine may have been inspired by Burney's post-operative difficulties following her mastectomy (*Iron Pen*, 56), but the emphasis in the drawing on Burney's arm and the suggestion of the spouting of steam from her head can also be taken as a comic commentary on Burney's unremitting devotion to the labor of writing.

desire is balanced by physical losses that aim for the reestablishment of equilibrium. In the most striking instance of this, Mrs. Delvile, in the midst of a heated argument with her son, spontaneously begins to hemorrhage. Mortimer promises to agitate her no more, and she "burst into an agony of tears" (682). As with Cecilia, this release of excess tension provides some relief, and although her "mouth still continued to fill with blood . . . it gushed not from her with the violence it had begun" (682). Here extravagant bleeding serves to signify emotional extravagance, becoming a grotesque physical reenactment of Mrs. Delvile's fixation on the Delvile lineage: the concern for the blood of the Delviles was ever in her mouth, and now it fills her mouth almost to the point of choking her. At the same time, this hemorrhaging serves as the balancing price of emotional extremity; Mrs. Delvile herself will later confess that her health nearly became "the sacrifice of emotions most fatally unrestrained" (700).

Thus *Cecilia* represents social and even emotional structures in terms of a liberal economic worldview, but one wherein the ideal of equilibrium and self-regulation becomes a moral desideratum imposed on individuals themselves. Indeed, the felt need to resolve social conflicts on an individual level points in the direction of a new individualism, an individualism not only of Smithean freedom but also of private suffering. The grand account sheet that structures *Cecilia* could, then, be said to prepare the way for the advocacy of personal suffering one finds in *Camilla*. In what Delvile calls "this expensive age" (757), the availability of pleasure is restricted by the need for equilibrium, the necessity of gains and losses. Gallagher notes that contemporary critics complained of the "paucity of pleasure" to be had in *Cecilia*'s ending (236); in her next novel Burney would be spurred to find new forms of pleasure in a world of self-imposed suffering.

III CAMILLA

Camilla is Burney's first Romantic-era novel, and while period boundaries are of course a matter of convention, in this case they dovetail nicely with an important shift in Burney's interests. As we have seen, in *Evelina* and *Cecilia* there is only one way of desiring, and the question is whether that desire will be constrained from without or from within. In *Camilla* and *The Wanderer*, however, it is the nature of desire itself that is at stake. *Camilla* is concerned with the self-regulation first explored in *Cecilia*, but in the later novel this regulation is manifested not in the form of restraint on desire but in the development of a new kind of desire altogether. In *Camilla* desire itself is experienced as a simultaneously painful and pleasurable version of self-management; limitations have become an aspect of desire rather than a barrier to it.

Like the earlier novels, *Camilla* links erotic desire to commercial desire, but in *Camilla* that commercial desire takes two distinct forms. Indeed, this novel establishes an opposition between two quite different modes of desire, and it struggles to choose between them. The first operates serially, avoiding overinvestment in any one object, and the second involves the fixation on and idealization of a single object. Burney seems to prefer the first mode; she presents it as the rational, sensible way to desire. Yet ultimately the events of the novel belie that choice, suggesting as they do that the second mode, while risky, is in fact the more noble and generous of the two. In effect, Burney embraces the speculator's desire, the gambler's desire, that Hogarth and Defoe had found so disquieting. *Camilla* suggests that speculative, idealizing, and self-abnegating desire combines the best aspects of traditional aristocratic culture with the most compelling features of a blossoming democratic one. At the same time, Burney highlights the vulgarity of serial desire, directly exposing its roots in contemporary retailing techniques. In *Camilla* Burney takes her first step towards an endorsement of eroticized submission.

The affective tone of *Camilla*, its emotional inflection, is striking and distinctive; the reader of the novel quickly becomes aware that she or he is immersed in a very different atmosphere from that of Burney's earlier novels. Reading the book for the first time, one is likely to feel there is something claustrophobic and even oppressive about it. Although roughly the same length as *Cecilia*, it feels much longer, oddly distended. This sensation arises largely from the fact that while the complications of the plot appear relatively minor, the anxieties generated by those complications feel exaggeratedly intense.[28] Burney's contemporary reviewers understood that the

---

[28]   Thus Julia Epstein notes the "paradox" of the fact that "financial crises . . . fuel a plot in which, in fact, none of the principals lacks substantial assets" (*Iron Pen*, 127). Whereas Cecilia and Mortimer have to struggle with well-defined and serious obstacles to their union, Camilla and Edgar seem always to be struggling with minor obstacles, ones that they should have been able to overcome within the first few hundred pages; Kristina Straub aptly describes the book as "an absurdist's vision of romance" (*Divided Fictions*, 186). The nonnecessity of their suffering is itself, of course, a primary theme of the novel. Margaret Doody argues that *Camilla* is an antilove story that demonstrates the dangers of making a courtship a more complicated and adversarial affair than it need be (*Life*, 221). This theme, however, might easily have been explored without being dramatized at such length. The narrative could, for instance, have signaled delays in the courtship simply by leaping forward in time – it does, after all, make such a leap when it shifts abruptly from Camilla's childhood to her adolescence. Or Edgar's suspicions and Camilla's indiscretions could have been made more immediately damaging through the perversity of events.

novel was to serve as a warning against "caution and suspicion on the part of the lover" and "juvenile heedlessness and precipitancy . . . on the part of the lady,"[29] but they also remark on the novel's length, sensing a disproportion between events themselves and the difficulty of bringing matters to a resolution. Thus, the reader for the *Analytical Review* notes that "The incidents, which are to mark out the errours of youth, are frequently only perplexities, forcibly brought forward merely to be disentangled; yet, there are many amusing, and some interesting incidents, though they have not a plot of sufficient importance to bind them together."[30] The more blunt reviewer for the *British Critic* confesses that "the story is doubtless spun out to an immoderate length."[31]

One could claim that these reviewers did not fully apprehend Burney's aims, and were therefore led to find the book's events less meaningful than they might have. Indeed, Doody argues that the tendency of both early and more modern readers to read the novel as a conduct book has blinded them to many of its peculiar merits.[32] Nevertheless, the three reviewers I quote above are all at least sympathetic to Burney's project and favorable overall in their assessment of it; I would argue that their vague discomfort with its length reflects something important about the novel. One of them tellingly remarks that "The reader's attention is throughout kept awake (*though indeed somewhat harassed*)."[33] For the reader who identifies or at least sympathizes with the heroine there *is* something literally harassing about getting through the book. Even Doody, who on one occasion describes the story as "festive," notes that the narrative "bustles with overdetermined anxiety."[34] I would argue that the foregrounding of anxiety and discomfort is a sign that anxiety itself forms an important part of the book. It is affect and not just incident that is important here.

This pervasive anxiety is reflected in the frequency with which characters within the book are described as being in suspense. Both emotionally and physically, they repeatedly find themselves "suspended": "Camilla stood suspended"; "Sir Sedley stood suspended, how to act, what to judge"; Camilla "stood suspended from her purpose."[35] Of course, the very word "suspense" suggests that the delays and anxieties the book generates have their

[29] *Monthly Review* 2:21 (October 1796), 157.   [30] *Analytical Review* 24 (August 1796), 142.
[31] *British Critic* 8 (November 1796), 536. The writer for the *Monthly Review* reluctantly admits that the reader may at times "experience some degree of lassitude, and be disposed to think the writer tedious" (158).
[32] See Doody, *Life*, 218.   [33] *Monthly Review*, 157, emphasis mine.   [34] Doody, *Life*, 217, 253.
[35] Frances Burney, *Camilla*, ed. Edward and Lillian Bloom (New York: Oxford University Press, 1983), 155, 559, 761. All subsequent references to this novel will be to this edition and will be given parenthetically in the text.

gratifications; suspense, after all, can be interesting and enjoyable, as the popularity of the Gothic novels of the period attests. But while suspense in the Gothic novel is a response to real or at least imagined terrors, the suspense here is a response to the complications of a relatively mild-mannered love plot. Powerful feelings of suspense are, for these characters, directly related to love and sexual desire; it is overwhelmingly the hero and heroine who feel the most suspense, and others feel suspense when they become themselves romantically entangled. Seeing this link between suspense and desire, we begin to understand the nature of the gratification offered by the strange distension of the plot. In this book romantic desire is experienced as suspense. For all that the characters suffer, it seems that they, like the novel's readers, are intended – whether self-consciously or not – to "enjoy their symptom,"[36] to find stimulation in anxiety itself. Thus the reader's sense of harassment and his or her appreciation of the book walk hand in hand.

The modern reader, accustomed to seeing danger eroticized in Romantic and post-Romantic art, might not be surprised to find suspense represented as central to sexual life. But the link between suspense and eroticism should by no means be assumed to be a universal feature of human psychology. Before the late eighteenth century, suspense, while it may have accompanied sexual desire, was not generally represented as erotic in itself. While delay does sometimes play a role in earlier accounts of desire, as for instance in many Renaissance sonnet sequences, it generally serves the function of justifying complaint or extending the sexual encounter rather than generating an eroticized form of anxiety. In *Camilla*, however, the characters' love lives seem to have very little to do with such matters as physical longings or the beauty of the beloved; instead, they revolve around anxiety and suspense. This rather unusual situation reflects the particular economic and political conditions of the 1790s. We can begin to understand this by noting that in *Camilla* delight in suspense – the fusion of deferral, anxiety, and desire – finds its purest form, its paradigm, in gambling. Significantly, the characters themselves describe their romantic risk-taking and suspensive suffering in terms of lottery metaphors. Hence Edgar exclaims, "'in how despicable a lottery have I risked the peace of my life!'" (571). One hundred pages later, still feeling emotionally entangled with Camilla, he remarks that "'the last of my intentions was any further essay in a lottery I had found so inauspicious'" (644).

---

[36] The phrase is Slavoj Žižek's, from his book entitled *Enjoy Your Symptom* (New York: Routledge, 1992).

Significantly, Camilla's entrance into the world is marked by her first participation in a lottery, and that lottery and its outcome remain emotionally significant throughout the novel. But before looking at the lottery scene more closely, it may be useful to say a few words about the significance of gambling in the period. As Rueven Brenner points out, gambling, betting, speculating, and investing were conceived as similar, and "speculation and gambling were linked and condemned together."[37] We saw in Chapter 1 that speculation was believed not only to be grounded in illicit desire but to generate such desire; the same was true of gaming. An epitaph written on the final state lottery of 1826 argued that

> As they increased, it was found that their
> continuance corrupted the morals,
> and encouraged a spirit
> of Speculation and Gambling among the lower
> classes of the people;
> thousands of whom fell victims to their
> insinuating and tempting allurements.[38]

Gambling was understood to have a quasi-sexual allure, and if its effect on a man was that it left him literally spent, enervated, its effect on a woman was to render her dissipated in the manner of an adulteress: "I come . . . to consider all the ill Consequences which Gaming has on the *Bodies* of our Female Adventurers . . . There is nothing that wears out a fine Face like the Vigils of the Card Table, and those cutting *Passions* which naturally attend them."[39] The perceived link between gambling and sexuality gave rise to an analogy between the uncontrolled losses and gains of gaming and rapacious and violent sexuality; as Sir James Courtly tells Lady Reveller in the play *The Basset-Table* (1705), a woman who loves play "passionately" should not be surprised to find herself threatened with rape.[40] For writers at the end of the century, the association of sexual violence with speculation was revitalized to the point of becoming a commonplace. For the 1790s, like the period of the South Sea Bubble, were years that witnessed accelerated change and an increase in speculation in all its forms. It is but a short step from Burke's scornful account of stockjobbers to his vision of the violation of Marie Antoinette.

---

[37] Reuven Brenner and Gabrielle Brenner, *Gambling and Speculation* (Cambridge: Cambridge University Press, 1990), 90, 63.

[38] Quoted in John Ashton, *The History of Gambling in England* (Chicago: Herbert Stone, 1899), 240.

[39] Quoted in *ibid.*, 54, second emphasis mine.

[40] Susannah Centlivre, *The Basset-Table* (London: W. Feales, 1736), 62.

At the level of plot, Camilla's first lottery is important to her romance with Edgar because it provides an opportunity for the manifestation of their common benevolence and their attachment to each other: Camilla, having felt pressured to put in for the lottery, feels distressed at having done so when she realizes that it has rendered her unable to offer charity to the poor. Edgar, in approbation of her repentance, promises to retrieve her half-guinea from the raffle, but, finding he cannot do so, he provides her with a half-guinea of his own. Camilla is then mightily surprised when she learns that she has won the prize after all. In her eagerness to deny her claim to it, it ends up in the hands of Indiana, but Edgar retrieves it and presents it again to Camilla as rightfully hers. The lottery and its outcome thus proleptically enact the shape of the courtship as a whole, but in a finer tone: Camilla stakes her claim to Edgar and then relinquishes it, both as a form of self-chastisement and for Indiana's sake. Ultimately, however, through penitence and good fortune, he is returned to her, fully hers. Tellingly, it is the locket itself that brings about Camilla's final reunion with Edgar. At the climax of the book, Camilla once again relinquishes the locket, and Edgar, finding it, thereby learns her whereabouts and saves her from madness and death. This "nick of time" happy ending, however, takes 900 pages and a fair amount of agonizing to accomplish. The emotional risk entailed in participating in the lottery for the locket and the lottery of romance is very real, even if all ultimately ends for the best.

The lottery and its prize in this way become rich in romantic meaning for Camilla and Edgar, but a closer look at the raffle scene itself reveals the extent to which the very structure of the lottery provides a paradigm for the workings of romantic desire. The raffle is first introduced thus:

a paper was handed about, to collect half guineas for a raffle. A beautiful locket, set round with pearls, ornamented at the top with a little knot of small brilliants, and very elegantly shaped, with a space left for a braid of hair, or a cypher, was produced; and, as if by magnetic power, attracted into almost every hand the capricious coin, which distress, but the moment before had repelled. (93)

The magnetic power of this object immediately links it to the desirable women of the book. Not only do we repeatedly see women in *Camilla* function as commodities, we see them function specifically like this commodity, as a magnet. Mrs. Berlinton, in particular, is a magnetic figure, and at assembly after assembly she functions as a "loadstone" (440). As the metaphor of magnetism suggests, the desire elicited by the locket and by certain women reflects not their absolute and inherent value but a primarily relational value. The relational character of desire is manifest, for instance, in the fact that simply being close to the loadstone of the party renders one interesting and desirable; Camilla, standing with Mrs. Berlinton,

> was now looked at by all present as if seen for the first time; every one discovered in her some charm, some grace, some excellence; those who, the minute before, had passed her with perfect indifference, said it was impossible to see and not be struck with her; and all agreed she could appear upon no spot under the sun, and not instinctively be singled out. (443)

Burney exposes this structural bias quite deliberately, and not always with such gentle satire as she uses here. In the paragraph following the first alluring description of the locket, the narrator proceeds to describe it quite differently: the raffle "was the mere common mode, of getting rid of a mere common bauble, which no one had thought worth the full price affixed to it by its toyman" (93). This deflation from magical object to mere bauble reveals the extent to which the structure of the raffle itself serves to elicit desire. Burney even goes so far as to make the raffled object a locket; it is "set round with pearls," and ornamented, but it is, of course, empty at the center. The locket's post-sale history continues this idea: Edgar tries to make the locket Camilla's own by filling it with her sisters' hair, while for Camilla it becomes a prized possession not because of its value in itself but because of the circumstances in which it was obtained.

The raffle thus serves to generate and focus desire – it provides a structure within which a mere bauble can function as a loadstone. In a raffle all eyes are focused on a single object, and participants display their willingness not just to pay for the object, but to risk paying for nothing. The lucky one who gains the object does not simply acquire it but wins it, and wins it away from others; although the lottery is a risky mode of acquisition, it is also a particularly exciting and ego-gratifying one. But it is not just the opportunity to win that makes participation in the lottery appealing. As it is represented here, lottery-pleasure lies not just in the having but in the getting, in the gambling itself. During the period in which the outcome is awaited, a single object commands complete attention, thereby heightening desire, while anxiety combines with that desire to produce a potent mixture of emotions that have their own powerful appeal. For the gambler, time is suspended, and desire itself becomes a source of uneasy pleasure. Camilla and Edgar become for each other singular objects of desire who not only merit but require risk-taking to obtain.

IV

While the lottery both structures and symbolizes the gratifying – if risky – side of romance, it is a different but related economic activity that will structure and symbolize romance at its worst: shopping without the intention to buy. Whereas the lottery scene occurs early in the book and helps to set the central courtship in motion, Camilla's dangerous outing with Mrs. Mittin comes at the height of her socializing, introduces her to other suitors, and brings in its wake an end to her engagement with Edgar. Newly arrived in Southampton, and eager for some distraction from her worries about Edgar, Camilla accompanies the "forward, vulgar" (606) Mrs. Mittin on what she expects to be a sightseeing trip. The sightseeing, however, turns out to be entirely in the form of window-shopping; Mrs. Mittin says that "'these shops are all so monstrous smart, 'twill be a pleasure to go into them, and ask the good people what there's to see in the town'" (607). Quickly enough, this method of getting information becomes an end in itself:

> This pretext proved so fertile to her of entertainment, in the opportunity it afforded of taking a near view of the various commodities exposed to sale, that while she entered almost every shop, with inquiries of what was worth seeing, she attended to no answer nor information, but having examined and admired all the goods within sight or reach, walked off, to obtain, by similar means, a similar privilege further on; boasting to Camilla, that, by this clever device they might see all that was smartest, without the expense of buying any thing. (607)

This unorthodox form of "shopping" can be opposed to the workings of the lottery at almost every point: it involves no risk and no expense, and it distracts the attention with multiple objects – objects that can then be compared – rather than focusing it on one, ostensibly superb object. While participation in a lottery and gaming more generally often function as signs of aristocracy or gentility, this appreciative looking without the intention to spend is patently considered vulgar.[41]

---

[41] It should be noted that this connection of gaming with gentility is largely an ideal one. That is, during the eighteenth century lotteries formed a part not only of high life, but of social life in general. It played a role even in common trade, where the purchase of the humblest goods from a lottery tailor, lottery staymaker, or lottery eating house brought with it a lottery ticket (see Ashton, *Gambling*, 228). Indeed, the new practice of providing "insurance" on lottery tickets, whereby the cost and rewards of a single ticket were subdivided among many people, made gambling available even to the poorest. But this diffusion of lottery mania was perceived as troublesome precisely because

To understand the significance of this scene, one must bear in mind that this book was written during a period of change in the meaning and practice of shopping. During the first part of the eighteenth century, commerce was rarely impersonal. Interactions between buyer and seller would not typically have been characterized by anonymity. For the rich at least, the merchant's practice of coming to call for orders or the payment of bills personalized, in the manner of a patronage relationship, commercial transactions. In-shop trade typically occurred at the home of the seller, and the shopkeeper's identity was often stamped on his goods.[42] Moreover, all buyers were affected by the fact that manufactured goods were not yet fully standardized and their quality was in no way guaranteed. In a time when old guild and civic controls had been weakened but not yet replaced by national legal safeguards, one's knowledge of a vendor was the best way of ensuring the quality of the goods one bought. On the other side of the counter, the shopkeeper had reason to be suspicious of the quality of the coin he received, in this era of insufficient and poor coinage. More importantly still, since the shopkeeper, like almost all other members of this society, operated largely on credit, he had to have knowledge of his customer and faith in his ability to pay his bills.

The turn of the century, however, was to witness a gradual shift toward a very different sort of retailing, one in which the relation between merchant and buyer became more and more impersonal, while the attraction of the goods themselves, magnified through display and competitive advertising, became increasingly important. By 1780 "an increasing number of shopkeepers sought to attract custom by listing prices; ticketing their wares with no abatement; offering special bargains or particularly low prices for ready money."[43] Neil McKendrick notes that

commercial practice was moving so rapidly then and the scale of change was so dramatic, that what James Lackington had tried to introduce in 1780 – fixed prices and no credit – was regarded as being established by 1800, and by 1821 a single fixed price 'NO ABATEMENT' linen draper was reported to be taking £500 a day and employing up to thirty assistants. All these figures are of course open to doubt, but the change of scale is unmistakable.[44]

gaming continued to be associated with noble privilege. It is this traditional association that we see at work in *Camilla*.
[42] See Carrier, *Gifts and Commodities*, 70–1.
[43] Hoh-Cheung Mui and Lorna Mui, *Shops and Shopkeeping in Eighteenth-Century England* (London: Routledge, 1989), 235.
[44] Neil McKendrick, "Commercialization and the Economy," in William Brewer, Neil McKendrick, and J. H. Plumb, eds., *The Birth of a Consumer Society: The Commercialization of Eighteenth-Century England* (Bloomington: Indiana University Press, 1982), 86.

Traditionally, prices had reflected social relations, such as the status of the buyer: "'What's to pay?'. . . 'What you Honor pleases,' was the answer, 'but gentlefolks gives half-a-crown'" (428). Fixed prices eliminated the need for negotiation, and cash sales permitted a more anonymous relation between buyer and seller.

By the Victorian era fixed pricing and cash sales were to change the aims and techniques of retailing. As a wholesaler explained to parliamentary commissioners in 1833, most modern retailers included price tickets on their goods because of "an entire change in the mode of carrying on the retail business, that is, that it has now become more casual and less dependent on regular constant customers."[45] But in the late eighteenth century, such techniques were considered not only extraordinary but also not quite "proper." Robert Owen, who worked in a fixed-price shop as a boy, described its customers as not very "genteel."[46] The anonymity and publicity of the excursion with Mrs. Mittin gestures toward this new and "vulgar" kind of commercial relationship. While it was common enough for members of the gentry to put a shopkeeper to considerable trouble, only, finally, to leave without making a purchase, Mrs. Mittin's rummaging suggests a new form of commerce that is not dependent on mutual recognition and that will ultimately thrive on the full display and ticketing of goods.

Just as the affective structure of gambling can serve to structure sexual desire, so this new attitude toward goods, the "objective" comparison of them on the basis of qualities understood to be inherent in them, promoted particular habits of courtship and romantic desire. In *Camilla* casual shopping provides the paradigm for a form of sexual desire that is self-serving, calculating, and fickle. The desire to see everything while focusing on nothing suggests both a promiscuity of interest and an ultimate aloofness. In a sense, then, it is fitting that this "indulging . . . unbridled curiosity" (607) does not pass with "impunity" (607), but elicits a perverse correlative; the women themselves become objects of unbridled curiosity, of a promiscuous and flippant attention:

every one perceiving that, whatsoever had been his recommendation . . . the two inquirers went no further than into the next shop, whence they regularly drew forth either the master or the man to make another starer at their singular proceeding.

---

[45] *Select Committee on Manufactures*, Q, 1415–21.
[46] Quoted in Dorothy Davis, *Fairs, Shops, and Supermarkets: A History of English Shopping* (Toronto: University of Toronto Press, 1966), 189.

Some supposed they were only seeking to attract notice; others thought they were deranged in mind; and others, again, imagined they were shoplifters. (608)

Matters are further complicated by the fact that, because Camilla is "of a figure and appearance" (607) that would seem to place her above such activity, her presence also stimulates the more focused attention characteristic of the lottery paradigm we have already examined. To the idle curiosity generated by the women's shopping is added a dangerous speculative element; the shopkeepers eventually make the women's identity the object of various bets, and "business gave way to speculation" (608). Before they are even aware that they have become an object of attention, Camilla and Mrs. Mittin find themselves threatened with insult by a party of three men; fortunately, Edgar steps in to protect Camilla before the danger has gone beyond the point of menace.

Thus the anonymity of the shopping trip with Mrs. Mittin leads to a dangerous sexual correlate: class divisions are blurred as everyone from a linen draper to a Lord observe and finally threaten to lay their hands on the two women. One is reminded here of a remark by the forward-looking Josiah Wedgwood; he refers to the effective display of goods not only as a way to generate desire, but also as an activity with a hint of impersonal aggressive sexuality about it: "I need not tell you that it will be our interest to amuse and divert & please & astonish, nay, even to ravish, the Ladies."[47] While the scene in *Camilla* does not end in rape, it does "introduce" Camilla to a number of men, all of whom will later presume upon their former "acquaintance." In the aftermath of this event, Camilla suffers indignities from these men while at the same time appearing to Edgar as a determined coquette, and therefore an object unworthy of his choice. "Sightseeing" with Mrs. Mittin therefore seems to establish Camilla's identity as a casual shopper in addition to stimulating the interest of other casual shoppers in her.

V

What we have, then, are two quite different paradigms for romance. The lottery model involves focus on a single object, a lofty superiority to the careful inspection of that object, and an imaginative absorption in the object's ostensibly ideal qualities. It requires expenditure without any assurance of winning the prize. Its association with aristocratic life reflects the assumption that the true nobleman is indifferent to the

[47] Quoted in *ibid.*, 201.

comings and goings of mere money. Shopping around, on the other hand, involves the stimulation of desire through sheer quantity; it lives on mundane calculation and the impulse to inspect; and it reflects an unwillingness to take a risk, or, in fact, to spend at all. The difficulty is that while the vulgarity and selfish calculation of shopping make it an unappealing model for romance, proceeding on speculation is patently risky. The romantic complications that the book takes such time to work out reveal a real, if subtle, struggle to define a suitable form of desire in a world where desire is linked either to aristocratic profligacy or petty-bourgeois stinginess.

Indeed, the novel's central courtship traces the constant push and pull between these two paradigms. Edgar refers to his romance with Camilla as a dangerous lottery, and he is constantly tormented with the suspense of the gambler; but his pursuit of Camilla sometimes takes on the character of mere shopping, and it is at those times that the greatest difficulties arise. In Edgar's first discussion of Camilla with his tutor, Dr. Marchmont, he appears quite ready to take a risk, but Marchmont is able to change Edgar's proclaimed "irrevocable choice" (157) by counseling what seems to be only a slight change in method: "'deception is easy, and I must not see you thrown away'" (158). By suggesting that Edgar does not yet know Camilla's intrinsic value, Marchmont introduces an insoluble problem: if Edgar must be certain of Camilla's value before acting, he will never be able to act – he will be forever inspecting the merchandise. At this point Edgar is still ready to proceed on speculation, willing to grant Camilla credit: "'Let me, then, be her guarantee!'" (158). The two discuss the matter, Marchmont persisting in arguing that Edgar take the approach of the careful shopper: "'do not mistake promise for performance'" (159). The result of this interview and an exchange of letters is the quelling of Edgar's impulse to act the generous part of the speculator: "The first blight [was] thus borne to that ardent glee with which the imagination rewards its own elevated speculations" (180). Just as there is something vulgar in Mrs. Mittin's shopping, so there is in the inspection Marchmont advises; Edgar himself describes such distrustfulness as "ungenerous" (160) – a word that captures its emotional, financial, and even class resonances. And, ironically enough, in accepting Marchmont's counsel to shop, Edgar makes his courtship a far more risky affair than it need have been: his first sensation of "suspensive discomfort" (162) follows upon his initial meeting with Marchmont rather than any disappointment from Camilla. Edgar rapidly becomes, as Mrs. Arlbery describes him, "a watcher," jealous of the object of his choice, "lest she should not prove good enough to merit it" (482). That Edgar is, however, ill-suited to be a "shopper" is manifested in the fact that he is unable to take an interest in more than one object; he is not capable of taking a dispassionate inventory of Camilla's qualities, and even less of comparing her with other potential brides. Never does he remind us of the true shopper: "gay shops afforded . . . to Miss Dennel a wonder and delight, that kept her mouth open, and her head jerking from object to object, so incessantly, that she saw nothing distinctly, from the eagerness of her fear lest anything should escape her" (395).

Camilla, meanwhile, though "unused to hazard" (93), is not only urged by circumstances to play in various lotteries but is also characterized by a highly developed imagination that leads her to speculate continually about Edgar. Like Edgar, Camilla has been warned against speculation, and is sometimes frightened to discover herself involved in it: "she now first weighed the hazard of what she was doing, the deep game she was inconsiderately playing" (589). But again, like Edgar, she only experiences new difficulties in her efforts to avoid speculation. Thus, while Marchmont unwittingly leads Edgar astray, Mr. Tyrold causes problems for Camilla. In a letter to his daughter, Tyrold equates the first sensations of love with the dangers of idle speculation; the letter opens by comparing Camilla's apparently unrequited affection for Edgar to bankruptcy:

The man who loses his whole fortune, yet possesses . . . an accommodation to circumstances, is less an object of contemplative pity, than the person who, without one real deprivation . . . is suddenly forced to recognise the fallacy of a cherished and darling hope.

. . . Nor is its downfall less terrible to its visionary elevator, because others had seen it from the beginning as a folly . . . its dissolution should be estimated . . . by its believed promise of felicity to its credulous projector.

Is my Camilla in this predicament? had she wove her own destiny in the speculation of her wishes? (355–6)

Camilla's love is here explicitly analogized with the patently dangerous activity of the visionary projector, the speculator. Tyrold goes on to sympathize with woman's peculiar lot in such matters. Although there is no reason in theory why women should not "be allowed to dispose of their own affections" (358) – the wording here suggests the analogy with financial expenditure – "disquisition on this point will remain rather curious than important, till the speculatist can superinduce to the abstract truth of the position some proof of its practicability" (358). Tyrold therefore advises that Camilla "vary those thoughts that now take but one direction, and multiply those interests which now recognise but one object" (359). The result: Edgar decides that Camilla is a coquette unworthy of his affection.

Thus it becomes clear that while gaming and all forms of hazard are derided and termed dangerous, the events of the novel nevertheless suggest their necessity. In part, this attraction to gambling reflects the traditional association of gambling and gentility. But in this age of a rapidly expanding industrialist consumer economy, gambling also has the merit of giving free reign to the dynamics of contemporary consumerist desire while remaining untainted by its vulgarity. That is, gambling thrives on expansive desire even as it enacts its own painful discipline – all while the abstract, ludic quality of the activity seems to raise it above the level of petty exchange, of pounds and shillings and *quid pro quo*. To this ideological advantage, moreover, must be added particular political virtues, virtues of special significance at the end of the century. For the importance of gambling in *Camilla* signals a new view of fortune, one that reflects political as well as economic change. The checks and balances of *Cecilia* are not operative here; this is a world dominated by destiny and luck. The high levels of anxiety and suspense signal the fact that this is not a society governed by an invisible hand, a self-correcting system, but one where one sister, Camilla, can be repeatedly pronounced "lucky" (and she does win both of the lotteries she enters, not to mention that larger lottery of courtship), while another, Eugenia, just as deserving if not more so, can suffer repeated indignities that seem simply to be her fate. The book may never explicitly mention the French Revolution, but its influence is there just the same; the world is no longer predictable, and while visionary speculation may be dangerous, there is also something irresistible and even necessary in it. In this world the delight in the vicissitudes of gambling is no more than a perversity appropriate to a volatile age. Burney opens the novel thus:

The historian of human life finds less of difficulty and of intricacy to develop, in its accidents and adventures, than the investigator of the human heart in its feelings and its changes. In vain may Fortune wave her many-coloured banner, alternately regaling and dismaying, with hues that seem glowing with all the creation's felicities, or with tints that appear stained with ingredients of unmixt horrors; her most rapid vicissitudes, her most unassimilating eccentricities, are mocked, laughed at, and distanced by the wilder wonders of the Heart of man; that amazing assemblage of all possible contrarieties, in which one thing alone is steady – the perverseness of spirit which grafts desire on what is denied. (7)

Fortune – throughout the eighteenth century the presiding deity of the varied forms of gaming and speculation – appears here in a guise that brings to mind the French Revolution. The economics of Fortune are now intertwined with politics, with Fortune a standard-bearer bringing not just wealth or poverty but unprecedented optimism and unprecedented barbarity. Of course, in this period economic and political speculation were often seen to go hand in hand, a combination bewailed by Burney's friend Burke in his *Reflections on the Revolution in France* (1790). Burke condemns the French for being

the very first who have founded a commonwealth upon gaming, and infused this spirit into it as its vital breath. The great object in these politics is to metamorphose France, from a great kingdom into one great play-table; to turn its inhabitants into a nation of gamesters; to make speculation as extensive as life; to mix it with all its concerns; and to divert the whole of the hopes and fears of the people from their usual channels, into the impulses, passions, and superstitions of those who live on chances.[48]

This association of gaming with revolution was not peculiar to Burke and marked a change in the political significance of gaming. As Thomas Kavanaugh argues, the probability theory developed by Enlightenment thinkers, which sought to rationalize and domesticate "hazard," originally had an antiauthoritarian character. Concerning itself only with odds in the present, probability theory began as "an ethics of the individual freed from the weight of the past."[49] That function, however, was gradually subordinated to "the far more oppressive ideologies of the probable and the normal." Thus, at the end of the eighteenth century, it was the irrationality and passion of gambling that was linked to the struggle against authoritarianism. The individual came once again to the fore and was interesting precisely in proportion to his eccentricities. In Kavanaugh's words, "To choose chance was to choose to understand the individual as a singular, isolated consciousness within a world of disorder and unpredictability shared with other, equally limited consciousnesses similarly stymied by the absence of any integrating principle."[50] As Burke's account suggests, there is in gambling itself an element of "latent rebellion" against "moderation

---

[48] Edmund Burke, *Reflections on the Revolution in France* (New York: Anchor Books, 1973), 209.
[49] Thomas Kavanaugh, *Enlightenment and the Shadows of Chance* (Baltimore: Johns Hopkins University Press, 1993), 25.
[50] *Ibid.*, 25, 5.

[and] morality"[51] – in late eighteenth-century terms, against "things as they are."[52]

While Burney does not openly support the French Revolution in *Camilla*, she does suggest that the speculation decried by Burke is an unavoidable part of life. The world of *Camilla*, sheltered as it is, is the world of "disorder and unpredictability" described by Kavanaugh, a place where the vicissitudes of Fortune find an appropriate analog in the perversities of human beings, who show a remarkable capacity to torment themselves with desire. Burke's use of the metaphor of grafting in *Reflections* hints at its resonance in Burney's introduction: for him, it is a sign of the artificiality of Revolutionary politics and economics.[53] For Burney, too, the image suggests something forced and artificial – but she presents this grafting as a constituent part of all human life, not simply a pastime of the French. Human beings, loving what is denied, have in them a masochistic impulse. Thus while at one level *Camilla* offers a moral/practical message – Camilla and Edgar should have sought one another more straightforwardly – at another level it teaches us the impossibility and even the undesirability of such straightforwardness; as everyone from Mrs. Arlbery to Marchmont to Tyrold is constantly noting, "'A certainty of success in many destroys, in all weakens, its charm'" (360). In this

---

[51] Edmund Bergler, *The Psychology of Gambling* (New York: Hill and Wang, 1957), 18. Bergler argues that the gambler unconsciously wants to lose, that gambling itself is an effort "to recreate omnipotence through [an] aggression against parents and educators" (32) for which the gambler desires punishment. Freud had himself found Oedipal and masochistic desires at work in gambling; he argued that Dostoevsky's parricidal impulses could be linked to his self-destructive interest in gambling ("Dostoevsky and Parricide," in *The Standard Edition of the Complete Psychological Works of Sigmund Freud*, 24 vols., vol. XXI, trans. and ed. James Strachey with Anna Freud [London: Hogarth Press, 1961], 177–94).

[52] Of course, the late-eighteenth-century world of fashion and shopping had tried, in its own way, to incorporate into itself an invigorating element of changefulness; novelty itself played a new and important role in eighteenth-century consumerism, as we will see in the next chapter. J. H. Plumb notes that the expanding consumption required by industrial production required a belief in the value of growth, change, and modernity ("The Acceptance of Modernity," in McKendrick et al., *Birth of a Consumer Society*, 316), and by the end of the century variety and novelty were primary characteristics of consumer goods themselves. But as Ann Bermingham points out, the "revolutions" embodied in fashion are very much contained: "fashion provided a comforting model of history, one that demanded, in an almost subliminal way, that 'revolution' be understood as both rupture – the myth of progress – and as continuity – the myth of historical repetition" (Bermingham, "The Picturesque and Ready-to-Wear Femininity," in Stephen Copley and Peter Garside, eds., *The Poetics of the Picturesque* [Cambridge: Cambridge University Press, 1994], 100). During the period, then, the world of shopping, while it traded on the idea of novelty, did not seem as truly and excitingly changeful as the gambler's world, the world of the hopeful speculator.

[53] Edmund Burke argues, for example, that "Upon that body and stock of inheritance [from our English forefathers] we have taken care not to inoculate any cyon alien to the nature of the original plant" (*Reflections*, 43).

world of change, one does best not to seek satisfaction directly but to take satisfaction in speculation itself.

Gambling and speculation, longtime recreations of the aristocracy, therefore became imbued with the spirit of a new age, linked to forms of political speculation that were, ironically enough, precisely opposed to aristocratic privilege. Surcharged with meanings both old and new, gambling in *Camilla* may in some ways seem like careless squandering, but it also appears generous and uncalculating. It may pose a threat to social stability, but it also signals an imaginative and idealistic investment in the future.[54] Thus the heroine of this Burney novel is represented as remarkable not for moral probity or powerful reason like Cecilia but for a well-developed imagination and a generous spirit. She is notable, moreover, not for the regularity of her features but for their expressiveness – their individuality – and her primary charms are "variety" and "elasticity" (15). In a delirious dream-vision Camilla feels an irresistible impulse to make out an account of her life: writing out her claims and her deserts, she cannot but acknowledge the moral bankruptcy of her current course and her wish for death. Camilla's anguish and the frequency with which the characters are tempted to suicide reflect the diminishing feasibility of rational moral accounting. The balance-sheet no longer provides answers, and risk is simply unavoidable. It makes sense, then, that visionary enthusiasm, imagination, and speculation – and the painful, suspenseful desire to which they give rise – exert a sort of magnetic influence in the novel; ultimately they are not to be resisted.

---

[54] The novel does, however, make an effort to delimit Camilla's speculative leanings by establishing an opposition between her and other, less rational and restrained characters. Mrs. Berlinton in particular serves as a foil designed to assure us of Camilla's essential respect for social norms and laws. Attractive as she is, this enthusiastic woman, who loves to read Akenside's "Pleasures of the Imagination" and inhabit visionary worlds, is immediately perceived by Edgar as a threat to Camilla. Camilla's "romantic new friend" (439) inspires a fanciful attachment – "Camilla quitted not this enchantress till summoned" (468). When Edgar ruminates over the various persons he perceives as threatening Camilla or his attachment to her, he runs through a series of male rivals but finally ends thus: "another rock was in the way, against which he apprehended she might be dashed, whilst least suspicious of any peril . . . for it was Mrs. Berlinton, the beautiful, the accomplished, the attractive Mrs. Berlinton, whom he beheld as the object of the greatest risk she had to encounter" (486). Whereas the ostensible threat posed by male rivals is clear enough, Edgar is unable to articulate the threat posed by Mrs. Berlinton; it remains a vague menace. Before arriving safe in Edgar's port, Camilla may be crushed upon this charming social loadstone. In fact, when Mrs. Berlinton does finally fall, Camilla is far too right-minded not to notice it; this friend never did pose a real threat. But that felt menace, I would argue, reflects the extent to which the novel itself feels the pull toward imaginative pleasures. Mrs. Berlinton is, potentially, too attractive, so Burney constantly gives the reader cues to keep her at arm's length, and depletes her of charm almost immediately when she begins to go astray. Fittingly, her fall involves both the development of a weakness for gambling and the cultivation of an illicit romance. And we are not surprised to learn that Bellamy, Mrs. Berlinton's beautiful friend, is a truly dangerous person, who actually grew up in a gambling house and is desperate to pay off his gambling debts.

VI

The perverse attraction to speculation, however, is more than simply a concession to a world dominated by fickle Fortune, or a sign of an idealistic
investment in the future. The novel makes not just a virtue but also a pleasure of necessity, for even at its most anxious the romantic lottery in which
Camilla and Edgar cast their stakes undeniably has its pleasures. The characters' accounts of their suffering are something more than mere gestures to
a traditional language of courtly love or heroic romance; the suspense that
forms such an important part of desire in the novel is developed to a masochistic pitch of enjoyment. Macdersey's description of pleasure's relation to
torment suggests how this may be so; when asked what he thinks of gaming,
he replies, "'I hold nobody to have an idea of life that has not rattled in his
own hand the dear little box of promise. What ecstasy not to know if, in two
seconds, one mayn't be worth ten thousand pounds! or else without a farthing! how it puts one on the rack!'" (480) Although slightly ridiculous
himself, Macdersey expresses a sentiment with which the novel ultimately
sympathizes. The man or woman of imagination and feeling is one who
loves gambling, who finds ecstasy on the rack of suspense. Thus Camilla
is drawn to Edgar although he appears to be distant, superior, severe, and
cold. Mrs. Arlbery tells Camilla outright that her fancy "'has hit upon a tor-
mentor'" (455) in Edgar. Yet in contemplating him Camilla often finds
herself "in a perturbation at once pleasing and painful" (156). Even as she

gave free vent to her tears, and thought herself the most wretched of human beings;
she found her heart, her aching heart, more than ever devoted to Mandlebert, filled
with his image, revering his virtues, honouring even his coldness, from a persuasion
she deserved not his affection, and sighing solely for the privilege to consign herself
to his remembrance for life. (542)

In *Camilla* Burney offers a full exploration of eroticized emotional distress.
Here desire and pleasure are always tied to pain: Edgar opens the long-
awaited proposal scene with the words "'O Camilla! torture me no
longer!'" (544). The central characters of *Camilla* show what Burney calls
"the customary ingenuity of sensitive minds to torment themselves" (681).
    It is worth noting, moreover, that while father figures predominate in the
world of *Evelina*, Camilla is the first of Burney's novelistic heroines to have
a living mother, and she is both powerful and righteous. Camilla's fear and
remorse, when she must return to her family after her debts have
been discovered, are, like her brother's, focused on her mother. To her

children at least, Mrs. Tyrold plays the role traditionally associated with the father: "Though unaffectedly beloved, Mrs. Tyrold was deeply feared by all her children" (238). The paternal sadism and maternal consumerism of *Evelina* have been transformed; here it is Mrs. Tyrold who represents punishing authority, even though it is clear that her will is ultimately always subordinate to her husband's. As with Burke's Marie Antoinette, power, while it remains with the father, is symbolically lodged in the mother. Such "transvestite authority," as Eagleton calls it, was well-suited to the 1790s, a period that saw important challenges to overt traditional power.[55] Fear and desire are no longer dissociated as they were in Burke's sublime father/beautiful mother binary; prohibition and consumption are now inextricably linked. Consumption is not only delayed, suspended, and anxious, but can be experienced and enjoyed only on those terms.

In this third novel, then, Burney tests the virtues of two very different ways of desiring. Like many other works of the 1790s, *Camilla* aims not only to square social protocols with individual desire, but also to explore and redefine "individual desire" itself. The new association of gambling and speculation with radical generosity, coupled with the development of impersonal trade practices and their association with vulgarity, encouraged the investment in a specific form of desire, one fraught with anxiety and discomfort and characterized by imagination, idealization, deferral, and suspense. Camilla and Edgar try to be objective, careful, and thrifty in their pursuit of one another, but they invariably reveal their true nature as generous, imaginative speculators. Pages and anxieties mount as they learn how best to desire in a new world where Fortune's eccentricities can be surpassed only by those of the human heart.

VII THE WANDERER

While in *Camilla* speculation in its political aspect is only indirectly touched upon, in Burney's 1814 novel *The Wanderer* both the economics and the politics of the Romantic age – and their influence on the shape of desire – are fully explored. The novel is set during the years of the Terror, and at its end the novel's hero remarks that the French Revolution

[55] Terry Eagleton, *The Ideology of the Aesthetic* (Oxford: Basil Blackwell, 1990), 58. Claudia Johnson makes a somewhat similar argument, claiming that the inversion of gender roles in Camilla's parents gives Mr. Tyrold, like many of the men in *Camilla*, access to the ideological power embodied in sensibility. Her main concern, however, is that this masculine usurpation of an erstwhile feminine sensibility renders women "grotesque," that it "aggravates the problem of female subjectivity" (*Equivocal Beings*, 148).

"has not operated more wonderfully on the fate and fortune, than upon the minds and characters of those individuals who have borne in it any share."[56] The composition of the novel occurred at a sufficient temporal distance from the Terror to permit its direct contemplation, and the result is an extremely complicated set of explicit and implicit reflections on politics, economics, and the dynamics of desire.

In *Camilla*, as we saw, speculation is represented as risky, but it is undeniably compelling. In *The Wanderer*, however, speculation in the political realm appears not only risky but downright dangerous – 1789 is now too far distant for the charms of Revolutionary enthusiasm to be remembered. Yet Burney is, perhaps more than ever, attracted to certain revolutionary values, especially ideals of equality. So she salvages speculation and the painful pleasures that accompany it by distinguishing political and economic speculation and then roundly denouncing political speculation while looking to economic speculation for the equalizing she seeks. Thus this narrative has not one but two heroines: a proper heroine and a secondary or antiheroine. Both Juliet and Elinor, as the novel opens, escape from France to England, and while each embodies revolutionary change, the two divide the field between them, Juliet embodying new economic relations, Elinor speaking for new political relations. Through Elinor, then, Burney is able to distance herself from overt revolutionary feminist and democratic doctrine, while using Juliet to espouse feminist and democratic economic arguments that are equally, if not as obviously, revolutionary.

Burney was able to do this only because she had changed many of her earlier opinions regarding labor, anonymity, and vulgarity. Her new appreciation for labor and production, and her sensitivity to contemporary changes in retailing, led her to dissolve the opposition between shopping and gambling with which she had concerned herself in *Camilla*. In *The Wanderer* even the commonest shop goods are capable of eliciting the painful and idealizing speculation associated exclusively with gaming in *Camilla*. Indeed, this book defines and celebrates a specifically Romantic-era form of commodity fetishism. Even while it develops a labor theory of value, the novel promotes a mystification of the commodity by insisting on the aloof independence of labor and its products. The apparent autonomy of things – which KarlMarx decries – is used by Burney precisely as a

[56] Frances Burney, *The Wanderer*, ed. Margaret Doody, Robert Mack, and Peter Sabor (Oxford: Oxford University Press, 1991), 869. All subsequent references to this novel will be to this edition and will be given parenthetically in the text.

means to argue for the autonomy of the makers of those things. For at the moment of the composition of *The Wanderer*, it seemed that the growing potency of the commodity could be used as a lever for asserting the political independence of the laborer/producer over against the aristocrat/consumer. For Burney, the commodity does and should appear aloof and exotic, and it merits idealizing, passionate, and painful desire. The erotic submission espoused here is no longer that of jaunty aristocrats or hot-blooded revolutionaries but of right-minded people who are willing to invest all labor and its products with the charisma once ascribed to kings.

We begin with the political doctrine eschewed through the figure of the antiheroine, Elinor. During her visit to France, Elinor is "infected . . . with the system-forming spirit" (157). Elinor sometimes speaks very movingly for the necessity of removing "outworn prejudices," especially with respect to women. Unfortunately, in practice this creed leads Elinor to make a spectacle of herself in the service of her own desires. For instance, Elinor pointedly chooses to perform her sacrificial suicide for Harleigh at a public performance, thereby putting Harleigh under public pressure to accede to her passion. Elinor herself describes her "liberated" efforts to attain Harleigh in theatrical terms: "'My operations are to commence thus: Act I. Scene I. Enter Ellis, seeking Albert . . . though I know not whether the catastrophe will be tragic or comic, I am prepared in my part for either'" (157). Embodied as they are in Elinor's actions, then, Revolutionary politics are represented as little more than the manipulative public display of desire. And in this, one might add, Burney did not simply develop a personal metaphor for Revolutionary activity; as Mona Ozouf, Lynn Hunt, and others have shown, Revolutionary *fêtes* and spectacles were not mere sideshows to the Revolution but were crucial to the Revolutionary project.[57] Burney's representation of Elinor's theatricality thus represents a crucial insight into the workings of the French Revolution – it is about desire made spectacular.

Despite her sympathies with certain aspects of Revolutionary and feminist thinking, Burney was deeply suspicious of this politicization of desire. Not only does Elinor play Lady Wronghead in the private theatricals she arranges, and act as a "principal buffoon" on the larger stage of Brighthelmstone social life, but her theatrical display of desire rapidly becomes a

---

[57] See, for instance, Mona Ozouf, *Festivals and the French Revolution*, trans. Alan Sheridan (Cambridge, Mass.: Harvard University Press, 1988), and Lynn Hunt, *Politics, Culture, and Class in the French Revolution* (Berkeley: University of California Press, 1984), Chapter 2, "Symbolic Forms of Political Practice."

miniature version of the Terror. Throughout the book she uses threats to manipulate Harleigh and Juliet: a letter addressed to the latter is explicitly described as a "memorandum of terror" (197). From the outset Elinor's proceedings have a bellicose character, as the word "operations" in the quotation above describing the first act of her drama suggests – the term seems better suited to the discussion of military strategy than the preparation for a play.

So while Elinor can be a moving spokeswoman for women's right to desire, she also reveals the dangers and paradoxes of that desire. And just as political ideals of equality and independence – and the political means of achieving them – are questioned and distanced through her, so, too, she becomes the representative of a "bad" form of self-abnegating eroticism. For while on the one hand she makes much of her independence, she no sooner does so than she gives herself over in abject subjection to Harleigh: "'you, O Harleigh! you I obey, without waiting for a command . . . To you, my free soul, my liberated mind, my new-born ideas, all yield, slaves, willing slaves'" (190). This "thraldom of an over-ruling propensity" (155) inspires a masochistic language even before it is clear that Harleigh does not reciprocate Elinor's affection. Once it is obvious that her affection is unrequited, Elinor lovingly describes Harleigh as "'the imperious, constant master of my mind'" (378). But while Elinor views her behavior as the natural expression of her romantic devotion to Harleigh, the reader is encouraged to see it as a sign of self-devotion. This subjection, after all, exists side by side with her efforts at domination by indirection. The spectacle of female political independence is one of extremes, of a masochistic terrorism.

VIII

But if Burney eschews overt political change in Elinor, she embraces the possibility of a new economic order through the figure of Juliet. Whereas Elinor openly reflects on politics, Juliet reflects internally on economic relations, and her experiences serve as object lessons in economics for the reader. To understand Burney's representation of economics in *The Wanderer*, we must turn again to the retailing world – this time the retailing world of the early nineteenth century. For this novel actively promotes a form of commodity fetishism, a fetishism shaped by changes in early nineteenth-century production and sales. Of course, many of these changes were part of a gradual development. Advertising, for instance, had long been evolving in terms of both quantity and quality or sophistication. From the time of its humble beginnings in the late eighteenth century, the increasing use of large-claim advertising had had the effect of lending goods greater powers than they could reasonably be said to possess. As Neil McKendrick points out, "by the turn of the century the art of puffing had reached such a pitch and commanded such a variety of techniques that a new vocabulary of description had been invented to do it justice."[58] During this period, many a newspaper was entirely devoted to advertisement, and such newspapers were typically met not with scorn but with delight, as we see in a poem by Isabella Lickbarrow:

> The "*Advertiser*," you must know,
> Fresh from the Mint not long ago,
> We welcomed with abundant pleasure,
> Impatient for the mighty treasure . . .[59]

Even the continual rise in the stamp duties and the high tax per advertisement during the early years of the war with France did not deter the advertisers' zeal; indeed, they began to seek not merely to inform but to impress. Looking back to his early years working for the *Morning Post*, Daniel Stuart describes the canniness of advertisers at the turn of the century:

Each was desirous of having his cloud of advertisements inserted at once in the front page. I would not drive away the short miscellaneous advertisements by allowing space to be monopolized by any class . . . I accommodated the booksellers as well as I could with a few new and pressing advertisements at a time. That would not do, they would have the cloud.[60]

Turn-of-the-century advertising aimed not simply to capture the attention but to overwhelm it.

This development was, however, only one of several that were to lend a peculiar power to the early nineteenth-century commodity. At the time of the composition of *The Wanderer*, large-scale industrial manufacture was on the rise, as was the standardization of goods for sale. Increasingly, commodities were ready-made, produced for a large impersonal market, rather than bespoke or tailor-made to the needs of a given person. The consumer world was one in which commodities seemed more and more to have a life of their own, an independent existence. Thomas Richards argues in *The Commodity Culture of Victorian England* that the Great Exhibition of

---

[58] McKendrick, "Commercialization and the Economy," 148, 182.
[59] Isabella Lickbarrow, "The Fate of Newspapers," in Lickbarrow, *Poetical Effusions* (London: J. Richardson, 1814), p. 73.
[60] The quotation is from an article written for the July 1838 issue of *the Gentlemen's Magazine*, in which Stuart gives an account of his early years with *the Morning Post*.

1851 presented commodities in a way that made them appear "autonomous and untouchable": they were set apart and illuminated, and while they were meant to be seen, they were surrounded by a barrier that asserted "the inviolability of the object."[61] But this new aura of autonomy did not spring full grown out of the magical spaces of the Crystal Palace; mass production itself made for a world where the existence of commodities preceded and appeared independent of consumer needs or desires.

The new autonomy of the commodity was, moreover, complemented by a novel form of commodity "individuality." For during the late eighteenth and early nineteenth centuries, the kind of particularity that was coming to be valued in persons was also becoming an important quality in consumer goods. Indeed, it was often the particularity of one's possessions that served to ground and give objective form to one's own individuality. The display value of fashionable objects, which from the seventeenth century had been measured primarily in terms of market value, was now complicated by the growing importance of "taste." To be surrounded by the material forms of wealth was no longer enough; one's consumer choices had to reveal, first and foremost, the refinement of one's faculty of judgment. One sees this at work, for instance, in the handling of domestic interiors. As Charles Saumarez Smith shows, over the course of the eighteenth century the semiotics of the interior gradually changed. Professional architects, who had previously concerned themselves almost exclusively with exteriors, gradually took over the task of interior design, and the plans in which they mapped out those interiors became increasingly sophisticated and detailed. The new weight given to such details can be clearly seen in the portraits of the period. Conversation pieces of the early part of the century typically represent families in settings that signify wealth without being themselves particularized: it was not uncommon to be painted on the grounds of a landed estate that was not one's own, in clothes that actually belonged to the painter's lay-figure and that appeared repeatedly in his works. By the end of the century, however, it was important that the objects surrounding the sitters be properly their own, and the number of those objects grew. This development would ultimately result in the Victorian penchant for bric-à-brac. Thus even the trend toward the standardization of goods, in the context of a general proliferation of commercially available objects, did not interfere with the consumer's sense of the specificity of the

---

[61] Thomas Richards, *The Commodity Culture of Victorian England: Advertising and Spectacle, 1851–1914* (Stanford: Stanford University Press, 1990), 32.

commodity. Indeed, the sense of this specificity was heightened, and this, in turn, helped to sustain new notions of individuality.

The early nineteenth-century commodity was thus endowed with a new species of autonomy and individuality, and it seemed to promise to foster those same qualities in its buyer. But changes in retailing tended to heighten one's sense that the new autonomy of the commodity belonged to it alone. As we have seen already, the Romantic period witnessed a gradual shift toward a modern form of retailing, one in which fixed prices and ready-cash sales permitted the relation between merchant and buyer to become more and more impersonal. But while that relationship became more impersonal, the customer's relationship with the commodity became increasingly important. That is, shopping was no longer a matter of engaging with the shopkeeper but of engaging with the commodity itself. The new practice of open ticketing enhanced this effect; it seemed that objects set their own terms for sale.[62] As the nineteenth century progressed, it was increasingly presumed that it was the value of goods themselves that established price.[63]

If goods now seemed to sell themselves, this was also because retailers were not only using entertainment to attract customers, as we saw in the discussion of *Evelina*, but also magnifying the attraction of goods through display. As with advertising, this use of display in retailing was part of a gradual development. At the beginning of the century, a London draper who went to work in the provinces discovered at first hand the difference between his and the more traditional way of doing business: "they had never been in the habit of displaying any quantity of goods in the windows and my style of window-dressing was looked upon as a decided innovation ... People seemed to depend more upon their connexion and usual customers than to seek for new ones."[64] Sophie von la Roche, a German visitor writing home in 1786, speaks glowingly of fashionable Oxford Street, brilliantly lit by oil lamps in the evening: "First one passes a watch-making, then a silk or fan store, now a silversmith's, a

[62] For a discussion of fixed pricing and open ticketing, see Carrier, *Gifts and Commodities*, 80.

[63] Thomas Richards argues that the absence of price tags on exhibition articles promoted a "transparency of exchange," in which things appeared to "sell themselves" (*Commodity Culture*, 38). I would argue that originally it was the *presence* of the "price ticket" that appeared to confer that power upon them.

[64] Anon., *Reminiscences of an Old Draper*, ed. William H. Ablett (London: S. Low, Marston, Searle & Rivington, 1876) p. 142. Since the early eighteenth century, new luxury items had begun to give rise to shops that relied on the display of goods to draw in customers. By mid-century luxury trades were increasingly making use of plate glass and constructing bow windows for the display of goods. As Alison Adburgham notes, by the end of the century "the more prosperous shopkeepers ... had 'patent lamps' trained on their windows from outside" (*Shopping in Style: London from the Restoration to Edwardian Elegance* [Over Wallop: Thames and Hudson, 1979], 73).

china or glass shop . . . Just as alluring are the confectioners and fruiterers, where, behind the handsome glass windows pyramids of pineapples, figs, grapes, oranges and all manner of fruits are on show."[65] The reputation of the shopkeeper remained extremely important, but the increased use of display to garner custom looks forward to a more modern form of retailing. When display became commonplace in shops that were not luxury shops, it seemed particularly offensive. In 1819 "Several Tradesmen" warned the public against price ticketing, complaining that it was a "deceptive practice," and going on to remark that "*Cheap shops* are a great evil, and a much greater eye-sore to the *regular* Trader." These "Imposter shops" were typically known for "the vehemency and number of their placards, signs and tickets."[66] By 1810 a provincial tradesman complained that in London one was "no longer able to discern the neat but unadorned shop . . . the windows were such as Gulliver would describe as a glass case in Brognibog . . . I could make out – and Co. Chemicals and Galenicals in that kind of distorted characters which are pourtrayed on the Egyptian monuments of antiquity."[67] Exotic show seemed to be replacing old-fashioned respectability. It is worth noting that the shop run by the heroine of *The Wanderer* is of a fully nineteenth-century kind. Juliet intends (though she forgets) to take immediate payment from the strangers who come into the shop, and she and Gabriella seek to attract passing trade, "decking out" the shop "to attract passers bye" (624). Although Burney sets her novel in the 1790s and in the provinces, she gives the shop a modern urban character.

In various ways then, the consumer's experience in the shop increasingly developed his sense of the centrality and autonomy of the commodity. As the "dropping trade" – the casual trade of strangers passing by – became more important and cash sales and fixed prices became more common, it seemed that one's relation was less with the shop vendor than with the object for sale. Even changes like the increase in the number of specialty shops contributed to this effect, since they organized shopping in terms of the objects sold rather than the convenience of the shopper. Here, in fact, one notes an important distinction between Romantic-era and Victorian retailing. In the latter period sales were reorganized around the comfort of the shopper, and stores became a kind of second home in which the needs and desires of the customer were specifically catered to. This was especially true of the department store: "Assistants in department stores . . . were

---

[65] Sophie von la Roche, *Sophie in London, 1786*, ed. Clare Williams (London: J. Cope, 1933), 141.
[66] Anon., *The London Tradesman* (London: Simpkin and Marshall, 1819), 118.
[67] *The Tradesman* 3:1 (July 1809), 31.

inclined to be flattering rather than argumentative: the customer was now to be waited on rather than negotiated with ... People could now come and go, to look and dream, perchance to buy, and shopping became a new bourgeois leisure activity."[68] The Romantic specialty shop, although it sought to attract customers, and operated on a system of fixed prices and cash sales, was not yet a haven for dawdling dreamers. Indeed, the initial effect of moving to a fixed-price, cash-sales policy was to make such stores appear distinctly user-unfriendly.

Turn-of-the-century forms of retailing were, moreover, not without their political implications. Cash sales and fixed prices challenged, and, in effect, flattened traditional social relations, a fact keenly and sometimes painfully felt by their first advocates. Thus there were times when James Lackington, whose "Temple of the Muses" became something of an institution, considered relinquishing his "favourite scheme" of cash-only sales because of the awkwardness of refusing credit "to the most respectable characters, as no exception was (or now is) made, not even to the nobility."[69] This kind of retailing seemed to many contemporaries to herald the breakdown of social relations. Lackington was told that he "might as well attempt to re-build the Tower of Babel as to establish a large business without giving credit."[70] This way of doing business had a revolutionary character that, at the end of the century, resonated with the influence of the French Revolution.

The breakdown or simplification of the buyer-seller relationship was, however, compensated for in the consumer-commodity relationship. That is, rather than struggle with a merchant over the price of an object, one mentally engaged with the object itself, which seemed to set its own terms for purchase. Thus, as relationships between persons became more anonymous and less obviously inflected by status differentials, the relationships of persons to objects became a substitute arena for interactions involving dominance and submission.[71] Marx argues that the belief that commodities "rule the producers instead of being ruled by them" is the result of a mystification

---

[68] Rachel Bowlby, *Just Looking: Consumer Culture in Dreiser, Gissing and Zola* (New York: Methuen, 1985), 4.

[69] James Lackington, *Memoirs of the First Forty-Five Years* (London: Whittaker, Treacher, and Arnot, 1830), 214. [70] *Ibid.*

[71] The very architecture of marketing during this period underscores this point. "Market reform in the late eighteenth and early nineteenth centuries was part of a revolution in both architectural form and the arrangement of public space"; the haphazardly developed street market came to be replaced by monumental market halls that served as a focus of civic pride – a pride that, at the beginning of the century, was reflected in the popularity of classical architectural forms for such markets. See James Schmiechen and Kenneth Carls, *The British Market Hall: A Social and Architectural History* (New Haven: Yale University Press, 1999), 47. The typical new market hall "acted as an advertisement for the activities of the market as noble and well-ordered ... The public market had joined the church and the town hall as an idealized

attendant upon the stable determination of a commodity's exchange value.[72] But the early nineteenth century was to witness a transfer of ostensible power from persons to commodities not because of a change in the determination of market value during that period but because the power relations that obtained between people were being, at least in appearance, flattened. As hierarchical social relations were increasingly challenged in the political sphere, those hierarchies were reinscribed in the economic realm both in practical terms – buying power became increasingly more important than lineage – and in purely emotional ways.[73] James Carrier notes that factory production made "objects more opaque to buyers, especially the buyers likely to be shopping in the emerging new-style stores in London around 1800. With this opacity it became easier for seller and buyer alike to impose new, symbolic meanings on commodities."[74] In the early 1800s, after the heated political debates of the 1790s, in which everything from monarchy to property and the institution of marriage was questioned, it was only the value of objects themselves that seemed secure, and it was the consumer's capacity to recognize or respond to the commodity's apparent autonomy that enabled him to reenchant his world.[75]

institution" (48). The imposing market halls and glamorous shops of the turn of the century provided an impressive context for the items sold there.

[72] Karl Marx, *Capital*, 2 vols., vol. I, ed. Frederick Engels, trans. Samuel Moore and Edward Aveling (New York: International Publishers, 1987), 79.

[73] Lynn Hunt has convincingly argued that in France during the Revolution the aura, the charisma attached to kingship, was transferred to language, both verbal and symbolic. The language and iconography of the period thus bore an unprecedented burden of meaning and feeling (see Hunt, *Politics, Culture*, 21). In England, of course, the monarchy remained. But the frugality and madness of George III did little for the prestige of the monarchy, and the fierce contention the French Revolution had sponsored did at least challenge the legitimacy of many traditional institutions. In England there was relatively little in the way of new political or social institutions to which to transfer the charisma of the old. One finds instead a tendency toward hero worship: figures such as Napoleon Bonaparte and Byron were invested with a great deal of feeling and desire. As Byron himself claimed, his was an age in which heroes were produced in abundance, though generally they ultimately failed to satisfy (see the first five stanzas of Canto 1 of *Don Juan* in Jerome McGann, ed., *Byron* [Oxford: Oxford University Press, 1986], 378–9). I would argue that in England, an island known for its commerce, charisma was increasingly transferred to economic goods, and that changes in retailing helped to make this transference possible.

[74] Carrier, *Gifts and Commodities*, 76. Richards argues that in 1887, the year of Queen Victoria's first Jubilee, advertisers "used traditional intimations of the immateriality of royal power to confer a vast and often uncontrollable significance on the material world" (*Commodity Culture*, 82); like the Queen's two bodies, objects were given both a material and a transcendental meaning. But as Richards himself suggests, Victoria was not so much mined for her innate charisma as simply represented as charismatic by advertisers: "Victoria did not have to be inherently charismatic to exercise a kind of acquired charisma by becoming a semiotic lodestone" (79). I would argue that this was because commodities were by that time already laden with charisma, a situation of which advertisers merely took further advantage by attaching that charisma to its traditional sources when possible.

[75] Thomas Richards offers a similar argument, though for a somewhat later period, claiming that "the legitimation crisis that followed in the wake of the French Revolution and the Napoleonic Wars" led

Increasingly, it was consumer goods that inspired the hopes and loyalties of the English subject.

IX

We return now to *The Wanderer*, a novel devoted to rumination on the nature and value of labor and the commodity. As Juliet passes through a range of occupations, from humble companion to mantua-maker to milliner, she and the reader are given ample opportunity to contemplate economic relations from the perspective of labor. Through Juliet's experience and Arbe's commentary, Burney constructs an elaborate labor theory of value and complains of the incommensurability of the value generated by the laborer and that recognized by the consumer. The aristocrats who owe Juliet money tend to delay payment or neglect it altogether, and they justify themselves by belittling the service or product they have received from her. As Juliet considers, "Alas! . . . how little do we know either of the labours, or the privations, of those whose business it is to administer pleasure to the public! We receive it so lightly, that we imagine it to be lightly given!" (321).

Thus Burney goes a step beyond linking value to utility, for use value, like exchange value, is measured at the point of consumption, not the point of production. The self-serving elites of Brighthelmstone argue the value of utility only to deny the value of labor; as Mr. Scope and Miss Bydel claim, 'if singing and dancing, and making images, are ever so pretty, one should not pay folks who follow such light callings, as one pays people that are useful' (324). Arbe responds with an impassioned diatribe on the short-sightedness of this view, explaining that "'because you, at idle hours . . . lounge in your box at operas and concerts . . . do you imagine he who sings, or who dances, must be a voluptuary? No! all he does is pain and toil to himself; learnt with labour, and exhibited with difficulty'" (325). Among Brighthelmstone elites, Arbe's notions are considered those of a madman, a big-hearted fool. But it is not only the aristocrats of the Brighthelmstone community who consistently fail to perceive the value embodied in labor. Even Miss Matson, Juliet's employer, judges her by her wealth rather than her labor. "Miss Matson, in unison with the very common character to which she belonged, had appreciated Juliet not by her worth, her talents, or her labours, but by her avowed distress, and acknowledged poverty" (450) – that is, she had not appreciated her at all.

---

to the "modulated transformation of the remnants of the high style into the basic tropes of a new commodity culture" (*Commodity Culture*, 54).

Both explicitly and implicitly, the novel argues that the value lodged in a service or product is derived from the value of materials and labor, and that price should reflect that value. At the milliner's Juliet is appalled to see "The most callous disregard to all representations of the dearness of materials, or of the just price of labour, was accompanied by the most facile acquiescence even in demands that were exorbitant, if they were adroitly preceded by, 'Lady *** . . . gave that sum'" (427). She learns that labor and its compensation often stand in an inverse relation, and that "The goods which demanded most work, most ingenuity, and most hands, were last paid, because heaviest of expense . . . though . . . their payment [was] the first required" (427). Nor do these inequities spring solely from consumer greed; when he can, the merchant aims at inequities that favor him: "every article was charged, not according to its value, but to the skill or ignorance of the purchaser; old goods were sold as if new; cheap goods as if dear" (427). By implication, commodities and services are possessed of an inherent value, a value that should be directly reflected in price. This value is determined at the point of production; it is established long before the consumer saunters into the shop.

The injustice and irrationality of the sales Juliet describes arise from the fact that in turn-of-the-century provincial England exchange is still generally not impersonal: price is not determined on the basis of a notion of inherent value but is instead the product of a give and take between merchant and buyer. Of course, the changes that had already transformed London would soon be felt in the provinces as well. Tellingly, Burney chose to set her tale in the quiet town of Brighthelmstone, a town whose very name would ironically signal, to Burney's readers of 1814, the transformation from a provincial to a modern commodity culture. By the time he had taken his oath as Regent in 1811, Prince George had made "Brighton" a center of fashion and taste. For Burney's readers then, Giles Arbe's vision of economic justice may well have appeared forward-looking rather than foolish. Arbe's vision is about more than just the abstract recognition of the value of labor: it is also about the reduction of relations of rank to impersonal monetary relations. In Brighthelmstone economic interactions are inevitably complicated by considerations of rank, family connections, and other social relations. The inequalities to which this gives rise are touched upon in an early exchange between Juliet and Arbe: Juliet refuses a gift of money from Arbe, explaining that "'I have been brought up to avoid all obligations with strangers.' 'How so? I don't at all see that. Have you not an obligation to that linen draper, and hosier . . . if you take their things, and don't pay for them?'" (281). Arbe refuses to recognize the personal and class distinctions that complicate, and, essentially, impede fair exchange.

By conceiving of monetary exchange in impersonal terms and setting it at the heart of social interaction, Arbe is able to imagine an equality grounded in economics: 'you have paid all your debts, you ought to hold up your head; for, where nothing is owing, we are all of us equal, rich and poor' (521). In essence, Arbe denies what one might call the *ancien régime* notion of rank that had traditionally inflected every social interaction. It is worth noting, however, that he never argues for strictly political change. By grounding equality in impersonal economic relations, Arbe offers an apparently more viable creed of equality than Elinor's political radicalism, even if that creed seems to be founded on an almost dreamy unawareness of social realities. And unlike Elinor's, Arbe's motives are entirely humane and unselfish, and he himself is generally "placid" (325) and gentle. Thus, while French political radicalism is distanced in the figure of the dramatic and often manipulative Elinor, Juliet and Giles Arbe quietly fasten our attention on the issue of the value of labor and the possibility of equality in economic relations. It makes sense, then, that Juliet's aristocratic *émigrée* friend Gabriella, while her character and situation suggest that the toppling of the French aristocracy was a misfortune, nevertheless speaks for the honor of economic independence through labor: "the French Revolution has opened our eyes to a species of equality more rational, because more feasible, than that of lands or rank; an equality not alone of mental sufferings, but of manual exertions" (639).

To achieve this "equality of manual exertions," the book argues for the necessity of the universal availability of the means of economic independence, particularly for women. Juliet quickly discovers the necessity of having some capital simply in order to work as a laborer: she needs money to give harp lessons, to fund a subscription concert, to do needlework orders, and even as a premium to work for the milliner: "Every species of business, however narrow its cast, however limited its wants, however mean its materials; required, she now found, some capital to answer to its immediate calls, and some steady credit for encountering . . . unforeseen accidents, and unavoidable risks" (425). In this more traditional economy, the necessity of capital forces Juliet to rely on patronage. The difficulty of achieving real independence in such an economy, especially for women, is a cause for constant lament in the novel. Burney insists that "FEMALE DIFFICULTIES" are the result of economic dependence, and that all persons, including women, should have recourse to some means for independence. Thus, just as a kind of democratic politics enters *The Wanderer* through the back door of economics, so the female independence that is condemned when sought through political means is boldly espoused in the economic domain.[76]

X

To the reader of *Evelina*, *Cecilia*, and *Camilla*, one of the most striking features of *The Wanderer* is its focus on an anonymous heroine, a heroine who remains, throughout the book, a sort of black hole of desire, attracting the wishes of others while expressing none of her own. But as we shall see, Juliet's peculiarities can be linked to the fact that she functions as an analog of the new, early nineteenth-century commodity.

The Wanderer opens with Juliet crossing the Channel to England and making the trip to Brighthelmstone. She is introduced to us, as to the people of Brighthelmstone, as an assemblage of strictly external features, and she immediately becomes a spectacle, a novelty, and an object of amusement. Apparently black, she therefore also seems exotic and bears the aura of a human reduced to the status of a possession. Even before Juliet's black arms are revealed, Elinor, amused by her unusual look, remarks to Harleigh that 'you would just as willingly find her a tawny Hottentot as a fair Circassian' (12). Nor does the removal of Juliet's disguise help matters; her persistent opacity fixes her in the role of exhibition object. At a gathering, Elinor "flew back to summon the Incognita to descend for exhibition" (53).

---

[76] It must be noted, however, that Juliet pays in security for the liberty she does achieve. She discovers the price of liberty at first hand when her employment with a mantua-maker comes to an abrupt end: "The pleasure with which she had considered herself free, because engaged but by the day, was changed into the alarm of finding herself, from that very circumstance, without employment or home; and she now acknowledged the providence of those ties, which, from only feeling their inconvenience, she had thought oppressive and unnecessary" (455). As she later remarks of the rural day-laborer, he "had no anxiety for the morrow" but he also "waked not to active hope" (699). The book does, then, occasionally express reservations about the flexibility and independence of anonymous wage-labor relations. Indeed, true independence, especially female independence, can sometimes seem antisocial. Juliet explains her unwillingness to perform in public thus: "who is so free, – I might better, perhaps, say so desolate, – as to consider themselves clear of all responsibility to the opinions of others?" (296). (Nevertheless, in spite of Harleigh's discouragement and her own reluctance, she finally agrees to perform publicly, determining that she must do whatever is necessary to enable herself to pay her bills.) Furthermore, the romance elements of the novel require a softening of the argument for independence; while most of the book focuses our attention on Juliet's struggle to support herself, resolution can still only be imagined in the form of marriage and family connections that would obviate all need for personal labor. When Harleigh makes his proposals to Juliet at the end of the novel, hoping her current independence (that is, her newfound wealth and her extrication from her false marriage) will leave her free to accept him, she responds by saying "No, Mr Harleigh, no! . . . I am not so independent . . . Had I an hundred hearts, – ten thousand times you must have conquered them all!" (861). Complete independence would make the romance resolution impossible.

During the time Juliet stays with her, Elinor "exulted in thus exclusively possessing [her], as a hidden curiosity" (55).

Having no money of her own, Juliet remains an object, and thus, ironically enough, is always connected with money. Because she has no place in a system of blood and patronage relations, her links with others are invariably economic in character, with the result that she is always of necessity a public rather than a private person. Her very presence signals a publicity inappropriate to female delicacy; when Elinor suggests that she be brought into Mrs. Maple's parlour, her aunt caustically responds, 'Because Mr. Harleigh was so kind as to make a hoy of my boat, does it follow that you are to make a booth of my parlour?' (56). The connection to prostitution, like that to blackness, suggests a vendible being. Miss Arbe, to prepare "Ellis" for a concert, buys her a pink gown with the unspoken aim of packaging and presenting her as a public performer. Miss Crawley, upon seeing the gown, remarks, 'Why then The Ellis will be The doll!' (314). Poverty, publicity, and objectification are insistently linked, and Burney goes on to connect all these to the state of the increasingly industrialized worker and his or her products. Juliet herself is treated as if she were a manufactured item: 'Why that new skin must have cost you more than your new gown. Pray which did you get the best bargain?' (45). Moreover, to be poor, to be a laborer, is to be like a machine; Mrs. Ireton complains of her dependants: 'How unfortunate it is to have such nerves, such sensations, when one lives with such mere speaking machines!' (481). Arbe later remonstrates against this: 'What can rich people be thinking of, to lay out their money in buying their fellow-creatures' liberty of speech and thought! . . . Tell a human being that she must only move to and fro, like a machine?' (524). To be a laborer is to be reduced to a machine, attached inescapably not just to the world of made objects but to the world of production more generally.[77] While we never see Juliet working with industrial machines, we do see her working in factory conditions, i.e. as part of a group of workers gathered under a single roof whose labor is overseen by a supervisor. At the milliner's shop "she was summoned early to the shop to take her work; but, when she begged leave to return with it to her chamber, she was stared at as if she had made a demand the most preposterous" (425–6). At the mantua-maker's she is surrounded by "still more

---

[77] We are reminded here of the figure in which Burney herself is represented as a machine. Indeed, it is likely that Burney's new sympathy for the laborer arises in part from her own experience – after her marriage in 1793 and the birth of her son a year later – as a woman who was largely responsible for the support of her family. The special attention she gives to the labor of artists and performers, moreover, can surely be related to her own status as a writer and her intimacy with other artists, especially musicians.

fellow-work-women" (452), and she finds the work even more tedious: "the unvarying repetition of stitch after stitch, nearly closed in sleep her faculties, as well as her eyes" (454). At the same time, to be a female laborer is to be not just a machine and a manufactured product, but a spectacular commodity: the women in Miss Matson's shop are quite deliberately put on display before its customers, and most of Juliet's "jobs," as music teacher, personal companion, and so forth, involve some element of display.

The peculiarly Romantic character of Juliet's commodity function inheres not just in her theatricality but in the fact that in spite of her spectacular qualities she is consistently anonymous and aloof. From the outset she is distant and her identity unstable. Her real name is unknown for most of the novel, through which she passes as the Incognita, L. S., Elless, Ellis, Julie, and Juliette until finally her surname of Granville is revealed. Her appearance, too, changes: in the first scenes of the novel, she is bandaged and appears to be black; she later astonishes those around her by her transformation into a fair Grecian-style beauty. Her capacity for metamorphosis is a source of constant comment: 'O! what, you have some other metamorphosis to prepare, perhaps?' (44); 'you metamorphose yourself about so, one does not know which way to look for you. Ovid was a mere fool to you' (771). These metamorphoses enhance Juliet's capacity to serve as exotic spectacle while simultaneously underscoring her independence of and distance from her audience. As we eventually learn, Juliet's secrecy about her birth and identity is a necessary practical measure. But her obscurity extends beyond the issue of her name, and encompasses the expression of her desires and beliefs. The polar opposite of Elinor, Juliet will not reveal her romantic desires, even when earnestly pressed to give the merest hint of them, and although constantly queried about the state of affairs in France when she left it, she never answers any questions about French politics or expresses her views on them. Like the commodity on display, she seems at once publicly available and of mysterious provenance. Like an automaton, she embodies the very essence of the commodity as Marx describes it; she is an object, but one that seems eerily possessed of a life of its own.

Juliet is, moreover, not a "bespoken" object; she does not exist for the sake of any given buyer but remains anonymous and aloof. As Epstein remarks of her, "to lack a name is to belong to no one, that is, to belong to oneself."[78] The absence of her family throughout most of the book ensures that she will not simply be "given away" on the marriage market, the prize of a bargain struck between others. Like the fixed-price commodity, Juliet

[78] Epstein, *Iron Pen*, 178.

appears to have an independent existence and value, and like well-advertised consumer goods (and tellingly enough, she is, at the end of the novel, advertised in newspapers), she seems to bear an enormous potential. One does not know who she is or where she came from, but that very ignorance permits one to imagine that she might be infinitely valuable. In feeling attracted to her, Harleigh proves himself a good modern man: he chooses a wife not on the basis of pedigree and traditional social relations but in the way one might pick something out in a shop. He knows nothing of its origin, and its virtues, at least initially, can only be guessed at, but he *feels* that it may be the most precious thing in the world. Harleigh thus enjoys not only the ultimate pleasure of obtaining Juliet but also the suspenseful intermediate pleasures of contemplating her, idealizing her, and desiring her.

In effect, then, Juliet has the charms not just of the commodity generally but of the early nineteenth-century commodity in particular. These peculiar charms speak not just to the workings of retailing in the Romantic period but also to the structure of Romantic-era fashion. The architecture, design, and clothing of this period have been described as reflecting a "cult of styles," a longing not just for exoticism but for varieties of exoticism, ranging over "the scenery of the world, suggesting themes now from Switzerland, now from Italy, now from Egypt, now from India."[79] Juliet's capacity for metamorphosis is ideally suited to make her a fashionable object given contemporary canons of taste: she is fair Circassian, tawny Hottentot, and Grecian beauty all at once. This taste for the exotic reflected, of course, a developing imperial trade, but it also helped to reinforce the distance and inscrutability of the commodity generally. Exotic goods from foreign lands simply represented the *ne plus ultra* of the autonomous, glamorously advertised new commodity with its unknown provenance. Moreover, it is not just particular exotic styles but variety itself that is attractive in Juliet. For it is precisely because of her constant transformations that Juliet appears to be such a fully individualized, *sui generis* creature. This changeableness also allows Juliet to embody in herself the dynamic character of a rapidly developing fashion system. That Juliet is a woman serves to enhance this effect; this was a period that saw an explosion of women's fashion magazines, a period in which the old association of women with superficiality and masquerade acquired new commercial dimensions as women came to be more firmly linked with the rapidly changing cycles of fashion itself. But, as Ann Bermingham demonstrates, this was also a period that saw the

---

[79] John Summerson, *Architecture in Britain, 1530–1830*, 9th edn (New Haven: Yale University Press, 1993), 447, 452.

triumph of the "natural" commodity, the ideological lynchpin of an "emerging commercial discourse which sought to identify appearances with essence."[80] Thus the love of the exotic, the novel, and even the mysterious coexisted with a new love of the natural. Juliet is able to satisfy all these apparently contradictory needs. She is honest and inartificial – her behavior is consistent and true to her character, she disguises herself only reluctantly and in the beginning, and she never lies – yet at the same time she represents all the opacity and variety that a love for the exotic and the fashionable could demand.

The plasticity and obscurity of Juliet's identity – the very features that make her officially unacceptable to Brighthelmstone society – make her centrally important to that society because they enable her to function as a screen for the projection of the desires of others. This imaginative engagement with Juliet is an activity in which all the elite consumers of Brighthelmstone take part. Indeed, for the most part they experience her as devoid of any but speculative value. Her apparent independence and the speculation it stimulates make her far more valuable than any mere servant, whose value is well-established, could possibly be. As the narrator remarks, speculation on Juliet's identity was a "species of commerce, always at hand, and always fertile" (429). It is not insignificant that the lower one moves down the social scale in Brighthelmstone, the less interest is shown in Juliet's "mystery"; it is not simply a "natural" human response to her situation. But what was separated in *Camilla* – the painful pleasure of speculation and the vulgarity of modern shopping – is here brought together. For, given her new sense of the value of labor, Burney now sees that the aura of magnetism should be perceived not just around lottery lockets but also around even the commonest shop goods. Hence while Juliet's aloofness and anonymity make her an object of the kind of speculation we saw in *Camilla*, they do so precisely by tying her to the typical commodity.

This speculative value lends Juliet a special charisma and generates powerful feelings in those around her, as Burney makes very clear from the outset. Riley claims that he seeks 'always for what is hidden. What is obvious soon surfeits me. If this demoiselle had named herself, I should never have of her again; but now, I'm all agog to find her out' (29). Juliet affords stimulation in a world where straightforward consumption leads to satiety. The hero Harleigh, who claims that his interest does not spring from 'a romantic admiration of mystery' (34), is nevertheless not interested in Juliet when she appears to be only an ordinary friend of

[80] Bermingham, "The Picturesque," 94–6, 90.

Elinor's: when she is unrecognizable after her change of costume, Harleigh looks for her "with striking eagerness, yet evident disappointment; and, slightly bow[s] to the scarcely noticed, yet marked courtsie of the stranger [Juliet]" (49). When he discovers who she is, Harleigh laughingly admits that if she had seemed such when he first met her, he would have been safer from her (52). This speculative curiosity, furthermore, typically has a passionate and erotic quality, a fact evidenced in Juliet's capacity to attract almost every aristocrat in Brighthelmstone, whether male or female. Certainly, her beauty plays an important role in this, but her beauty is not all; the fact that she appears to be distant and reserved, a "thing of alabaster" (444), makes her more desirable. The young Lady Aurora uses a highly charged romantic language with Juliet: 'Do not talk thus, my dear, dear Miss Ellis! Oh! if I were my own mistress – with what delight I should supplicate you to live with me entirely! to let us share between us all that we possess; to read together, study our musick together, and never, never to part!' (136). But the fascination is felt even by the old and cruel Mrs. Ireton: "her desire was so inflamed to develop the secret" of Juliet's identity (41), that it becomes an "insatiable passion" (46), and she is unwilling to let Juliet leave her service.

Thus, just as the buyer-commodity relationship gradually became a new arena for power relationships, if only in the imagination, so Juliet's relationships with those around her become the locus of unexpected power dynamics. Indeed, just as Burke had argued that obscurity and distance are appropriate to royalty because they are productive of sublime effects, so here the obscurity of labor and the commodity renders them amenable to the sublime. While Juliet is, in practical terms, almost completely powerless in Brighthelmstone society, she tends to inspire a sort of reverence in those around her, many of whom take a delight in her of a strikingly submissive kind. Granting Juliet this power is, moreover, represented as the most ethical response to her. Generally speaking, the more sympathetic the character, the more he or she idealizes and imaginatively empowers Juliet. Harleigh, who is most passionately and "properly" attracted to Juliet, idealizes her most fully, and her virtues elicit in him a submission that is often painful: 'You must clear this terrific obscurity, that threatens to involve me, once more, in the horrours of excruciating suspense!' (595). He asks if she will 'not be generous enough to relieve a perplexity that now tortures me? Is it too much for a man lost to himself for your sake, – lost he knows not how, – knows not to whom, – to be indulged with some little explanation?' (204). But Juliet "gives fascination even to repulse" (205), and Harleigh admits that he 'must admire, must respect the decree that tortures me'

(348). Harleigh's attachment to Juliet, like so many of his characteristics, has a slightly old-fashioned quality that brings to mind the conventions of courtly love. These conventions, although appropriate to the romance genre, stand out starkly against the realistic narrative of Juliet's hardships. This context serves to highlight the extent to which Harleigh's distresses are, as it were, arbitrary, freely chosen. In the "modern" world of realism, such behavior appears not simply old-fashioned but vaguely baffling. This helps to explain Harleigh's relative unpopularity among critics, to whom he has often seemed weak, feeble.[81] Feeble though Harleigh may seem to the modern reader, however, he is nevertheless the hero of the story because the erotic submission he practices, unlike Elinor's, involves the generous appreciation of the labor and therefore the value of others.[82]

In this self-effacing reverence for the commodity, then, we see a signal difference from the commodity fetishism of the eighteenth century. For in a text such as *The Rape of the Lock*, the spoils of imperial capitalism, while they seem to have a life of their own, never truly challenge the autonomy of the people they serve.[83] Belinda is empowered rather than disempowered by her possessions, and while Pope argues that she is more attached to these objects than she should be, he is clearly most concerned not with their autonomy but with the autonomy they permit Belinda to enjoy. Juliet, on the contrary, has no possessions to empower her, and yet insofar as she herself is a commodity-like object of desire, she is strikingly autonomous and powerful. This power of the commodity – and of the

---

[81] Margaret Doody, for instance, notes that it is old Sir Jaspar who "acts the part of the love-story hero – finding Juliet in London, following her, rescuing her in the nick of time from abduction by the villain – all of which activities Harleigh, who should be the hero, refrains from with his own kind of impotence" (*Life*, 347).

[82] Thus, although desire is, to a certain extent, inherently about self-satisfaction, here only desire that is generous and selfless is good. Elinor's essentially selfish masochism is exposed as false while Harleigh's desire, which involves real self-abnegation, is represented as right-minded and attractive. In this novel proper desire can never express itself positively, as a desire for personal possession, since to do so would be a mark of absorption in self rather than the beloved. Indeed, not only self but even personality is to be lost rather than expressed in the act of desire, so that the virtues of the beloved can more surely be reflected in the lover. For the display of personality is not simply morally misguided; it tends to be linked, as in Elinor's case, to dangerous political interests, a showy form of masochism that functions as a kind of political terrorism. Elinor reveals these links in their extreme form; the display of her character is also a display of erotic desire and political conviction. For Elinor, a person who does not express desire is a "non-descript"; as she says of Harleigh to Juliet, "I heartily congratulate your apathy . . . for he is so completely a non-descript, that he would else incontestably set you upon hunting out for some Rosamund's Pond" (68). But in this book to be such a "non-descript" is to be a hero. Burney herself, in her introductory letter to Doctor Burney, claims that her book is "a composition upon general life, manners, and characters; without any species of personality, either in the form of foreign influence, or of national partiality" (4). Again, distinct personality tends to be tied to a politicized form of desire.

[83] On the fetishism of the spoils of imperialism in *The Rape of the Lock*, see Laura Brown, *Alexander Pope* (Oxford: Basil Blackwell, 1985), Chapter 1.

woman-as-commodity – is represented in various arts of the early nineteenth century. Edward Copeland notes that as she moves from *Sense and Sensibility* (1811) to *Pride and Prejudice* (1813) "[Jane] Austen shifts her attention from the *loss* represented by acquisition to the *power* invested in material items that convey meaning," and argues that this new emphasis on the potency of goods is common in women's novels of the early nineteenth century.[84] Elizabeth Kowaleski-Wallace, drawing a "historical connection between the visual pleasures of consumption and the visual thrill of pornography," argues that the rise of consumerism and the development of modern pornography find a common link in "a fiction or fantasy about female commodity." But as she notes of Thomas Rowlandson's Regency-era pornography, "as commodity, Rowlandson's women are often very mysterious, elusive, and powerfully self-sufficient. If these women represent a cultural fantasy about female commodiousness, the message is that woman as commodity may very well be inaccessible."[85] Although Burney is well aware of the danger to women of appearing to be nothing more than an object on the marriage market – characters in her earlier novels learn this lesson at some cost – she also shows some sympathy with those women writers who found in urban commerce and spectacle a source of power. Judith Pascoe notes that "critical writing about women in the eighteenth and nineteenth centuries has tended to assume their exclusion from the world of commerce", "despite evidence of women's active presence in the city." Pascoe argues instead that "The last decades of the eighteenth century quite possibly provided a window of opportunity for female denizens of the city which would no longer be available by the middle of the nineteenth century."[86] Mary Robinson, for instance, in a poem of 1804, "London's Summer Morning," celebrates the energy of the city and the power of female display:

> Now, spruce and trim,
> In shops (where beauty smiles with industry)
> Sits the smart damsel; while the passenger
> Peeps through the window, watching every charm.
> Now pastry dainties catch the eye minute
> Of humming insects, while the limy snare
> Waits to enthrall them.[87]

[84] Edward Copeland, *Women Writing about Money: Women's Fiction in England, 1790–1820* (Cambridge: Cambridge University Press, 1995), 97.
[85] Elizabeth Kowaleski-Wallace, *Consuming Subjects: Women, Shopping, and Business in the Eighteenth Century* (New York: Columbia University Press, 1997), 99, 101, 104.
[86] Judith Pascoe, *Romantic Theatricality: Gender, Poetry, and Spectatorship* (Ithaca: Cornell University Press, 1997), 134.
[87] In Roger Lonsdale, ed., *Eighteenth-Century Women Poets* (Oxford: Oxford University Press, 1990), 473.

The peeping passenger risks enthrallment just as the insects do. Commercial display has its risks, to be sure, as Juliet discovers when she must work on display in Miss Matson's shop, but it also comes with powers of its own.[88]

In an age when increased anonymity was beginning to limit the uses of personal credit, Juliet widens the bounds of belief and inspires faith in the potential of an impersonal society; as Elinor puts it, 'You are such a compound of mystery, that one extraordinary thing is not more difficult to credit in you, than another' (161). Juliet's elderly "suitor" Sir Jaspar Harrington asks, 'What is it you have about you that sets one's imagination so to work?' (435), and speaks of the 'magnetism of mystery and wonder' that (544) she exudes. He describes Juliet in her 'nameless state' as 'an exquisite, but nearly visionary being!' (628), a being 'straight descended from the clouds' to whom no one has presumed to give a 'human genealogy' (629). He confesses to Juliet that he used to view 'all females with the scrutiny of a bargain-maker' (631), whereas she appears to him as a transcendental creature, one whose value could never be fixed. In his conversations with her, he repeatedly invokes a Swedenborgian supernatural machinery that calls to mind the machinery of Pope's *The Rape of the Lock*. Claiming that he is troubled by 'imps of darkness' (626), he describes their painful ministrations in terms that are reminiscent of the sylphs' dressing of Belinda; the machines used to support him almost sound like the corsets and other instruments used to shape the female body: they 'jammed my lean, lank arms into a machine of whale-bone, to strengthen and invigorate them for offering support, in cases of difficulty or danger, to my fair one: others fastened elastic strings to my withered neck and shoulders, to enable me, by little pulleys, to raise my head, after every obsequious

---

[88] The fantasy world to which Juliet gives others access is pleasing not only in its substance but also in its very form: the mystery that envelops her affords her an escape from the practical rationalism of everyday life in the early industrial age. Harleigh, "wrapt up in the contemplation of an object thus singular, thus excelling, thus mysterious, [found that] all ambition of personally shining was forgotten" (95). Elinor, while she claims to love rationality, clearly enjoys mystery; asking Harleigh where he has been secreting his common sense, she adds "Not that I mean to look for it! – 'twould despoil me of all the dear freaks and vagaries that give zest to life!" (29). Just as much early nineteenth-century poetry proposes an escape from the deadening effects of industrialization and urbanization through the stimulation of the imagination, *The Wanderer* offers imaginative revitalization. The *locus classicus* of this idea is of course Wordsworth's 1800 "Preface" to *Lyrical Ballads*, in which he argues that he hopes to "enlarge this capability" of his fellows to respond imaginatively and sympathetically to humble subjects in an age in which urbanization and the French Revolution were operating "with a combined force to blunt the discriminating powers of the mind" (Wordsworth, "Preface," in *Lyrical Ballads*, ed. R. L. Brett and A. R. Jones [London: Methuen, 1963], 249). But in the novel it is the romance heroine/Romantic commodity that revives torpid minds and thrills active ones. Juliet tells Harleigh that she knows that the mystery surrounding her has, by occupying his imagination, made her harder to forget (776).

reverence to my goddess' (627). These flights of fancy were unknown to Harrington before meeting Juliet; as he says, 'my sylphs all reserved themselves for my meeting with you!' (631). Juliet thus inspires Harrington to become, not just fanciful, but, like Pope's Belinda, a good consumer, one who has entered a magical world of commodities come to life. Burney makes it clear that just as women, as well as men, should have opportunities to be producers, men, as well as women, act the part of consumer. At the same time, the shift from sylphs who provide service and attendance to imps who enforce submission reflects the distance between the early eighteenth century and the early nineteenth. The world of commodities is still a fanciful one, but one in which those fanciful pleasures arise from submission rather than empowerment.

That this aura of mystery and autonomy that serves to reenchant modern life is old regime "charisma" in its new, modern home is revealed most directly in the tendency of characters to respond to Juliet, in her "spectacular" mode, as if she were royalty: after her dramatic performance, she is "followed by all the youthful part of the company, to whom she seemed the sovereign of a little court which came to pay her homage" (100).[89] And while in practical terms Juliet's experiences represent the height of Burneyan novelistic realism (we see her lonely and desperate, fatigued by tedious labors, hungry and thirsty, and threatened in the woods with rape), for the people of Brighthelmstone Juliet, although officially considered a mere object of amusement, functions as a visitor from the glamorous world of romance.

Burney's striking decision to make Juliet an incognita not just within the book but for the reader as well serves to further *The Wanderer's* economic and moral argument. For by these means the reader is forced to respond to Juliet under the same conditions that govern the responses of the people of Brighthelmstone. Like many a Wordsworth poem, the book aims not just to tell a story, or even to offer up a moral, but to train the reader in the forging of sympathetic ties by encouraging him or her to form them in the act of

---

[89] Juliet's monarchical charisma has important generic implications, for it aligns her with the traditional heroine of romance. When she refuses Elinor's gift of clothes, Elinor remarks that "that's more romantic . . . and so 'twill be more touching; especially to the little peer; for as you won't say who you are, he can do no less than, like Selina, conclude you to be a princess in disguise" (110). Of course, one reason why Elinor claims to despise mystery is its *ancien régime* overtones. She is thus able to disapprove of Harleigh's interest in Juliet on implicitly political grounds: "But you, Harleigh, will you, also, practisce disguise? and fall so in love with mystery, as to lose your nobler nature, in a blind, infatuated admiration of the marvellous and obscure?" (180). For Harleigh and others – even, at times, Elinor herself – the desire for the traditional world of romance and its stable hierarchies is very powerful.

reading. In this respect the book itself functions as an aloof commodity, an object that does not simply satisfy a preexisting need but elicits a personal imaginative investment.[90] Juliet's meditations and Arbe's commentary provide an explicit lesson in economic relations: one must respect and believe in the value of independent labor and its products. But readers are not simply offered these facts as truths: they are forced to prove them on their pulses in their relationship to Juliet, for that relationship embodies those truths.[91] The consumerism that is a guilty if straightforward pleasure in *Evelina* can now be imagined as generous and right, if at the cost of complicating the pleasure it affords. In *The Wanderer* the early nineteenth-century commodity's novelty, autonomy, and its indifference to rank figure forth the promise of a new, more universal independence and an equality grounded in the anonymity of new economic relations. This commodity's potency serves not to empower the consumer but to signal the merits of labor. At the same time, the mystery that surrounds the commodity and the charisma that characterizes it serve to revive the enchantment of a fading world, producing a new one where hierarchies and submission persist only in the form of enjoyable fantasies, and where a "speaking machine" (481) can exert 'a magnetism of mystery and wonder!' (544).

---

[90] It is worth noting that by this point in her career, Burney had a keen sense of the place of her novels in the market. She had given up on subscription funding, with its kinship to patronage, and had learned to negotiate very lucrative deals with the booksellers, making arrangements that would allow her to reap the benefits of rapid sales and multiple editions.

[91] The book has, of course, all the qualities of a fairy tale designed to teach generosity: be kind to everyone, because you never know how important they might turn out to be. And Burney, for all the sympathy she shows for the laborer, does sometimes heighten Juliet's fairytale glamour by setting her against the foil of laborers who are unglamorous in the extreme. In some respects Burney wants to have her cake and eat it, too – to argue for the value of labor and goods, to write a fully realist novel thick with commentary on the importance of economic independence, while at the same time offering a romance in which the incognita heroine is finally revealed as the aristocratic woman *par excellence*. Nevertheless, as a laborer Juliet confronts her fellows and us as a person without social connections or a past, and they and we are asked to judge her on the basis of her exertions alone. At the same time, the book presents us and the people of Brighthelmstone with a person who in herself functions as a kind of modern commodity, independent and aloof, and challenges us to respect her on her own terms, and even to enjoy a kind of submission to her powers. Some characters in the book stand up well to this challenge. Harleigh and Aurora in particular can see, as it were, the labor that has gone into the making of Juliet, and although, like the visitors to Miss Matson's shop, they could deny the labor and quality of which they cannot have proof, they choose instead to grant her an inherent value. They are willing to believe and they teach readers by example that they, too, should believe – believe in the value of independence, in the value of the laborer, in the value of the commodity.

CHAPTER 3

The aesthetics of passion: Joanna Baillie's defense of the picturesque in an age of sublimity

> The characters over whom [the passions] are made to usurp dominion, must be powerful and interesting, exercising them with their full measure of opposition and struggle . . . Though belonging to such characters, they must still be held to view in their most baleful and unseductive light.
>
> –Joanna Baillie, from the "Introductory Discourse" in *Series of Plays on the Passions*[1]

While Frances Burney was ultimately to find in the charismatic magnetism of the commercial world of the early nineteenth century a solution – albeit a purely affective, fantastic one – to the political quandaries raised by the French Revolution, many of her contemporaries regarded submission, especially submission in the domain of the emotions, as necessarily suspect. As is clear from the quotation above, Joanna Baillie, the preeminent dramatist of the 1790s,[2] regarded the dominion of passion over reason as nothing short of disaster, and her theory of human nature is premised on a faith that even in an age of social turmoil a certain command of the objects of the external world was in fact possible to those who were masters of their inner lives. Indeed, Baillie's theoretical writing ultimately turns on the question of who shall be master, and aims to prove that rational control – at least in the form of an intellectual mastery of oneself and the world – is essential not just for practical but also for moral reasons. But as the quotation also suggests, the specter of seduction, and an awareness of the appeal of being dominated, lurk behind and seem in fact to motivate Baillie's argument on behalf of the right rule that is rational mastery. It is

---

[1] Joanna Baillie, *A Series of Plays* (1798), (rpt. Oxford: Woodstock Books, 1990), 59. Unless otherwise noted, all subsequent references to Baillie's work will be to this volume and will be given parenthetically in the text.

[2] In the words of Stuart Curran, Joanna Baillie "exerted the most direct practical and theoretical force on serious drama written in the Romantic period." ("Romantic Poetry: The 'I' Altered," in Anne K. Mellor, ed., *Romanticism and Feminism*, [Bloomington: Indiana University Press, 1988], 186).

precisely because passion and usurpation appear so seductive to Baillie that they elicit a powerful counter-narrative on behalf of reason and independence.

Baillie was not alone in her efforts to develop a model of desire that could serve as an optimistic and masterful counterpart to accounts of pleasurable submission such as Burney offers in *Camilla* (1796) and *The Wanderer* (1814). In fact, as we shall see, the logic of intellectual mastery that structures Baillie's dramatic theory lay at the heart of the aesthetic mode that was to pose the most serious challenge to the self-abnegating pleasures of the sublime aesthetic: the picturesque. For while the sublime involved intense, sustained interest in a single object, and, like gambling in Burney's novels, generated feelings of suspense and even pain, the picturesque promoted the pursuit of one object after another in succession and argued that possession in the form of knowledge could afford sufficient gratification. The picturesque drew upon the serial desires of the shopper, but purged them of the taint of vulgarity; it was an aesthetic ideology perfectly suited to the support of middle-class commercial values and an anti-French political conservatism. To prefer one of these aesthetic modes over the other was thus not only to make a claim regarding the proper nature of the aesthetic object but also to make assumptions regarding the desire and politics of the aesthetic subject. These two conceptions of desire – as fixated or successive – were often described by contemporaries as not simply unlike but actually in opposition with each other.

Baillie's writings literally stage just such an opposition. She champions a picturesque aesthetic that, while premised on the intensity of human longing, is nevertheless designed to shape it into regular, predictable, and immediately gratifying forms. In essence, Baillie made use of a logic of desire and satisfaction that supported a fantasy of economic abundance even as she sought to reimagine its objects as noncommercial. She explicitly opposes this picturesque aesthetic to the aesthetic of the sublime, which she strenuously derides. But as we will see, the seductiveness that leads men and women to forfeit dominion over their hearts and minds was to work its "baleful" effects even among Baillie's admirers, who, in spite of her derision of it, were ultimately most drawn to those of her plays that dramatized sublimely obsessive and painful desire.

I

Baillie's "Introductory Discourse" to her *Series of Plays* begins with an explanation of her "ideas regarding human nature" (2). Speaking as a theoretician, she begins with first principles, and in the opening pages of her "Introductory Discourse" she lays out the bold premise of her essay and her project: the most fundamental and universal human impulse is a sympathetic curiosity regarding other people. According to Baillie, the observation of human character provides the "native and favourite aliment" (19) of persons of all kinds, from little children to village gossips to great wits. This curiosity, moreover, gives rise to an urge not just to observe and know but also to classify: "From this constant employment of their minds, most people, I believe, without being conscious of it, have stored up in idea the greater part of those strong marked varieties of human character, which may be said to divide it into classes; and in one of those classes they involuntarily place every new person they become acquainted with" (3). For Baillie, the human mind is ceaselessly occupied with the classification of fellow humans. It is this interest in classification that, according to Baillie, gives rise to a strong and natural desire to see character artistically embodied in the form of drama.

The observant and curious people Baillie describes do, however, sometimes let their natural tendencies take a wrong turn. Sympathetic curiosity can easily be perverted from an interest in classifying people on the basis of character into a focus on the things, the material objects, that had for centuries served as reliable signs of social classification. In fact, as one moves through the "Introductory Discourse" it becomes clear that Baillie conceives her project as being in competition, not with the work of other playwrights, but with the popular interest in fashion. She describes numerous instances of the misdirection of sympathetic curiosity into a fascination with fashionable distinctions and the world of goods. Thus, in the first pages of her account of sympathetic curiosity, she notes that it often leads to mere gossip about dress and manners. Still, Baillie insists that the interest in passion will ultimately prevail over the interest in fashion:

Anger is a passion that attracts less sympathy than any other, yet the unpleasing and distorted features of an angry man will be more eagerly gazed upon, by those who are no wise concerned with his fury or the objects of it, than the most amiable placid countenance in the world. Every eye is directed to him; every voice hushed to silence in his presence; even children will leave off their gambols as he passes, and gaze after him more eagerly than the gaudiest equipage. (10)

The comparison being drawn here, however unselfconsciously, is remarkable and encapsulates the logic of the discourse as a whole. The fascination with goods and the external signs of rank is to be replaced by the healthy, natural interest in human states of mind.

Nowhere does this antifashion discourse appear more clearly than in Baillie's discussion of genre. She argues that drama is the most natural and fundamental of genres; as quoted above, she notes that even children will spontaneously play the role of spectator. She defines most of the other popular genres of her day as derivative and overrefined: essentially, as fashionable exotics. Baillie's account of the desires satisfied by the romance and the novel puts one once again in mind of gaudy equipage: "Our love of the grand, the beautiful, the novel, and above all of the marvellous, is very strong; and if we are richly fed with what we have a good relish for, we may be weaned to forget our native and favourite aliment" (19). By the paragraph's end Baillie has explicitly linked the pleasures of the "higher sentimental novel" to the delight in exotic collectibles and the formal garden: it "is a dressed and beautiful pleasure-ground, in which we are enchanted for a while, amongst the delicate and unknown plants of artful cultivation" (20). Similarly, poetry is described as a "fair field," "enriched" with beauties (20), and she attributes to it superficial charms, "decoration and ornament" (21).

What one begins to see, then, is that Baillie's conception of human nature is structured in terms of a competition between passion and fashion. But while she disparages consumerist modes of thinking, the very fact that Baillie sets passion and her plays in competition with the world of fashionable goods suggests an affinity with that world. That is, her own procedure implies that consumerist voyeurism and the theater of sympathetic curiosity must somehow be comparable. In particular, one is immediately struck by the fact that Baillie's focus is not on passions as internal experiences but rather as discrete "things" to be viewed from without and evaluated. It is, moreover, noteworthy that Baillie sometimes describes even the observation of character not as an activity of cold reason but as a sort of fascination: "What human creature is there, who can behold a being like himself under the violent agitation of those passions which all have, in some degree, experienced, without feeling himself most *powerfully excited by the sight*?" (9–10, emphasis mine).

As Baillie describes it, then, "sympathetic curiosity" operates as a powerful form of desire and is linked to consumption at its most basic. Baillie's resistance to consumerism cannot hide the extent to which her own project and her understanding of human nature are shaped by its logic. Her very language reflects the common commercial ground between passion and fashion: if people end up talking about "how a man wears his wig and cane, what kind of house he inhabits, and what kind of table he keeps" rather than "slight traits in his words and actions" (4), this is because "in communicating our ideas of the characters of others, we are often called upon to support them with more expence of reasoning than we can well afford, but our observations on the dress and appearance of men, seldom involve us in such difficulties" (4). One thus pays in reasoning for the pleasure of storing up character types. Baillie insists on the value of exploring those marks of personal distinction that do not involve purchasing power or consumer clout – the capacity to buy and display the wig, house, and table. What she offers is, in effect, a better buy for one's classifying labor. Opinions on subtle distinctions of character may demand "more expence of reasoning," but it is clear that for Baillie such reasoning is a small price to pay for access to what she elsewhere calls a "rich vein" (3) of knowledge.

This dual relation to consumerism is reflected even in Baillie's strictly technical dramaturgical interests. On the one hand, she complains of the need for smaller theaters and more naturalistic acting styles, hoping to create a form of drama that is not simply a larger-than-life glorious spectacle but an intimate revelation of the nuances of character. At the same time, however, she wants to discourage the people-watching that was a traditional part of theatergoing and suggests staging innovations that would serve to circumscribe the drama proper, offering it up not as just another part of human life but as a delimited object of consumption: "the removal of the stage-boxes itself would be a great advantage. The front-piece at the top; the boundary of the stage from the orchestra at the bottom; and the pilasters on each side, would then represent the frame of a great moving picture, entirely separated and distinct from the rest of the theatre."[3] Drama is thus flattened out, turned into a spectacle of a wholly new and modern kind: a "great moving picture."

We can better understand the link between sympathetic curiosity and consumerism if we consider the broader social resonances of the terms "sympathy" and "curiosity." The first of these – "sympathy" – has, of course, a venerable eighteenth-century heritage. The philosophical tradition that focused on sentiment and its communication can be dated from the Earl of Shaftesbury's 1711 *Characteristics*. Even as Shaftesbury warns against the performances and impostures of the world, and even as he tries to distance himself and his text from the marketplace, his language reveals the centrality of both to his argument. Thus, for instance, he argues that through soliloquy, a sort of performance to oneself, one is able to assess

---

[3] Joanna Baillie, *The Dramatic and Poetical Works* (1851) (New York: Georg Olms Verlag, 1976), 235n.

or "audit" one's own morality: "A person of profound parts, or perhaps of ordinary capacity, happens on some occasion to commit a fault. He is concerned for it. He comes alone upon the stage; looks about him to see if anybody be near; then takes himself to task, without sparing himself in the least ... By virtue of this soliloquy he becomes two persons."[4] The assessment of one's morality thus becomes a matter not simply of contemplation but of private performance. One can proceed only through dramatic indirection, applying one's capacity for sympathetic responsiveness to oneself. At the same time, Shaftesbury speaks of emotional matters in commercial terms: it is by "taking an inventory of the same kind of goods within ourselves, and surveying our domestic fund" that we learn to understand both ourselves and others.[5] From the outset then, the sympathy on which this theory of morality was founded had powerful ties to both the theater and the marketplace.[6]

Adam Smith, after Shaftesbury the most important figure in the philosophical treatment of the issue of sympathy, speaks of it as both a sign of the irreducible separateness of persons and the force that ties people to one another. Unlike Shaftesbury, however, Smith openly acknowledges the links between sympathy, theatricality, and commerce; he argues that it is the "original desire to please ... [their] brethren," a desire to garner sympathetic feeling, that urges men to obtain wealth, since "[t]he man of rank and distinction is observed by all the world. Every body is eager to look at him, and to conceive, at least by sympathy, that joy."[7] The growing importance of sympathy in the eighteenth century therefore both reflects the development of commerce and played a crucial role in its ideological success. It comes as little surprise that by the end of the eighteenth century the ability to respond sympathetically to sentiments in others and to feel them in oneself came to be valued in and of itself. So, while for Smith sympathy allows us to translate an image of wealth

---

[4] Anthony, Earl of Shaftesbury, *Characteristics of Men, Manners, Opinions, Times*, ed. John Robertson, 2 vols., vol. I (rpt. Indianapolis: Bobbs-Merrill, 1964), 105.   [5] *Ibid.*, 124.

[6] Indeed, as Jean-Christophe Agnew argues, the growth of the marketplace and the sense of the world as a stage are linked developments: life in a developing capitalist society seemed increasingly to be a matter of performance. For Shaftesbury and those who were to follow, it was sympathy that was to bind an increasingly atomistic society together. Agnew argues that in the eighteenth century, "the theatrical perspective entered into the ideological mainstream as an amusing gloss on the literate ideal of the detached and impartial observer of life, the discriminating consumer of the urban spectacle. More controversially, it became, at the hands of Adam Smith, a startlingly novel, wholly secular, and decidedly functionalist social psychology of market society (*Worlds Apart: The Market and the Theater in Anglo-American Thought, 1550–1750* [Cambridge: Cambridge University Press, 1986], 13).

[7] Adam Smith, *The Theory of Moral Sentiments*, ed. A. L. Macfie and D. D. Raphael (Indianapolis: Liberty Classics, 1982), 51.

into an abstract but satisfying feeling, for Baillie, at the end of the century, sympathy allows us to translate an image of feeling into an abstract form of wealth.

This gradual objectification of feeling toward the end of the century can be related to the particular form that sympathy takes in Baillie's writing: as a modifier for "curiosity." For during the period curiosity often functioned not simply as a desire for knowledge but as a desire for possession. Baillie's interest in classification and the "storing up" of types lends her project an austere, scientific appearance, but it also ties it to one of the most powerful consumerist logics of her day. Here we must note that Baillie spent many years – after the death of her father when she was a girl – under the protection of her uncle, John Hunter, the foremost natural historian of Britain of his time. In the late eighteenth century, natural history no longer propounded a system of fixed hierarchies, and John and his brother William Hunter were involved in developments in that science that were to change the face of it forever.[8] But naturalist classification was linked not just to abstract scientific endeavors but also to breeding and the display of natural curiosities; it formed part of that great eighteenth- and nineteenth-century consumerist pastime: collecting. From flowers to books to outdated coins, classifying and collecting made objects valuable. Marcia Pointon remarks of Grangerism, the fad for collecting and catalo-ging portrait heads (originally stimulated by the publication of James Granger's *Biographical History of England* in 1769), that

The economy of collecting "heads" is interesting historiographically for, whilst undoubtedly individual collectors gained great pleasure from browsing among their albums of pasted engravings, the dynamics of collecting were determined more by a notion of plenitude, by a desire to fill in all the gaps and produce a complete map which, like the world of plants, would be open to taxonomic investigation.[9]

---

[8] As W. D. Ian Rolfe puts it, William Hunter "broke the chain of being" in two places with his argument for the extinction of the mastodon and the Irish "elk" ("Breaking the Great Chain of Being," in W. F. Bynum and Roy Porter, eds., *William Hunter and the Eighteenth-Century Medical World*, [Cambridge: Cambridge University Press, 1985], 315.) Rolfe notes that "although allegiance to the Chain continued throughout the eighteenth century, new progressivist thinking inspired scientists to 'temporalise' the Chain and view it as a ladder that organisms might climb rather than a rigid ranking of immutable entities" (302). Indeed, John Hunter's museum distinguished itself by arranging material according to a "dynamic concept" rather than "systematically," with classification "based on a rigid static concept" (see George Qvist, *John Hunter 1728–1793* [London: William Heinemann, 1981], 67).

[9] Marcia Pointon, *Hanging the Head: Portraiture and Social Formation in Eighteenth-Century England* (New Haven: Yale University Press, 1993), 58.

Of course, during the politically unstable early years of the Romantic period such exercises in taxonomy had a special appeal; in the 1790s one bookseller even provided a ready-made Granger, since some portrait heads were so difficult to find that it required "almost the work of one person's life to get them together."[10] These fads were no small-scale affairs; as Robert Southey's Espriella, in *Letters from England* (1807), remarks, "since a clergyman some forty years ago published a biographical account of all persons whose likenesses had been engraved in England . . . you rarely or never meet an old book here with the author's head in it; all are mutilated by the collectors." But then, as he also noted, "There is, perhaps, no country in which the passion for collecting rarities is so prevalent as in England."[11]

Chandra Mukerji argues that the "passion for collection was dependent upon a refiguring of the meanings of curiosity and greed."[12] Baillie's own formulation of "sympathetic curiosity" is quite striking in this regard; she describes man's fundamentally sympathetic impulse as leading not to love or concern about others but simply curiosity.[13] Moreover, Baillie's larger plan, to publish a series of plays on the passions, with a comedy and a tragedy devoted to each, can be viewed not just as a quasi-scientific research project but also as a clever marketing device. Her "extensive design" is, after all, not to be taken for granted as an obvious way of proceeding; as she remarks herself,

How little credit soever, upon perusing these plays, the reader may think me entitled to in regard to the execution of the work, he will not, I flatter myself, deny me some credit in regard to the plan. I know of no series of plays, in any language, expressly descriptive of the different passions; and I believe there are few plays existing in which the display of one strong passion is the chief business of the drama, so written that they could properly make part of such a series. I do not think that we should, from the works of various authours, be able to make a collection which would give us any thing exactly of the nature of that which is here proposed. (71)

---

[10] W. Baynes, *Catalogue of Richardson's Collection of English Portraits . . . as described in Granger's Biographical History of England* (London: W. Baynes, 1792–9).

[11] Robert Southey, *Letters from England* (1807) (London: The Cresset Press, 1951), 117, 115.

[12] Chandra Mukerji, "Reading and Writing with Nature: A Materialist Approach to French Formal Gardens," in John Brewer and Roy Porter, eds., *Consumption and the World of Goods* (London: Routledge, 1993), 441.

[13] The tension generated by this yoking of sympathy and curiosity is more fully felt at other moments in the "Discourse." At one point Baillie goes so far as to remark that the desire to see a person in calamitous circumstances can lead to the triumph of curiosity *over* sympathy: "often will a returning look of enquiry mix itself by stealth with our sympathy and reserve" (9).

Baillie's interest in character can be linked to a new conception of drama as the representation of character rather than action, and, as Jeffrey Cox argues, Baillie's plays have much in common with the contemporary mono-drama, with its focus on passion in a single person.[14] It is true, too, that the codification of the passions and their external expression had played a role in shaping the aesthetics of eighteenth-century acting, so that Baillie's interest in the passions *per se* is not without precedent.[15] But to build whole plays around the display of a single passion was unusual indeed. That the plan stood out as anomalous in the dramatic world is reflected in the response of a writer for the *Edinburgh Review*: "to confine the whole interest of the story to the development of a single passion, seems to us to be altogether impracticable."[16] In the context of the theater, then, Baillie's plan represented no obvious organizational choice, but in the context of collecting it makes perfect sense. As Baillie herself underscores, the plan she offers to the world is a rarity, a product not to be found elsewhere. Moreover, since the plan itself is for a series, Baillie stimulates the urge to master a series that fuels the collector's desire. The aim is possession and plenitude; the existence of the scheme produces the drive for completion. Thus Baillie's first volume, which did not include the comic companion to *De Montfort* (1798), a tragedy on hatred, leaves the reader's (and the collector's) appetite whetted for more. And, as was generally true in the contemporary world of collecting, the collector's taxonomy is flexible and accommodates additions. So, while Baillie's original "Introductory Discourse" suggests that she will focus on three passions – love, ambition, and hatred – she is able to introduce more later, claiming in her third volume, for instance, that remorse is the passion best suited to dramatic representation.

Setting Baillie's work in the context of the turbulent 1790s can help us to better understand why she expects the external expression of passion and character to take the place of the fashionable objects of the earlier part of the century. In a world where traditional signs of hierarchy no longer seem fully operative, it is not surprising that new, workable systems of classification should have a considerable market value. In fact, I would

---

[14] Jeffrey Cox, *In the Shadows of Romance: Romantic Tragic Drama in Germany, England, and France* (Athens: Ohio University Press, 1987), 44.
[15] See Alan Hughes, "Art and Eighteenth-Century Acting Style, Part III: Passions," *Theatre Notebook* 41:3 (1987), 128–39.
[16] *Edinburgh Review* 4 (July 1803), 271. Baillie's plan can give even modern readers discomfort; W. L. Renwick condescendingly remarks that "no real dramatist would deliberately sit down to write a whole series of *Plays on the Passions*. It is an odd and not unsympathetic spectacle, but – however her friends and the patients of her well-loved brother might admire it – it is not drama" (*English Literature 1789–1815* [Oxford: Clarendon, 1963], 232).

argue that Baillie's interest in the expression of character is part of a general search during this period for ever more intimate and inalienable signs of hierarchy. Simply put, if in the eighteenth century one generally relied on dress and accoutrements to determine a man or woman's rank immediately, in the nineteenth century one often went one layer deeper, relying on signs of status embedded in the flesh itself. Hence the growth of interest at the end of the eighteenth century and the beginning of the nineteenth in such sciences as phrenology and physiognomy.[17] This development began with the publication in 1774–8 of Johann Casper Lavater's *Essays*, which by 1810 was available in ten English editions. Lavater tried to develop the study of physiognomy in the context of modern taxonomic science, and after him, Franz Joseph Gall and Johann Spurzheim and numerous others took up his insights and explored them in the context of natural history. Physiognomic assumptions about the determined and readable quality of human character were, by the Victorian period, ubiquitous. The distinctions that would in the early eighteenth century have been legible in one's costume were, by the nineteenth century, legible in one's body and especially one's face. Roy Porter points out that this new system had the added advantage of being true to "Nature," thus satisfying another interest of Baillie's and of the Romantics more generally.[18]

Physiognomy is a taxonomic system that, like Baillie's, aims at the classification of external expressions of character and retains its link to amateur collecting. Baillie's description of the expression of passion is reminiscent of the engraved studies of faces so common in works on pathognomy and physiognomy (figure 3). Baillie argues that whereas in the past poets "have made use of the passions to mark their several characters, and animate their scenes," she will endeavor to "open to our view the nature and *portraitures* of

---

[17] Of ancient origins, physiognomy was very popular during the Renaissance, and its usefulness in reinforcing hierarchies was already clear then, as Juliana Schiesari shows with respect to della Porta's influential *Della fisionomia dell'uomo* ("The Face of Domestication: Physiognomy, Gender Politics, and Humanism's Others," in Margo Hendricks and Patricia Parker, eds., *Women, "Race," and Writing in the Early Modern Period* [London: Routledge, 1994], 60). For Renaissance thinkers, the link between physiology and emotion was direct and coordinated by what Michel Foucault calls a logic of resemblance; one sees this clearly in the popular conception of the four temperaments, originally an element of Greek physiognomic theory. During the seventeenth century, however, the practice of physiognomy waned with the development of the Cartesian notion of the self and the rise of inductive, secular modern science, what Foucault terms "classical thought." On the logic of resemblance and its opposition to classical thought, see Foucault's *The Order of Things* (New York: Vintage, 1973). But in spite of the difficulties of reconciling this traditional system of analogies with modern science, the late eighteenth and early nineteenth centuries were to witness a new flowering of physiognomic theory.

[18] Roy Porter, "Making Faces: Physiognomy and Fashion in Eighteenth-Century England," *Etudes Anglaises* 4 (October–December 1985), 392.

Figure 3. Johann Casper Lavater, "Rage," from *Essays on Physiognomy*
(London: Printed for John Murray, 1789).

those great disturbers of the human breast, with whom we are all, more or
less, called upon to contend" (38, emphasis mine). Baillie's promotion of
more naturalistic acting styles directly reflects this interest: she consistently
argued for a "natural and genuine" style of acting,[19] and even suggested technical innovations in such matters as overhead stage lighting in the hope that
her plays would be performed in ways that revealed the nuances of human
expression more fully. In 1812 she argued that small theaters were best
because in them actors "were encouraged to enter thoroughly into the characters they represented, and to express in their faces that variety of fine
fleeting emotion which nature in moments of agitation assumes."[20] For in

---

[19] Baillie, *Works*, 233. In this attention to the nuances of expression and gesture, Baillie's work reflects
the ideals of contemporary acting. In his "Essay on the Drama," Sir Walter Scott was to compare an
older to the preferred modern style of acting thus: "Declamation seems to have been more in fashion
in the school of Booth and Betterton than that vivacity of action which exhibits at once, with word,
eye, and gesture, the immediate passion which it is the actor's part to express" (*The Miscellaneous Prose
Works of Sir Walter Scott*, 28 vols., vol. VI [Edinburgh: Robert Cadell, 1834], 370).

[20] Baillie, *Works*, 232.

her plays – plays she hoped to have performed – Baillie offers the dramatic equivalent of the series of engravings that invariably served as the backbone of those bestsellers, pathognomic and physiognomic texts.

We begin to see that even as Baillie extolls the advantages of passion over eighteenth-century consumer goods, passion as she presents it has many features in common with other consumer goods of the Romantic era. For Romantic-era consumer goods, called upon to mark distinctions at a time when distinctions were everywhere being challenged, bore an unprecedented semiotic burden; while in the eighteenth century the representative and identifying function of goods operated more or less straightforwardly, in the Romantic period, when this function was arguably of more importance than ever, its workings had to be effaced. That is, while goods often still served to define persons, they had to do so in "natural," subtle ways.[21] It comes as little surprise, then, that among her contemporaries Baillie's codified passions proved, ultimately, to be among the most fashionable of collectibles.

II

The difficulty of maintaining the distinction between passions and consumer goods creates a tension that is at the very heart of Baillie's project. Given that even passions can become consumables, it is perhaps unsurprising that, while she is undoubtedly their champion, Baillie's own feelings about the passions are patently ambivalent. On the one hand, Baillie elevates the passions in importance, arguing that they are the center and circumference of social life. But on the other hand, she is clearly fearful of the very intensity of passion that she argues is so compelling to the observer. We have already seen that the overall structure of the *Series of Plays* is designed to stimulate the enthusiasm of the collector, but the treatment of individual passions within the plays further underscores the fact that Baillie's passions are intended to be got but not had, truly "collectibles" in the sense that they

[21] It is arguably at this moment that we see the emergence of the consumer society described by Jean Baudrillard. Baudrillard argues that in the modern world "objects are no longer tied to a function or to a *defined* need. This is precisely because objects respond to something different, either to a social logic, or to a logic of desire, where they serve as a fluid and unconscious field of signification"; needs "are produced as elements of a system and not as a relation between an individual and an object" (*Selected Writings*, ed. Mark Poster [Stanford: Stanford University Press, 1988], 44, 42). In the early eighteenth century, the social logic of objects, their signifying role, was clearly understood – kept, as it were, at the level of consciousness. It was only at the end of the century that this role, while of more importance than ever, came to seem of ambiguous value, its operation sent underground. It was then that objects came increasingly to serve as an "unconscious field of signification."

are to be enjoyed not in themselves but as part of a series. For while Baillie clearly wants her audience to take pleasure in the passions they see performed on stage, the plays themselves suggest that passions are deeply threatening when experienced at first hand, and that one will be undone – in both moral and practical terms – if one gives oneself over to them. The ethical, rational consumption of the passions is necessarily done at one remove. Thus, even when speaking of the display of dramatic character rather than commodities *per se* Baillie reveals her awareness of the danger of experiencing consumer spectacles in any but a distanced and curatorial way.

This ambivalence regarding passion is at least partly a product of Baillie's moderate, middle-class politics. We have noted already the antiaristocratic character of the antifashion, anticonsumerist language of the "Introductory Discourse": the gaudy, ornamental, refined, and artificial world of aristocratic goods and fashions comes under continual attack. The essay aims to develop our taste for the simple and natural, and Baillie argues that it is in the middling and lower classes that those values thrive. As she claims in a passage that may well have influenced William Wordsworth,

Those works which most strongly characterize human nature in the middling and lower classes of society, where it is to be discovered by stronger and more unequivocal marks, will ever be the most popular. For though great pains have been taken in our higher sentimental novels to interest us in the delicacies, embarrassments, and artificial distresses of the more refined part of society, they have never been able to cope in the publick opinion with these. (20)

But if Baillie belittles the "artificial distresses" of the elite, implicitly comparing them unfavorably to "real passions," which are ostensibly natural and universal, she is hampered by the fact that real passion still seemed in many ways to be an exclusive property of the elite. Indeed, Baillie herself is not quite able to challenge the generic protocol that requires that the heroes and heroines of tragedy be upper-class figures. This constraint, of course, was not simply a formal matter but reflected longtime attitudes regarding rank and feeling; passions had long been associated with, and were in fact considered the prerogative of, the aristocracy: "according to a long tradition, it was primarily the aristocracy that is animated by numerous noble or ignoble passions which clash with the dictates of duty and reason or with one another."[22] A contemporary reviewer's puzzlement regarding

---

[22] Albert O. Hirschman, *The Passions and the Interests: Political Arguments for Capitalism before Its Triumph* (Princeton: Princeton University Press, 1977), 111.

Baillie's professed intention to represent passion as it appears in the everyday domestic life of the middle classes reveals that even during the 1790s passions were still often conceived as akin to aristocratic dress, a form of "splendid drapery" that is "usually laid aside" "in private life, and on trifling occasions."[23] In her "Introductory Discourse" Baillie insists on the universality of passion, but she tends to revert to a more traditional view of it when she turns to the composition of her plays, where she generally does link grandeur of passion with nobility. In *Count Basil* (1798), the hero, a count, falls in love with the daughter of a duke, and in *De Montfort* the hero, a man of wealth and position, struggles against his hatred for the Marquis Rezenvelt.

This generic limitation would not be overcome until the development of the melodrama on the nineteenth-century stage, and the problems it causes for Baillie can at times be felt even in her theoretical "Introductory Discourse." Thus, for instance, in spite of her plan to represent each passion she treats in both tragic and comic form, it is clear that she does not find it easy to import tragic passions into the realm of comedy: it is comedy's "task to exhibit [men] engaged in the busy turmoil of ordinary life, harassing and perplexing themselves with the endless pursuits of avarice, vanity, and pleasure; and engaged with those smaller trials of the mind, by which men are most apt to be overcome, and from which he, who could have supported with honour the attack of greater occasions, will oftentimes come off most shamefully foiled" (44). Somehow the great passions of ambition, hatred, and love that Baillie tends to center on in this essay are hard even for her to imagine in the comic mode; we hear instead of avarice, vanity, and pleasure. In this context it makes sense that the *Edinburgh Review* writer should remark that "Passion, perhaps, is not essential to comedy at all; but the distribution of passion into tragical and comical, is so old, so obvious, and so natural, that we really are at a loss to conceive what strange caprice could have tempted this ingenious writer into so wanton a violation of it."[24] As much as Baillie wants to represent passion as a natural and universal object of interest, she unavoidably feels its links to an elite culture whose powers of fascination were precisely what she had set out to undermine by focusing on emotion in the first place.

But if Baillie's belief in the value of passion is complicated by her forward-looking distrust of aristocratic culture, it is further challenged by her conservative nationalist leanings. For while in certain respects Baillie's

[23] *Edinburgh Review*, 273.   [24] *Ibid.*, 277.

work has a radical character, that radicalism is always tempered by a keenly felt anxiety vis-à-vis the French. Baillie's British nationalism is reflected not only in her investment in the notion of native land,[25] but even in her literary allegiances. Thus she argues for the value of drama over poetry and the novel in part because of its popularity among the lower classes and its communal reception:

A play, but of small poetical merit, that is suited to strike and interest the spectator, to catch the attention of him who will not, and of him who cannot read, is a more valuable and useful production than one whose elegant and harmonious pages are admired in the libraries of the tasteful and refined. To have received approbation from an audience of my countrymen, would have been more pleasing to me than any other praise. (66)

The impressions made by [the drama] are communicated, at the same instant of time, to a greater number of individuals, than those made by any other species of writing; and they are strengthened in every spectator, by observing their effects upon those who surround him. (58)

The drama was thus a truly public entertainment, and it defined, moreover, a public opinion that was, in this period, becoming more inclusive and more self-consciously British.[26]

The community-minded character of Baillie's interest in drama is further reinforced by her devotion to Shakespeare, a devotion that, during the French Revolution, was widespread and often nationalist and conservative in its bearings. Baillie herself speaks very forthrightly of her "attachment to the drama of my native country, at the head of which stands one whom every British heart thinks of with pride."[27] Baillie's use of Shakespeare as a model is obvious; indeed, at times she clearly fears that it is too obvious. Not a writer who tended to gloss her own works, on two occasions in *Ethwald* (1802) she offers a footnote that is clearly intended to deflect charges of excessive influence. In the first case she says of the lines "How like a ship, with all her goodly sails / Spread to the sun, the haughty princess moves" that "Probably I have received this idea from Sampson Agonistes,

---

[25] Throughout her life Baillie acted as a champion of the arts of her native Scotland, but vis-à-vis Europe she practiced a broader British nationalism. As Linda Colley reminds us, during the period the two roles were not considered incompatible (*Britons: Forging the Nation 1707–1837* [New Haven: Yale University Press, 1992], 6).

[26] See Colley, *Britons*, and John Klancher, *The Making of English Reading Audiences, 1790–1832* (Madison: University of Wisconsin Press, 1987).

[27] Quoted in Margaret Carhart, *The Life and Work of Joanna Baillie* (New Haven: Yale University Press, 1923), 72. (From *The Dramatic and Poetical Works of Joanna Baillie*, 2nd edn [London, 1853]).

where Dalila is compared to a stately ship of Tarsus 'with all her bravery on, and tackle trim,' & c."[28] Given that John Milton's lines are patently drawn from Shakespeare's famous passage on Cleopatra, it would seem that Baillie proclaims a debt to Milton only to obscure a debt to Shakespeare. Similarly, a footnote is provided in Bertha's mad scene, a scene obviously influenced by Ophelia's mad scenes, right down to the love-lorn songs. Baillie remarks of one of Bertha's songs that "For this third Song, *which is the only literary assistance either in verse or prose that I have ever received*, I am indebted to the pen of a friend."[29] But Baillie's discomfort was for the most part not shared by her readers and her many champions, who were very happy to dub her the new Shakespeare.[30]

This nationalistic, somewhat conservative strain in Baillie further exacerbates her ambivalence regarding the value of passion. For just as French artifice and fashion are linked to the fascinating but outmoded and stifling spectacle of elite passion, so French revolutionary fervor is linked to the antisocial potential of the radical liberation of popular passions. We see the effects of the latter connection in Baillie's tendency to describe passion in terms of military invasion: "looking back to the first rise, and tracing the progress of passion, points out to us those stages in the approach of the enemy, when he might have been combated most successfully; and where the suffering him to pass may be considered as occasioning all the misery that ensues" (43). This conception of feeling clearly owes much to a tradition of viewing passion as a kind of suffering visited upon a

---

[28] Joanna Baillie, *A Series of Plays: in which it is attempted to delineate the stronger passions of the mind* 3rd edn, 3 vols., vol. II (London: Longman, 1806), 163.

[29] *Ibid.*, 220, emphasis mine.

[30] The *Edinburgh Review* reviewer, for instance, after noting the many parallels between *Ethwald* and scenes from Shakespeare, simply expresses a kind of pleasure that scenes have been "borrowed" from this "great author" (*Edinburgh Review*, 279) and calls *Ethwald* a "correct transcript of Macbeth" (279). In an age when originality was coming to be increasingly valued, this delight in repetition signals the workings of ideological need: Baillie's talent, combined with the Shakespearean quality of her work, qualified her to serve as another Shakespeare just when one was most wanted. Ultimately then, Baillie's loyalties and ambitions take her down a complicated and somewhat winding middle road. The same reviewer describes just such a middle course in her diction: "The diction and poetry of those tragedies is certainly entitled to very considerable praise. There is no part of Miss Baillie's introductory remarks better founded, than that in which she condemns the artificial stateliness and wearisome pomp of our modern tragedy. This lofty vein, indeed, has of late years been very generally ridiculed: but it has been supplanted by an opposite excess; and the plain vulgarity and prose ecstasies of the German drama deserve still less indulgence, than the mellifluous majesty of our native dramatic poetry. The writer of these plays has attempted a more temperate reform; and, taking for her model the middle style of Shakspeare's versification, has ventured to bespeak the public attention to a species of composition in which so many of her contemporaries have miscarried" (282). Baillie observes a stylistic medium that, in political terms, avoids the extremes of the artificially lofty and the plain vulgar; this is a writer for reform, but of a temperate kind.

person, a thing to which one is subjected. It also has affinities with a quasi-religious understanding of passion in which extremes of emotion function as what Baillie calls "visitations of the soul" (43), something akin to a spirit possession. Nevertheless, Baillie's continued references to invasion, usurpation, and domination, at a time when the British were experiencing intense fears of a French invasion, seem rather more pointed in their implications. Baillie wants to argue for the commonality and intensity of human passion, but she is fearful that such passion brings revolution in its train.

That Baillie should reconceive anxieties about literal invasion as a problem in the realm of feeling does, of course, make sense in the context of the 1790s. Baillie discovers an enemy to British stability in the great passions – love, ambition, hatred, enthusiasm – that moved the French to optimism, the Terror, and finally a battle for empire. This view was not uncommon among the British; Richard Payne Knight, for instance, noted in his 1794 poem *The Landscape* that in France one saw "private passions triumphing over public policy."[31] For Baillie, passion itself can sometimes operate like a foreign body with an agency of its own, and no physical invasion is as damaging as that which follows on the seduction of the feelings:

The characters over whom [the passions] are made to usurp dominion, must be powerful and interesting, exercising them with their full measure of opposition and struggle; for the chief antagonists they contend with must be the other passions and propensities of the heart, not outward circumstances and events. Though belonging to such characters, they must still be held to view in their most baleful and unseductive light; and those qualities in the impassioned which are necessary to interest us in their fate, must not be allowed, by any lustre borrowed from them, to diminish our abhorrence of guilt. (59)

We see again that Baillie's ambivalence regarding passion runs deep. For passions are not only dangerous insofar as they can become too like spectacular elite commodities, but also in their capacity to "usurp dominion" over even powerful and interesting characters.[32] Baillie directs our attention to the

[31] Richard Payne Knight, *The Landscape, a Didactic Poem* (London: W. Bulmer & Co., 1794), 77. We see the same concern with the role of passion in public affairs among Francophile writers, and even they show some suspicion of it. In a highly laudatory biographical sketch of Napoleon Bonaparte in 1797, a writer for the *Monthly Magazine* claims that "great events produce great characters" because "they excite the passions" (373), but goes on to argue that Napoleon himself was great because he had "in a great measure obtained, the mastery over his passions" (377) ("Original Anecdotes and Remarks of Eminent Persons: Napoleon Buonaparte," *The Monthly Magazine and British Register* no. 17:3 [May 1797], 373, 377).

[32] This concern with passion's relation to invasion and usurpation is further explored in *Count Basil*, in which the Count's soldiers, who are seduced into mutiny, are described as treacherous because "impassion'd" (141). In the one mutinous officer this seduction occurs entirely at the level of

passions at the same time that she keeps them at arm's length, deliberately representing them in an "unseductive light." Her very use of the word "seductive," of course, suggests the power of attraction she believes the passions to have as well as the dangers of that attraction.

By representing passions as external to human beings, Baillie highlights their sinister foreignness in addition to reinforcing their connection with clothes, equipages, and other accoutrements of commodity culture. But cordoning off the passions does serve to keep them safely external to the individual. A man may experience passion, but that passion is not an intrinsic part of him:

To endeavor to interest the mind for a man under the dominion of a passion so baleful, so unamiable, may seem, perhaps, reprehensible. I therefore beg it may be considered that it is the passion and not the man which is held up to our execration; and that this and every other bad passion does more strongly evince its pernicious and dangerous nature, when we see it thus counteracting and destroying the good gifts of heaven, than when it is represented as the suitable associate in the breast of inmates as dark as itself. (65)

That Baillie has some difficulty defining the relation between passion and character precisely is, however, felt even here. While the first man would be forgiven for harboring one bad passion on the grounds that the passion is not truly part of him, the second man is considered bad in himself for harboring many bad passions. Thus a quantitative has suddenly become a qualitative distinction, and the second man's passions define his character. We see this kind of equivocation throughout the "Discourse." Baillie usually describes the passions as transient, external forces; in the following instance passions are merely a storm that passes over the native landscape of true character:

To hold up for our example those peculiarities in disposition, and modes of thinking which nature has fixed upon us, or which long and early habit has incorporated with our original selves, is almost desiring us to remove the everlasting mountains, to take away the native land-marks of the soul; but representing the passions brings before us the operation of a tempest that rages out its time and passes away. (42–3)

feeling: "No cunning traitor did my faith attempt, / For then I had withstood him; but of late, / I know not how – a bad and restless spirit / Has work'd within my breast" (153).

But at other moments it is clear that Baillie sees the passions as having complicated links to character: "Though a *native trait of character or of passion* is obvious to [the generality of mankind] as well as to the sage, yet to their minds it is but the visitor of a moment; they look upon it singly and unconnected" (13, emphasis mine).

For Baillie, then, passion serves as the nodal point of a number of contradictory interests. In passion aristocratic grandeur and plebeian energy meet, making it a threat to the moral integrity of those who experience it. Nevertheless, Baillie would have our desire to see passions in others be the foundation of a sense of community that would defy elite culture without undermining the foundations of British society as a whole. Thus, although for Baillie passions, like fashions, can be imagined as external and even invasive, she argues that it is our vicarious interest in them that defines human character.

III

Ultimately, then, it is desire to which Baillie turns in an effort to manage the passions. Since for Baillie the great danger of emotional life is invasion by or fixation on a single passion, she suggests that passions are best experienced not only vicariously but also serially, one after another. In Baillie's world it is only by lightly skipping from one passion to the next that one can safeguard oneself emotionally. The logic of collecting thus serves not only to order the passions into a coherent, flexible system, but also provides a dynamic model for their appropriate enjoyment.

This model of desire, which undergirds Baillie's dramatic aesthetic, is, moreover, not peculiar to her, but provides the emotional foundation for one of the most important aesthetic theories of the period, the picturesque, to which we will therefore now turn. Eighteenth-century Britain saw the development in many realms of a fashionable antifashion, antiartifice discourse; in this discourse "nature" and "the natural" were privileged categories. We have already seen this language at work in Baillie; its importance in the culture at large is most clearly seen in the domain of landscaping and gardening, where "naturalness" was a primary desideratum. Early in the eighteenth century, the royal gardeners George London and Henry Wise drew on Dutch, Italian, and especially French influences, but as the century progressed "nature" was gradually reconceived in opposition to "culture," and the landscaping style for which the English became famous reflected this change. The English landscape garden defined itself against more formal garden designs, especially the intricate geometries of the French garden, epitomized by the grounds at Versailles designed by André le Nôtre. As Horace Walpole put it, devices like the ha-ha allowed "the contiguous ground of the park without the sunk fence . . . to be harmonized with the lawn within, and the garden in its turn was to be free from its prim regularity, that it might assort with the wilder country without."[33]

This logic was carried even further at the end of the century by writers on the picturesque. During the years of the French Revolution, older, entirely "unimproved," British parks and woodlands came increasingly to be linked to the power of property and nostalgic ideals regarding English land and English landed families. Among conservatives in particular these parks and woods were often associated with a past paternalistic age, an age when the relation between propertied and unpropertied seemed more secure. Uvedale Price, who had been alarmed by the news of a party of French landing in Wales, warned that the landscape park, though originally designed to mimic nature, was too severe, too threatening, the clumps of trees resembling "compact bodies of soldiers," and recommended that landscape be managed according to ideals of paternalistic benevolence and painterly intimacy – i.e., that it be designed to look less like an emblem of status and more like a natural landscape.[34] Price's investment in the ideal of ancient English liberties underwrites his attraction to an aesthetic characterized by naturalness and freedom of movement: "by its variety, its intricacy, its partial concealments, it excites that active curiosity which gives play to the mind, loosening those iron bonds, with which astonishment chains up its faculties" (I, 89). The picturesque was to afford freedom from the bonds of the sublime, bonds that, because of their visibility, seemed to threaten the stability of the very hierarchies on which they relied. Both Price and Knight, while they read a hierarchy in the interrelations of trees and other elements of the landscape, argue for more natural and "connected" landscapes, what Stephen Daniels calls "a landscape with distinctions but not divisions."[35] As Knight puts it, "nature still irregular and free, / Acts not by lines, but gen'ral sympa-

---

[33] Horace Walpole, *The History of the Modern Taste in Gardening*, in *Horace Walpole: Gardenist*, ed. Isabel Chase (Princeton: Princeton University Press, 1943), 25.

[34] Uvedale Price, *Essays on the Picturesque*, 3 vols., vol. I (London: J. Mawman, 1810), p. 246. Further references will be given parenthetically in the text. For a discussion of Price's response to news of the invasion, see Stephen Daniels, "The Political Iconography of Woodland in Later Georgian England," in Denis Cosgrove and Stephen Daniels, eds., *The Iconography of Landscape* (Cambridge: Cambridge University Press, 1988), 59.   [35] Daniels, "Iconography," 61.

thy."[36] Grounds that appeared to be natural woodlands thus served as signs of both a kind of liberalism and a nostalgic conservatism for good old England.[37]

Given Baillie's own politics, it comes as little surprise that the form of fashionable consumption that appears most frequently in the "Introductory Discourse" is one that brings into focus the difference between French and British style and is centered on an ideal of native land: gardening and landscaping. In her gardening metaphors Baillie opposes "bad" *ancien régime*-style artifice to "good" British natural landscapes. In this she reveals both her progressive commitment to changing hierarchies and signs of status and her somewhat conservative British nationalism. Baillie, like writers in the English landscaping tradition, makes frequent use of the discourse of the natural and free; we have seen that one of her central arguments is that people have an innate desire to see representations of character that are faithful to "nature." Meeting with a "natural" representation of character is for Baillie like coming upon "some humble cottage, resembling the dwellings of our own native land," and we naturally "gaze upon it with affection" (23). Significantly, Baillie often uses elaborate conceits centering on landscaping to make her point:

The one [novels focused on the refined part of society] is a dressed and beautiful pleasure-ground, in which we are enchanted for a while, amongst the delicate and unknown plants of artful cultivation; the other [works which characterize human nature in the middling and lower classes] is a rough forest of our native land; the oak, the elm, the hazle, and the bramble are there; and amidst the endless varieties of its paths we can wander for ever. Into whatever scenes the novelist may conduct us, what objects soever he may present to our view, still is our attention most sensibly awake to every touch faithful to nature. (20)

Baillie's metaphor is structured according to the opposition that structured British thinking about estate planning, and in contrasting the pleasure-ground to a forest Baillie specifically applies the logic of the picturesque. In her play *The Alienated Manor* (1836) we see this logic at work in an interchange between landscape gardener Sir Level Clump, who works in the style of Lancelot ("Capability") Brown, and Crafton, a young man with a taste for the picturesque, whose ancestral grounds Clump intends to "improve." For Clump, the relation of forest to landscape park is analogous to that between a "rude, untamed clown" and a "gentleman," while for

[36] Knight, *Landscape*, Book 1, ll. 143–4.
[37] See Alan Liu's *Wordsworth: The Sense of History* (Stanford: Stanford University Press, 1989) for an excellent discussion of the complicated politics of the picturesque (84–115).

the sympathetic Crafton the difference is, rather, like that between "a savage chief" and "a posture-master."[38] In this language Baillie echoes Knight's description of a forest's "savage pride" while she succinctly shows how the principles of the picturesque take the ideals of Brownian landscaping one step further.

While the British landscape garden and the picturesque estate set themselves in opposition to formal sophistication and artificiality, they also served to make the natural itself a possessible commodity and a sign of status. In Mukerji's words, eighteenth-century French gardens can be viewed as "sites for conspicuous collection," but the same can be said even of Baillie's forest.[39] Here the collectibles are not exotics but "natural" specimens of English flora: the oak, elm, hazel, and bramble, lovingly inventoried. One must bear in mind that by 1800 England was the least forested of northern European nations, and because of the need for timber for shipbuilding, trees were particularly valuable so planting was considered a patriotic activity.[40] This catalog of trees thus suggests more than simple enthusiasm for nature; in fact, even Baillie's choice of trees is telling. English hardwoods, especially the oak, were part of an iconography, both verbal and visual, dear to conservatives, who linked the slow-growing and stately oak with the idea of great families and their hereditary properties. Elms, also popular as parkland trees, tended to be associated with the working countryside. Just as telling is the absence in Baillie's catalog of conifers, which, because they were fast-growing and tolerant of thin soils, became increasingly popular at the end of the century. Price and even the liberal Knight complained about conifers, which they and others associated with a vulgar middle-class taste and the ambitions of parvenus. As Stephen Daniels notes, the more Humphrey Repton "was forced to take on parvenus as clients, the more he identified them with conifers. Of one of them he complained: 'how could I hope to suggest an idea to this man who shewed me what he called "the LARGEST ACORN he had ever seen!" at the same time producing the CONE of a STONE PINE that grew near an oak and had fallen among the acorns! (fit emblem of him I thought who had fallen among Gentlemen but could NOT be mistaken for one)'."[41] Baillie's inventory thus accurately specifies those plants that would be fashionable in the realm of the picturesque and in the eyes of adherents to old English ideals.

[38] Joanna Baillie, *Dramas*, 3 vols., vol. I (London: Longman, 1836), 126.
[39] Mukerji, "Reading and Writing," 441.   [40] See Daniels, "Iconography," 43, 47.
[41] *Ibid.*, 69.

Of course, not just trees but the forest itself was in its way a fashionable object. In an age when the rate of enclosure was increasing, natural grounds such as Baillie describes were becoming ever more closely tied to the idea of property. Ann Bermingham argues that as with enclosure "the real land-scape began to look increasingly artificial, like a garden, the garden began to look increasingly natural, like the preenclosed landscape. Thus a natural landscape became the prerogative of the estate, allowing for a con-veniently ambiguous signification, so that nature was the sign of property and property the sign of nature."[42] And as Bermingham notes of the pictur-esque, it not only "aesthetically packaged the landscape" but also offered "a discourse that was as easily consumed as the scenery it described."[43] Although they aspired to the appearance of the spontaneous, the unpro-duced and unbought, the landscape garden and then the picturesque forest became fashionable commodities and signs of status. In the scene described above, Crafton confesses that his perception of "sylvan beauty" in the land he sees before him is perhaps due to his partiality for "the ancient possessions of [his] forefathers" (125). Baillie's forest may not be a sophisticated pleasure-ground, but the nature it represents may ultimately be an even more fashionable commodity.

As I suggested earlier, moreover, a closer look at Baillie's work and the picturesque reveals a kinship that goes beyond a fashionable stand against fashion, or a rhetoric of natural property; both incorporate a new attitude toward possession itself. One is not surprised to find that Baillie and Price value similar things: he argues that violent emotion renders creatures pictur-esque (I, 60), and that the picturesque is an effect of character generally, and especially "marked and peculiar character," which renders even "a disagree-able mind" interesting (I, 203). But more importantly, Baillie and Price argue for a similar form of interest in and attachment to these valuable things. Thus Price speaks of the workings of "sympathy" and "curiosity" in response to picturesque landscape.[44] For him, "intricacy" in landscape involves a partial obfuscation of its charms, a concealment that generates and nourishes curiosity; the picturesque is "the coquetry of nature" (I, 89). The bald display of power and property in the Brownian park is thus for Price not only impolitic but also deprives one of the pleasure of dis-covery, a pleasure that involves "uncertainty" (II, 200), a subtle pleasure and

[42] Ann Bermingham, *Landscape and Ideology: The English Rustic Tradition, 1740–1860* (Berkeley: University of California Press, 1986), 13–14.
[43] Ann Bermingham, "The Picturesque and Ready-to-Wear Femininity," in Stephen Copley and Peter Garside, eds., *The Politics of the Picturesque* (Cambridge: Cambridge University Press, 1994), 85.
[44] See, for instance, Price, *Essays*, I, 122.

one that is enacted over time. Baillie, too, opposes movement and discovery to a kind of static reverie in the presence of artifice, an opposition reminiscent of what John Dixon Hunt describes as a new "dedication to process rather than product" in British garden design and landscape painting at the end of the century.[45]

With this in mind, we begin to recognize that the consumerism that informs Baillie's work is not simply about ownership; Baillie's aesthetic, like Price's, is an aesthetic not just of possession, but of acquisition. Picturesque theorist William Gilpin was well known for his tourism; Baillie's work records a kind of emotional tourism. She discovers and collects nuances of character and passion, and that act of discovery and collection is interminable – the collector's work is never done, the tourist is ever on the move. As Mary Shelley puts it in Frankenstein's account of a journey through picturesque scenes: "a traveller's life is one that includes much pain amidst its enjoyments. His feelings are forever on the stretch; and when he begins to sink into repose, he finds himself obliged to quit that on which he rests in pleasure for something new, which again engages his attention, and which also he forsakes for other novelties."[46] Gilpin remarks that "The variety of nature is such, that *new objects*, and new combinations of them, are continually adding something to our fund, and inlarging our collection."[47] Like Gilpin's hunger for picturesque scenes, Baillie's "sympathetic curiosity" functions as an unflagging form of desire.[48]

This formulation of desire served the expanding economy in at least two ways. On the one hand, the desire sponsored by the picturesque shows its affinities with capitalist-industrial production, for this is a form of desire which involves both reason – in the form of active curiosity – and work – in the form of an energetic and unceasing search for charming objects. The picturesque experience thus has the ideological advantage of being a form of consumption that nevertheless looks like a mode of production, an active experience that demands energy, the effective use of time, and a regular shifting of attention from one object to the next. On the other hand, and at the same time, the picturesque, like sympathetic curiosity, argues for the value of intense desire while managing it in such a way as to promote optimum consumption.

---

[45] John Dixon Hunt, *The Figure in the Landscape: Poetry, Painting, and Gardening during the Eighteenth Century* (Baltimore: Johns Hopkins University Press, 1976), 198.

[46] Mary Shelley, *Frankenstein*, ed. Maurice Hindle (New York: Penguin, 1985), 202.

[47] William Gilpin, *Essays on Picturesque Beauty* (London: R. Blamire, 1794), 50.

[48] Alan Liu, too, notes that in the picturesque the accent is not on consummation, but his focus on Wordsworth leads him to develop this insight into an argument regarding arrested desire rather than sustained desire (*Wordsworth*, 63).

IV

As the repeated appearance of the terms sympathy, curiosity, nature, collection, and variety suggests, this "picturesque" mode of desire stands in an overdetermined relationship to other aspects of Romantic culture. I would argue that in fact it represents one of the most important paradigms for desire in Romantic-era England. Thus, for instance, we find its characteristic dynamic at work even in the realm of architecture, a relatively conservative and static art by its nature. This can perhaps be seen most clearly in the work of Sir John Soane, who was, with John Nash, one of the most successful architects of the Romantic period. From 1806 to 1821, and under the influence of Knight and Price, Soane expanded and reworked elements of his earlier style "to obtain new and picturesque effects, which [he] called the 'Poetry of Architecture.'"[49] Indeed, his interest in "literary" effects led Soane, tellingly enough, to baroque architect and dramatist Sir John Vanbrugh, whom he praises in terms very like those used by Baillie and other Romantics in their acclamation of Shakespeare: "For Invention," Soane argues, he "has had no equal in this country. Boldness of Fancy, unlimited Variety and Discrimination of Character mark all his productions . . . The young Architect, by studying the picturesque effects of his works will learn to avoid the dull monotony of minor Artists, and be led to think for himself and acquire a Taste of his own."[50] Again we see a concern with variety, novelty, and discrimination of character. Nor are these concerns simply a matter of theory; they are borne out in fascinating ways in Soane's work of this period, which is, in its effects, fully as "theatrical" as Vanbrugh's, as we will see.

In practice, of course, the picturesque in architecture is most obviously made manifest in buildings that aspire to the virtues of simplicity or naturalness. Thus, for instance, Nash built cottages, while Soane often suggested the natural in subtler ways; in the Bank Stock Office, for example, he employs vertical strips in relief in such a way as to make the pilasters that were part of the classical vocabulary suggestive of a primitive hut.[51] But the picturesque was also allied with what architectural historian John Summerson terms the "cult of styles,"[52] a relish for the indiscriminate

---

[49] John Summerson, *Sir John Soane* (London: Art and Technics, 1952), 17.
[50] Quoted in *Ibid.*, 36.   [51] See *Ibid.*, 27.
[52] See John Summerson, *Architecture in Britain, 1530–1830* (New Haven: Yale University Press, 1993), Chapter 29. Further references will be given parenthetically in the text.

duplication of types which is evidenced most clearly in Nash's work, which reproduces Chinese, Indian, Gothic, and classical models, among others. Soane's eclecticism is not as immediately apparent as Nash's, but it could be argued to run even deeper in that it reduces exotic "styles" to their constituent elements and then recombines those elements so as to produce various and novel effects.

One begins to see, then, a surprising sympathy between Soane's temperament and Baillie's: both have an interest in subtlety, variety, and novelty. But this sympathy extends further still, for both are also notable for their emphasis on life indoors. As Summerson notes, "it is no accident that one always thinks of Nash in terms of exteriors, Soane in terms of interiors" (*Architecture*, 461). Just as Baillie's interest in interior spaces, what Catherine Burroughs calls "closet drama,"[53] can be linked to her interest in the nuances of individual character, so Soane, a rather shy and private man, is at his best in the design and decoration of interiors, and those interiors tend to be highly individualized and even eccentric. Inside Soane's buildings, moreover, one sees the collecting mentality once again at work, for they are individualized by means of the proliferation of minor stylistic elements and small varied objects. An east-west cross-section of 13 Lincoln's Inn Fields nicely suggests this proliferation (figure 4).

The Romantic interest in differentiation and individualization extended not just to decorative features and display objects but to the layout of buildings as well. It was during this period that common rooms were "individualized," made to serve separate functions for which they were equipped with specialized furniture. As Alan and Ann Gore explain,

Sofas, formerly placed against walls, were now arranged at right angles to or facing the fireplace. The newly introduced sofa table was designed to stand in front of a sofa and to be used for reading or writing. The chairs, which formerly were replaced against the walls after use, remained firmly in position. One contemporary correspondent unacquainted with this new fashion was convinced that her hostess's servants had left, when she saw the chairs scattered around the room . . . This was a period when much new and specialist furniture was introduced, such as quartetto tables, canterburies to accommodate the plethora of magazines, ladies' work tables, chiffoniers and so on.[54]

---

[53] Catherine Burroughs, "English Romantic Women Writers and Theatre Theory: Joanna Baillie's Prefaces to the *Plays on the Passions*," in Carol Shiner Wilson and Joel Haefner, eds., *Re-Visioning Romanticism: British Women Writers, 1776–1837* (Philadelphia: University of Pennsylvania Press, 1994), 281.

[54] Alan and Ann Gore, *The History of English Interiors* (Oxford: Phaidon, 1991), 105–6.

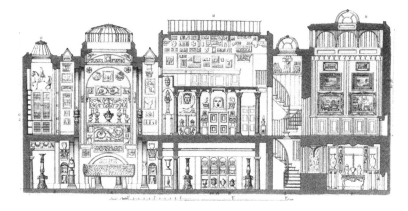

Figure 4. Sir John Soane, section from west to east through the Dome, Colonnade, and Picture Room, 13 Lincoln's Inn Fields.

Garden designer Humphry Repton illustrates the social significance of this change with a poem – "A Modern Living-Room" – accompanied by a pair of images in his 1816 *Fragments on the Theory and Practice of Landscape Gardening*:

> No more the *Cedar Parlour's* formal gloom
> With dulness chills, 'tis now the *Living Room*;
> Where Guests, to whim, or taste, or fancy true,
> Scatter'd in groups, their different plans pursue.[55] (figure 5)

Not only did specialized rooms encourage specific and varied activities but a new informality allowed for the pursuit of particularized interests. Of course, this new freedom was not complete; the new rooms arguably served to define the activities of the household more thoroughly. Indeed, other new forms of domestic organization seemed clearly to have a defining and regulating function. For, as Leonore Davidoff argues,

In the period from about 1800 to 1840 meals changed in character. Dinner began to be eaten later in the evening. Instead of having one or two large courses, including a selection of as many as twenty-five different dishes, set on the table at once in a mixture of roasts, "made-up" dishes, sweets, tarts and jellies, the meal began to be served sequentially, starting with soup and moving through a variety of tastes

[55] Humphry Repton, *Fragments on the Theory and Practice of Landscape Gardening* (London: T. Bensley and Son, 1816), 58.

Figure 5. Humphry Repton, "The Cedar Parlour" and "A Modern
Living-Room," from *Fragments on the Theory and Practice of
Landscape Gardening* (London: T. Bensley and Son, 1816).

and textures to a sweet, a savoury and finally dessert. This order was accompanied by
the proliferation of specialized utensils and dishes to prepare and present
the extended meal and much more labor was needed to serve it. At the same time
there was, at least for family meals, a move to make food predictable. Increased
resources were not used to allow choice to run riot. Rather the sentiment was that
"it was an excellent plan to have certain things on certain days."[56]

---

[56] Leonore Davidoff, "The Rationalization of Housework," in Davidoff, *Worlds Between: Historical Perspectives on Gender and Class* (New York: Routledge, 1995), 85.

Again, then, we see that specialization was not only implemented syn-chronically but diachronically, and served both to organize the objects of desire and to regulate that desire over time. If we return to Soane's archi-tecture, we see that even there the same effect is sought. As Summerson remarks, Soane's mind was "departmental and particularizing" (*Architec-ture*, 461), and this departmental quality functions not just statically but dynamically. Soane's own home provides a striking example of this. The house at 13 Lincoln's Inn Fields is designed, on every level, to provoke unceasing movement, a sort of tourism of the interior. As Sum-merson describes it, Soane aimed for "a disposition of planes in such a way that the eye was drawn through one after another instead of being halted by inert consciousness of a wall or ceiling. It is exactly analogous to some of the landscape effects most valued at the time" (462). In Soane's library

> there are hanging arches, Gothic-inspired, which "detach" the ceiling from the walls; tall bookcases, inset with strips of mirror, stand beneath and beyond the arches, while above the bookcases, and remoter still, is a deep mirror-frieze which, reflecting the whole ceiling, hints at yet further receding planes. It is imposs-ible to say on which plane the actual wall exists; for all aesthetic purposes it is not there (466).

This effect of recession is clearly not put in the service of grandeur in the eighteenth-century manner. The aim is not to make the space look bigger than it is; in fact, devices such as the hanging arches effectively divide and diminish the space. The aim, rather, would seem to be the perpetual stimulation of interest. Thus the floor plan of the house does not, like the grand houses of the seventeenth and eighteenth centuries, lead via what Mark Girouard terms the "axis of honour" toward a conclusion in the form of a private closet (see figure 6, a plan of the ground floor of nos. 12, 13, and 14 Lincoln's Inn Fields). Nor are rooms arranged in a simple circuit, a style that became popular for town homes in the mid-eighteenth century, and that reflected the importance of socializing with one's own class rather than offering selective patronage to persons of various ranks.[57] Instead, Soane's house is broken up into small, discontinu-ous spaces: tiny corridors that call attention to themselves with their little colored-glass skylights, windows and cut-out walls that provide unexpected views of other rooms, whose elevation relative to one's own vantage point

[57] Mark Girouard, *Life in the English Country House* (New Haven: Yale University Press, 1978), 144, 194.

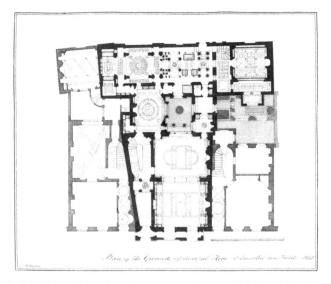

Figure 6. Sir John Soane, plans of numbers 12, 13, and 14 Lincoln's Inn Fields, drawn by C. J. Richardson, 1825.

often has a disorienting effect. There is no straightforward way to make one's way through the house, and, given its small size, it is surprisingly easy to get lost in.

If the picturesque landscape embodies the "coquetry of nature," then, this house enacts the coquetry of culture. Soane himself describes the Breakfast Room as follows: "the views from this room into the Monument Court and into the Museum, the mirrors in the ceiling, and the looking-glasses, combined with the variety of outline and general arrangement and the design and decoration of this limited space, present a succession of those fanciful effects which constitute the poetry of architecture."[58] This effect of succession is, however, most fully manifested in the Print Room. A small square room hung with paintings, it appears at first to be perfectly traditional in design. But, as one discovers, its "walls" open out, like flat vertical shelves, to display still more paintings behind them. On one wall in particular, this perpetual opening of new vistas leads finally to a surprising view through two floors down to the "Monk's Room." Once again, collection and the stimulation of curiosity and desire go hand in hand. One valuable

[58] Quoted in John Summerson, David Watkin, and G. Tilman Mellinghoff, *John Soane* (London: Academy Editions, 1983), 34.

Figure 7. Sir John Soane, detail of the east respond of the arches separating
the Library from the Dining Room, 13 Lincoln's Inn Fields.

visual object opens onto another in an apparently endless succession.
Mirrors, which are scattered throughout the house, produce a similar proliferation of goods and images – small, and hung at odd angles, they are
clearly not intended simply to enlarge the space. (See figure 7, a detail of
the east respond of the arches separating the Library from the Dining
Room, in which the design of cut-open spaces, the display of objects, and
the use of mirrors are all apparent.) These mirrors reveal once again the
relationship between proliferating goods and images and the establishment
of self-consciousness and individuality. It comes as little surprise that
Soane himself was to become an avid collector, and it is perfectly fitting
that he left his house to the nation as a museum, that great nineteenth-
century site for collection in the service of identity-formation. Soane's
architecture of this period, is, in Summerson's words, "intensely original"
(*Architecture*, 462), and thus achieves one of the preeminent aims of
Romantic art, but it is also a beautiful material reflection of the ideals
of Romantic consumerism.

V

As popular as the picturesque was, and as "natural" as the serial consumption it described seemed to be, it was ultimately unable to displace the sublime, and the obsessive, overwhelming desire it sponsored. This is revealed in the fate of the two plays Baillie used to dramatize the competition between these two major Romantic aesthetic modes, her plays on the passion of love: the tragedy *Count Basil* and the comedy *The Tryal* (1798). *The Tryal*, as I will demonstrate, shows us "picturesque" desire at work, and underscores its many social and personal advantages. *Count Basil*, however, explores a very different kind of desire, one that has masochistic elements and finds its aesthetic foundation in the sublime. Read as pendants, then, these two plays could be said to act out a contest between the two most important models of desire at the turn of the century. Both these models had their grounding in contemporary commerce, and both were described by their admirers so as to mask that fact. For Baillie, however, the model of desire that underwrites the sublime is both culpably aristocratic in tenor and linked to plebeian rebellion. As I will show, Baillie condemns the "sublime" love of Count Basil, representing it as an aristocratic mode of desire characterized by the overidealization of a single object, stagnation, and loss of self. In *The Tryal* she offers as its healthy counterpart the image of a bourgeois love which is characterized by curiosity, liveliness, and self-substantiation rather than self-loss.

To understand Baillie's handling of this opposition we return briefly to Price to examine his foundational treatment of the relationship of the picturesque to the sublime. For Price, the *locus classicus* of the theory of the sublime was Edmund Burke's *A Philosophical Enquiry into the Origin of Our Ideas of the Sublime and Beautiful*. Burke's theory simultaneously looks backward to a time when the social hierarchy was relatively fixed and differences of rank were the medium through which life was daily conducted, and forward to a time when extended notions of liberty would make the display of power a somewhat less straightforward affair. Thus, on the one hand, Burke works according to very old assumptions when he takes as one of his premises the notion that relationships are *always* inflected by power differentials: "Whenever strength is only useful, and employed for our benefit or our pleasure, then it is never sublime; for nothing can act agreeably to us, that does not act in conformity to our will; but to act agreeably to our will, it must be subject to us, and therefore can never be the cause of a grand and commanding conception."[59] Burke takes for granted that nothing can please us without being subject to us; the possibility of a mutually beneficial equality of power or even a chance coincidence of interests is not even thinkable here. One is either subject to power and therefore experiences sublime pain, or one subjects another to one's own power and thereby experiences beautiful pleasure:

for the enjoyment of pleasure, no great efforts of power are at all necessary; nay we know, that such efforts would go a great way towards destroying our satisfaction; for pleasure must be stolen, and not forced upon us; pleasure follows the will; and therefore we are generally affected with it by many things of a force greatly inferior to our own. (*Philosophical Enquiry*, 111)

Again, Burke cannot imagine that a more powerful person or thing could please us, for pleasure necessarily involves the exertion of power over something else: pleasure must be "stolen." On the other hand, however, Burke's theory looks forward to the very period in which the sublime was to become a central aesthetic category – the turn of the century – in that it also takes for granted that those ubiquitous power relations were gradually becoming aestheticized, distanced. As he explains in his first chapter on the sublime, "When danger or pain press too nearly, they are incapable of giving any delight, and are simply terrible; but at certain distances, and with certain modifications, they may be, and they are delightful, as we every day experience" (59–60). It makes sense that Burke's theory, although a product of the mid-eighteenth century, should have been so important to artists of the Romantic period, an era enlivened by new notions of liberty and equality. In Romantic art power relations are reproduced in a distanced and therefore enjoyable form.

But the Burkean and the Romantic sublime are concerned not only with power relations but also with desire. It is by now a critical commonplace that Burke's theory grounds itself on a notion of gender difference. By gendering the sublime masculine and the beautiful feminine, Burke is able to make a space for a resuscitated sublime in an aesthetic system that had largely been dominated by notions of beauty, especially classical beauty. According to the logic of Burke's argument, just as there are two genders, so must there be two significant aesthetic categories. Indeed, by aligning the sublime with the masculine, he is able not only to provide it with an

[59] Edmund Burke, *A Philosophical Enquiry into the Origin of Our Ideas of the Sublime and Beautiful* (London: Rivington, 1812), 114. Further references will be given parenthetically in the text.

entrée into the world of modern aesthetics but to secure it the position of honor there. Yet the effects of Burke's gendering go further still, for it shapes the desire provoked by beautiful and sublime objects. Beauty in general draws us to it; we enjoy its proximity, whether in a person, animal, or plant. It elicits a quiet but continuous desire, conservative and gentle in its effects. In human sexual relations beauty serves the further function of individualizing lust, for it is

fit that [man] should have something to create a preference, and fix his choice . . . The object therefore of this mixed passion, which we call love, is the *beauty* of the *sex*. Men are carried to the sex in general, as it is the sex, and by the common law of nature; but they are attached to particulars by personal *beauty*. (66)

The desire stimulated by beauty is therefore very like marital desire as Burke imagines it: steady, temperate, and reliable.

The experience of the sublime, however, has a narrative, and brings into play what Burke calls the "stronger" passions – those relating to pain and fear. Objects that impress us with their sublimity "suspend" the motions of the soul (95): the "mind is so entirely filled with its object, that it cannot entertain any other, nor by consequence reason on that object which employs it" (96). One's sense of self is held in abeyance and even reason is overcome, but this suspension then gives way to sensations of "delight" as one recognizes that the threat is, after all, only ideal. It would seem, then, that the sublime object does not elicit desire at all, since it appears to be the sole agent in this interaction. But its very status as an aesthetic *object* confirms its passivity, its lack of intentionality, within the paradigm of the sublime itself. Sublime objects and experiences were, moreover, actively sought for the pleasurable *frisson* they afforded. The sublime, then, describes a form of desire that, although active in itself, poses as passive, helpless.[60] "This mixed sense of pleasure I have not called *pain*, because it turns upon actual pleasure" (86) – it is this paradoxical, even masochistic mode of desire that fuels the sublime.

With this in mind, we return to Price and the picturesque. For if Burke's theory allows for two forms of desire, Price's will add a third between the two, and in so doing redefine all three. In essence, if sublime and beautiful correspond to father and mother in Burke, Price's picturesque is aligned

---

[60] Indeed, Frances Ferguson argues that while "the beautiful associates itself with a slow and almost imperceptible movement toward death," "the sublime becomes linked with labor." Thus both the sublime and the picturesque enjoy the ideological benefit of being related to production. (*Solitude and the Sublime: Romanticism and the Aesthetics of Individuation* [New York: Routledge, 1992], 52.)

with the lover: the young, unmarried woman, the coquette. In the presence of the picturesque, the viewer experiences neither fear nor quiet pleasure but a playful sense of excitement:

If we examine our feelings on a warm genial day . . . pleasure then seems to be our natural state; to be received, not sought after; it is the happiness of existing to sensations of delight only; we are unwilling to move, almost to think, and desire only to feel, to enjoy. In pursuing the same train of ideas, I may add, that the effect of the picturesque is curiosity; an effect, which, though less splendid and powerful, has a more general influence. Those who have felt the excitement produced by the intricacies of wild romantic mountainous scenes, can tell how curiosity, while it prompts us to explore . . . by its active agency keeps the fibres to their full tone; and thus picturesqueness when mixed with either of the other characters, corrects the languor of beauty, or the tension of sublimity. (I, 88–9)

As we have already seen, Price describes the picturesque as the coquetry of nature, and he recurs to this metaphor as a means for explaining the dynamic character of picturesque charm. Thus, for instance, he illustrates the curiosity-provoking quality of partial concealment by distinguishing between forms of female attractiveness: "Many persons . . . may have experienced how differently the passions are moved by an open licentious display of beauties, and by the unguarded disorder which sometimes escapes the care of modesty, and which coquetry so successfully imitates" (I, 22).

Price's insertion of the picturesque into Burke's scheme, however, necessarily transforms it. In his efforts to clear a space for and define the category of the picturesque, Price opposes it to both the sublime and the beautiful, with the result that those two categories are drawn closer together. In the quotation above, for instance, we see that beauty, like the sublime, induces a state of passivity, almost of helplessness. Given this, the reader is not entirely surprised to hear Price describe beauty as "splendid and powerful" in its effects, even though in Burke's paradigm splendor and power would be considered salient features of the sublime. Furthermore, whereas Burke's gendering of the sublime and beautiful renders the two categories completely incompatible, Price's examples reveal that for him even the feminine may partake of the sublime: "Juno, however beautiful, had no captivating charms, till she had put on the magic girdle [Venus's cestus]; in other words, till she had exchanged her stately dignity, for playfulness and coquetry" (I, 87). While Price's main concern is to demonstrate that beauty is improved by the addition of picturesque charm, he suggests by implication that beauty and sublimity can coexist in a woman.

Price, then, implicitly regenders the aesthetic field as a whole. Like Burke, he takes for granted that it is most pleasurable to play a masculine role and therefore defines the enjoyment of the picturesque as the most manly, vigorous form of aesthetic enjoyment. But he also loosens the connections between masculine and sublime, feminine and beautiful that Burke had worked so hard to establish. This loosening is arguably a result of the changed political context in which Price's theory was produced: if for Burke traditional images of masculine power produced a pleasurable *frisson*, for Price the propriety of traditional male authority was too beleaguered and important a notion to serve as the grounds of a merely aesthetic pleasure. More importantly, Price needed to argue that such authority was gentle and benevolent, not terrifyingly sublime. By the 1790s the embodiment of the sublime in a figure like a king was too politically vexed to be entirely workable: conservatives wanted to accent the kindliness of such figures, and radicals were loath to find anything attractive in the power they wielded. At the turn of the century, therefore, it was generally those persons and phenomena that stood outside the traditional realm of human authority that served as sublime objects: weather, landscapes, and animals, but also criminals and women. When Burke was to write his *Reflections on the Revolution in France* (1790), he himself combined the sublime and the beautiful so as to make the former more palatable. While the power of France and the French monarchy was arguably masculine and sublime, Burke embodied it in the beautiful form of Marie Antoinette, thus resolving for political reasons the respect/love opposition he had established in his earlier treatise. As Terry Eagleton puts it, "The law is male, but hegemony is a woman; this transvestite law, which decks itself out in female drapery, is in danger of having its phallus exposed."[61] By the 1790s, then, masculine and feminine and sublime and beautiful were no longer *ipso facto* opposed, and the sublime could in fact be more readily embodied in a female figure than a male one.[62] This reconception of the sublime and beautiful reflects a more fully Romantic notion of the sublime, one that is important to the configuration of eroticized submission at the turn of the century.

---

[61]   Terry Eagleton, *The Ideology of the Aesthetic* (Oxford: Basil Blackwell, 1990), 58.

[62]   For the flipside of this formulation, see Claudia Johnson's *Equivocal Beings: Politics, Gender, and Sentimentality in the 1790s* (Chicago: University of Chicago Press, 1995). Johnson argues that in the 1790s men coopted traditionally feminine sensibilities, leaving women with no domain of their own.

If we return now to Baillie, we see that in *Count Basil* and *The Tryal* she dramatizes and opposes love in the sublime/beautiful mode – self-abasing love for a woman perceived as both beautiful and powerful – and love in the picturesque mode – love for a woman who is neither beautiful nor powerful but engagingly playful. Baillie suggests that the former kind of love is both politically destabilizing and linked to false aristocratic values. Love as we have it in *Count Basil* is associated with a loss of autonomy and is analogous to the old-fashioned consumerist habits that Baillie complains of in her "Introductory Discourse." The pitfalls of such desire are immediately felt in the representation of marriageable women in the play. Throughout *Count Basil* the love that leads to passive rapt admiration is vilified: Rosinberg says of Basil and his men that

> They must not linger who would quit these walls;
> For if they do, a thousand masked foes,
> Some under show of rich luxurious feasts,
> Gay, sprightly pastime, and high-zested game;–
> Nay, some, my gentle ladies, true it is,
> The very worst and fellest of the crew,
> In fair alluring shape of beauteous dames
> Do such a barrier form t'oppose their way,
> As few men may o'ercome. (93)

This passage illustrates the set of metaphoric equations to which the play repeatedly returns: desire in this world is an aristocratic pleasure, it is false and deceitful, and it is as dangerously confining and even invasive as enemy troops. Rosinberg, who conflates these pleasures with women themselves, is revealed in the play to be a misogynist. But the play supports his contention that the world Basil has entered is not only a feminine one, but one where women dominate, using their beauty to exercise a power that renders them sublime.

At the center of this courtly world of pleasure stands Victoria, who is consistently linked to desire, power, spectacle, and enchantment; as Valtomer says of her, "She should be queen of revelry and show" (83). Indeed, she becomes just that when she and her father host a masquerade. In the masquerade scene Basil rhapsodizes about finding himself "in the region of delight" (125), and sets out to find Victoria. Here he recapitulates the events of an earlier scene – in which he publicly honored the worthy veteran Geoffrey – but in a feminine world and at the level of desire: dressed as a wounded soldier, he arguably comes "as" Geoffrey. This costume expresses his wish both to have his military glory already secured and to have himself and his honor fully recognized by Victoria. Victoria, similarly, enters in a costume that represents a wish fulfillment: she is dressed as a female conjuror. But her wish, unlike Basil's, will be fulfilled in fact: she longs for the power to enchant, and she exercises just such a power. Although she does admire Basil, in her interactions with him she aims only to test her power over him, and, despite his better judgment, Basil accedes to all her manipulations. It is no accident that her adopted son is a playful, mischievous fellow who appears at the masquerade as Cupid, thereby suggesting Victoria's affinity with Venus. Little Mirando earns treats by rattling off a list of his surrogate mother's conquests and including himself among them.

Victoria's oft-discussed ravishing beauty and her powers of enchantment make her, in the eyes of Basil and others, the embodiment of the sublimely beautiful, but for Baillie this is no virtue. Victoria's attractiveness is analogous to that of the refined, showy, and idealized consumer objects Baillie complains of in her "Discourse." It is telling that in her triumph over him Victoria takes Basil to a beautiful forest grove that seems so magical that "'Twere sacrilege with horses hoofs to wear / Its velvet turf, where little elfins dance, / And fairies sport beneath the summer's moon" (167). This place has much in common with the "beautiful fairy ground" of the "Introductory Discourse," that unhealthy place of enchantment and stasis. Victoria, as an idealized object of desire, holds Basil suspended in time, and he finds himself in that most dangerous position of being "enthralled by a woman" (156).

Victoria, then, elicits a willing and pleasurable submission, one that is threatening because it partakes of an old, reverential attitude toward things of beauty and signifiers of power and position. Such submission leads to a loss of autonomy that has not only personal but also political ramifications: ultimately, it is Basil's unwillingness to deny Victoria her wishes that leads him to neglect his soldierly duties. Nor is this problem specific to the relationship between Basil and Victoria; in this play the power of beautiful young women to elicit love is repeatedly denominated "tyranny." The good Albini warns Victoria against the exercise of this tyranny, reminding her that beauty is transient and that exercising power over a man is inappropriate. Albini condemns "she / Who vainly on her transient beauty builds / A little poor ideal tyranny" (109). Albini thus both condemns the tyranny of the ideal and suggests that this tyranny is ideal, that it is illusory. But Victoria, vain and inexperienced, fails to heed this advice and continues to enjoy deliberately manipulating Basil. It is fitting that when she is not at a procession or entertainment she is often found hunting. Her lust for the hunt reflects her desire for power just as the pleasure she takes in riding reveals her drive to provoke passion and turn it to her own uses: "I vault already on my leathern seat, / And feel the fiery steed beneath me shake / His mantled sides, and paw the fretted earth; / Whilst I [sit] aloft, with gay equestrian grace" (165). Basil's disguise as a wounded soldier tells more truth than he knows, for he has been wounded by this *victorious* huntress and tyrant.

The political tenor of the play's central romance, is, however, even more complicated than this language of tyranny suggests. For in this play Baillie's association of passion with enemy invasion and rebellion is writ large. Enemy spies are given the task of "simple untaught soldiers to seduce / From their sworn duty" (151) – a seduction that mirrors the women's seduction of the officers. This seduction leads to mutiny: "*The Soldiers are discovered drawn up in disorderly manner, hollaing and speaking big, and clashing their arms tumultuously*" (142). Basil's own seduction, furthermore, by distracting him from his role as leader, makes him vulnerable to this sedition. Seduction, then, is linked not only to tyranny but also to plebeian rebellion; the psychological and physical threat represented by republican France is played out here in the form of seduction scenes.[63] In her account of submissive desire, then, Baillie's concerns regarding the potential dangers of passion are made fully manifest. Love as we see it here is linked to a form of consumerism that Baillie argues is outmoded: an apparently ideal object enchants the viewer, destroys his will, and leaves him with no thought other than the desire for possession. Like a "masked foe," this love can hold a man prisoner, exercising a tyranny over him that leaves even a military leader helpless to defend himself. At the same time, this love is associated with political instability generally, with revolutionary enthusiasm. Little wonder then that love, generally considered a benign or even vital passion, is represented here as in itself destructive.

In this light comments of Baillie's such as the following take on added significance: "It is much to be regretted . . . that the eternal introduction of love as the grand business of the Drama, and the consequent necessity for making the chief persons in it such, in regard to age, appearance, manners, dispositions, and endowments, as are proper for interesting lovers, has occasioned so much insipid similarity in the higher characters" (51). Her claim, moreover, that "it is not my intention to encourage the indulgence of this passion, amiable as it is, but to restrain it" (63–4) is

---

[63] It is not insignificant that Basil was to aid his allies in a battle against the French.

something of an understatement. The peculiar form of Basil's punishment for his indulgence of this passion makes this strikingly clear. Given false information about the state of affairs in Pavia, Basil allows Victoria to detain him for two days in Mantua, with the result that the battle of Pavia takes place without him, his allies winning alone. Basil, overwhelmed by despair and convinced that his military reputation is ruined, finds a desolate cave and shoots himself. What is remarkable here is that although he was deceived regarding the situation in Pavia and committed only an error of omission that caused his allies no harm, Basil is insistent that his military honor is irretrievably lost. But if Basil's suicide seems incomprehensible given traditional codes of honor, it can be easily comprehended given Baillie's conception of the passions. Basil may have lost no military campaign, but he did allow himself to be captured, wounded, and tyrannized by his passion, and for Baillie the loss of one's self-control is not much different from loss on the battlefield.

Baillie makes her indictment of this kind of love not only severe but also broad in application. While the play condemns uxoriousness in men and associates women with love and men with work, thus offering a traditional and even misogynistic view of gender roles, it also inverts typical gender relations in some striking ways. The first sign of this is the analogy drawn between Basil's military reputation and a woman's sexual reputation. Basil remarks at the beginning of the play that "A soldier's reputation is too fine / To be expos'd e'en to the smallest cloud" (90). This gesture to the language of sexual reputation foreshadows Basil's professional undoing due to passion. But more importantly, it signals the fact that the play performs a gender switch on what might be considered a more typical love-tragedy plot. Here a man, simply by harboring passion for a woman, feels that his reputation has been destroyed and that he has no choice but to kill himself. His female beloved, who has been honestly attracted to him but who has played with his feelings, finally learns her lesson with his death and devotes herself to a punitive celibacy thereafter. The exacting mores that usually prohibit passion in women alone are generalized. In this world, for a man to have given in to passion is enough to lend his suicide a certain weight of legitimacy.

So resistant is the play to the threat that romantic love represents that it is often channeled into the ostensibly safer context of familial relations. Thus Rosinberg speaks of his devotion to "but one of all the sex, / Who still shall hold her station in my breast," only finally to reveal her as his "own good mother" (88). Even Basil's relationship to Victoria is prodded in this direction: when they are alone together Basil describes himself as repeating Victoria's words "As mothers on their lisping infants gaze, / And catch their broken words" (168) and Victoria says that she wishes Basil were her brother. Victoria's relationship to her charge Mirando, being structurally the "safest" of all, is perhaps the most openly erotic in the play, full of teasing, embracing, and kissing (113). In fact, Baillie often offers familial, and particularly maternal, affection as the model for safe, healthy love. Jane De Montfort's essentially maternal affection for her erring brother in *De Montfort* serves as a type for Baillie's preferred form of love. It is the same love that Albini has for Victoria, and that Marian has for Alice in Baillie's play *The Phantom* (1836); in each case the older woman specifically comments that she likes the younger the better for her weaknesses. Albini, for instance, tells Victoria that she loves her better than she loved Victoria's mother not only in spite of but even because of Victoria's flaws. The fact that the beloved does not appear ideal and elicits no desire for possession – at least in the eyes of these mother figures – makes her a healthy object choice. These maternal figures, who often play only a limited role in the plot, enjoy a level-headedness and distance from events that makes them the closest representatives on stage of the godlike spectator of the passions:

A man of this contemplative character partakes, in some degree, of the entertainment of the Gods, who were supposed to look down upon this world and the inhabitants of it, as we do upon a theatrical exhibition; and if he is of a benevolent disposition, a good man struggling with, and triumphing over adversity, will be to him, also, the most delightful spectacle. (14)

Ultimately, then, it is the dramatist and members of her audience who experience love best, precisely because they experience it only as a spectacle in the distance.

As striking as her maternal figures are, however, Baillie does not go so far as to thwart the conventional expectation that a play on love will focus on romantic love. In her comedy on love, therefore, she sets herself the task of defining a form of romantic love that is not disastrous in its consequences. What she gives us in *The Tryal* is a love that is coquettish and playful, curious and active – a love that involves a devotion to its object but an unwillingness to relinquish the self and its principles. She shows us, in essence, a picturesque form of love. Agnes, the heroine of *The Tryal*, is unlike Victoria in almost every respect. She is repeatedly described as plain or downright homely, and even her good uncle allows that "there is not one feature in thy face that a man would give a farthing for" (197). Agnes has, therefore, nothing in common with showy consumer goods. Because she is an heiress, however, she has found that she nevertheless draws men who are perfectly ready to take advantage of her capacity to serve as a static symbol of value, even if the image they would form together is no very attractive one: as she dryly remarks, "One would swear I were made of amber, to attract all the dust and chaff of the community" (196). She therefore determines to switch roles with her humble cousin so that, both plain and penniless, she can elicit the right kind of affection. She assures her uncle that as flighty as the plan may seem, "It is a reasonable woman's desire" (196). Indeed, although very playful, it is clear from the outset that Agnes is a practical and intelligent woman.

The man who becomes Agnes's lover does indeed love her in spite of what she lacks, and actively approves of the fact that she is not a thoughtless slave to fashion. When other men, such as Sir Loftus Prettyman, fail to see her charms, he is astonished: "Good god! what a contemptible perversion of taste do interest and fashion create! But it is all affectation" (208). Agnes, for her part, finds Harwood desirable largely because he has "a sensible counte-nance" and "so little of the foppery of the fashion about him" (204). While others may look for outward signs of wealth in their lover, Agnes, as if she were a good reader of Baillie's "Introductory Discourse," focuses on his face, and the fact that when near her "many a varied expression his countenance assumed" (205). As a lawyer, moreover, Harwood has the merit of being a man professionally concerned with the study of human character: as Agnes's uncle remarks;

I perfectly agree with you, Mr Harwood, that the study and preparation requisite for your profession is not altogether a dry treasuring up of facts in the memory, as many of your young students conceive: he who pleads the cause of man before fellow-men, must know what is in the heart of man as well as what is in the book of records, and what study is there in nature so noble, so interesting as this? (228)

Given the disdain for wealth and fashion revealed in this play, it is unsur-prising that the Withringtons are not represented as straightforwardly aris-tocratic. Agnes is an heiress, but her cousin is penniless and their uncle does not elicit great respect from the men of fashion in the play. That the play is set in Withrington's house in Bath makes sense, since Bath was notoriously a place where class lines were rather fluid. Agnes is as rational and scrupu-lous as any good bourgeoise, and the play that centers on her is entirely in plain prose. When Agnes assures her uncle that her cousin will be financially secure even without marrying into money, he teases her by suggesting that she and the man she loves "will get a prize in the lottery, or find out the philosopher's stone, and coin their old shoes into guineas" (199), thereby implying that Agnes's whims are those of a thoughtless girl. But Agnes responds by teasing him back: "it is not that way the fortune is to come" (199), she says, and she goes on to urge her uncle to provide for her cousin's financial security by settling a provision upon her. As this example suggests, Baillie is careful to distinguish Agnes's aims not only from the single-minded selfish pursuit of wealth and fashion of a Sir Loftus Prettyman, but also from the nervous greed of the true bourgeois. Here, for instance, Agnes manages to obtain very practical ends, but all through "frolicksome" (202) means. In this she is opposed to Mr. Royston who, always dickering over small sums and speaking of the "great deal of management" (215) that his affairs require, is too scattered in his pursuit of his goals ever to be successful. Indeed, Baillie suggests that the nervous money manager ends up looking very like the fashionable aristocrat; Royston finds his counterpart in the chatterbox Miss Eston, who describes her similarly busy schedule thus: "I'm sure I have been all over the town this morning, looking after a hundred things; till my head has been put into such a confusion!" (233).

The desire that Agnes elicits in Harwood is as sensible and playful as she is herself. Agnes is, in effect, like the coquette of the picturesque. As Withrington remarks, "allow me to say all this playing, and laughing, and hoidening about is not gentlewomanlike, nay, I might say, is not mai-denly. A high bred elegant woman is a creature which man approaches with awe and respect; but nobody would think of accosting you with such impressions, any more than if your [sic] were a couple of young female tinkers" (240). Despite Withrington's complaint, it is this eager and energetic love that the play espouses. While such love does involve a commitment to its object, it never develops into a state of passive enchantment; it stimulates the mind and its curiosities rather than lulling them into a stupor.

Harwood's public and private personas therefore not only do not come into conflict but are mutually reinforcing. For it is his task to attend to the niceties of human character not only in his work but also in his courtship; as the play's title indicates, love and the lover are put on trial here. Indeed, Harwood undergoes not one but two trials. Having passed the first test in loving Agnes for her playful character alone, he gradually becomes too smitten with her, granting her too much power over him. The hardest trial he undergoes, then, is a test of his capacity to resist the temptation to give in to sublime love. His friend the Colonel warns him of his danger, letting us know just enough about himself to reassure us that he is a fitting advisor, one who knows not to overvalue romantic love: "I was early cha-grined with the want of promotion, and disappointed in my schemes of ambition, which gave my countenance something of a melancholy cast, I believe, and the ladies have been kind enough to attribute it to the effects of hopeless love; but how could you be such a ninny, my dear Harwood?" (259). The Colonel, a friend of Harwood's father, plays a quasi-paternal role in warning Harwood of the dangers of excessive love and the horrors of having a tyrannical wife. But excessive love is rep-resented as equally unhealthy for the woman who is its object, and With-rington advises his ward against accepting such a love: "there are men whose passions are of such a violent over-bearing nature, that love in them, may be considered as a disease of the mind" (276). Modern love in the picturesque mode is constantly in danger of slipping into the sublime/beautiful mode of aristocratic, courtly love. In essence, we have here the opposite of the situation in *Camilla*: Agnes and Harwood, like Camilla and Edgar, are advised by paternal figures to avoid excessive, sub-missive love, but here that advice ultimately proves to be sound rather than misguided.

So determined is Agnes to avoid eliciting submissive love that she resolves to put Harwood to another test to see if he would love her even if he believed her to be unprincipled, firmly pledging that she will give him up if he does. Fittingly enough, this trial is accomplished by means of a play within the play: "I wish . . . we could conceal ourselves somewhere in his apartments, where we might see Harwood have the letter put into his hands, and observe his behaviour" (279). We thus see Baillie's theoretical interest in the role of reason and curiosity in the stimulation of desire enacted within the play itself, and we are reminded once again of the kinship between healthy love and sympathetic spectator-ship. Desire for another should lead to an impulse not simply to observe the beloved – to lose oneself in superficial spectacle as Basil does – but to observe the beloved from a sufficient distance to allow the rational con-templation of him or her. It is not by chance that *Count Basil* – a play full of processions, masquerades, and spectacles – is tragic, while *The Tryal* – in which spectacle is put in the service of a rational search for truth – is comic. For Harwood and Agnes do survive this second trial; they both show a willingness to renounce their love and thereby prove the health of that love. Harwood learns that even when Agnes "pretended to be careless" of him, she thought of him "all the day long" (293), but he learns, too, that she was not so immobilized with love for him that she would have accepted him had he been immobilized with love for her. The play closes with Harwood affirming that although his wife is an heiress, he will never be "an idle gentleman" (299), for which Agnes thanks him, adding that his good work as a judge of character "will be our nobility" (299).

Romantic love, situated at the intersection of passion and desire, was for that reason an emotion of particular consequence to Baillie, and its proper regulation was a felt necessity. Ironically enough, however, for all her efforts to define and promote a safe and healthy form of love in *The Tryal*, it was to her tragedies that Baillie's contemporaries were consistently drawn. Her votary Sir Walter Scott, in recommending her tragedies to a friend, added that "the comedies you may pass over without any loss,"[64] and a reviewer tellingly remarked that there was "too little *danger* in these comedies."[65] Indeed, it is significant that Baillie began her *Series of Plays* with *Count Basil*, for in spite of her indictment of sublime, self-abasing love, and her claim that it is both economically outmoded and politically unsound, it was in fact a form of love that was of central importance to Romantic-era culture. Although set in the sixteenth century, *Count Basil* maps out patterns of desire that were of profound contemporary relevance, and Baillie's condemnation of Basil's love often met with incomprehension: "The love of *Count Basil* . . . for an accomplished and virtuous princess, has nothing in it that should lead the readers of that tragedy to stifle such an honourable and successful passion in their own bosoms, or to shut the avenues of their hearts to the approaches of beauty and merit."[66] Baillie's celebration in *Count Basil* of the submissive homoerotic love that Basil's men feel for him reveals her own attraction to an ideal of charismatic leadership of the kind for which Napoleon was just beginning to be known. It is thus less surprising than it might seem that in the period before her death, when "her mind was controlled largely by her imagination," she told friends that "she had seen Napoleon ride up the hill to her."[67] And in a final irony, Baillie's own fame as a tragic writer tinged her with the aura

---

[64] From a letter to Mrs. Bentley, quoted in Donald Carswell, *Scott and His Circle* (New York: Doubleday, 1930), 290. [65] *Edinburgh Review*, 278. [66] *Edinburgh Review*, 275–6.
[67] Carhart, *Life*, 67.

of the sublime, and the admiration she elicited from men like Lord Byron, combined with her reserve, put her in the role of the aloof, commanding woman. Scott discovered no contradiction, and in fact found it perfectly fitting, that it should be "A retired female, thinking and writing in solitude, [who] presented to her countrymen the means of regaining the true and manly tone of national tragedy."[68]

[68] Scott, *Prose Works*, 387.

CHAPTER 4

Practicing politics in the comfort of home

Joanna Baillie's notion that submissive eroticism was allied to both traditional hierarchies and revolutionary principles, whether or not that notion was borne out historically, was shared by writers of subsequent decades. For many writers of the early nineteenth century, scenes of erotic self-abasement proved to be a useful forum for manipulating and interrogating power relations generally. As we will see, Romantic-era representations of eroticized submission often dramatize a fascination with and an ambivalence toward power inequities, for they celebrate hierarchy, while, through their excesses, making it appear absurd. These representations were thus an ideal vehicle for thinking through political ambivalence at a time of acute political instability. Moreover, by reducing the scale of the struggle for power to the confined dimensions of personal life, they both intensified that struggle and made it appear more manageable. Especially for those attracted to democratic ideals, imagining hierarchy at home was a safe way of exploring its costs and its pleasures.

This chapter follows the vicissitudes of this exploration in the self-representations and the fictions of three writers: the essayist William Hazlitt, the poet Lord Byron, and the novelist Lady Caroline Lamb. All three writers produced semi-autobiographical accounts of their own erotic lives, and all three drew both implicit and explicit connections between erotic life and early nineteenth-century politics. Byron, dismayed to see political power resolved into mere monetary relations, deliberately eroticized it in an effort to make it once again palpable and material. Lamb, on the other hand, suggested in her writing that both the virtue and the danger of modern political life lay precisely in the fact that radical politics were unavoidably erotic – that they were, in fact, fueled by submissive desire. Hazlitt, meanwhile, attempted to work through his political disaffection after Waterloo with a remarkable account of the political value of his self-abasement before a girl half his age. For this stalwart radical, such romance seemed the best – indeed, the only – way to keep the hope of democracy alive.

I

Hazlitt's 1823 *Liber Amoris* recounts, in fictionalized form, the story of 45-year-old Hazlitt's infatuation with Sarah Walker, the nineteen-year-old daughter of his landlord. Hazlitt's reason for publishing this history is a matter to which we will turn later, but it is important to note from the outset that while the book was inspired by real events, it was not presented to the public as an autobiography, but as the posthumously published papers of a "native of North Britain"[1] – with the result that, given literary convention, it appeared to be a novel. As recent critics have hastened to point out, this collection of ostensibly historical documents does indeed function as an artfully contrived whole. The precise character of that whole has, however, been a subject of some debate: Marilyn Butler argues, for instance, that it is first and foremost a satire of the sentimental novel, while John Kinnaird describes the book as the story "of a writer struggling to come to terms with an unfulfilled dream of destiny and with the hopeless conviction of his incurable lovelessness."[2] The difficulty of determining the genre and tone of the piece is in part a product of the book's rather unconventional subject, failed courtship. Just as the protagonist vacillates between obsessive love and jealous rage, unable to "develop" his attachment in a progressive and coherent way, so the book itself seems to move in fits and starts, as if unsure how to proceed. Indeed, the materials from which the book is constructed are themselves various, a hodgepodge of letters, conversations in the form of dramatic dialogues, and vignettes built around literary allusions. Matters are further complicated by the fact that for Hazlitt's modern critics, the autobiographical character of the book has been a source of embarrassment; even those who have devoted entire monographs to Hazlitt's work often gloss over *Liber Amoris* in a few paragraphs or even a few sentences.[3] But as I will argue, the book's relentless focus on ill-governed passions, as well as its generic and tonal eccentricities, reflect the workings of a comprehensible internal logic. For *Liber Amoris*

[1] William Hazlitt, *Liber Amoris or The New Pygmalion*, intro. Michael Neve (London: Hogarth Press, 1985), from the "Advertisement." Further references will be given parenthetically in the text.
[2] Marilyn Butler, "Satire and the Images of Self in the Romantic Period: The Long Tradition of Hazlitt's *Liber Amoris*," in G. A. Russo and Daniel P. Watkins, eds., *Spirits of Fire: English Romantic Writers and Contemporary Historical Methods* (Rutherford, N.J.: Associated University Presses, 1990), and John Kinnaird, *William Hazlitt: Critic of Power* (New York: Columbia University Press, 1978), 266. Further references to *Critic of Power* will be given parenthetically in the text.
[3] This is true, for instance, of David Bromwich's *Hazlitt: The Mind of a Critic* (Oxford: Oxford University Press, 1983), and Kinnaird's *William Hazlitt: Critic of Power*.

represents a fully developed and self-conscious aesthetic of erotic submission, one that juxtaposes idealism and cynicism and privileges uncertainty and suspense. As in Frances Burney's *The Wanderer*, this aesthetic derives in part from early nineteenth-century economic habits. But it also derives from Hazlitt's investment in early nineteenth-century politics, and his belief in the future as a realm in which altruism and democracy would finally be possible. As we will see, in his attraction to submissive role-playing Hazlitt shows himself to be not just a man of private foibles but, here as in his essays, a spokesman for his age.

In *Liber Amoris* Hazlitt and Walker are reproduced in abstract, fictional form as simply H and S, their interactions becoming paradigmatic of the interactions of any "he" and "she," and, indeed, of any two people of unequal power. For Hazlitt, as for Burney, such interactions are founded on a dynamic of desire learned in the marketplace. Indeed, similarities in the courtship dynamics of the central couples of *Liber Amoris* and *The Wanderer* are immediately apparent. S, like Juliet, is a woman of the working class whose lover imagines her to be someone extraordinary. In *The Wanderer* Juliet embodies the appeal of the early nineteenth-century commodity: apparently common and of obscure origin, her aloofness and exoticism allow her to serve as a cipher onto which other characters can project their desires and ideals. Her opacity places her beyond the ordinary tests and measures of value, making her appear to be a person of incalculable value capable of exerting power over her admirer. If this paradigm is adumbrated in *The Wanderer*, it is fully developed in *Liber Amoris*, and raised to a higher degree of self-consciousness. H's idealization of his beloved, more determined even than Harleigh's, is represented as excessive and unwarranted. His self-abasement, moreover, is passionately pursued, sometimes to the point of absurdity.

To a certain extent, this difference simply reflects differences between Burney and Hazlitt as persons and as writers. But this raising of the ante in the representation of masochistic behavior also reflects the entrenchment of modern urban consumerism. This change is visible first of all in the fact that although he is S's champion, H avidly objectifies her and readily imagines her as debased. Even H's grammar suggests such objectification; in a letter to S he addresses her in the third person, explaining that he is happy that he has had "two letters from Sarah" (40). H's sexual desire for S is indistinguishable from a desire literally to consume her: "I could devour the little witch. If she had a plague-spot on her, I could touch the infection: if she was in a burning fever, I could kiss her, and drink death as I have drank life from her lips" (61). As the image of the plague-spot suggests, S's insistent objectification is linked to her debasement. Whereas Juliet truly is superior to the class she inhabits, the reader of *Liber Amoris* is never given sufficient reason to believe that S is, in spite of H's celebration of her "sovereign grace and beauty" (8). H himself ultimately speaks of her as a "common lodging-house decoy, a kissing convenience, [whose] lips were as common as the stairs" (20). But even in the early pages of the book, pages that show H at his most adoring, we see him attached to the notion of S's commonness. In fact, as Hazlitt's biographer Stanley Jones points out, Hazlitt tended to exaggerate the lowliness of the historical Walker: "Writers on Hazlitt have generally accepted too readily his own prejudiced view in *Liber Amoris* and assumed that the [Walker] family were lower in the social scale than they actually were."[4] Although H repeatedly denies that S could be in any way humble or debased, it is clear that he needs or wants to consider it a real possibility: "Wert thou all that I dread to think – wert thou a wretched wanderer in the street, covered with rags, disease, and infamy, I'd clasp thee to my bosom, and live and die with thee, my love" (29). Whereas Harleigh wants his dream of his wanderer's noble origins to be realized, it is clear that H wants no such thing for his S, whom he would imagine a wanderer if she cannot actually be one.

Furthermore, it is necessary to the erotic dynamic Hazlitt establishes here that S be, in some sense, in H's employ. As Hazlitt was to write in "On Great and Little Things," an essay composed around the time of the Walker affair, "I admire the Clementinas and Clarissas at a distance: the Pamelas and Fannys of Richardson and Fielding make my blood tingle."[5] The servant girl is understood to be the fair – if resistant – object of her master's lust, his to possess, and S's work in H's boarding-house is insistently underscored so as to render her similarly available. No aristocrat, and not even a man of considerable means, H must make much of his mistress's servant status in order to secure her object-function for him. But unlike Mr. B, H is a tenant, not an owner by hereditary right, and S is not part of his retinue and available only to him, but a woman whose labor is available for hire to any man. Thus H constantly worries that S has been conducting affairs with other lodgers. The thought of S actually being with someone else sends H into a jealous rage, but his recurrent tendency to believe that such a thing is likely reflects a deep readiness to do so.

---

[4] Stanley Jones, *Hazlitt: A Life* (Oxford: Oxford University Press, 1991), 310. Further references will be given parenthetically in the text.

[5] William Hazlitt, "On Great and Little Things," in *The Complete Works of William Hazlitt*, 21 vols., vol. VIII, ed. P. P. Howe (London: J. M. Dent and Sons, 1930–4), p. 236. Further references to this edition will be given parenthetically in the text by volume and page number.

H understands that S does not exist for his sake alone and that her avail-ability to him presupposes her availability to others; she is not like the pos-session of a nobleman but modern, urban merchandise.

The urban and worldly character of this courtship is signaled not only in the public nature of S's object status but also in the extent of H's idealiz-ation of her; while S is depressed lower than Juliet, she is also raised higher. H sometimes idealizes her in a manner reminiscent of Harleigh's idealization of Juliet: "Talk of a tradesman's daughter! you would ennoble any family, thou glorious girl, by true nobility of mind." She responds that she knows "her inferiority to most," to which he answers: "To none; there is no one above thee, man nor woman either. You are above your situation, which is not fit for you."[6] But H usually goes much further than this, calling S a sovereign to whom he would be a slave, describ-ing her as an angel, a saint, an idol. Since the narrative never provides a basis for these claims, they cannot but appear to be the willful projection of a con-sumer, wise in the ways of the world, who knows he must use his imagin-ation to invigorate an otherwise dull reality. Hazlitt understood that sustaining such imaginative idealization requires the deferral of the moment of taking possession. As he writes in "Of the Past and Future" in *Table-Talk* (1821): "The good that is past is in this sense like money that is spent, which is of no further use, and about which we give ourselves little concern. The good we expect is like a store yet untouched, and in the enjoyment of which we promise ourselves infinite gratification" (*Works*, VIII, 25). Hazlitt consciously and straightforwardly regards the period prior to purchase as the moment of greatest satisfaction. Similarly, H's pro-tracted courtship of S allows him to imagine that she could provide infinite gratification. That Walker spoke and wrote little, a fact often deridingly noted by Hazlitt's biographers and critics, would have made her all the more aloof and remote, and therefore, for Hazlitt, an ideal object of desire.

Altogether, then, the relationship between H and S would seem to rep-resent a further development of the commodity paradigm discussed in relation to *The Wanderer*. Like Juliet, S is changeable and various, and inscrutable in spite of her spectacular qualities. But in *Liber Amoris* the aloofness of the object of desire arouses not only interest but also suspicion; H, worldly and middle-class, understands the impostures of the urban market. Hazlitt's involvement with Walker was characterized by a relentless barrage of questions and tests to determine her "real" identity; in *Liber*

---

[6] Frances Burney, *The Wanderer*, ed. Margaret Doody, Robert Mack, and Peter Sabor (Oxford: Oxford University Press, 1991), 34.

Amoris H constantly asks S if she has "two characters, one that you palm off upon me, and another, your natural one, that you resume when you get out of the room, like an actress" (28). S seems to H not just unknowable but even deliberately theatrical, an object offered for display and consumption whose essence is quite other than what it appears. Thus we find in *Liber Amoris* a wry self-consciousness that is absent in *The Wanderer*, for H knows that his idealized vision of S is largely his own creation. H is like the consumer who, while he knows that advertising is manipulative and that a single commodity cannot satisfy his deepest wishes, nevertheless enjoys believing in such fictions. At the same time, he takes for granted that possession can never live up to anticipation – performance will always fall short of promise.

The paradoxes of the modern market not only lead H to postpone possession but change his conception of it altogether. Although Hazlitt desires the Pamelas of the world it is clear that H is no Mr. B who will be rewarded with physical possession once he recognizes the full value of S's character. The difference between possession as manifested in *Pamela* (1740) and possession as we find it in *Liber Amoris* is touched upon by Hazlitt himself in *Characteristics* (1823):

I think men formerly were more jealous of their rivals in love – they are now more jealous of their mistresses, and lay the blame upon them. That is, we formerly thought more of the mere possession of the person, which the removal of a favored lover prevented, and we now think more of a woman's affections, which may still follow him to the tomb. To kill a rival is to kill a fool; but the Goddess of our idolatry may be a sacrifice worthy of the Gods. (*Works*, XI, 203)

Physical possession alone is no longer enough; it does not of itself eliminate a mistress's aloofness. Her affections might still belong to another, heightening her desirability while eliciting painful and even violent emotions in her lover. The sudden shift to the language of sacrifice signals the irreducible problem here: to remain an idol the beloved must maintain her distance, with the result that she never can be "possessed" except in the transient moment of her sacrifice. While in *The Wanderer* possession is still the ultimate goal, even if the focus of the narrative is on the feelings of idealization, anxiety, and desire that precede it, in *Liber Amoris* possession is subject to an infinite regress, to the point that it comes to seem unimaginable. As Hazlitt argues in his essay "On Will-Making," modern man's desire for wealth is and should be abstract and speculative; he admiringly describes the aims of a will in the Thelusson family, designed to allow for the unlimited extension of the family property, as "purely imaginary, romantic – one might almost say, disinterested."[7] Wealth as a subject of the imagination, something to be enjoyed in the indefinite future, loses its taint of materiality. Similarly, H's desire for S is so hopeless that it becomes, like S herself, "ideal."[8] A reviewer for the *Examiner* wryly remarked of *Liber Amoris*: "We are not aware of the publication of anything so indicative of the Ideal theory of Bishop Berkeley . . . nothing so approaching to a demonstration that mind is the great creator."[9] This speculative relation to objects of desire, while it allows for the idealization of those objects and renders the desire itself "romantic" and "disinterested," also makes the enjoyment of possession an impossibility.

H's ambivalence regarding possession is encapsulated in the book's opening dialogue, entitled "The Picture," in which H shows S an image to which he likens her. It seems at first that the picture serves primarily as a vehicle for practicing possession. When apart from S, H writes in a letter to her "I think I must send to him [Mr. P–] for the picture to kiss and talk to" (39). Indeed, H goes even further in his effort to make S like the picture and therefore "his." The episode closes with H saying, "Thou art heavenly-fair, my love – like her from whom the picture was taken – the idol of the painter's heart, as thou art of mine! Shall I make a drawing of it, altering the dress a little, to shew you how like it is?" (4). H quite consciously sets himself up as not only the owner but also the creator of the idol he adores. Nevertheless, his use of this picture to mark his possession of S is complicated from the outset. H makes much of the fact that the miniature is of obscure origin – he does not know if it reproduces a Guido or a Raphael – and subject – some say it is a Madonna, and some a Magdalen,

---

[7] William Hazlitt, "On Will-Making," in Hazlitt, *Table-Talk*, ed. William Carew Hazlitt (London: George Bell & Sons, 1900), 158.
[8] This new, Romantic-era conception of desire thus goes hand in hand with a new conception of value, one that not only influences the perception of commodities and women but also gives rise to new categories of value, such as that of "genius." Romantic "genius," unlike Augustan "wit" or late eighteenth-century "sensibility," signals a thing of special value precisely because it is not simply high on the scale of standard values but off the scale entirely. In the latter part of the century, David Hume represented poetic genius as valuable for its rarity: "If refined sense and exalted sense be not so useful as common sense, their rarity, their novelty, and the nobleness of their objects make some compensation and render them the admiration of mankind, as gold, though less serviceable than iron, acquires from its scarcity a value which is much superior" (*An Inquiry Concerning the Principles of Morals* [New York: Macmillan, 1957], 65). But Hazlitt goes one step further and describes genius as a quality that cannot be brought to market at all: "A little originality is more esteemed and sought for than the greatest acquired talent, because it throws a new light upon things, and is peculiar to the individual. The other is common; and may be had for the asking, to any amount" (*Table-Talk*, 61). It is no longer enough to be very valuable; a truly fine thing must be "priceless." Not surprisingly, H tells S, "I owe you more than I can ever pay" (38).
[9] *Examiner* (May 11, 1823).

while he thinks that it resembles Raphael's St. Cecilia, "with looks commercing with the skies" (3). That is, not only does H underscore the fact that the miniature is enveloped in mystery, but he increases the distance of its female subject by noting her entire indifference to mundane matters. It would seem that a Magdalene or even a Madonna would be too much of this world for his purposes, so he links his "goddess" to the ecstatic patron saint of the most abstract and disembodied, the least representational, of art forms. (Later in the narrative he further develops S's connection to St. Cecilia by giving S a musical instrument, a flageolet.)

In Raphael's painting of St. Cecilia, the figures of St. Paul, Mary Magdalene, St. John, and St. Augustine all look down, out toward the viewer, or toward one another, while St. Cecilia looks up toward the sky, where a vision of heavenly musicians is revealed. So rapt is she by this heavenly music that her earthly instruments go unnoticed at her feet and even the one she holds seems to be slipping from her fingers. As Giorgio Vasari describes it, she is "wholly absorbed in the harmony; and in her countenance is seen that abstraction which is found in the faces of those who are in ecstasy."[10] For H, such abstraction serves as a figure for S's distance, the difficulty of capturing her – even of capturing her attention. H wants in S a palpable object, something to have and to hold; but it is clear that he also wants S to be the image of abstraction and the unattainable. Thus, although H often likens S to a statue, the epitome of the solid and palpable, he also describes her in terms that highlight her immateriality, referring to her by sobriquets such as "the sweet apparition" (59). The miniature focuses this contradiction in H's drive for possession. It thus functions as a fetish as Anne McClintock defines it, "the displacement onto an object (or person) of contradictions that the individual cannot resolve at a personal level."[11] The miniature embodies the tension inherent in H's desire to define S as unattainable on the one hand and his own property on the other. Like the locket in *Camilla*, the miniature fascinates because it dramatizes the workings of desire in the marketplace. But whereas the locket serves to bring into focus the problem of the social determination of value, the miniature embodies contradictions in the ideology of urban marketplace desire in the 1820s. The antinomies of that desire, even more extreme than they were in *The Wanderer*, make the use of such fetishistic displacement particularly eligible.

---

[10] Giorgio Vasari, *The Great Masters*, trans. Gaston de Vere, ed. Michael Sonino (New York: Park Lane, 1986), 167.

[11] Anne McClintock, *Imperial Leather: Race, Gender and Sexuality in the Imperial Contest* (New York: Routledge, 1995), 184.

H's construction of S as deeply embodied on the one hand and remotely ideal on the other returns us to the aesthetic issues raised in the Prologue, for the marked division between material sign and ideal significance gives the representation of S a quasi-allegorical quality. Theresa Kelley argues that "modern [post-sixteenth-century] allegory is a metafigure for the rule of abstractions over particulars (or the reverse)"[12]; it is a figure for equivocal referentiality. It is just such equivocation that is at stake here, whether H represents it as inhering in S herself or simply in his view of her. Determining the aesthetic and ethical value of such equivocation in the world of *Liber Amoris* is, however, no easy matter. The canonical Romantic account of allegory, summed up in Samuel Taylor Coleridge's *The Statesman's Manual* (1816), patently privileges the symbol over allegory because the symbol fuses sign and referent, whereas in allegory "picture-language" and "abstract notions" jostle for pride of place.[13] But if for Coleridge symbolism was patently superior to allegory, Hazlitt understood that this evaluation had everything to do with Coleridge's conservative politics of the 1810s. In his review of *The Statesman's Manual*, Hazlitt underscores Coleridge's association of "mechanic philosophy" with political radicalism, so that Coleridge's complaint that "the mechanical understanding . . . confounds SYMBOLS with ALLEGORIES" must be regarded as a political and not simply an aesthetic claim (*Works*, VII, 121). Wryly referring to his own "mechanical understanding," Hazlitt implies that the value Coleridge sets on the organic fusion characteristic of symbolism is little more than an aestheticized, mystified version of the impulse to quash dissent. Hazlitt does not quote Coleridge's definitions of symbolism and allegory but simply remarks that Coleridge "labours very learnedly" to set right the confusion between the two, "and so he goes on for several pages, concluding his career where the Allies have concluded theirs, with the doctrine of Divine Right; which he does not however establish quite so successfully with the pen, as they have done with the sword" (121). Better a mechanical understanding, one that "recognizes no medium between *literal* and *metaphorical*,"[14] than mediation and unification by the sword.

Not only does Hazlitt regard the "problem" of allegory as specious and even politically suspect, but he suggests elsewhere that female allegorical figures in particular effectively resolve any readerly difficulties with allegory

---

[12] Theresa Kelley, *Reinventing Allegory* (Cambridge: Cambridge University Press, 1997), 11.

[13] Samuel Taylor Coleridge, from *The Statesman's Manual*, in *Lay Sermons, The Collected Works of Samuel Taylor Coleridge* 16 vols., vol. VI, ed. R. J. White (Princeton: Princeton University Press, 1972), 30.

[14] Coleridge, quoted in Hazlitt's review, *Works*, VII, 121.

by virtue of the pleasure they give. In his 1818 lecture on Chaucer and Edmund Spenser he remarks on the contemporary discomfort with allegory: referring to particular scenes in Spenser, he notes that "some people will say that all this may be very fine, but that they cannot understand it on account of the allegory. They are afraid of the allegory, as if they thought it would bite them: they look at it as a child looks at a painted dragon, and think it will strangle them in its shining folds." Hazlitt responds:

This is very idle . . . It might as well be pretended that, we cannot see Poussin's pictures for the allegory, as that the allegory prevents us from understanding Spenser. For instance, when Britomart, seated amidst the young warriors, lets fall her hair and discovers her sex, is it necessary to know the part she plays in the allegory, to understand the beauty of the following stanza? . . . Or is there any mystery in what is said of Belphoebe, that her hair was sprinkled with flowers and blossoms which had been entangled in it as she fled through the woods? (*Works*, V, 38).

Female beauty in particular has the power to render the gap between sign and signified unimportant, for the "picture-language" of that beauty seems quite naturally to signify the ideal. Thus, for Hazlitt, female beauty and allegorical figuration are perfectly suited to each other.

It is not surprising, then, that H, in his account of S, quite deliberately slips into the allegorical mode. For allegory in *Liber Amoris* embodies at once the contradictions inherent in the modern desire for possession and the necessity of dissent and contradiction in all forms of representation – a point to which we will return later. S's quasi-allegorical character registers, at the level of representation, the painful contradictions and tensions of the desire she elicits in him, even as her beauty reconciles him to that pain. It thus makes sense that in another scene of *Liber Amoris*, H almost ecstatically likens S to an explicitly allegorical figure: "Do you know I saw a picture, the very pattern of her, the other day, at Dalkeith Palace (Hope finding Fortune in the Sea). . . and the resemblance drove me almost out of my senses" (112). Hazlitt's biographer notes that "the naked figure of Fortune conjured up so overwhelmingly the image he cherished of her that on the following Monday, haunted by the memory of it, he hurried down to [John Robertson] Bell's house in Pilrig Street to get his friend to accompany him on a second visit to Dalkeith" (*Hazlitt*, 332–3). *A Catalogue of the Pictures at Dalkeith House* describes the painting thus: "Fortune, a nude female figure, lies on the sea, on a raft on which are objects emblematical of riches. Truth, a flying figure, slightly draped, raises her. In the right hand of the painting are fairy and satyr children, some swimming"

(333). That the figure that drew Hazlitt's attention should be Fortune is fitting; we are returned to Joseph Addison's fickle virgin, William Hogarth's queen of the lottery, and Burney's dismaying standard-bearer. S *is* Fortune, notorious for her fickleness, and for the pleasures and pains she brings. That Hazlitt should take the figure rescuing her in the painting to be Hope and not Truth makes perfect sense: it is not truth but simply wishfulness that will save Fortune now, for speculation is no longer feared but willfully embraced. H does sometimes worry that S will prove to be another "bubble" – "no object in nature is substantial, real, but false and hollow, like her faith on which I built my trust" (68) – but he constantly gives signs that he knows that it is his own imagination, his hope, that sustains the image of S, the woman who is at once his Pamela, his St. Cecilia, and his Fortune.

II

The masochistic eroticism of *Liber Amoris* can, then, be linked to a further development of the marketplace logic of desire at work in *The Wanderer*. But while the political is subsumed in the economic in Burney's treatment of erotic life, in Hazlitt's treatment of it the opposite tends to be true. Burney focuses on demonstrating the dignity of labor and the value of its products. But for Hazlitt, who does not distance himself from revolutionary politics the way Burney does, the issue of the dignity of the common people is first and foremost a political one. H himself is fully conscious of the fact that his courtship of S functions as a form of political critique. This critique is most obviously manifested in his straightforwardly egalitarian pronouncements:

H. Yes, you told me yourself he left you . . . because "the pride of birth would not permit a union." – For myself, I would leave a throne to ascend to the heaven of thy charms . . . S. If the proud scorn us here, in that place we shall all be equal. H. Do not look so – do not talk so – unless you would drive me mad. I could worship you at this moment. (13)

H responds with affection and excitement upon hearing S's remark on equality, and sometimes even construes her resistance to his overtures in the terms of 1790s radicalism: when S speaks of her attraction to the single life H asks, "Do you mean on account of its liberty?" (33).

Liber Amoris invokes not only the language of liberty and equality but also the notion of political consent and the related economic category of contract. Walter Benn Michaels argues that the masochistic contract represents the logical extension, even to the point of absurdity, of capitalistic, democratic contract relations.[15] The "absurdity" here lies in the fact that the masochist demands for himself absolute power of contract but with the goal of rendering himself powerless.[16] H's relationship with S reveals just such a paradox; he sets his own self-abasement within a framework of mutual consensuality. As we have seen, Hazlitt argues that the sexual possession of a woman is not enough for the modern lover: only a fully consensual relationship can gratify him. Thus H struggles to forge a relationship with S through agreements. We see this from the first vignette, in which H convinces S to consider her likeness to the painted miniature. S's every concession, however trivial it might be, functions for H as a covenant, a tacit agreement to permit him to continue "worshiping" her. Although S is typically reluctant to agree to H's quirky "contracts," he experiences them as the very stuff of their relationship. When there is trouble between them, H complains, not that S does not love him, but that she does not "[keep] her faith with [him]" (43).

The language of liberty, equality, and contract notwithstanding, the book's political commentary inheres mainly in its reproduction of hierarchy in deliberately provocative forms. H grants a lower-class woman sovereign powers, thereby challenging "Legitimacy" – hereditary monarchy and its institutional and cultural supports. Although Hazlitt's biographer Stanley Jones assumes that Walker was simply wishy-washy, unsure of her desires, Hazlitt himself represents her not as flighty but as possessed of a dominating willfulness. If S neglects H or offers favors to others it is not because she is a lighthearted coquette but because she is tyrannical with her affections, offering them only when and where she will, and making clear through the alternation of giving and withholding that both are entirely in her control. After all, S's fickleness is not the fickleness of an ordinary girl but of Fortune herself; she is not simply whimsical but deliberately coldhearted. Although Hazlitt's interest in the historical Walker was initially piqued by her forwardness, and although he did what he could to secure her in marriage, it was her distance, her power over him, that provided her lasting charm. As H explains to S, "Your charms are irresistible as your will is inexorable" (9). Much as H laments this tyrannical quality, it is clear

[15] Walter Benn Michaels, "The Phenomenology of Contract," in Michaels, *The Gold Standard and the Logic of Naturalism* (Berkeley: University of California Press, 1987).

[16] In the case of male masochism, this apparent absurdity is further heightened by the inversion of typical gender relations. If, as Carole Pateman argues, contract theorists "transformed the law of male sex-right into its modern contractual form," founding modern civil society on an unstated sexual contract, masochism both reveals and mockingly inverts this state of affairs (*The Sexual Contract* [Stanford: Stanford University Press, 1988], 3).

that he is also drawn to it; even in the final pages of *Liber Amoris*, H admits that "the ascendancy of her will, her determined perseverance in what she undertakes to do, has something admirable in it, approaching to the heroic" (178). Enjoying S's ascendant will, H gladly plays the complementary role of abased minion: "you see how I droop and wither under your displeasure! Thou art divine, my love, and canst make me either more or less than mortal. Indeed I am thy creature, thy slave – I only wish to live for your sake – I would gladly die for you – " (8). H's language exceeds the rhetoric of sensibility, just as the autobiographical facts of Hazlitt's infatuation reveal more than just a keen desire for love. H does not love S in spite of her scornfulness; he loves her because of it. He asks of S, "How can I escape from you, when every new occasion, even your cruelty and scorn, brings out some new charm. Nay, your rejection of me, by the way in which you do it, is only a new link added to my chain" (12–13). This inversion of typical power relations – one expects the middle-class man to have power over the lower-class girl – constitutes a direct challenge to social norms.

Liber Amoris challenges hierarchy not only directly, by means of inversion, but also ironically, by rendering hierarchical relations ridiculous in themselves. Sarah, with her sublime power and inexorable will, is insistently likened to a monarch: "Your power over me is that of sovereign grace and beauty" (8); "by her soft looks and queen-like grace (which men might fall down and worship) I swear to live and die for her!" (43); "above all, tyrannous love sits throned, crowned with her graces" (79). But whereas we are encouraged to see and appreciate the sovereign charms of Burney's Juliet, Hazlitt gives us enough negative information about S to make a mockery of this language.[17] Even as he celebrates her queenly charms, H suggests that S is really just a common young woman: selfish, devious, and immodest. Her habit of sitting on H's lap, for instance, does not easily accord with his description of her as regal in bearing. Extreme self-abasement before this woman undeniably has an element of the absurd in it, with the result that the reader begins to imagine that "sovereignty" is simply the product of the foolish self-abasement of those who support it. H's coupling of the language of sovereignty with the language of slavery works to heighten

---

[17] Both Gilles Deleuze and Theodor Reik speak of the element of contempt in the masochist's submission; his pursuit of punishment is too enthusiastic, so that it finally functions as a "demonstration of the law's absurdity" (Deleuze, "Coldness and Cruelty," in *Masochism* [New York: Zone Books, 1989], 88; see also Reik, *Masochism in Modern Man*, trans. Margaret Beigel and Gertrud Kurth [New York: Farrar, Straus and Co., 1941]). In *Liber Amoris* we sense a similar contempt, though its object is not the law but "tyranny."

this effect, for it suggests that monarchy is sustained not by the loyalty of citizens or subjects, proud of their English liberties, but by the imposition of inhuman constraints upon hapless, abject slaves. Although superficially similar to the courtly love rhetoric of vassalage, the language of slavery is distinctive, and in the early nineteenth century it could not but sound uncomfortably literal given the recent battle for abolition and the passage of Lord Grenville's abolition bill in 1807. Lines like the following would be apt to rasp against the nerves of readers accustomed to hearing accounts of the pernicious effects of slavery: "Ah! if you can never be mine, still let me be your proud and happy slave" (39). Indeed, Hazlitt regarded Castlereagh's willingness to accede to Tallyrand's request for a continuation of the slave trade in France as one of the more galling outcomes of the reassertion of legitimacy in France. It is fitting then that H adopts the posture of a slave at the same moment that he finds in S a monarch to adore. Hazlitt would have us understand that monarchy and slavery go hand in hand, so that the willing support of monarchy must appear absurd.[18]

Hazlitt's assessment of hierarchy in *Liber Amoris* is in fact even more complicated than this preliminary sketch suggests. For as deeply distrustful of hierarchy as he was, he also found it compelling; he challenged tyranny throughout his life, using his essays as a medium through which to complain of everything from the decisions made at the Congress of Vienna to William Wordsworth's political "apostasy," but there was always a part of him uncomfortable with contemporary models of democracy. In *William Hazlitt: Critic of Power*, Kinnaird argues that Hazlitt was fascinated by the idea of power and that this fascination is reflected in all aspects of his thought. Hazlitt speaks of the love of power as the original sin (*Works*, XII, 348), and Kinnaird argues that Hazlitt considers "this subjection of human personality to the 'innate perversity' (12.136) of its passions" the fundamental weakness of humans (*Critic of Power*, 88). The problem is not that people are essentially evil; it is simply that the love of power produces evil effects: "There is a love of power in the mind independent of the love of good, and this love of power, when it comes to be opposed to the spirit of good, and is leagued with the spirit of evil to commit it with greediness, is wickedness" (*Works*, XII, 348). Hazlitt loves the idea of democracy in part because he believes so fully in the strength of the individual desire for

---

[18] While Burney would have us take seriously the power exerted by an apparently common woman, Hazlitt never quite allows us to do so. In this respect, then, we do see a lurking conservatism within Hazlitt's radicalism, as he makes use of one traditional notion regarding proper social relations (working-class women do not deserve the submission of middle-class men) to undermine another (monarchs deserve the submission of their subjects).

dominion – even as he recognizes that that very desire makes democracy difficult to achieve. He claims, moreover, that to the extent that ordinary men are relatively powerless, they tend to identify with and enjoy the power of those who have dominion over them. And this is not always and only bad; as Kinnaird explains:

a king provides a "royal self" for the love of power among his subjects, and since this compensatory image of unconscious desire appeals to all members of society and transcends envy, it "baffles" civil discord and fosters a mutual accommodation of interests, interposing a barrier in the will itself "to the tormenting strife and restless importunity of the passions in individuals."(*Critic of Power*, 108)

The vicarious identification with power is one of the few safe ways for individuals to manage their love of power. *Liber Amoris* puts this theory of monarchical relations into erotic practice. The book does not simply offer a carnivalesque subversion of normative power relations; the power imaginatively conferred upon S serves as a guard against egotism even as it makes available a mediated pleasure in power. The private character of this relationship makes it a safe forum for the indulgence in tyranny. At the same time, H's obeisance has a therapeutic value: submission to the will of another serves to baffle his own. It makes sense, then, that as important as freedom is to Hazlitt, in *Liber Amoris* H is eager to relinquish his freedom to S; his divorce is represented as a freedom which he can then offer up to her: "I will take my Freedom (a glad prize) and lay it at her feet" (85).

Hazlitt goes further still, to suggest that suffering has, in itself, a liberating effect. In "On the Love of Life," Hazlitt argues that the desire for power makes us cling to life in a way that only extraordinary suffering can challenge: "Passion, imagination, selfwill, the sense of power, the very consciousness of our existence, bind us to life, and hold us fast in its chains, as by a magic spell"; only "an extremity either of bodily or mental suffering" can break these chains.[19] The love of power is itself a subjection of sorts, one that can be ended only by a painful subjection to something else. If the selfwill is linked to "restless desires" and "tormenting passions" (*Works*, IV, 1), H's relationship with S is a practical experiment in the management of such passions. H's selfish desires, when focused on S, can never be satisfied and thus become the means – necessarily painful – of their own undoing. Paradoxically, then, the battle against "selfwill" can be sustained through acts of willfulness. Thus even as H presents himself as victim, his efforts to manipulate S through "contracts," gifts, and the display of his suffering, are fully apparent. This manipulation has played no small part in rendering the

[19] From *The Round Table* of 1817, in Hazlitt, *Works*, IV, 3.

book distasteful to many modern critics. Indeed, Hazlitt's friend Peter
George Patmore found his treatment of Walker deliberately provocative
and inappropriate. In *Liber Amoris*, H writes in a letter of response to
Patmore, "You say it is my own 'outrageous conduct' that has estranged
her; nay, I have been *too gentle* with her" (80). Ultimately, H's conduct provokes even Patmore himself, so that he, too, can serve H as disciplinarian. H
writes in another letter to him, "I received your letter this morning, and I
kiss the rod not only with submission, but gratitude" (57).

It is not only in its representations of hierarchy that *Liber Amoris* comments upon the issue of social equality that so obsessed Hazlitt the political
essayist. Even the suspense that is so fundamental to H's eroticism has, for
Hazlitt, a philosophical and political import. For Hazlitt believed that post-
poning gratification and focusing one's interest on the future could, in itself,
have the effect of curbing one's egotism and thirst for power. One of
Hazlitt's first and longest essays was on the relation of altruism to time.
Written when his goal was to be a philosopher, it remained throughout
his life one of the essays of which he was most proud. "An Essay on the Principles of Human Action" was intended to serve as a refutation of the materialist view of the innate selfishness of man. Hazlitt's argument runs as
follows: we all take a personal interest in events of the past and present,
measuring them against our own needs and desires. But since the future
is uncertain, an imaginary realm, our private interest in it can be no
greater than our interest in the future welfare of others:

I admit that you have a peculiar, emphatic, incommunicable and exclusive interest
or fellow-feeling in the first two of these selves [those of past and present]; but I
deny resolutely and unequivocally that you have any such natural, absolute, unavoidable, and mechanical interest in the last self, or in your future being, the interest
you take in it being necessarily the offspring of understanding and imagination
(aided by habit and circumstances), like that which you take in the welfare of
others, and yet this last interest is the only one that is ever the object of rational
and voluntary pursuit, or that ever comes into competition with the interests
of others.[20]

The self we imagine in the future, because it exists only in imagination, does
not interest us any more than the future selves of others. Our interest in self
and other being thus balanced, it should be possible – at least with regard to
the future – to act in accordance with genuinely altruistic motives. This

---

[20] William Hazlitt, "Self-Love and Benevolence," in *William Hazlitt: Selected Writings*, ed. Jon Cook
(Oxford: Oxford University Press, 1991), 167.

thesis, one of the first fruits of Hazlitt's intellectual labors and one to which he returned over the course of his life, was of foundational importance to him. It had, moreover, profound political implications: as Kinnaird argues, "fortified by his own theory of 'disinterestedness'" (*Critic of Power*, 9) Hazlitt was able to avoid complete disenchantment in the face of political setbacks. In Kinnaird's words, Hazlitt strove to maintain "the loyalty to the future . . . that a commitment to ideal values required" (40). For while Hazlitt wrote as a moral philosopher, and as the child of dissent, concerned with benevolence and human freedom in purely abstract terms, he also wrote from the point of view of a man who, all his life, would support democracy and reform. The future was for him the realm of democratic possibility. Of course, given the anxious English retaliation against the revolutionary French, the advent of an egalitarian social order in England seemed indeed to have been postponed indefinitely. But Hazlitt's interest in the future *qua* future involved him in a paradox the complications of which extend beyond any such practical considerations. For to be fully mindful of an imaginary future where all interests are equal requires an absorption in the future as such, with the result that the actual achievement of equality comes to seem unimportant.

Given Hazlitt's fascination with the future, the representation of time in *Liber Amoris* takes on additional meaning. Within the text itself H's capacity to enjoy the present is very limited; whatever kindness S shows him serves only to stimulate anxiety about the likelihood of her kindness in the future. H's obsession with the future highlights a familiar paradox: once arrived, the future is simply the present. S's distance and independence, much as H bemoans them, serve the vital function of ensuring that her potential to gratify him will never be realized, that it will remain safely lodged in futurity. Hence the stifled character of the narrative: the advent of the future is breathlessly awaited but the arrival of the ideal must be perpetually postponed. H not only directly relinquishes power in his relationship with S but also uses the relationship to orient himself toward the future – the domain where self and other stand side by side – so as to lose himself in its rich possibilities. Even if the future, in its ideal form, can never arrive, the consciousness of it, the waiting posture itself, becomes a useful exercise in the management of the self. Hazlitt the philosopher is determined to shatter not just what he calls the "rock" of self-interest but also the "rock" of the self: "if I do not (round and smooth as it is) cut it into three pieces, and show that two parts in three are substance and the third and principal part shadow, never believe me again" (166). To relinquish our self-interest requires taking apart the very self we imagine to be the bedrock of that interest. By adopting a submissive posture, H enlists the help of another in this act of undoing.

This self-shattering orientation to the future shapes not only H's actions within the book but also the form of the book itself. The "plot" of *Liber Amoris* is devoid not only of consummation but even of substantial action, and the book's organization is designed to heighten the sensation of waiting, of suspense. If we look at Part I, for instance, we see that the chapter titles are suggestive of some kind of linear development or progression: "The Picture," "The Invitation," "The Message," "The Flageolet," "The Confession," "The Quarrel," "The Reconciliation." In fact, however, these chapters are not arranged in chronological order; thus, for instance, the confession recounted in the fifth vignette occurs before the scene described in the fourth, in which the subject of that confession is already common knowledge. The result of this organizational scheme is that it forces the reader to enter H's world of suspense, a world where events, though heavy with meaning, do not lead, in progressive fashion, toward a definitive end. This is, in effect, a world where causal relations have been disarticulated; individual scenes do not form part of a larger development – rather, each one embodies in itself the larger story, a story of ungratified desire. Thus Hazlitt makes his own art like his vision of Shakespeare's, in which "years are melted down to moments, and every instant teems with fate."[21] Parts II and III of the book, unlike Part I, each consist of a series of letters to a single correspondent, and each series is chronologically arranged. But even here the return to events we have learned of already in earlier parts of the book creates a feeling of retrograde motion. The form of the book itself serves in this way to underscore the pleasure but also the pain and even the tedium of suspense.[22]

---

[21] Lecture 3 on Shakespeare and Milton, in Hazlitt, *Works*, V, 51.

[22] In its handling of temporality, *Liber Amoris* brings to mind another of the fundamental characteristics of masochism as defined by psychoanalysts, what Reik calls the "suspense factor." "Masochistic tension vacillates more strongly than any other sexual tension between the pleasurable and the anxious, and it tends to perpetuate this state" (*Masochism*, 59). Throughout *Liber Amoris* H complains of the suffering that suspense causes him; he writes to his friend that he "can bear any thing but this cruel suspense," but goes on to confess that "I sit and indulge my grief by the hour together; my weakness grows upon me" (55). Reik remarks that being hung or suspended is a favorite masochistic practice because "it gives a functional objectivity to the sensation of suspense" (*Masochism*, 60); *Liber Amoris* lacks the paraphernalia of masochism at its most dramatic, but H does say that "I cannot describe the weakness of mind to which she has reduced me. This state of suspense is like hanging in the air by a single thread that exhausts all your strength to keep hold of it" (60). Reik argues that the attraction to suspense reflects the fact that for the masochist the tension of anxiety has become intertwined with sexual tension, until finally it has become pleasurable in itself and serves as a substitute for release or orgasm (*Masochism*, 64). The masochist meets punishment or discomfort first so as to dispense with them and clear the field for pleasure, but that pleasure

Hazlitt's determination to shatter the rock of self-interest is played out not only within the book but also in the very fact of its publication. His indiscretions regarding his attachment to Walker were notorious, and have been variously accounted for by critics and biographers, who themselves often show signs of embarrassment at his behavior. The inclusion of ruminations on Walker in essays he was composing at the time of his involvement with her sometimes seems to be a matter of simple carelessness but at others to be a meaningful mistake. Jones writes that "Ever since his return to London he had been unable to resist the melancholy temptation to pour out his troubles to anyone who lent a sympathetic ear; in his loneliness and misery he responded to the slightest encouraging word or look, from friend, from acquaintance, from stranger" (*Hazlitt*, 334). Further, Hazlitt sometimes deliberately exaggerated elements of his story and invented "outrageous details, partly no doubt from perverse bravado" revealing "a perverse impulse to exaggerate his degradation" (332). The culmination of this perverse bravado was the decision to publish *Liber Amoris*. The book is presented as the collected papers of an anonymous man now passed away. But given the advance publicity that Hazlitt's own talking produced, it took only eight days for the attribution to be made and the autobiographical reference recognized (337). One of Hazlitt's Victorian editors, Richard Le Gallienne, wonders how even a need for money could have driven Hazlitt to an act of such disastrous imprudence: "a man could hardly have done a more deliberately stupid injury to his fame."[23] Not surprisingly, the publication elicited an explosion of hostility from Hazlitt's enemies, who took every advantage of the opportunity to lambast him, not just as a writer but also as a person. Marilyn Butler has suggested that all such attacks are founded on a fundamental misapprehension of Hazlitt's aims in *Liber Amoris*, which she describes as satiric. Butler is quite right to underscore the satiric and ironic qualities of the text, but given its autobiographical element there was little chance that it would not redound negatively upon its author. Hazlitt's humiliation was thus witnessed not just by Walker but by a broad public.[24]

---

tends increasingly to be deferred. For Hazlitt, on the other hand, this deferral can be accounted for in terms of economic and political motives.

[23] Reprinted in Hazlitt, *Liber Amoris*, 220.

[24] Butler, "Satire and the Images of Self." Hazlitt's attraction to publicity and intersubjectivity – both political commitments – give a special significance to the presence of what Reik would call the demonstrative feature: "the suffering, discomfort, humiliation, and disgrace are being shown and so to speak put on display" (*Masochism*, 72); "Even in cases where there is no question of a perversion in the grosser meaning of the word, where masochism signifies an attitude toward life, this

Kinnaird argues that the "most original and least perishable part of Hazlitt's theory of 'disinterestedness'" is "his sense of self as always in some mode or degree *intersubjective*, as existing and acting only in tension with real or imagined otherness" (*Critic of Power*, 58). H intentionally sets about losing his own sense of self in S: "I feel that I could grow to her, body and soul" (62). But it is precisely S's ultimate unattainability that guarantees H's self-loss: "Ah! if you are never to be mine, I shall not long be myself. I cannot go on as I am. My faculties leave me: I think of nothing, I have no feeling about any thing but thee: thy sweet image has taken possession of me, haunts me, and will drive me to distraction" (2). Indeed, the complete loss of S leaves H as insubstantial and ghostly as the "future self": "She was my life – it is gone from me, and I am grown spectral!" (68). As the book draws to a close H tells J. S. K. that "I was transformed too, no longer human . . . I was taken out of myself, wrapt into another sphere" (156).

This self-abnegating commitment to intersubjectivity has broad formal implications. It helps us to understand, for instance, Hazlitt's championship of dramatic literary modes. Drama, being constitutively intersubjective, both in itself and as performed before an audience, seemed to Hazlitt to provide a happy alternative to the politically dangerous "egotism" of contemporary poetry, embodied at its best in the poetry of Wordsworth. For Hazlitt, such egotism urges people to put their own interests above the public good, which in turn leads them to seek power over others to ensure their ability to gratify those interests. Much as he admired Wordsworth, Hazlitt feared that "Wordsworth's claim to be representative is at odds with his withdrawal from those engagements with audiences and with other writers which would validate that claim."[25] Thus it was drama and not lyric poetry that ultimately provided the template for Hazlitt's own style as essayist, which aimed at a "disinterestedness" founded on its openness to multiple points of view, multiple interests. For Hazlitt, it was not possible simply to rise above the fray of political argument, as Wordsworth sometimes claimed to do; liberty and democracy relied upon open and sustained contestation. Hazlitt proclaimed that he had "little ambition 'to set a throne or chair of state in the understandings of other men'" (*Works*, VIII, 6–7); his essays were therefore designed to have the quality of an exchange rather than a sermon or lecture. Hazlitt's conversational and flexible style, and even his habit of frequent quotation, approach his ideal of democratic

---

demonstrative feature is distinctly recognizable" (74). Again, Hazlitt provides a political logic for understanding what psychoanalysts would consider a typical feature of masochism.
[25] Cook, from his Introduction to *William Hazlitt: Selected Writings*, xxxiii.

exchange as closely as is possible in the writing of a single man. In *Liber Amoris* this attraction to dramatic conversational style is even more fully and variously indulged. Not only does H describe his encounters with S in dramatic terms – "We had a famous parting-scene" (48) – but he writes the bulk of Part I in the form of dramatic dialogues. Even in Parts II and III, the emphasis on intersubjectivity is generically preserved by means of the epistolary format. Within those letters, moreover, Hazlitt sometimes lets events unfold through dialogue: "S. 'Is it nothing, your exposing me to the whole house in the way you did the other evening?' H. 'Nay, that was the consequence of your cruel reception of me'" (150).

The dramatic forms to which Hazlitt is drawn have the further virtue of enacting a type of role-playing that makes not just relationships generally but power relations in particular appear attractively labile. The dramatic nature of *Liber Amoris* extends well beyond the use of speech prefixes; it shapes characterization itself. The representation of H and S does not aim at psychological verisimilitude. The characters are not only described by means of a heightened rhetoric that makes them appear larger than life, but their own speeches are often little more than a tissue of literary allusions. It is as if these highly artificial characters – these ciphers, H and S – are conscious of the fact that they are merely playing a part: the part of the Romeo-like lover, willing to sacrifice his life for his beloved; the lover made mad, like Othello, with jealousy; the faithless woman, heartless as Cressida; the reluctant servant-girl, chaste like Pamela.[26] Insofar as these roles are presented *as* roles, power relations appear to take the form of a game, and insofar as the players can find pleasure even in powerlessness, this is a game they cannot lose.

---

[26] The artificiality of these roles denaturalizes ordinary hierarchies, including even gender hierarchies. In *Liber Amoris* H's ostensibly feminine emotional qualities are actually given a physical correlative; he closes a letter to Patmore thus: "I must break off here; for the *hysterica passio* comes upon me, and threatens to unhinge my reason" (91). Those of Hazlitt's early critics who had an animus against him used *Liber Amoris* to argue that he was emasculated; Hazlitt's late nineteenth-century admirer Richard Le Gallienne, sensing that the problem is a formal and stylistic one, wondered with dismay at the absence in *Liber Amoris* of the "bracing manliness" and "virile English" that he so admired in Hazlitt's other writings (from Le Gallienne's 1893 Introduction to *Liber Amoris*, reprinted in Hazlitt, *Liber Amoris*, 229). Claudia Johnson argues that "whereas many literary and social historians hold that sentimentality spelled the 'feminization' of culture in general and of men in particular, I will maintain that [during the 1790s] sentimentality entailed instead the 'masculinization' of formerly feminine gender traits, and that the affective practices associated with it are valued *not* because they are understood as feminine, but precisely and only insofar as they have been recoded as masculine" (*Equivocal Beings: Politics, Gender and Sentimentality in the 1790s* [Chicago: University of Chicago Press, 1995], 14). The feelings of which H is so proud in *Liber Amoris* accomplish just such a recoding; Hazlitt's H is not just a creature of sensibility but a downright hysteric. But whereas Johnson claims that the man of feeling is preeminently a conservative man, we can see that indulgence in passionate feeling can also be put in the service of a democratic program.

It is fitting, then, that Hazlitt finds in drama a source of suspenseful erotic pleasure, a pleasure reminiscent of the pleasure H takes in his interactions with S. In spite of the transience of performance, Hazlitt experiences the drama as time-stopping; as Jones describes it, "Playgoing had a unique sense for him: the privilege of inhabiting a special region of time arrested between past and future, the paradox of a real suspension of events bodied forth in an ideal succession of incidents" (*Hazlitt*, 85). Hazlitt believed that the works of his favorite dramatist, Shakespeare, called into play

all the resources of the understanding and all the energies of the will; irritated by obstacles or yielding to them; rising from small beginnings to its utmost height; now drunk with hope, now stung to madness, now sunk in despair, now blown to air with a breath, now raging like a torrent. The human soul is made the sport of fortune, the prey of adversity: it is stretched on the wheel of destiny, in restless ecstacy. The passions are in a state of projection. Years are melted down to moments, and every instant teems with fate. (*Works*, V, 51)

This passage could as easily describe H's affair with S as a Shakespearean play. As in Hogarth and Burney, fortune plays an important role, acting as a tyrant who provides ecstasy through adversity. The reversals of fortune can be linked, moreover, to another feature of drama – and erotic submission – that was dear to Hazlitt: its dialectical quality. Jones notes that Hazlitt had a powerful "sense of passional dialectic at work in drama, especially Shakespearean tragedy" (*Hazlitt*, 192). This is dialectic of a particular kind, a master-slave interchange that does not necessarily work its way forward toward greater freedom.[27] Instead, *Liber Amoris* suggests that practical democracy is an ongoing drama, a public debate rife with reversals and shifts of power.

It makes sense therefore that Hazlitt took a kind of pride in his feelings for Walker. Although most modern and contemporary critics regard Hazlitt's behavior with Walker, if not disturbing, at least distasteful, his account of it in *Liber Amoris* cannot be reduced to a silly story about frustrated desire or a case study in personal pathology. The book simultaneously challenges hierarchy and shows the difficulty of truly eliminating it; it recapitulates the power relations of absolutism as it mocks them; and it provides a forum in which to practice the abandonment

---

[27] Deleuze describes a similar phenomenon at work in Masoch's writing: "the masochistic hero appears to be educated and fashioned by the authoritarian woman whereas basically it is he who forms her . . . Dialectic does not simply mean the free interchange of discourse, but implies transpositions or displacements of this kind, resulting in a scene being enacted simultaneously on several levels with reversals and reduplications in the allocation of roles and discourse" ("Coldness and Cruelty," 22).

of self to another and to the vagaries of a future in which altruism and democracy, however difficult of realization in a concrete present, can enjoy at least a shadowy existence.

III

Recognizing the political valence of the eroticism of *Liber Amoris* helps to make sense of it in terms of Hazlitt's larger oeuvre. The book is not simply an anomaly, an autobiographical eyesore in the larger landscape of Hazlitt's writings, but intimately linked to his development as a political thinker and writer. It was composed during a period of crisis in Hazlitt's political thinking, a crisis centered on the figure of Napoleon Bonaparte. Hazlitt's attachment to Napoleon in his prime was itself an uneasy compromise solution to his ambivalence regarding power. Napoleon was a self-made man of talents who fought on behalf of a new republic. At the same time, he was the very incarnation of the man of power, someone with whom others could pleasurably identify and in whom they could lose their own "selfwill." This latter appeal helps to account for Hazlitt's continuing attachment to him even after he crowned himself Emperor. Napoleon's losses at Leipzig and Waterloo, and his death in exile in 1821, were great blows for Hazlitt. It is not by chance that the death of Napoleon and the reassertion of legitimacy were followed by the Walker affair. Not only have biographers tended to link the two – Jones titles his chapter on Napoleon's defeat "The End of Public Hopes" and his chapter on the Walker affair "The End of Private Hopes" – but Hazlitt himself did, remarking that he hoped to find in his relationship with Walker some compensation for political disappointments: imagining her face of "angel sweetness," he is recalled to "years that are fled . . . I am in the Louvre once more. The sun of Austerlitz has not set. It still shines here – in my heart; and he, the son of glory, is not dead, nor ever shall [be], to me . . . All that I have thought and felt has not been in vain."[28] *Liber Amoris* represents an effort to work through political quandaries on an emotional and erotic level.

Since Napoleon both embodied and reconciled the contradictory impulses of Hazlitt's politics – his longing for equality and democracy on the one hand, and his attraction to charismatic leaders on the other – the loss of him meant the collapse not only of Hazlitt's hopes but even of his means of constructing those hopes. The result was that Hazlitt's political thought after Waterloo began to take two extreme, and opposed, forms.

[28] From "On Great and Little Things"; Hazlitt, *Works*, VIII, 237–8.

On the one hand, he wanted more than ever to believe in the power of common men to eradicate tyranny and establish egalitarian social institutions, while on the other he suspected that he should relinquish his old beliefs altogether and give himself over to a thoroughgoing cynicism. This internal contradiction led to a stalemate that functions as yet another determining factor in the already overdetermined stagnation or suspensefulness of *Liber Amoris*. The book strives to validate Hazlitt's faith in Napoleon by recapitulating the self-denying idealization of a powerful figure – in this case, a beautiful woman – while simultaneously trying to renounce that idealization as absurd. Insofar as the book does trace a "development," it is a development that moves in two opposed directions. *Liber Amoris* aims to imagine and represent the ideal, but each new incarnation of the ideal quickly proves untenable, so that the book comes to seem an argument for skepticism. Especially at the beginning of the book, we often see H pushing in the direction of greater idealization and abstraction, as if desperate to avoid the apparently inevitable rupture of belief. As the idealization of S becomes increasingly unworkable, H comes to seek the ideal in his act of loving her. When S proves changeable, H becomes increasingly adamant, and his heart takes on the petrified character once attributed to S: "Is my love then in the power of fortune, or of her caprice? No, I will have it lasting as it is pure; and I will make a Goddess of her, and build a temple to her in my heart, and worship her on indestructible altars, and raise statues to her: and my homage shall be unblemished . . . and when that fails the memory of it shall survive" (101). Ultimately, that merely metaphoric solidity gives way to the more perfect abstraction of memory. This movement away from materiality even at the level of artistic representation is encapsulated in a chapter entitled "Perfect Love":

> Perfect love has this advantage in it, that it leaves the possessor of it nothing farther to desire. There is one object (at least) in which the soul finds absolute content . . . The truth of passion keeps pace with and outvies the extravagance of mere language. There are no words so fine, no flattery so soft, that there is not a sentiment beyond them, that it is impossible to express, at the bottom of the heart where true love is . . . Perfect love reposes on the object of its choice, like the halcyon on the wave; and the air of heaven is around it. (102–3)

The loved object affords not only absolute content, or happiness, but also absolute content or substance – it is the one essentially real thing. But again, gradually this substantiality becomes a quality of the love itself, to which mere representation is inadequate. In the end, love becomes a more concrete, stable thing than its object, which is as changeable and formless as the sea. Hazlitt's perpetually receding idealism is thus refined to the point of vanishing.

Over the course of the narrative, the loss of faith in the ideal is simultaneously passionately felt and wryly disavowed, and this contradiction is negotiated by granting certain figures in the narrative an almost magical ability to contain such tension. The first of these figures is clearly S herself. She is not only idealized and objectified but is also associated with a series of idols, the most important of which are the allegorical figure of Fortune and the miniature portrait reminiscent of St. Cecilia. She is both giver and taker and divine intercessor. But the outstanding talisman of the tale is, tellingly, a bronze figure of Napoleon that H refers to as "the little image." This figurine appears intermittently throughout the narrative. S tells H that it resembles a former lover to whom she remains devoted, and he insists that in that case she should keep it. Thereafter, H speaks of it as if it had the power to keep him and S together, and is surprised when it seems no longer to have that power: "'Well, then, for the sake of *the little image!*' The appeal seemed to have lost its efficacy; the charm was broken; she remained immovable" (131). Such moments dramatize the extent to which H's romantic life is shaped by his political investments rather than his understanding of the inner life of his beloved.

The focus of H's romantic idolatry, S is thus but another version of the man he calls "the God of my idolatry" (36).[29] H links S to Napoleon not only by entrusting her with the "little image," but also by insisting upon her likeness to it; he repeatedly refers to S as "the statue." The figurine reproduces S's power and coldness, as well as her object-function, in intensified and miniaturized form; it serves, as it were, as a second-order fetish, just as money is arguably a sort of second-order commodity fetish. For like money, "the little image" is not only desirable in itself but mediates between H and the object of his desire. These various links between S and the little image reveal just how complicated the relation of the personal to the political is in this book. That is, personal relations are not simply

---

[29] For Freud, the fetish is the image of or substitute for the female phallus, and the choice of the fetish object is determined by the last object seen before the absence of the maternal penis is discovered. Deleuze describes the fetish as a "frozen, arrested, two-dimensional image, a photograph to which one returns repeatedly to exorcise the dangerous consequences of movement, the harmful discoveries that result from exploration; it represents the last point at which it was still possible to believe" ("Coldness and Cruelty," 31). Hazlitt's fetish, too, is an emblem of female power, but it signifies that power in political terms: Napoleon represents the power that can be achieved by the common man, and this is the power that H grants S. Napoleon had died in exile just a year before Hazlitt's infatuation with Walker. The figure of Bonaparte does, then, represent for Hazlitt the radical the "last point at which it was still possible to believe."

like political relations, analogues for them, but become in themselves a venue for political experience. Given this fact, H's belief that giving S the figure will help him to secure her enjoys a plausibility that is absent on the surface; under ordinary conditions, after all, a man does not try to advance his own courtship by giving his beloved the image of another man. Considering the weight of meaning borne by the little figure, it is no surprise that the moment of its first appearance, when its significance is determined, should function as the happiest moment in the book, while the moment of its destruction should function as the bitterest. In a climactic scene towards the end of the book, H finally rejects the masochistic arrangement emblematized by the figure: "I was still to be tantalized, tortured, made the cruel sport of one, for whom I would have sacrificed all . . . I then dashed the little Buonaparte on the ground, and stamped upon it, as one of her instruments of mockery" (135). In this scene H formally gives up on the possibility of finding love with S and proclaims that he has renounced her forever. But he also renounces the idealized object (both S and Napoleon) through which he had mocked tyranny and relinquished his own drive for power. The destruction of the figure has the status of a crisis moment within an otherwise stagnant narrative precisely because it not only enacts H's loss of faith in Napoleonic politics but also ruptures the suspense that reflects Hazlitt's faith in the future as an ideal realm.

It is largely on this scene that any sense of narrative conclusion must rely, for H's destruction of the figure, followed by his piercing scream and abrupt exit, seems to mark a definitive change in his relationship to S. And yet, dramatic as it is, this moment is not so definitive as it first appears. In subsequent scenes H gives the broken pieces of the figurine to S, who, much to his delight, has them mended. H's discovery that S has been meeting another man, an ex-lodger, serves as the final reason to end the affair, and the book ultimately closes on a note of dismissal, but even the book's conclusion does not sound particularly conclusive: "Her image seems fast 'going into the wastes of time,' like a weed that the wave bears farther and farther from me. Alas! thou poor hapless weed, when I entirely lose sight of thee, and forever, no flower will ever bloom on earth to glad my heart again!" (182). There is something abstract and forced in this ending, with its exclamation marks and high-flown rhetoric trying to do the work of real conviction. Indeed, in Hazlitt's life the infatuation was to linger on. He had a friend stay at the boarding-house to make a test of Walker's chastity, a test that was, not surprisingly, to prove inconclusive. As late as September 1823, when Hazlitt was in town he spent nights watching Walker's door (*Hazlitt*, 348). At the same time, Hazlitt never entirely renounced his

attachment to Napoleon, and late in life he devoted himself to writing a cel-
ebratory biography of him.

It seems, in fact, that in the end no act of Walker's could have caused
Hazlitt to relinquish entirely his attachment to his fictional notion of S.
For in the theatrical world of H and S, consummation is, finally, beside
the point: what one wants is to inhabit a world where power is labile and
even the person who is not in control can find pleasure in its exertion. It is
a world where suspension in political quandaries could be experienced as
titillating rather than simply demoralizing. Hopeless romance was, for
Hazlitt, not just a useful venue for the disciplining of desire but one that rendered the effectiveness of that discipline ultimately inconsequential, for
through erotic submission one learned to take pleasure precisely in the contradictions and uncertainties of modern power relations. In *Liber Amoris*
Hazlitt would suggest that the "sun of Austerlitz" could indeed continue
to shine, but only in a "heart" prepared to take pleasure in disappointment.

IV

Quirky as he might have been, Hazlitt was not the only Romantic writer
notorious for producing an autobiographically charged account of sex and
politics. In *Don Juan* (1819–24), Byron combined teasingly revelatory
erotic narrative with withering political satire. This combination, as
critics have long understood, aims at more than simply *épater les bourgeois*.
While Hazlitt uses erotic relations to explore issues of equality, Byron, in
Don Juan, uses them to explore the concept of freedom. What Byron's
poem reveals is the extraordinary difficulty of defining – indeed, even of
imagining – the ideal of freedom that was the shibboleth of the political
progressives of his age. Given the novelty and extent of the ideological
work the term was expected to perform, this difficulty should perhaps
come as no surprise. After all, as Theodor Adorno reminds us, it was
not until the early nineteenth century that the groundwork was even
laid for the birth of the modern idea of freedom: "Before the formation
of the individual in the modern [Hegelian] sense . . . it is an anachronism
to talk of freedom, whether as a reality or as a challenge."[30] But for
Adorno, at least, the moment of the birth of the idea of freedom is also
the moment of its conscription; he notes that the greater the freedom
of the Kantian subject, the greater his responsibility – "Like the idealists
after him, Kant cannot bear freedom without compulsion."[31] In Byron's

---

[30] Theodor Adorno, *Negative Dialectics*, trans. E. B. Ashton (New York: Continuum, 1987), 218.
[31] *Ibid.*, 221, 232.

case, this paradox is registered first of all in the fact that, as often as the word "freedom" appears in *Don Juan*, it never describes an achieved state of being. "Freedom" takes its shape, and even its status as an ideal, only in opposition to that other charged category of the period, "tyranny." It was this opposition that, in the early phase of Byron's career, gave "freedom" its meaning, if only negatively. But this oppositional tension was to lose much of its force after the exile of Napoleon in 1814. For Byron, from that point on tyranny would appear not just malevolent but grotesquely impotent, as it does in his emasculated figures of Southey and Castlereagh. On the surface this impotence is a great boon for freedom:

> Fair Freedom! We may hold thee dear,
> When thus thy mightiest foes their fear
> In humblest guise have shown.
> Oh! ne'er may tyrant leave behind
> A brighter name to lure mankind![32]

But these lines, in their bitterness, reveal very clearly that freedom is clung to only insofar as tyranny has become unimpressive. Worse still, with the loss of its potency, tyranny can no longer generate meaningful oppositional energy. All that is left is matter without spirit, undifferentiated and meaningless:

> Weigh'd in the balance, hero dust
> Is vile as vulgar clay;
> Thy scales, Mortality! Are just
> To all that pass away;
> But yet methought the living great
> Some higher sparks should animate,
> To dazzle and dismay;
> Nor deem'd Contempt could thus make mirth
> Of these, the Conquerors of the earth. (ll. 100–8)

Tyranny, deprived of its sublimity, is superseded not by freedom but by a form of power that is not only contemptuous but contemptible.

These lines betray an important feature of the early nineteenth-century freedom/tyranny opposition: it can be used precisely to avoid thinking about the practical specifics of republicanism or democracy. As Byron's

---

[32] Byron, "Ode to Napoleon Bonaparte," ll. 86–90, in Jerome McGann, ed., *Byron* (Oxford: Oxford University Press, 1986).

lines reveal, tyranny did in fact have in the period another relatively well-defined antonym: equality. But as we saw above, the image of men having equal weight is, for Byron, literally morbid. Thus he, like many of his contemporaries, chooses to speak of the two poles of political possibility as tyranny and freedom. Unlike equality, freedom was linked to privilege. Historically, it had described not only exemption from despotic control but also immunity, franchise, nobility, and the power of self-determination. Adorno points out that "it is the nature-controlling sovereignty and its social form, dominion over people, that suggest the opposite to our consciousness: the idea of freedom. Its historical archetype is he who is topmost in hierarchies, the man who is not visibly dependent."[33] As a form of privilege, freedom is precisely not equality; it is thus no contradiction that Byron calls for freedom even as he celebrates hierarchy.

Byron's crucial insight was that his was an age in which, in the face of the diminished potency of tyranny, freedom itself had lost much of its heroic oppositional integrity. The years following Napoleon's exile were years that left many English thinkers stranded between a fear of and a nostalgic longing for genuinely sublime and compelling leaders. This longing was compounded by the fact that, at this time, even those with power did not seem to be free; in fact, Byron suggests in *Don Juan*, they were the least free of all. Even as he rails against tyranny – "I will teach, if possible, the stones / To rise against Earth's tyrants. Never let it / Be said that we still truckle unto thrones"[34] – the narrator proclaims that freedom is a practical impossibility, especially for those in power: "Most men are slaves, none more so than the great, / To their own whims and passions, and what not" (V, 195–6). This latter is a point the narrator makes repeatedly; he asks why England "boast[s] herself the free, / Who is but first of slaves? The nations are / In prison, – but the jailor, what is he? / No less a victim to the bolt and bar" (X, 537–40). The slave, in recognizing his subjection, enjoys as much freedom as is available in this age of slavery.

Deprived of its sublimity, political power becomes a matter of mere form, a force that can be conveniently measured in pounds sterling. In *Don Juan* the English cantos describe a society in which money functions as the *primum mobile*:

> Who hold the balance of the world? Who reign
> O'er Congress, whether royalist or liberal?

[33] Adorno, *Negative Dialectics*, 220.
[34] McGann, ed., *Byron, Don Juan*, Canto VIII, ll. 1076–8. All subsequent references to *Don Juan* will be to this text and will be given by canto and line number.

. . .
Who keep the world, both old and new, in pain
Or pleasure? Who make politics run glibber all?
The shade of Bonaparte's noble daring? –
Jew Rothschild, and his fellow Christian Baring. (XII, 33–40)

Nobility has been lost, and only the cold calculus of money remains. Feelings, in such a culture, are rendered as measurable quantities, pleasure and
pain, and the ability to command this pleasure and pain becomes the
only clear mark of power. Jerome Christensen, who offers the most
nuanced exploration of the ramifications of Byron's rank in an increasingly
commercialized society, argues that Byron's writing is characterized by
"strength," a virtue to be distinguished from commercialist power, one
that functions instead according to "an aristocratic symbolic economy of
expenditure."[35] This is an economy that relies on the generation of
surplus meaning, and it generates this surplus in part by virtue of its reference to a full-bodied symbolism of blood rather than the allegory that is
money. Christensen argues that "to link meaning and the body is not to
incarnate meaning but to assert that the body is more than the physical."[36]
This something "more," possessed of a potency that demands a response, has
the power to elicit the attitudes and actions that constitute freedom. I will
argue that in *Don Juan* Byron uses two quite different forms of eroticized
submission to comment on the status of freedom in his day. First, he endeavors to reanimate tyranny, to rediscover its "strength," precisely in order to
rediscover freedom, and he does this by resituating power relations in the
erotic domain so that they can be rendered fully corporeal and easily put
to the test of literal potency. To this end, he sets the bulk of his poem in
exotic locales that allow full play to an eroticized fantasy of Oriental
tyranny, a tyranny marked not by "commercialist power" but by "strength."
The poem's second vision of eroticized submission, however, is both subtler
and darker. When the eponymous hero travels to England, he discovers a
culture dominated by commercialist power, and he finds in the English a
people who delight in submitting to that power, with the result that even
their erotic lives become not only unfree but also abstract and disembodied.
Unlike Hazlitt, Byron finds these idealized forms of submission – and the
representational practices that accompany them – deeply disturbing. Yet we
find his Don Juan inexorably drawn to practice them.

---

[35] Jerome Christensen, *Lord Byron's Strength: Romantic Writing and Commercial Society* (Baltimore:
Johns Hopkins University Press, 1993), 5.
[36] *Ibid.*, 47.

V

That the resistance to abstract form in the name of freedom should seem peculiarly aristocratic is not incidental. The very formalism of the new legal and political systems of the early nineteenth century was, after all, designed to be productive of equality: "Though failing to provide us with a positive casuistry for future action, [Kant's] formalism humanely prevents the abuse of substantial-qualitative differences in favor of privilege and ideology. It stipulates the universal legal norm, and thus, despite and because of its abstractness, there survives in it something of substance: the egalitarian idea."[37] Byron's literalization of freedom as illicit sexuality serves the cause of freedom in a markedly inegalitarian way; it is not by chance that the liberating eroticism of the first part of *Don Juan* is generally fueled by hierarchical difference. Unlike earlier Jacobin writers who had treated sexual topics, and for whom sexual gratification was typically linked to the breakdown of hierarchy, Byron finds the *frisson* of sexual freedom to be most potent when experienced in the context of erotic domination. In Byron's hands eroticized submission can serve as an ideal means of practicing freedom in an age dedicated not only to hypocritical proclamations of chastity but also to abstraction, money, and the multiplication of petty tyrannies.

We see one such use of this eroticism in Canto V, in which Juan is made the love-slave of the empress Gulbayaz. The pleasure of the scene in which Juan is brought before Gulbayaz arises from its capacity to elicit in the reader two seemingly incompatible emotional responses to power. The first involves the enjoyment of seeing the protagonist – the European with whom the reader identifies in this Oriental(ist) scene – rendered a slave. Indeed, this scene is the most fantastic and dramatic of the representations of erotic submission we have seen thus far. After so many metaphoric slaves, we finally have a real one; after so much talk of men being reduced to feminine subservience, we see a man actually in drag. But the scene also provokes laughter by virtue of presenting a young man put in a position where he is forced to do precisely what the reader assumes he would most like to do: have sexual relations with a beautiful woman. The scene allows the reader both to indulge vicariously in subservience to real, corporeal power, and to scoff at such power. This doubleness is heightened by the fact that the pleasure to be derived from Juan's subservience belongs only to Juan's reader, and, perhaps, his author. Juan himself is no masochist; he is,

---

[37] Adorno, *Dialectics*, 236.

instead, a vehicle for the masochistic fantasies of others. While Juan proclaims that his "'soul loathes / The effeminate garb'" (V, 603–4), the
poem's readers are treated to a five-stanza point-by-point description of
how he looks in it. It is clear that the reader is meant to enjoy the image
of his enslavement; indeed, the reader is explicitly enjoined to fantasize
about the scene:

> Her presence was as lofty as her state;
> Her beauty of that overpowering kind,
> Whose force description only would abate:
> I'd rather leave it much to your own mind,
> Than lessen it by what I could relate
> Of forms and features; it would strike you blind
> Could I do justice to the full detail;
> So, luckily for both, my phrases fail. (V, 769–76)

This facetious stanza encodes the larger logic of Byron's Orientalist eroticism, in which dramatic scenes of submission are buffered by powerful distancing mechanisms. This distancing occurs both at the level of
characterization – Juan himself takes no delight in servitude – and at the
level of representation – lacunae, digressions, and narratorial flippancy all
protect the reader from becoming completely immersed in the erotic
fantasy. The canto simultaneously indulges the reader's longing to be con-
fronted with a fully corporealized power and his or her desire, as a free
English subject, to see that power rendered ridiculous. The tale's exotic
setting provides the perfect ground for the achievement of such opposed
ends; for the English reader, Oriental despotism seems at once a compelling
fact of nature and an absurdity. It is against the background of these two
very different perceptions of the scene that Juan's proud claim that
"'Love is for the free!'" (V, 1012) marks him at once as a hero and a
figure of fun. Both roles revitalize the spirit – at once heroic and cynical
– of opposition to tyranny.

But while the early cantos boldly make use of scenes of sexual submission to prompt the attitudes and acts that constitute "freedom," the
final cantos reveal, in strikingly pessimistic terms, that most Englishmen
practice a much more subtle and genuine form of sexual submission, a
form that, far from being productive of freedom, is actually a sign that
it has long since been renounced. While the first cantos indulge in a
dramatic but distanced fantasy of pleasurable subordination and jaunty
resistance, the final cantos abandon both drama and distance to offer a
precise analysis of English eroticism, an analysis that looks very much

like those offered by Burney and Hazlitt. Juan finds himself in the cold, formal world of English high society, where pleasure and pain are interconnected:

> And hence high life is oft a dreary void,
>   A rack of pleasures, where we must invent
> A something wherewithal to be annoy'd.
>   Bards may sing what they please about *Content*;
> *Contented*, when translated, means but cloyed;
>   And hence arise the woes of sentiment,
> Blue devils, and Blue-stockings, and Romances
> Reduced to practice and perform'd like dances. (XIV, 626–32)

Whereas Burney and Hazlitt can both find racks of pleasure that are truly compelling, for Byron the painful pleasures of high life have become routinized to the point of being empty. It is not just contentedness but content itself – meaning – that is absent here. This is a world not of "strength" but of "commercialist power." When change does occur in this place of dull routine, it takes the form of moneyed speculation:

> Every loan
> Is not a merely speculative hit,
>   But seats a nation or upsets a throne.
> Republics also get involved a bit;
>   Columbia's stock hath holders not unknown
> On 'Change (XII, 42–7)

Where power is not the privilege of wealth, it is merely the byproduct of speculation. Throughout the English cantos, the narrator refers to lotteries of various kinds: he speaks, for instance, of a powerful coterie of women as enjoying a rule of right "Which hath a little leaning to a lottery" (XIII, 650), and remarks of a widower's luck in obtaining a new bride, "I / See nought more strange in this than t'other lottery" (XII, 295–6). One response to this unjustified vacillation of power is simply to become a speculator oneself, to learn to enjoy, in Burneyesque fashion, the pleasures of risk. The narrator does indeed adopt this stance at times, indulging himself with aristocratic insouciance. After describing the common "secret prepossession" (XIV, 46) to "plunge with all your fears" (47) to the unknown, he describes his own composition as an act of speculation:

> But what's this to the purpose? you will say.
>   Gent. Reader, nothing; a mere speculation,

> For which my sole excuse is – 'tis my way . . .
>   This narrative is not meant for narration,
> But a mere airy and fantastic basis,
>   To build up common things with common places. (49–56)

He goes on to explain, "I think that were I *certain* of success, / I hardly could compose another line" (89–90), for, like Camilla and Edgar, he knows very well that "In play, there are two pleasures for your choosing – / The one is winning, and the other losing" (95–6).

But the narrator's jaunty assertions cannot entirely mask his discomfort with these insubstantial forms of power:

> I'm serious – so are all men upon paper;
>   And why should I not form my speculation,
> And hold up to the sun my little taper?
>   Mankind just now seem wrapt in meditation
> On Constitutions and Steam-boats of vapour;
>   While sages write against all procreation,
> Unless a man can calculate his means
> Of feeding brats the moment his wife weans. (XII, 161–8)

The vapourousness here modifies not just the steamboats but even the constitutions in question – everything in this culture threatens to dematerialize. The implicit reference to Thomas Malthus at this moment underscores the risk that this abstraction poses to the life of the body. Juan cannot even see England, the nation of "haughty shop-keepers" (X, 518), through this vapor, which is also a form of pollution:

> Each wreath of smoke
>   Appeared to him but as the magic vapour
> Of some alchymic furnace, from whence broke
>   The wealth of worlds (a wealth of tax and paper). (657–60)

In *Don Juan* money, that second-order fetish, never compels belief; there is no equivalent to Hazlitt's "little image" here. In this poem the idealization that undergirds the eroticism represented by Burney and Hazlitt is not trusted, either in its political or its personal form. Whereas H can at least imagine the soul "find[ing] absolute content" (102), Byron's narrator cannot. Tellingly, Canto XI, which begins the English cantos, opens by debunking idealism in its loftiest form: ostensibly admiring talk of George Berkeley's "sublime discovery" (XI, 9) is followed by a discussion of indigestion and finally death. The body is reintroduced here not simply, in the tradition of eighteenth-century satire, to challenge human pride, but in the hope that it could serve as a more viable ground for value than mere ideas, just as blood and the activity of the body are represented as more meaningful than money.

Thus, unlike the Orientalist eroticism of Canto V, the eroticism of the English cantos functions not as a cure for, but as a symptom of, the disease of a money-driven culture. This "rack," rather than being liberating, serves as a sign of the frustration of bodily pleasure. In England Juan finds himself living among specters, courted by "sylph-like" (XIII, 859) women "All purged and pious from their native clouds; / Or paper turned to money by the Bank" (636–7). The closest Juan comes to sensual gratification is when he finds himself frightened by one of these specters in the form of the spirit of the "Black Friar." While Juan resisted enslavement in the East, in England he is complicit in this more insidious and subtle form of subjection. In England his love-interests tend to the ideal; they are beautiful and intelligent but also chaste and distant. Whereas in the earlier cantos sexual relations were available to Juan in many forms, in these final cantos idealized, unconsummated sexuality is the only game in town, with the single exception of the Gothic dalliance with the Countess Fitz-Fulke. Juan is as attractive as ever, but the niceties of British high society require the suppression of bodily desire. Adeline Amundeville and Aurora Raby, the two most compelling female figures in these cantos, are both virtuously remote. Juan's relation to Adeline is therefore teasingly represented by the narrator as suspenseful:

> Whether Don Juan and chaste Adeline
>   Grew friends in this or any other sense,
> Will be discuss'd hereafter, I opine:
>   At present I am glad of a pretense
> To leave them hovering, as the effect is fine,
>   And keeps the atrocious reader in *suspense*;
> The surest way for ladies and for books
> To bait their tender or their tenter hooks. (XIV, 769–76)

Aurora, the most serious of Juan's love-interests in these cantos, is also the most remote. She is described by the rivalrous Adeline as "prim, silent, and cold" (XV, 392), and indeed, she initially responds to Juan with "indifference" (609), nor does she ever visibly thaw. If Haidee was a "flower," Aurora is a "gem," beautiful but hard (464). Juan responds as if he were a boy once again, unsure of himself and of how to proceed: "Juan, on retiring for the night, / Felt restless, and perplexed, and compromised; / He thought

Aurora Raby's eyes more bright / Than Adeline (such is advice) advised"
(XVI, 89–92). That Juan should have no physical satisfaction from these
women makes sense given the fact that, like the money to which they are
so often compared, the women of England's "gynocracy" are creatures of
form rather than substance; Adeline's heart is "vacant, though a splendid
mansion; / Her conduct had been perfectly correct" (XIV, 74–5). Aurora
gives promise of more but remains mysterious: "in her / there was a
depth of feeling to embrace / Thoughts, boundless, deep, but silent too
as Space" (430–2).

This empty formalism generates an unease that is felt in the poem's
formal features. For this elite society had been Byron's world, and the
danger is that his writing might betray its origins in that world, that it,
too, might be an empty form. After all, it could be said that it was not
just the romances of others that had been "Reduced to practice and perform'd like dances." The narrator himself admits that his narrative is a
"mere airy and fantastic basis" on which to build his commonplaces. The
anxiety is that Byron's own art might lack genuine passion and substance.
The poem's digressive style has the virtue of signifying freedom from the
dictates of mere form: "I don't know that there may be much ability /
Shown in this sort of desultory rhyme . . . Of this I'm sure at least,
there's no servility / In mine irregularity of chime" (XV, 153–8). Nevertheless, the narrator's insistent claims that he is not bound by forms or inhib-
ited from doing what he likes – that he is no submissive Englishman – do
not always ring true. The poet might be the preeminent man of passion but
he might also be the preeminent man of form; and after all, subverting
forms makes their very presence more apparent. There is no solution to
this quandary, so ultimately Byron, like Hazlitt, simply clings to the ideal
of Napoleon; "Bonaparte's noble daring," at least, is undeniable, a true
instance of embodied power, even in defeat. Like Hazlitt, Byron owned a
bust of Napoleon, and as a boy at Harrow he had fought to defend it, a
fact he was to recall with pleasure as a man. Even after his power had
waned, Napoleon continued to represent the efficacy of representation
itself, its capacity to produce physical effects. It is worth noting that
Byron speaks of himself not as defending what Napoleon stood for
but literally as defending a statue of Napoleon: he describes having
"fought for his bust at school."[38] Years later, during the composition of

---

[38] From the journal entry for November 17, 1813, in Leslie A. Marchand, ed., *Byron's Letters and Journals* 12 vols., vol. III (Cambridge, Mass.: Belknap Press, 1974), p. 210. I am grateful to Bob Folkenflik
for directing me to this entry.

Don Juan, the memory of that representational efficacy was still warm, and it still seemed that under the sign of Napoleon even imaginary things could become as palpable as a fist fight, even if the fight was ultimately to be lost:

> In twice five years the "greatest living poet,"
>   Like to the champion in the fisty ring,
> Is called on to support his claim, or show it,
>   Although 'tis an imaginary thing.
> Even I – albeit I'm sure I did not know it,
>   Nor sought of foolscap subjects to be king, –
> Was reckoned, a considerable time,
> The grand Napoleon of the realms of rhyme. (XI, 433–40)

VI

Peter Graham argues that Byron's representation of Juan as the hapless victim of feminine manipulation took shape, in part, in response to Lady Caroline Lamb's representation of the eponymous hero/villain of her novel *Glenarvon* (1816) as a conniving seducer.[39] This notorious *roman-à-clef* rendering of Lamb's brief affair with Byron, long dismissed as little more than the ravings of a scorned woman, has often been regarded as simply "unreadable."[40] But it is worth noting that the novel very deliberately sets its narrative of personal erotic suffering in a fully defined political context. That context, moreover, is no superfluous addition to an essentially personal confession. To understand *Glenarvon* one must understand that it is an argument precisely for the interrelation of the personal and the political in early nineteenth-century British society. To a certain extent, this interrelation is immanent in one of the book's generic lineages: Nicola Watson argues that *Glenarvon* is an anti-Jacobin novel that relies on the familiar figure of the seductive revolutionary.[41] But I would argue that *Glenarvon* transforms the anti-Jacobin plot to the point of inverting its aims. For it finds in Jacobinical eroticism not a yearning for sexual freedom or fulfillment, but an attraction precisely to sexual frustration. *Glenarvon* suggests that political radicals, even more than conservatives, rely on the power of particular leaders to produce change. But since for the proponent

[39] Peter Graham, *Don Juan and Regency England* (Charlottesville: University Press of Virginia, 1990), 91.
[40] Frances Wilson, "Caroline Lamb and Her Critics," in Wilson's edition of *Glenarvon* (London: Everyman, 1995), 376.
[41] Nicola Watson, *Revolution and the Form of the British Novel 1790–1825* (Oxford: Clarendon Press, 1994), 177.

of liberty, equality, and fraternity subordination to a leader is difficult to justify in rational terms, it must be justified at the emotional level. For the rebels of *Glenarvon*, subordination finds a necessary support in eroticism. Thus, in addition to making the point that the personal is political, an insight implicit in many of the feminist writings of the period, the novel suggests that the political had become deeply personal, and that the eroticism of private life was being transferred to the public domain. Lamb then turns this insight into the pleasurably self-abasing character of modern politics to women's advantage by suggesting that women, because of their superior capacity for selfless devotion, should play a central role in modern political life.

Politics were, in Lamb's own experience, central to private life. Lamb might not have actively campaigned in the way that her mother, Lady Henrietta Frances Spencer, and her aunt, the Duchess of Devonshire, did, but she was genuinely interested and invested in her family's Whig principles. During her childhood, she showed "a precocious interest in Whig politics, and would drink confusion to the Tories in mugs of milk";[42] later in life she would develop a friendship with William Godwin. Private devotion and public devotion were, for her, the same; she claims to have fallen in love with William Lamb sight unseen because he was "a friend of Charles Fox, a friend of liberty."[43] Indeed, in her romantic life Lamb actively subsumed the public in the private. During her dramatic ritualized burning of (copies of) Byron's letters, she had a page read aloud the following lines:

> Is this Guy Fawkes you burn in effigy?
> Why bring the traitor here? What is Guy Fawkes to me?
> Guy Fawkes betrayed his country and his laws,
> England revenged the wrong: his was a public cause.
> But I have private cause to raise this flame,
> Burn also these, and be their fate the same,
> Rouge, feathers, flowers, and all those tawdry things,
> Beside those pictures, letters, chains, and rings,
> All made to lure the mind and please the eye,
> And fill the heart with pride and vanity.[44]

Lamb's dramatization of her feelings, typically represented by biographers as mere childishness, very pointedly serves to give her private experience public

---

[42] Elizabeth Jenkins, *Lady Caroline Lamb* (London: Victor Gollancz, 1932), 29.
[43] *Ibid.*, 38.   [44] *Ibid.*, 142.

meaning. In her theatrical ritual Byron's instruments of seduction are as treacherous as any plot to overthrow the government and therefore merit public recognition. At the same time that Lamb's wellbeing is analogized to national wellbeing, her motivation is represented as analogous to Fawkes's: his was a "public cause" while she has "private cause." Lamb thus presents herself as a private sufferer whose sufferings have a public significance; she casts herself as both victim and rebel.

In *Glenarvon*, however, Lamb goes beyond merely proclaiming that private erotic suffering can be publicly meaningful, for she also suggests the inverse, that public relations can often be resolved into instances of private desire. She does this most obviously by equating Glenarvon's political success with his sexual appeal. Lamb would have known of Byron's early parliamentary speeches on behalf of liberal Whig interests and his more general attraction to the spirit of rebellion. But this fact of Byron's biography is not sufficient to account for Lamb's decision to make her hero/villain a leader in the cause of Irish Emancipation. She very pointedly suggests that Glenarvon's eroticism cannot be understood apart from modern politics, for the emancipatory aim of those politics is actually the liberation of desire. For Glenarvon's Irish male followers, the desire at stake is the desire for material wealth, while for his female followers it is the desire for sexual fulfillment. Glenarvon indulges the men by talking of the money and goods they will enjoy, while seducing the women not by displaying his desire for them but by allowing himself to be an object of their desire.[45] That is, what he provides is not an opportunity to gratify desire but simply an opportunity fully to experience it.

Thus bound together at the nodal point of desire, the personal and the political are completely inextricable in the world of *Glenarvon*. It is not by chance that Glenarvon's sexual seduction of Elinor St Clare is indistinguishable from her seduction to the nationalist cause. Even Calantha, although a member of the English aristocracy, is attracted not only to Glenarvon's person but also to his politics; over the course of the novel, her sympathy for the nationalist movement is an exact register of her feelings toward

---

[45] *Glenarvon* is in fact remarkable in its representation of a man as the object of sexual longing; as Frances Wilson, the editor of the Everyman edition of the novel, remarks, "In this story the *masculine* is treated as the object of desire, while the *feminine*, as desiring subject, is analysed" ("Introduction," *Glenarvon*, xxiv). Glenarvon appeals to women, at least initially, with charms that would traditionally have been considered feminine: much is made of his beautiful face and his wistful, melancholy singing. When Calantha first sees him it is in the manner of a voyeur: he is alone, singing and playing a flute, and she takes him to be a "youth, for he had not the form or the look of manhood" (120). Peter Graham describes Glenarvon as an "*homme fatal*"(*Don Juan*, 108) – an epithet that reminds us just how unexpected, how unfamiliar, female "masochism" can be.

Glenarvon. Just as a figurine of Napoleon binds H and S in *Liber Amoris*, so a ring with the nationalist symbol of a harp serves to bind Calantha to Glenarvon. This conflation of forms of seduction is of course common in the anti-Jacobin novel. But the freedom of desire that is sought in this book never takes the credulous, optimistic form typical of that genre. Calantha, for instance, neither experiences nor represents her affair with Glenarvon as straightforwardly liberating; as she tells her husband's uncle, "I love another, and had rather be a slave in his service than Lord Avondale's wife."[46] The desire that is liberated here is a desire at one remove: a desire simply to experience desire itself. The rebels of *Glenarvon* assert not so much their right to have wealth or sexual freedom as their right to want them.

The erotic inflection of rebel politics is thus itself politically significant, and serves to distinguish those politics from traditional ones. As represented in this novel, hereditary rule is neither erotic nor sensational; it has no need of the arts of seduction. Avondale, Calantha's husband and a figure for William Lamb, is possessed of an authority so legitimate that it has no need of justification; accosted by a party of rebels, he has only to assert his superiority:

"We'll have no masters, no lords: he must give up his commission, and his titles, or not expect to pass." – "Never," said Lord Avondale, indignantly: "had I no commission, no title to defend, still as a man, free and independent, I would protect the laws and rights of my insulted country. Attempt not by force to oppose yourselves to my passage. I will pass without asking or receiving your permission." "It is Avondale, the lord's son," cried one: "I know him by his spirit. Long life to you! and glory, and pleasure attend you." – "Long life to your honour!" exclaimed one and all; and in a moment the enthusiasm in his favour was as great, as general, as had been at first the execration and violence against him. The attachment that they bore to their lord was still strong. (317)

When the rebels do reject this conventional subordination, they do so not by refusing to be subordinate but by making their subordination passionate rather than a mere reflex. Lamb's rebels call each other "Citizen," and speak much of the rights of man, but they tend to seek, even in the act of rebellion, a single, authoritative leader. Their chief of choice is Glenarvon, and because Glenarvon's lineage, unlike Avondale's, is tainted, he must ground his authority in charisma. The rebels' passionate attachment to him serves both to fix

---

[46] Lamb, *Glenarvon*, ed. Frances Wilson (London: Everyman, 1995), 250. All subsequent references to this novel will be to this edition and will be given parenthetically in the text.

their loyalties and as an expression of their capacity for desire. Glenarvon's beautiful face, his enchanting singing, and his dashing manner serve as the basis of a peculiarly modern authority that secures its power by appealing to the senses and desires of the masses. One character "enthusiastically" describes the way the "whole country are after" Glenarvon as "a rage, a fashion," while another denounces it as a "frenzy" (111). His meetings with his followers, many of whom are women, are compared to bacchanalian orgies (111). He is not merely attractive but elicits a pleasurable submission. Whether they are sympathetic to Glenarvon or not, all the characters agree that people follow him about "as if he were some God" (111). This is true of both Glenarvon's male and his female followers. In Lamb's world of charismatic radicalism, both men and women experience an erotic pleasure in submission, because to *desire* subjection is not feminine or masculine but socially progressive.

For all their progressive claims, however, in *Glenarvon* the revolutionaries are distinguished from the conservatives only in that they experience authority not as a given, a neutral fact of existence, but as a source of erotic pleasure. Like Leopold von Sacher-Masoch's characters, Lamb's rebels demand the right to use contractual relations to subordinate themselves, to show, as they do to Glenarvon, "the most obsequious devotion" (258). Even Elinor, in spite of her attraction to the idea of independence, can imagine the success of the Irish rebellion only in terms of a new hierarchy; she pictures "a servile world bowing before" Glenarvon, "old men forget[ting] their age and dignity to worship" him, and "kings and princes trembl[ing] before the scourge of [his] wit" (294).

Glenarvon argues not only that modern politics incorporate sexuality, but also that modern sexuality incorporates politics insofar as it is first and foremost about power. Hierarchy, no longer taken for granted, has become, quite literally, sexy. Sexual desire in this novel is always experienced in terms of power relations, typically those of master and slave. Calantha rapturously exclaims to Glenarvon, "I love but you: be you my master" (221) and later resolves to run away with him. When she wavers Glenarvon reminds her that "Thou art mine, wedded to me, sold to me" (254). Like S in *Liber Amoris*, Glenarvon appears to Calantha as no mere mortal but as both angel and demon: "Calantha felt the power, not then alone, but evermore. She felt the empire, the charm, the peculiar charm, those features – that being must have for her. She could have knelt and prayed to heaven to realise the dreams, to bless the fallen angel in whose presence she at that moment stood" (121). Glenarvon delights in reminding Calantha of his power over her, making clear that her mortification during the course of their affair is not simply the unhappy effect of living in a repressive society but a constituent part of the eroticism of their relationship:

"Calantha," said Lord Glenarvon, taking her hand firmly, and smiling half scornfully, "you shall be my slave. I will mould you as I like; teach you but to think with my thoughts, to act but with my feelings, you shall wait nor murmur – suffer, nor dare complain – ask, and be rejected – and all this, I will do, and you know it, for your heart is already mine." (192)

Glenarvon says this after having humiliated Calantha by showing her friends and family the love letters intended for his eyes only, and although she swears to herself that she will never forgive him, she does. For the modern reader, such moments of voluptuous self-abnegation are likely to be disturbing. But within the world of the novel, this eroticism of subordination and frustration actually seems the most natural and deeply felt kind. Moreover, all characters with radical sympathies practice such an eroticism, even those who elicit it in others; thus radical leaders, like radical followers, express their own desires in masochistic terms. When Glenarvon dictates Calantha's desire to her, he underscores her subordination to him, but when he expresses his own desire it, too, takes the form of a self-abasing reverence. He describes himself as a soul "conquered and enchained" by her (222), and the narrator explains that "Her coldness seemed but to increase his ardour" (223). Calantha repeatedly speaks of the "empire" Glenarvon has over her, but he claims that it is she who has the "empire" over him. This vacillation in power is as close as the book comes to imagining an equality of power: genuine mutual masochism figures as a kind of ideal order, if a painful and conflicted one. Graham remarks of the novel that "the pace and tone of the literary affair are if anything too faithful to the torturous and incredible real one – the result of this fidelity being that volumes 2 and 3 (the parts of the book given over to the liaison) are nearly unendurable."[47] But this torturous quality is of course an apt narrative expression of the eroticism that drives the characters. During the period of her attachment to Glenarvon, "remorse and suspense alternately agitated her [Calantha's] mind" (183), yet this is the most exciting and significant time in her life. Even peripheral characters take for granted that such suffering is constitutive of love; when Glenarvon claims that he has forsworn love, Doctor Everard remarks that it injures the health by causing suspense and fretting (164).

In spite of their avowed devotion to principles of equality, then, Lamb's rebels are not only unable to make equality an effective reality but cannot

---

[47] Graham, *Don Juan*, 111.

even make it an affective one. They therefore recast the hierarchy that seems an ineluctable part of their lives as the product of their own desire. If they must be dominated, they can at least choose who shall dominate them. But the rebels' eroticized submission to their leaders carries within it the means to bring about more significant change. Frances Wilson argues that "Byron's danger lay in his enticement to identification";[48] "within the terms of her own fantasy, Lamb can not only be seen to refashion herself in her romantic heroines, she also identifies herself with the hero, and she therefore presents her desire *for* Byron as a desire *to be* him."[49] According to Wilson, this slippage between desire and identification works within the text as well: "There is no such thing as an 'original personality' in *Glenarvon*"; the characters of the novel are essentially variations of each other.[50] I would argue further that this identification and tendency to similitude are generally represented as empowering. Elinor, for instance, becomes like Glenarvon to the point of taking a lover of her own, dressing in men's clothes, and finally leading the Irish rebellion herself. Ironically enough, however, it is precisely self-abnegating attachment that serves as the means for these transformative acts of identification. Lamb describes the mechanism thus:

When we love, if that which we love is noble and superior, we contract a resemblance to the object of our passion; but if that to which we have bound ourselves is base, the contagion spreads swiftly, and the very soul becomes black with crime. Woe be to those who have ever loved Glenarvon! Lady Avondale's heart was hardened; her mind utterly perverted; and that face of beauty, that voice of softness, all, alas! that yet could influence her. (264)

Here Lamb dutifully decries Calantha's seduction, but she also absolves her of responsibility for it. The more intense and self-abnegating the love, the greater its capacity to transform the lover. Such love enables a redefinition of the self so that it actually comes to resemble the powerful object of its devotion. In such a context, James Soderholm's remark that Lamb, by means of her forgeries and imitations of Byron, became "his miniature writ large" takes on a new significance.[51]

This transformative power of selfless desire has special implications for women, for it provides them with an acceptably "feminine" means of

[48] Wilson, "Introduction" to *Glenarvon*, xxi.
[49] Frances Wilson, "'An Exaggerated Woman': The Melodramas of Lady Caroline Lamb," in Wilson, ed., *Byromania: Portraits of the Artist in Nineteenth- and Twentieth-Century Culture* (Basingstoke: Macmillan, 1999), 216.
[50] Wilson, "Introduction" to *Glenarvon*, xxx.
[51] James Soderholm, "Lady Caroline Lamb: Byron's Miniature Writ Large," *Keats-Shelley Journal* 40 (1991), 28.

empowerment. Indeed, *Glenarvon* dramatizes a shift from older to newer forms of female power. The novel's two representatives of traditional female power are the Princess of Madagascar and Lady Margaret Buchanan. Both are influential, and between them they reveal the range of action available to the women of the generation preceding Lamb's own. In her portrait of Lady Holland as the Princess of Madagascar, Lamb's satire reaches its most daring heights: described as the "wife of the great Nabob," the Princess of Madagascar lives in a Gothic building known as Barbary House, where reviewers and men of talents, appearing at first to be "a black hord [*sic*] of savages," wear collars and chains around their necks (94). Calantha is told that if she, too, will wear a chain, she will find it gilded. When the Princess approaches her death, she asks her high priest, "Hoiaonskim," if she can be saved by sacrificing her followers, and her dying request is that all her attendants should be sent after her. Lamb thus indicts the female-run literary coterie with every cliché of Orientalism, while at the same time the ambiguity of the title "Nabob" leaves open the possibility that the despotism being practiced here is that of the Western colonizer. The salient point is that the Princess's power is tyrannical and, in the broadest sense, unchristian. But although the Princess's commands are carried out "with surprising alacrity" (93), for "Such is the force of fashion and power" (93), they have little effect on the larger world, because she sets her followers only "trifling task[s]" (93).

Indeed, great as the Princess of Madagascar's power is, it is markedly limited in scope: it is a tyranny in the domain of arts and letters only. Since the establishment in the late eighteenth century of the female-dominated salons and "bluestocking" circles, women had enjoyed authority in this realm, and initially at least this authority had extensive ramifications. As Anne Mellor shows, in the period from 1780 to 1830 women contributed actively and importantly to public discourse through their writing. This authority, however, gradually came to be circumscribed. As Mellor points out, "by the mid-nineteenth century, in a period of anti-feminist backlash . . . the figure of the Mother of the Nation . . . was rewritten as the Angel in the House, a woman whose moral and intellectual roles were entirely confined to the private household."[52] A look at the dates of Mellor's examples of authoritative Romantic-era women's writings – the bulk of which are derived from the first half of the Romantic period – reveals that the diminution in the boldness of female claims to influence

---

[52] Anne Mellor, *Mothers of the Nation: Women's Political Writing in England, 1780–1830* (Bloomington: Indiana University Press, 2000), 144.

public life had begun before mid-century; by the 1810s, the decade of *Glenarvon*'s composition, women's claims to direct public opinion had already become more muted and indirect.[53] Gone were the boldness of radical writers such as Mary Wollstonecraft and the influence of such conservative ones as Hannah More. The most famously direct comment by a woman on public life, Anna Barbauld's biting indictment of national policy in "Eighteen Hundred and Eleven," generated intense criticism. The Princess of Madagascar embodies a form of female power that was in the course of becoming privatized. She is represented as all-powerful within her own coterie, but never influences persons or actions outside of it. Little wonder, then, that Lamb represents her methods as not only tyrannical but also obsolete, as ancient as Eastern despotism and as unfashionable as endorsing slavery. The Princess of Madagascar practices a Gothic form of power that *should* properly be confined to such places as "Barbary" House.

But if the power of the society hostess seems outmoded, it appears that for an older generation of women, female power outside the literary circle could take only underhand forms, as it does in the machinations of Lady Margaret Buchanan, who uses her sexual appeal to manipulate others in ways that are not only selfish but also cruel. The clearest example of this is her manipulation of Viviani, Glenarvon's Italian persona. In his relation to Lady Margaret, the man who, as Glenarvon, is universally irresistible finds himself the victim of an unrequited infatuation that renders him so desperate that he is willing to commit any act, even murder, to obtain the object of his desire. The discovery, at the end of the novel, that Viviani and Glenarvon are one and the same is surprising to the point of lending credence to complaints that the novel is incoherent, "unreadable." But this lapse in verisimilitude enables Lamb to make a strong point about the capacity of relationships to change the very nature of those involved in them. In his connection with Lady Margaret, Glenarvon becomes an Italian not only literally but also generically. That is, he comes to resemble the Radcliffean "Italian," a figure with a Gothic propensity for evil. Lamb thus accuses Lady Margaret of wielding power in a manner that is positively malevolent – in scenes that feature her, the novel often shifts abruptly into a fully Gothic mode, complete with conspiracy, sadistic cruelty, and murder.

---

[53] Dena Goodman has shown that in France, the classic domain of the salonière, the centrality of the salons – and the power of the women who ran them – were already being challenged as early as the 1780s ("Regendering the Republic of Letters: Private Association in the Public Sphere, 1780–1789," in Dario Castiglione and Lesley Sharpe, eds., *Shifting the Boundaries: Transformation of the Languages of Public and Private in the Eighteenth Century* [Exeter: University of Exeter Press, 1995], 22–40).

Lady Margaret's climactic death scene, in which we see her knifed to death, enacts the fitting retribution for her guilty abuse of covert power.

While the power of the older generation of women in *Glenarvon* is at once limited and sadistic, the power of the younger generation is achieved through masochism. Lady Margaret scornfully chides Calantha for behavior that she perceives as a form of weakness: "now that you love, instead of rendering him you love your captive, you throw yourself entirely in his power, and will deeply rue the confidence you have shown" (238). The prescience of the warning notwithstanding, Calantha's self-abasing relation to power is represented far more sympathetically than Lady Margaret's scheming. Although the narrator berates Calantha and especially Elinor for allowing themselves to be sexually corrupted, she also goes to some pains to underscore their original innocence and natural goodheartedness. Unlike the Princess of Madagascar and Lady Margaret, who never feel for others, Calantha and Elinor "fall" only because of their susceptibility to such feeling. Creatures of sensibility, if they end up neglecting their domestic duties, donning men's clothes, or enjoying masculine freedoms, it is only because their feminine devotion to Glenarvon has ultimately made them like him. Even in their submission, moreover, they reveal a certain strength. Karmen MacKendrick argues that the masochist's suffering can in fact be a mark of her or his potency, a practice of power,[54] and Lamb would have us understand that that is the case here. For there is something heroic in the anguish of Glenarvon's lovers. Lamb's decision to name her adulterous protagonist after the heroine of John Ford's *The Broken Heart* (1633) – a princess who is guilty of no moral or social infractions – makes more sense in the light of this fact. Ford's Calantha is notable precisely for her ability to combine outward strength and sovereignty with inward suffering so deep that she ultimately dies of it. Charles Lamb, in his *Specimens of English Dramatic Poets* (1808), compares her sufferings to those of Christ, even as he notes that "the dilaceration of the spirit" and "inmost mind" are far worse than any form of "bodily suffering."[55] Caroline Lamb may well have been familiar with the play from this volume; at any rate, she certainly makes her Calantha a noble martyr whose sufferings are internal. Calantha herself remarks on her strength in suffering; she proudly exclaims to Glenarvon, "You may torture me as you please, if you have the power over me which you imagine, but I can bear torture, and none ever yet

---

[54] See Karmen MacKendrick, *Counterpleasures* (Albany: SUNY Press, 1999).
[55] Charles Lamb, ed., *Specimens of English Dramatic Poets Who Lived about the Time of Shakespeare* (London: Henry G. Bohn, 1854), 228.

subdued me" (192). Ultimately, Calantha's heroism takes obvious outward forms, and she does more than simply "suffer and be still";[56] she flouts convention and openly defies the wishes of her family and friends. But it is her self-abasing devotion that enables this extraordinary defiance: flinging her wedding ring from her hand, she tells her husband's uncle, as we observed earlier, that she "had rather be a slave in [Glenarvon's] service, than Lord Avondale's wife" (250).[57]

B`old as Calantha becomes, the most remarkable of Glenarvon's lovers is Elinor St Clare. Because Calantha is the primary figure for Lamb herself, she, along with Glenarvon, has tended to monopolize the attention of readers and critics. Indeed, Elinor is a somewhat shadowy figure, appearing only intermittently, and the narrator seems unsure what to do with her: at times she is represented as unspeakably base, at other times as almost superhuman. Elinor herself partakes of this uncertainty, moving in a single scene from being beautifully happy to proudly defiant to tearfully regretful of her own corruption. But I would argue that if Elinor's identity never takes a comprehensible, coherent shape, it is because she represents an ideal of female power and freedom that even Lamb is fearful to embrace. So she hovers about the margins of the book in spite of signs that she should be regarded as centrally important. After all, at the beginning of the novel it seems that she will be its heroine: the first pages recount her arrival at Belfont as a child, carried through wind and storm by her wild but visionary father, and we soon learn that she herself is a "prophetess" (355). Similarly, the narrative ends with her dramatic death – the final two chapters, which describe the deaths of several others, including Glenarvon, are presented as merely a "short" "sequel of the history" (357). I would argue that Elinor is a figure of female power at once so compelling and so disturbing that the narrator cannot watch her unblinkingly. Essentially, Elinor achieves the goal to

---

[56] This line, famous from Hemans, actually appears in a contrite poem that Lamb wrote shortly before her death: "For I have learned when others sigh / To suffer and be still" (Jenkins, *Lamb*, 272).

[57] That the novel is about forging an appropriate and effective form of female power was certainly recognized not only by Byron, who arguably responded to it in *Don Juan* (see Watson, *Revolution*, and Graham, *Don Juan*), but also by a female parodist of the novel, "an old wife of twenty years," who actually addresses her novel, *Purity of Heart*, to Lamb. One expects the book, subtitled "Woman as She Should Be," to take exception to the characterization of Glenarvon on moral grounds, but it focuses instead on the issue of the status of women. The problem with Lady Calantha Limb is that, in allowing herself to be manipulated by her lover, she becomes a disgrace to her sex. The novel's heroine, on the other hand, knows instinctively that a good woman should relinquish no control to a suitor and all control to a husband. Courted by one man, who insists on her subjection, she refuses him, later marrying a cruel and adulterous man who, at the end of the novel, finally recognizes her extraordinary merit in being willing to suffer a Griselda-style subjection to him (Anon., *Purity of Heart* [New York: Oram and Mott, 1818]).

which the other devotees in the book only aspire: she becomes so like the object of her devotion that she can take his place in the political arena. Elinor is not only beautiful, and a beautiful singer, just like Glenarvon, but she ultimately takes a second lover, wears male clothing, and leads her fellow Irishmen to rebellion. When Glenarvon loses his public credibility, she is ready to step in and take his place.

If we return now to the issue of democratic revolution, we see that it requires more than men and women whose satisfaction in devoting themselves to charismatic leaders can counterbalance the risk involved in challenging the status quo. A revolution also demands genuinely masochistic leaders, leaders devoted to an ideal of service rather than personal glory. In spite of his intermittent romantic subjection to Calantha, Glenarvon is not such a man. Although he teaches Calantha's son Harry Mowbray to say "we have no crown; we want no kings" (245), it is clear to all that he is deeply invested in his own status as "rebel chief" (245). Glenarvon claims that he would renounce everything for the cause, but his impulse is ultimately to dominate. It is his sort that Burke speaks of when he remarks that "often the desire and design of a tyrannic domination lurks in the claim of an extravagant liberty."[58] That Glenarvon eventually goes over to the English side comes as no real surprise. But Elinor, his acolyte – "so apt a scholar, for so great a master" (261) – very naturally steps into his role when he turns coat, and makes herself a true martyr to the cause. She is able to do this precisely because her masochistic devotion to Glenarvon has effectively turned her into what he only seemed to be.

Lamb's conception of revolution has important implications for the status of women in public life. If masochists are the truest radicals and women the best masochists, then it is women who should be at the forefront of political change. Lamb had witnessed at first hand her aunt's efforts on behalf of Charles James Fox's campaign in the Westminster election of 1784, and she had seen those efforts criticized for being unfeminine and morally suspect. Lamb's novel, by embracing charisma and the devotion it inspires as the basis of modern authority, not only endorses such dedication to a cause but makes it a preeminently and properly feminine trait. At the same time, she foregrounds the transformative potential of this dedication, its capacity to make women themselves charismatic. The women of the narrative are its best masochists, and Elinor the best among them – even after she refuses to follow Glenarvon as his mistress, she says that she

[58] Edmund Burke, "An Appeal from the New to the Old Whigs," in *The Works of Edmund Burke*, 6 vols., vol. VI (London: Oxford University Press, 1906), p. 49.

will do so as his slave, and she describes her relation to her new lover as similarly subordinating: "I am his, to follow and obey him" (261). Yet, at the moment of insurrection, it is Elinor, beautiful and mysterious, who leads the people. It is ultimately women who are best suited to leadership in a new democratic order.

Unfortunately, however, the strength of erotic submission is also its undoing, for it does not allow for successful consummation, and therefore renders both female leadership and political equality unsustainable. To dramatize this point, Lamb twice suggests that a revolution has begun, only to reveal that it is conservative forces rather than progressive ones that are truly in control. When a mob appears on the Altamonte estate, bearing torches and yelling "murder," "the inhabitants of the castle heard it as a summons to instant death" (336). But they soon discover that the "rebels" fury is actually directed at those they believe to be guilty of the kidnapping, years before, of the true heir of Delaval and their rightful lord. That is, they are rioting in defense of the old order. A similar, more comical version of such a mistake had occurred earlier in the narrative:

A small fleet had been seen approaching the coast: it was rumoured that the French in open boats were preparing to invade Ireland; but it proved, though it may sound rather ludicrous to say so, only the great Nabob and the Princess of Madagascar. Their immense retinue and baggage, which the common people took for the heavy artillery, arrived without incident or accident at Belfont. (166)

Lamb's satire aims to mortify Lady Holland by representing the powerful Whig hostess as a bungler who is more concerned with her own wealth and power than real social issues. At the same time, it reveals a nostalgia for a time when revolution did indeed seem immanent. But if rebellion seems ever more about to be and never actually to come, it is in part because the logic of erotic submission does not allow for its advent. Even Elinor can conceive of rebellion only as an exercise in futility: "What though our successors be slaves, aye, willing slaves, shall not the proud survivor exult in the memory of the past!" (354). The epithet "willing slaves" undermines the ostensible premises of this argument, revealing the underlying perversity of revolutionary thought. At the end of the day, the rebellion must fail, because failure is embedded in the self-abnegating logic that sustains it. And thus, in spite of Lamb's attraction to democratic masochism, she also condemns it as pathological; the narrator remarks that the most "fierce and daring" rebels are often but "disturbed characters": "martyrs and fanatics," they "attach a degree of glory to every privation and punishment in the noble cause of opposition to what they conceive is unjust authority" (161). At the novel's end, Elinor commits suicide by blindfolding her horse and galloping off a cliff. Her death enacts the paradox of her life: it is dramatic, heroic, self-destructive, and ultimately senseless. For all its self-serving fantasy elements, *Glenarvon* cannot finally imagine freedom either for Ireland or for women.

VII

In their very different ways Hazlitt, Byron, and Lamb all explore the role of masochistic eroticism in bringing about change; they use masochistic scenarios to think through the complicated and often ambivalent contemporary conceptions of equality, liberty, and authority. But masochistic scenarios could also be made to serve explicitly conservative ends. Such is the case in a poem titled *The Rodiad*, attributed to the pseudonymous George Coleman. Published in 1810 as part of the *"Library Illustrative of Social Progress,"* it displays its awareness of changing times on its title page. Although the series title functions as both a euphemism and a joke, it does touch on one of the principal themes of *The Rodiad*: modern notions of philanthropy and equality have come to interfere with traditional hierarchies and their pleasures, in particular the pleasure of flogging. The poem begins with a complaint that "All corrections cruel"[59] have been eliminated, and suggests that this change will effect an inversion, not a healthy leveling, of social relations:

> . . . A nice look out in truth,
> For us, the Teachers of ingenuous youth;
> Who, when we must not mark our discipline
> In bright red letters on their hinder skin,
> And once have lost command of their posteriors,
> Will soon be taught who are the true superiors. (7–8)

Of course, the tone throughout – as the title *The Rodiad* suggests – is light and humorous. This is no serious, sustained attack on modern politics or philanthropy. And despite the narrator-schoolteacher's lust for striping boys' bottoms, the poem is also not an ironic attack on corporal punishment; the lubricious delights of flagellation are fully described by the narrator and offered up for the pleasure of the reader. It is not without reason that the work has traditionally been classed with pornography

---

[59] George Coleman (pseud.), *The Rodiad* (London: Cadell and Murray, 1810) 7. Further references will be given parenthetically in the text.

rather than social commentary. The poem's commentary on social hierarchy is usually delivered with a wink:

> Some pedagogues are only strict for books;
> My bottoms blush for manners, words, and looks –
> Nothing a gentleman's demeanor teaches
> More than a graceful downfall of the breeches. (23)

The maintenance of social hierarchy is, however, essential to the genuine pleasures of the poem. This fantasy world is fueled by distinctions of rank. The narrator describes in particularly heady terms his rough treatment of "my orphan boy, my Portuguese" (26), a boy doubly disenfranchised, one whose "legal" rights are explicitly mocked: "In the school months, when native bums supply / My virgol muscles, he's a licensed boy; / But when no other lad at school remains, / I read his bill of 'penalties and pains'" (27). The teacher's secondary object of interest during these months is a lower-class boy, a "parish 'prentice" (31). In describing his treatment of this apprentice, the narrator again mocks the notion of legal democratic rights: "But my desire for equal rights to shew, / I mainly leave him to the gods below –" (32). The narrator goes on to explain that "Work'us," as the apprentice is called, already suffers much at the hands of all the servants and maids in the area; every time they are scolded by their superiors, they in turn vent their anger upon his "baseborn tail" (33). Flogging thus comes to seem a "natural" expression of social hierarchy: the great chain of being is reconstructed as a great chain of beating. The narrator is quick to point out that this violence does Work'us no harm: he remains not only physically vigorous but socially and sexually bold. *The Rodiad* presents a utopia in which the strict hierarchies of the past are revived as sexual fantasy.

The narrator does, however, claim to be sympathetic to the plight of the lower classes, though that sympathy is of a perverse kind: he suggests that flogging must not be lost as a practice because it is one of the few pleasures available to the poor man. "The rudest boor who labours late and hard / To feed his children, finds his just reward / When he corrects them royally at night" (38). The narrator thus uses the modern investment in an ideal of social equality to argue for the value of hierarchy. The poem's final tale is of a happy clerk "Saying he'd rather whip them [his children] at his ease, / Before his frugal meal of bread and cheese, / Than have the grandest supper in the land, / And be debarred from taking rod in hand" (54). Not surprisingly, the narrator finds the greatest threat to the flogging hierarchy in the ostensibly socially progressive attitudes of the middle ranks:

> 'Mid folks of high degree, the rod's astir –
> At Eton, Harrow, Rugby, Westminster,
> . . .
> But in the middle rank, I'm grieved to say,
> The Rod scarce holds its honourable sway; –
> Tradesmen I know with many a blooming boy
> Who scarce the privilege of the birch employ,
> And for whole months, through innocence or pride,
> Never discuss a prentice's backside. (45–6)

In the narrator's eyes this attitude is itself but a hypocritical expression of a hierarchical impulse; the tradesmen are actually motivated by pride to produce their "philanthropic trash" (49).

Flagellation, in this nostalgic incarnation, might appear to be largely sadistic in spirit, but it is, in fact, indifferently sadistic or masochistic. The poem ends with a final reverie on the vicissitudes of hierarchy. The narrator explains that he never wants to go where "*unbottomed* cherubs haunt the air; / Rather, methinks, I could with better grace / Present myself at some inferior place" where he could torture Queens, Bishops, and Deans (60). Pleasure thus makes the low high and the high low. It is the mobility of such categories that makes hierarchy, as it is imagined here, a game, a changeable domain of pleasure and pain rather than a restrictive and burdensome system. Even the narrator, for all his love of beating others, says that he will not complain if the "Eternal Schoolmaster" (60) dooms him to correction, for to "Flog and be flogged – is no bad fate at last" (62). From the vantage of a culture increasingly devoted, at least in principle, to individual autonomy and merely formal legal social bonds, the fantasy of a great chain of beating had the virtue of using the personal desires of individuals to make an abstract social order once again an organic whole.

Whether Jacobin or Tory, female or male, aristocrat or commoner, many thinkers and writers of the early nineteenth century found in scenes of erotic submission the means for thinking through the terrors and hopes of an age of revolution. Turning to courtly love, images of Eastern despotism, or memories of the schoolroom to fuel their fantasies, they explored the varied effects of eroticizing the hierarchies that had become the center of public debate at the turn of the century. The fictions they produced served sometimes to resuscitate hierarchy and sometimes to render it ridiculous. They provided a stimulus for liberty or functioned as the sign of its absence. And they argued for the central role of pleasurable submission in both revolutionary commitment and the nostalgic dreams of an organic society. In the first decades of the nineteenth century, when the moment of political change seemed at once immanent and to have passed irretrievably, such fictions were possessed of a particular urgency. When the public realm disappointed, or when it seemed disarmingly unstable, hierarchy at home, with all its nuances, frustrations, and satisfactions, seemed the best way to practice modern politics.

CHAPTER 5

Mastery and melancholy in suburbia

"To unperplex bliss from its neighbor pain . . ."
–John Keats, "Lamia," (1820)

For all their insight into the political and economic ramifications of the eroticization of power relations, Romantic-era writers themselves did not treat erotic submission systematically or taxonomically, and therefore have no single word to describe it. But in the latter part of the Romantic period, one writer did famously give a name to the pleasurable suffering he described, and that writer is John Keats. In this chapter I argue that Keatsian melancholy describes a form of eroticized submission peculiar to late Romanticism. This is an eroticism grounded less in the deferral of pleasure than in the awareness that the transitory nature of pleasure makes the experience of it always, of necessity, painful.

To trace the logic of this melancholy, one must first understand the contexts, both social and aesthetic, in which it developed. Romantic melancholy defined itself in part in opposition to a contemporary aesthetic of mastery, just as the picturesque had encoded a masterful form of desire that offered an alternative to the self-abnegation of the sublime. Indeed, to understand Romantic-era melancholy we must return to that earlier pair of prestigious aesthetic categories. For dwellers in the cities and suburbs of the early nineteenth century, the picturesque and the sublime, grounded in rural life and tourism, increasingly seemed less compelling than two more modern and affordable aesthetic modes: the empowering aesthetic of the synoptic and the melancholy aesthetic of the ephemeral. In essence, these aesthetics served as the picturesque and sublime of the city and suburbs.

The synoptic can be understood as an updated, suburban version of the picturesque. While the picturesque involved the exploration of vast tracts of space, suburban nature lovers began to admire art forms and landscaping techniques that made intensive rather than extensive use of space. This trend was epitomized in the gardenesque, which aimed to represent plenitude in the confined space of the suburban garden. This aesthetic of synopsis, though it did not emphasize exploration and movement as did Uvedale Price's picturesque, was still an aesthetic of consumption and mastery. Like many of his fellow suburbanites, Keats found this aesthetic deeply attractive, and its influence on his early poetry is pervasive. But increasingly he found himself more compelled by the melancholy beauty of ephemera. If the suburbs and cities seemed inappropriate settings for the traditional sublime experience, the sublime of mountains and cataracts, their restless energy provided the basis for a new way of feeling pleasurably overwhelmed.[1] The very pace of life in the city made urban experience impossible to master; if the aesthetic of the synoptic was one of intensified space, the aesthetic of the ephemeral was one of intensified time. In an age characterized by a "new sense of historical movement,"[2] an age more and more aware of the bustling quality of its burgeoning cities and the speeding-up of transportation and communication, time itself seemed to move at an unprecedented pace. As Byron wryly remarks in *Don Juan* (1819–24), "I knew that nought was lasting, but now even / Change grows too changeable, without being new."[3] Objects that were themselves fleeting became the focus of intense interest. Transient effects seemed to embody the very spirit of modern temporality, even as they eluded the often distressing materialism of modern life. These fleeting objects elicited a painful, unquenchable desire, the desire that Keats would so memorably define as melancholy.

This chapter explores the responses of two urban/suburban writers to these changes in the perception of space and time. After opening with an account of the aesthetics of the synoptic and the ephemeral, the chapter turns to Keats, whose struggle between those aesthetics shaped his most important poetry. For Keats, the masterful comforts of the synoptic increasingly gave way to the melancholy pleasure of worshiping the transient. Meanwhile, in the poetry of his years in Highgate, Samuel Taylor Coleridge was to expand the purview of Romantic melancholy by suggesting that even the aesthetic of the synoptic was disempowering. For Coleridge, the intensification of time and space was cause for profound philosophical concern: in his late poems it is impossible to experience the beloved except as a two-dimensional, ephemeral image, so that the act of loving becomes nothing

---

[1] Of course, even in the eighteenth century cities were sometimes described in terms of the sublime, just as scenes of modern industry sometimes were. Traditional connoisseurs of the sublime, however, generally represented cities like London as large in scale without being sublime.

[2] James Chandler uses this phrase in relation to the period of the Peterloo massacre, but his study of England in 1819 suggests a more general consciousness of historical change during the early nineteenth century (*England in 1819* [Chicago: University of Chicago Press, 1998], 20).

[3] Jerome McGann, ed., *Byron* (Oxford: Oxford University Press, 1986), Canto XI, ll. 653–4.

but a repeated mourning for the inaccessibility of the beloved. In Coleridge's hands, then, eroticized submission became a highly refined, self-conscious, and abstract exercise. In his late writings we witness a pursuit of melancholy so thoroughgoing it might have made even Keats shudder.

I

To understand the development of the synoptic ideal out of the picturesque, we must turn first to early nineteenth-century landscape and garden design, and to its most successful practitioner, Humphry Repton. Attacked by Richard Payne Knight and Price early in his career, after the mid-1790s he emerged as victor in the so-called "picturesque controversy," enjoying the endorsement of Edmund Burke and George III, among others. The investment in a notion of forward momentum, which Repton shared with the theorists of the picturesque, was gradually transformed during the early years of the new century. The picturesque of Knight and Price, because it involved perpetual forward movement attended by novelty, required extensive grounds, and was therefore ill-suited to the smaller-scale landscapes of the lesser gentry and the bourgeoisie. Inevitably, Repton was called upon to design landscapes on a more modest scale, and this change created a subtle shift in his management of forward motion, a change recorded in the aquarelle images he provided for his patrons. Relying as they did on traditional landscape painting, the dynamics of the picturesque were founded on compositional motifs that drew the eye into depth. In Repton's hands this depth came to be truncated, the picture plane rendered increasingly shallow. His illustrations of the approach to Woburn Abbey in Bedfordshire before and after alteration reveal this tendency quite clearly (figures 8 and 9). In the former a serpentine, undulating road draws the eye toward the Abbey. In the latter a new approach has been devised, one that makes the buildings appear larger and more impressive. But this "approach" hardly seems an approach at all, since both the road and the river lead the eye out of the picture frame rather than in toward the house. Although the picture retains a sense of depth, here as elsewhere Repton directs the eye to the middle ground. Repton considered one of the advantages of this new approach to the Abbey to be that it offered the eye no opportunity to travel to the spaces beyond the house; now "the whole seems embosomed in a magnificent wood."[4] It is telling that in his

---

[4] Humphry Repton, *Fragments on the Theory and Practice of Landscape Gardening* (London: T. Bensley and Son, 1816), 164.

APPROACH TO WOBURN ABBEY, AS IT HAS BEEN ALTERED

Figure 8. Humphry Repton, "Approach to Woburn Abbey, before
It Was Altered," from *Fragments on the Theory and Practice of
Landscape Gardening* (London: T. Bensley and Son, 1816).

discussion of the grounds at Armley in Yorkshire, Repton spoke of the
"three distances of the painter" not in the manner of his predecessors, as
"Fore-ground, the intermediate Part, and the Off-skip," but as "the
foreground – the landscape – and the offskip."[5]

Because of this middle-grounding tendency, Repton's work in the grand
manner of the old formal gardens often feels forced or awkward. We see
this, for instance, in his design for the cottage at Endsleigh in Devon
(figure 10). His painting of the grounds as he proposed to transform
them makes use of perspectival recession to suggest their extent. But the perspective organization of the picture is not consistent. The modified *allée* on
the left, for instance, is designed in a way that implies that the spectator is
standing exactly in front of it, while the handling of the cattle on the

---

[5] First quotation from Charles Avison, 1752, as reprinted in the OED in the entry for "offskip." Repton
quotation in Stephen Daniels, *Humphry Repton: Landscape Gardening and the Geography of Georgian
England* (New Haven: Yale University Press, 1999), 247.

APPROACH TO WOBURN ABBEY, BEFORE IT WAS ALTERED.

Figure 9. Humphry Repton, "Approach to Woburn Abbey,
as it Has Been Altered," from *Fragments on the Theory and Practice
of Landscape Gardening* (London: T. Bensley and Son, 1816).

GENERAL VIEW FROM THE SOUTH AND EAST FRONTS OF THE COTTAGE AT ENDSLEIGH, DEVONSHIRE.   DUTCHESS OF BEDFORD

Figure 10. Humphry Repton, "General View . . . of the Cottage at Endsleigh," without
overlay, from *Fragments on the Theory and Practice of Landscape Gardening* (London:
T. Bensley and Son, 1816).

right-hand side of the picture, combined with the strong horizontal axes of
fence and river, make sense only if the viewer is imagined to be standing in
front of them. Indeed, the picture falls visually into two halves, one arranged
vertically, the other horizontally, and each undermining the grandeur of the
other. The difficulty would seem to be that while the long perspectival *allée*
suggests grandeur by traditional means, Repton's more modern inclination
is to focus on middle-ground objects, as he does on the right side of the
print. As if to indicate that we really should be focusing on the middle
expanses of the terrain, the most striking human figures in the scene –
the family group in the middle ground – stand with arms extended to
either side.

Repton's tendency to work horizontally signals a new conception of
space that had profound social implications, for it reflected not just an aesthetic change – a transformation of the picturesque and a mistrust of the
sublime – but also a democratization of point of view. The horizon line
figured a kind of "leveling" both in itself and in that it offered a view of
the world that seemed to be more generally available. The "prospect," so
long linked to aristocratic privilege, could now be enjoyed by almost
anyone, for even a shallow space could be enlarged if one simply gazed
from side to side. This new, more egalitarian representation of space was
institutionalized in various forms: at the turn of the century, the popularity
of the manmade panorama blossomed, and mountain climbing became a
popular pastime. Rather than experience the awesomeness of a mountain
from afar, people wished to climb the mountain and experience the panoramic view *from* it.[6] For Price, the social implications of this change were clear
enough and quite alarming; the longstanding connection to a place, with
knowledge of "the local geography and history of an extensive prospect,"
was giving way to a vulgar form of landscape appreciation, that of the "prospect hunter (a very numerous tribe)."[7] Repton responded with a defense of
the prospect hunter:

in spite of the fastidiousness of connoisseurship, we must allow something to the
general voice of mankind . . . In the valley, a thousand delightful subjects present
themselves to the painter, yet the visitors to [Matlock Bath] are seldom satisfied
till they have climbed the neighbouring hills, to take a bird's eye view of the
whole spot, which no painting can represent.[8]

[6] See Stephan Oettermann, *The Panorama: History of a Mass Medium* (New York: Zone Books, 1997),
11. Further references will be given parenthetically in the text.
[7] Daniels, *Humphry Repton*, 123.
[8] Humphry Repton, *A Letter to Uvedale Price, Esq.* (London: Printed for G. Nicol, 1794), 15.

What we have here, then, is a bourgeois revision of the sublime: as Stephan Oettermann remarks of the panorama, "The bourgeoisie insisted on 'seeing things from a new angle,' an angle that made all members of the paying public equal" (*Panorama*, 24). Oettermann argues that the panorama figured as the opposite of the dungeon, that image of Absolutist oppression. The panorama was a "painting without borders" (15), and although it did rely on perspectival recession, it fundamentally altered its workings. Rather than presupposing a single point from which the landscape radiates in rational order, with all receding orthogonal lines meeting at a point opposite the fixed point of a single eye, the panorama utilized a system of perspective that presupposed a series of viewpoints along a horizontal line. In this theater it was not just the monarch who would see everything in correct perspective. It is fitting, then, that the subjects of these panoramas reflected a bourgeois, urban sensibility. Although Robert Barker, the first important producer of commercial panoramas, originally described them – as if in deference to the picturesque tradition – as "La Nature à coup d'oeil," they were in fact almost invariably representations of cityscapes or recent political events. Moreover, the implied point of observation was very often a commercial building; thus, for instance, Barker's view of London was taken from the roof of Albion Mills.

This interest in the panoramic view can be clearly seen in Repton's own work. In some of his Red Books, Repton includes pull-out panoramic views of his patron's grounds. In the Red Book for Sufton Court, in Herefordshire he explicitly distinguishes the panoramic view from the traditional compositions so beloved of his rivals Knight and Price: "I should no more advise the Landscape Gardener in laying out a place to affect the confined field of vision . . . of a Claude or a Poussin, than I should recommend to a landscape painter the quincunx . . . My sketches, if they were more finished, would be a sort of Panorama."[9] Indeed, Repton's images often reflect the logic of the panorama even when he is not working in an explicitly panoramic format. We see this for instance in his *General View of Longleate from the Prospect Hill* (figure 11). Once again, Repton accents horizontals rather than drawing the eye into depth; with the exception of Longleate itself, the only item of interest in the scene being viewed is the river mirroring the horizon. The pointing man in the foreground directs our eye into depth, but the members of his group all look elsewhere, prompting the viewer to imagine the scene not in terms of a straightforward view of the

---

[9] From the Red Book for Sufton Court (1795), private collection. Quoted in Daniels in *Humphry Repton*, 129.

GENERAL VIEW OF LONGLEATE FROM THE PROSPECT HILL:

Figure 11. Humphry Repton, "General View of Longleate," from *Fragments on the Theory and Practice of Landscape Gardening* (London: T. Bensley and Son, 1816).

house, but in terms of a circular panoramic vista. The foreground fringe of shrubbery makes a circle of the picnic area, which further heightens the impulse to imagine the scene in relation to a panorama. Indeed, the plate's power lies almost entirely in its capacity to suggest that panorama. The treatment of the house and the surrounding countryside is abstract to the point of being boring; the picture is not about them but about the pleasure of having a panoramic prospect.

The desire for mastery, coupled with a spirit of thrift, is taken to its extreme by Repton's successor, J. C. Loudon. Although he launched his career by setting himself against Repton, by the 1820s Loudon had come to appreciate Repton's work, and ultimately positioned him centrally in a landscaping tradition that he represented as having culminated in his own gardenesque style. Loudon actively preferred the suburban garden to the rural estate because a man could, in such a garden, have maximum enjoyment at a minimum cost.[10] Loudon's garden designs and drawings are not

[10] John Claudius Loudon, *The Suburban Gardener, and Villa Companion* (London: Longman, Orme, Brown, Green and Longmans; Edinburgh: W. Black, 1832), 10.

View from the Entrance Portico at Kenwood.

Figure 12. John Claudius Loudon, "View from the Entrance Portico of Kenwood,"
from *The Suburban Gardener, and Villa Companion* (London: Longman,
Orme, Brown, Green and Longmans; and W. Black, Edinburgh, 1832).

simply on a smaller scale than Repton's but reveal that the logic of Repton's
use of space has been taken a step further: Repton's focus on the middle
ground has now given way to a penchant for crowding the foreground.
Pictorial space in Loudon tends to be very shallow indeed. Thus, for
instance, he offers an "approach" to a house that has practically no depth
at all, so that forward movement toward the desired object is hardly possible; the object is already there. He even speaks of "views" in cases where
there is no prospect in the traditional sense, as in his view from the entrance
portico of Kenwood, which consists of a single large tree (figure 12).

For Loudon, ownership and control are of the utmost importance; his
writings reveal an anxious possessiveness. The owner of a small villa, he
argues, has the advantage that "his grounds lie more in his hands": he not
only owns them, but can design and maintain them himself.[11] This is a

---

[11] *Ibid.*, 9.

businessman's garden not only because of its affordability but also because of its manageability, its function as both an object of pleasure and an object of labor. Unabashed in their bourgeois sensibilities, Loudon's manuals preach an ethic of unrelenting work, and they argue that the reward for this work is a garden that, like the panorama, reproduces the world at large for the purpose of personal consumption. The aim of Loudon's "gardenesque" is complete mastery over this simulacrum of the natural world, a mastery that is not just legal but practical and intellectual. It is telling that most of Loudon's works appeared in the form of encyclopedias. Ponderous tomes, they purport to be exhaustive, to contain everything pertaining to their subject. Loudon's ideal gardener is a man who spends every free moment in study, and Loudon's volumes are there to provide him with all available knowledge on the natural world that it is his task to control.

This drive to be all-inclusive is in fact the leading characteristic of the gardenesque aesthetic. For the suburban gardener not only wants complete control over his land but also wants that land to contain everything worth having. Loudon repeatedly makes the point that on a modest estate one can cultivate not simply all the plants grown on a large one, but all the plants that are amenable to cultivation in England.[12] A typical gardenesque design demonstrates this ambition to reproduce the world in miniature. The numbers in figure 13 are keyed to a long list of plants; this landscape has more in common with a museum than a picturesque estate. The emphasis is not on the garden's beauty but on its botanical inclusiveness. Like Loudon's crowded foregrounds, this garden is designed for the man who wants to have it all, and to have it all within reach. The picturesque desire to experience variety has metamorphosed into a desire to experience everything. Just as the word "encyclopedia" derives from a notion of a circle of arts and science, an all-encompassing education, so Loudon's garden paths are often circular, leading the viewer past a "complete" set of plants.

Here again, then, we see a link with the contemporary panorama, which offers a circular, comprehensive view, one that aims to show everything. Although Loudon usually screens in his miniature world – with vegetation or with a wall – in order more fully to assert its completeness, when he does look beyond the boundaries of a property he looks panoramically. Thus, for instance, he suggests using an anamorphic panoramic drawing to get a sure sense of the surroundings of a given spot when one is choosing a place to build (see figure 14). It was precisely this kind of drawing that served as guides for visitors to the early panoramas. Indeed, such drawings were

---

[12] *Ibid.*, 4.

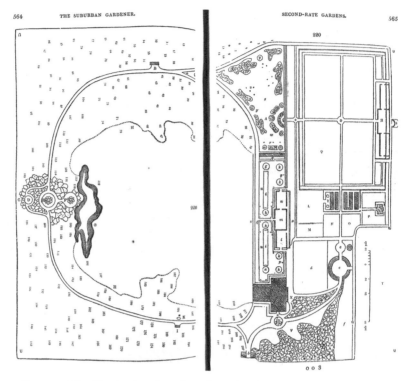

Figure 13. John Claudius Loudon, plan of a garden, from *The Suburban Gardener, and Villa Companion* (London: Longman, Orme, Brown, Green and Longmans; and W. Black, Edinburgh, 1832).

sometimes sold independently as "cycloramas," returning us once again to the notion of a complete circle. The gardenesque, like the panorama, functioned according to a logic of synopsis: it reproduced the richness of the world in a condensed format. The arts that operated according to this logic pleased precisely by virtue of this condensation and intensification.

For all its popularity, however, the synoptic aesthetic suffered from shortcomings that were visible even to the eyes of contemporaries. As William Galperin notes, the panorama may offer a commanding vantage, but that command cannot be complete since one must move about to experience it.[13] Similarly, the gardenesque had to compromise between the desire to "have it all" and the difficulty of fitting it "all" into the foreground.

---

[13] William Galperin, *The Return of the Visible in British Romanticism* (Baltimore: Johns Hopkins University Press, 1993), 46.

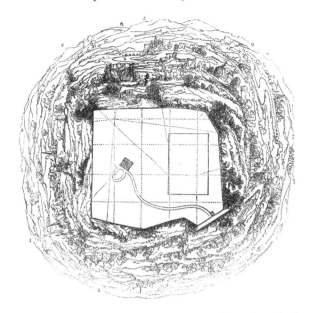

Figure 14. John Claudius Loudon, plan of a building site, from *The Suburban Gardener, and Villa Companion* (London: Longman, Orme, Brown, Green and Longmans; and W. Black, Edinburgh, 1832).

Underlying these difficulties is an even more serious problem: visual mastery in itself has limitations. Oettermann claims that

> after land reform, one might even see a parallel between the displaced farmer and the panorama visitor: the one was separated from the land by a fence, the other from the painted landscape by the "false terrain" and a railing . . . One contemporary expressed his discomfiture in this situation quite succinctly when he wrote, "You have the whole before you, so fine and so near that you want to reach out and touch it . . . but must refrain." (*Panorama*, 45)

Such complaints reveal the difficulty of satisfying the longing for "the whole" that gave rise to the synoptic aesthetic in the first place, just as they reveal an urban, hands-on bias that the traditional notion of visual mastery of a prospect could never quite gratify.

These shortcomings were not, however, sufficient to undermine the extraordinary popularity of the synoptic aesthetic. The suburban villa with its circular path, like the panorama and cyclorama, provided a comprehensive, controlled experience of the world for large numbers of the urban and suburban bourgeoisie. These consumers had a powerful appetite for this new aesthetic of intensified space, a space made smaller but richer. The owner of the suburban villa might have had only a small plot of land, and the visitor to the panorama might have had to bump shoulders with other fee-paying city dwellers as he enjoyed his artificial view, but both were able to derive from these reduced spaces a sensation of pleasurable mastery. The synoptic aesthetic gave visible form to democratic impulses, and, like the picturesque from which it was derived, it encoded a masterful, rather than a submissive, form of desire. Indeed, it offered the opposite of the submissive eroticism we have analyzed in previous chapters, since, without idealizing any one object of desire, it purported to provide the immediate gratification of a generalized desire to possess. But from 1810 through the 1830s this aesthetic would increasingly be displaced by another urban aesthetic, one that reflected the fact that in the modern city and its suburbs not only space, but also time, had been intensified.

II

Historians of nineteenth-century visual culture have suggested that inventions such as the moving panorama, the pleorama, and above all the diorama arose in response to complaints about the static quality of the panorama, especially the unnaturalness of still human and animal figures.[14] I would argue that what was at stake was not just movement *per se* but the representation of change. For these new visual technologies reflected a new taste, one that was to become more and more important over the course of the nineteenth century: a taste for the ephemeral, the fleeting. The diorama, which enjoyed its peak of popularity in the 1820s, did not provide an image of movement so much as it suggested the passage of time through the imitation of subtle changes of light and atmosphere. A transparent canvas and suspended colored screens were lit from behind so as to give the effect of alternations of sunlight and passing clouds, seasonal changes, and so forth. One of the diorama's forerunners, a slide show devised by the Swiss Niklas König, captures the spirit of these technologies in its name: the diaphanorama. Indeed, the diorama was less an offshoot of the panorama than a further development of the "moonshine transparencies" and magic lantern displays that had become so popular at the turn of the century (*Panorama*, 14). If the panorama provided a view of the world at a glance, the diorama revealed that no one

---

[14] See Oettermann, *Panorama*, 7, and Ralph Hyde, *Panoramania!: The Art and Entertainment of the "All-Embracing" View* (London: Trefoil Publications in association with the Barbican Art Gallery, 1988), 109.

glance could capture transient beauties. Even a single landscape, when subjected to meteorological flux, could never really be mastered. The very structure of the diorama theater, with its set of two "picture rooms," underscored the partiality of the views it offered. The displacement of one scene by another made it impossible to imagine either as "complete" or representative. What Galperin calls the "peculiar indeterminacy" of the dioramic experience was further heightened by the subjects that Louis Daguerre chose; he was particularly attracted to ruins.[15]

As with the panorama, the vogue for the diorama was not an isolated or accidental phenomenon but reflected a more general trend. Painters such as John Constable and J. M. W. Turner sought to capture the transient effects of light and weather in their paintings. Constable explained that in his *English Landscape Scenery* project he aimed "To give 'to one brief moment caught from fleeting time', a lasting and sober existence, and to render permanent many of those splendid but evanescent Exhibitions, which are ever occurring in the changes of external Nature."[16] Constable visited Daguerre's diorama, and, like Daguerre, often produced multiple versions of a single landscape under varying atmospheric conditions. Ann Bermingham, speaking of this practice, argues that it was intended in part to consolidate the identity of those landscapes. Yet, as she notes, "If the repetition of subjects establishes their universal essence, the tonality of Constable's late works – what he called the chiaroscuro of nature – reduces this essence to a ruin."[17] During the 1820s, the fugitive quality of the atmosphere itself became an important subject for Constable; this was the period of his cloud studies, quick sketches that were labeled with precise dates, times, and meteorological conditions.

Of course, it is Turner even more than Constable who is known for his interest in evanescent qualities of color and light. This interest is manifest as early as the 1810s and arguably functions as a high-art version of a similar trend in the domain of popular art. In a review of the 1842 Royal Academy Exhibition, a writer for *Blackwood's* drew precisely that connection:

[Turner's paintings] are like the "Dissolving Views," which, when one subject is melting into another, and there are but half indications of forms, and a strange blending of blues and yellows and reds, offer something infinitely better, more grand, more imaginative than the distinct purpose of either view presents. We

---

[15] Galperin, *Return of the Visible*, 64.
[16] John Constable, *John Constable's Discourses*, ed. R. B. Beckett (Ipswich: Suffolk Records Society, 1970), 9–10.
[17] Ann Bermingham, *Landscape and Ideology: The English Rustic Tradition, 1740–1860* (Berkeley: University of California Press, 1986), 150.

would therefore recommend the aspirant after Turner's style and fame, to a few nightly exhibitions of the "Dissolving Views" at the Polytechnic.[18]

Over the course of his career, Turner's paintings, like Constable's, increasingly attempted to reproduce sensation rather than represent clearly defined objects. As critics such as Jonathan Crary have shown, this replacement of an empiricist by a subjectivist view was a formative step in the development of modern art, and the relation of this subjectivism to canonical Romantic poetry is clear.[19] But it is not enough to say that Romantic-era painting is concerned with subjective sensation. For the sensations these paintings reproduce are specifically of the evanescence of the world. That is, it is important to recognize that what we are seeing here is as much a change in the valuation of objects as a change in the valuation of subjects. Painters such as Constable and Turner were not only concerned with the vagaries of sensation but were deeply attracted to ephemeral phenomena in themselves. The poem that Turner appended to a painting of 1843, *Light and Colour (Goethe's Theory) – the Morning after the Deluge – Moses writing the Book of Genesis* runs thus:

> The ark stood firm on Ararat; th' returning Sun
> Exhaled earth's humid bubbles, and emulous of light,
> Reflected her lost forms, each in prismatic guise
> Hope's harbinger, ephemeral as the summer fly
> Which rises, flits, expands, and dies.[20]

The title itself is enough to suggest the insubstantiality of the painting's ostensible subject matter. As the reference to Goethe implies, the painting is concerned with subjectivist optics, but it is also concerned with the particular attraction of ephemeral phenomena. While traditionally minded critics complained that Turner's paintings were "pictures of nothing, and very like,"[21] champions of the modern, like John Ruskin, argued that it was precisely their effort to capture the uncapturable, to suggest the mysterious, that constituted their virtue.

Even the theater, which was often criticized for its materiality by writers such as William Hazlitt and Charles Lamb, strove to become the haunt of

---

[18] *Blackwood's* 52 (July 1842), 26.
[19] See Jonathan Crary, *Techniques of the Observer: On Vision and Modernity in the Nineteenth Century* (London: MIT Press, 1990).
[20] Quoted in Michael Bockemühl, *J. M. W. Turner: The World of Light and Colour*, trans. Michael Claridge (Cologne: Taschen, 1993), 87.
[21] Quoted by Hazlitt, in *The Complete Works of William Hazlitt*, 21 vols., vol. XVIII, ed. P. P. Howe (London: J. M. Dent, and Sons 1930–4), p. 95.

evanescent characters and effects. Again, this evanescence had in part to do with a new conception of subjectivity, and in part with a new conception of the object world. Joanna Baillie's interest in dynamic change in characterization, and even her tendency to describe it in terms of meteorological fluctuation, looks forward to the deep attraction to characterological volatility that was to govern acting technique in the early nineteenth century. Edmund Kean was of course the actor most renowned for such volatility, but the spectacle of change was appreciated in all performances. In an 1814 review in *The Champion* of Miss Eliza O'Neill's Juliet, Hazlitt lauds her capacity to exhibit quick changes of passion: "We remember her manner in the Gamester . . . The look, first of incredulity and astonishment, then of anger, then passing suddenly into contempt, and ending in bitter scorn, and a convulsive burst of laughter, all given in a moment, and laying open every movement of the soul, produced an effect which we shall never forget."[22] By mid-century the taste for such spectacles was simply a given, and had been codified in the form of "Transformation Scenes," "marvels of intricate design and development, of subtle changes of light and colour, that were created to decorate the fairy-plays of Planché for Madame Vestris at the Lyceum."[23] Early nineteenth-century ballet, even more than the drama, aimed at lightness and ephemerality. In an 1817 review for the *Examiner* of "Two New Ballets," Hazlitt speaks of "lusty lovers flying in the air, nests of winged Cupids, that start out of bulrushes, trees that lift up their branches like arms."[24] The popularity of fairies, sylphs, wilis, and ghosts was even more firmly established after the phenomenal success in 1832 of *La Sylphide*. Marie Taglioni's light and airy pointework was complemented by her diaphanous white costume; indeed, Romantic ballets are still often referred to as *ballets blancs*. The very plot of *La Sylphide* thematizes transience: the hero, James, attempts to use an enchanted scarf to capture a sylph, but the loss of her wings means the loss of her life, and she dies in his arms. The ephemeral cannot truly be grasped. Nevertheless, artists continued to try to capture fairies well into the Victorian period, flying them across stages, scoring

[22] *Works*, V, 198–9. Such changeability was as appealing in "real" characters as it was in dramatic ones; Lady Caroline Lamb, for instance, was consistently described as a fairy or sprite, and described herself as "some rare night-flying moth he [Byron] had pinioned to dissect" (quoted in Doris Leslie, *This for Caroline* [London: Heinemann, 1964], 107).

[23] Martin Meisel, *Realizations: Narrative, Pictorial, and Theatrical Arts in Nineteenth-Century England* (Princeton: Princeton University Press, 1983), 184.

[24] William Hazlitt, "Two New Ballets," *Examiner* (February 9, 1817), reprinted in *Works*, V, 353.

music to represent their light and rapid movements, and painting them flitting by in many a moonlit scene.[25]

As Constable's phrase "catching a moment" suggests, the interest in fleeting objects was often linked to the desire to capture them. Indeed, even photography arguably developed out of precisely this impulse. Geoffrey Batchen notes that "the basic components of photography – the images formed by the camera obscura and the chemistry necessary to reproduce them – were both available in the 1720s, quite some time before the photograph was officially 'invented' in 1839."[26] The reason for the delay of this invention, he argues, is that the *desire* to photograph did not become widespread until the turn of the century. And this desire had everything to do with a love of evanescence; the early photographic experimenters did not simply want to capture a scene but to capture images they considered beautiful for their transience. William Henry Fox Talbot, who showed samples of his "photogenic drawings" at the Royal Institution in 1839, described his early endeavors in these terms:

[Using a camera obscura, I tried] to trace with my pencil the outlines of the scenery depicted on the paper. And this led me to reflect on the inimitable beauty of the pictures of nature's painting which the glass lens of the Camera throws upon the paper in its focus – fairy pictures, creations of a moment, and destined as rapidly to fade away. It was during these thoughts that the idea occurred to me . . . how charming it would be if it were possible to cause these natural images to imprint themselves durably, and remain fixed upon the paper![27]

[25] See Jane Martineau, ed., *Victorian Fairy Painting* (London: Holberton, 1998). The works of the Victorian painter E. T. Parris, who painted fairy subjects over the whole course of his career, exemplify this tradition. His 1832 *The Visit at Moonlight* clearly reveals the influence of the Romantic ballet on the nineteenth-century handling of fairy subjects: his fairies, flying or lightly perched on the tips of their toes, gleam in their translucency. This interest in things imperfectly defined, not quite perceived, even influenced the making of mundane domestic goods. The popularity of filmy muslins around the turn of the century reflected more than just a revival of neoclassical design in dressmaking. These same fabrics were used for window curtains and lampshades (see Wolfgang Schivelbusch, *Disenchanted Night: The Industrialization of Light in the Nineteenth Century*, trans. Angela Davies [Berkeley: University of California Press, 1988], 169). Translucent materials seemed both to capture light itself and to render diaphanous the objects seen through them. This love of translucency was later to find expression in the development of glass architecture; Schivelbusch remarks that "the impression of glass architecture can be summed up in one word: evanescence" (*The Railway Journey: The Industrialization of Time and Space in the Nineteenth Century* [Berkeley: University of California Press, 1986], 47).

[26] Geoffrey Batchen, *Burning with Desire: The Conception of Photography* (London: MIT Press, 1997), 26.

[27] From Fox Talbot's "Introductory Remarks" to *The Pencil of Nature* (London: Longman, Brown, Green, and Longmans, 1844).

Fox Talbot described the photographic process itself thus: "The most transitory of things, a shadow, the proverbial emblem of all that is fleeting and momentary, may be fettered by the spells of our '*natural magic*,' and may be fixed for ever in the position which it seemed only destined for a single instant to occupy."[28] Against earlier historians of photography, Batchen argues that both the calotype and the daguerreotype, like Daguerre's diorama, were fundamentally oriented toward the "contingency of appearance," not a positivist notion of reality.[29]

Photography, then, like the panorama, was not so much a quirk of technological development as the practical manifestation of a desire for a particular kind of visual experience. The aesthetic of the synoptic sought to provide an experience of having it all, and underwrote a masterful form of subjectivity. The diorama, on the other hand, along with various other technologies that were to become increasingly important over the course of the first half of the nineteenth century, functioned according to an aesthetic of the ephemeral. Both aesthetics catered to an urban/suburban class that increasingly had money to spend on art, whether in the form of a photograph or in a well-designed garden. The aesthetic of the ephemeral, however, was the more fully modern of the two, for the synoptic had its grounding in aristocratic habit and pretension. It took its shape from a traditional subjectivity founded in estate ownership and the experience of the grand tour, a subjectivity rooted in masterful possession, and especially the possession of real estate. This subjectivity was of course modified, trimmed down to an affordable suburban scale, even as its excesses, its claim to have it all, proclaimed its bourgeois anxieties. Its orientation, however, was fundamentally traditional.

The ephemeral, on the other hand, served to define a truly modern subjectivity, one that took its shape from fleeting and therefore highly particularized experiences. The identities formed in a fast-paced modern world, one steeped in history and contingency, were themselves more malleable, more flexible, and more individualized than those old-fashioned identities associated with Enlightenment norms and hierarchies. Fox Talbot's photographic reproduction of a "Specimen of Byron's Hand," which he intended to use in a memorial publication on the poet, ironically reveals the instability of the identity of even a famous poet and a Lord. By reproducing part of a manuscript version of an already published poem – the final stanza of a poem on

[28] William Henry Fox Talbot, "Some Account of the Art of Photogenic Drawing" (1839), in Beaumont Newhall, ed., *Photography: Essays & Images* (New York: Museum of Modern Art, 1980), 25.
[29] Batchen, *Burning with Desire*, 143.

the passing of great men, "Ode to Napoleon" – Fox Talbot reminds us of Byron's absence as much as he conjures his presence.[30]

Modern identities seemed by their nature mutable, and, increasingly, they were grounded not in relation to permanent objects but in relation to impermanent ones. In the economic realm this was related to a shift in emphasis away from ownership to that more modern activity, "consumption." For the growing numbers of people in the middle and lower ranks of society, a rise in purchasing power meant an increase in consumption in the literal sense of "consuming." There was a difference, after all, in the identity-conferring powers of goods depending on one's class: a possession such as real estate is lasting, unchanging – it is called "real" for a reason. But the goods that the public at large were able to afford usually came in the form of semi-durables and foodstuffs. Studies in the so-called consumer boom of the eighteenth century point to the fact that coffee, sugar, and tea were the luxuries in which the poor were most likely to indulge. Carole Shammas argues that while the early modern period saw a boom in groceries, one does not find the evidence one might expect of a boom in consumer durables. One reason for this, she suggests, is that

many of the new consumer goods were of a more ephemeral nature. The textiles were lighter, whether made of the new draperies, linen or cotton. Chapbooks and other paper products might not make it through the years. Pottery could be destroyed much more readily than wood or glass or pewter.[31]

Shammas concludes that "a combination of falling prices and substitutions of less permanent goods for more durable ones probably account for most of the increased accumulation of consumer goods in the eighteenth century."[32] This change can be related to the shift away from valuing objects first and foremost for what Grant McCracken calls "patina," or the signs of age, to valuing them for their novelty, their fashionableness.[33] By the nineteenth century institutions like the fashion system made obsolescence a structurally necessary part of the economy. Hazlitt explained to readers of the *Edinburgh Magazine* in an 1818 essay "On Fashion" that "The real and solid will never do for the current coin, the common wear and tear of

---

[30] Photogenic drawing negative, reproduced in Larry J. Schaaf, *The Photographic Art of William Henry Fox Talbot* (Princeton: Princeton University Press, 2000), 79.

[31] Carole Shammas, *The Pre-Industrial Consumer in England and America* (Oxford: Clarendon Press, 1990), 191.

[32] *Ibid.*, 200.

[33] See Grant McCracken, *Culture and Consumption: New Approaches to the Symbolic Character of Consumer Goods and Activities* (Bloomington: Indiana University Press, 1988), Chapter 2, "'Ever Dearer in Our Thoughts': Patina and the Representation of Status before and after the Eighteenth Century."

foppery and fashion"; fashion "contrives to keep up its fastidious preten-
sions . . . by the rapidity and evanescent nature of the changes."[34] For
members of the gentry and aristocracy, ownership largely still took the
form of lasting possession, but to those in the classes below, consumption
was literally that – it was about eating something or otherwise using it
up. A specialty food item might be considered a luxury and might mark
its consumer as a person of some means, but it did so in a very different
way from a piece of fine furniture. This new way of conceiving of objects
in time effectively inverted traditional notions of object value and the
stable, rooted social identities that value underwrote.

The aesthetic of the ephemeral celebrated this new relation to objects,
finding a beauty in their fugitive qualities at the same time that it recognized
the pathos inherent in their transience. It embodied the logic of the modern
in artistic form, reproducing the temporal signature of the modern commodity even as its immaterial qualities gave it the appearance of transcending the
market. Like the modern commodity, it underwrote a form of subjectivity
that was changeable, variable. But as we will see, it also gave rise to a
peculiarly modern form of melancholy, for attaching oneself to ephemeral
objects meant lamenting the very transience that made them lovely.

III

Nowhere are the aesthetics of the synoptic and the ephemeral more fully
considered than in the poetry of John Keats. As Marjorie Levinson has
shown, Keats's work was deeply influenced by his position as a petty-
bourgeois suburbanite, a man who felt himself to have an outsider's relation
to the fine arts in general and the elite poetic tradition in particular.[35] I
would argue that Keats's class status influenced not only his style and his
choice of subject matter but also the peculiar temporal dynamics for
which his poetry is so renowned. For the problem of consumption as an
"eating up" is one with which Keats struggled throughout his career. The
epigraph to his poem "On Fame," (written in 1819), states the problem
in its proverbial form: "You cannot have your cake and eat it too."[36]
You can have your chair and sit in it, or have your garden and walk in it,
but the more homely forms of consumption, those available to a man of

---

[34] William Hazlitt, "On Fashion," in *William Hazlitt: Selected Writings*, ed. Jon Cook (Oxford: Oxford University Press, 1991), 151, 150.
[35] Marjorie Levinson, *Keats's Life of Allegory: The Origins of a Style* (Oxford: Basil Blackwell, 1988).
[36] *John Keats: Complete Poems*, ed. Jack Stillinger (Cambridge, Mass.: Harvard University Press, 1978), 278. Further references will be given parenthetically in the text.

Keats's class, were more fleeting and potentially more vexed. In Walter Jackson Bate's words, Keats was a man who was "homeless, and, after the death of Tom and the departure of George, was to be largely homeless until the end."[37] But if Keats had little in the way of lasting comforts, he did enjoy some perishable ones. In the happier days of his boyhood, his grandfather fancied himself "a complete gourmand" (*John Keats*, 5), and the Sunday dinner was an important event in the Keats household. As a man, the consumer items that Keats most often discussed in his letters were foodstuffs:

> If I can [find] any place tolerably comfitable I will settle myself and fag till I can afford to buy Pleasure – which if [I] never can afford I must go Without – Talking of Pleasure, this moment I was writing with one hand, and with the other holding to my Mouth a Nectarine – good god how fine – It went down soft pulpy, slushy, oozy – all its delicious embonpoint melted down my throat like a large beatified Strawberry. I shall certainly breed.[38]

If for the aristocrat you are what you own, for the petty bourgeois you are what you eat:

> beef – beef . . . The Coachman's face says eat, eat – I never feel more contemptible than when I am sitting by a good looking coachman – One is nothing – Perhaps I eat to persuade myself I am somebody. You must be when slice after slice – but it wont do – the Coachman nibbles a bit of bread – he's favour'd – he's had a Call – a Hercules Methodist – Does he live by bread alone?[39]

Food is, moreover, a peculiarly social consumer item, one that establishes not just private identity but social relations:

> How came milidi to give one Lisbon wine – had she drained the Gooseberry? Truly I cannot delay making another visit – asked to take Lunch, whether I will have ale, wine take sur g ar, – objection to green – like cream – thin bread and butter – another cup – agreeable – enough sugar – little more cream – too weak 12 shillin & &c &c lord I must come again. (260)

According to Benjamin Robert Haydon, Keats's experiments in consumption made deliberate use of the fleeting character of taste; he tells an anecdote in which Keats covers his tongue in cayenne pepper to heighten the sensation of the contrasting "coolness of claret."[40]

---

[37] Walter Jackson Bate, *John Keats* (Cambridge: Harvard University Press, 1963), 89. Further references will be given parenthetically in the text.

[38] *Letters of John Keats*, ed. Robert Gittings (Oxford: Oxford University Press, 1970), 302.

[39] *Ibid.*, 293.

[40] *The Diary of Benjamin Robert Haydon*, 5 vols., vol. II, ed. Willard B. Pope (Cambridge, Mass.: Harvard University Press, 1960), p. 317.

As important as perishables were in the world of Keats's luxuries, however, he began his poetic career with a focus on the more traditional, synoptic experience. As Elizabeth Jones has shown, Keats's poetry has much in common with the gardenesque.[41] Not only does he make extensive use of horticultural imagery in his poems, but he works on a suburban scale, cramming as many different plants as possible into a small nook or bower. This respect for traditional landed values – albeit in their modern suburban form – is the less surprising given his reverence for poetic tradition, a tradition that would, after all, have appeared anything but ephemeral. One of Keats's first long poems is thus written in the tradition of the loco-descriptive poem, while it modifies the genre to focus on the specifically synoptic qualities of the scene described. In "I stood tip-toe upon a little hill," the imperatives of both the panorama and the gardenesque are satisfied: "There was wide wand'ring for the greediest eye, / To peer about upon variety."[42] In the 1805 *Prelude* Wordsworth describes the panorama painter as having a "greedy pencil";[43] here Keats unabashedly enjoys the satisfaction of such greed. That the urge to have it all binds together the gardenesque and the panoramic – the first an art of small, enclosed spaces and the second an art of wide open ones – is aptly proven in this poem. Although the speaker begins by skimming "Far round the horizon's crystal air" (l. 17), he quickly turns to the precise cataloguing of plants, remarking that "no tasteful nook would be without them" (1.30), as if the scene were not of a wide prospect but of a man-made garden. The speaker even uses the language of garden planning: "there too should be / The frequent chequer of a youngling tree" (ll. 38–9). The desire to take possession of the landscape for the sake of self-transformation is immediately made clear:

> I gazed awhile, and felt as light, and free
> As though the fanning wings of Mercury
> Had played upon my heels: I was light-hearted,
> And many pleasures to my vision started,
> So I straightway began to pluck a posey
> Of luxuries bright, milky, soft and rosy. (ll. 23–28)

Such possessiveness is apparently warranted by nature's own doings; the sweet peas, for instance, reduplicate the speaker's posture: "Here are sweet

[41] See Elizabeth Jones, "Keats in the Suburbs," *Keats-Shelley Journal* 45 (1996), 23–43.
[42] Keats, *Complete Poems*, 48, ll. 15–16.
[43] William Wordsworth, *The Prelude: 1799, 1805, 1850*, ed. Jonathan Wordsworth, M. H. Abrams and Stephen Gill (New York: Norton, 1979), 1805 Prelude, Book 7, l. 258.

peas, on tip-toe for a flight: / With wings of gentle flush o'er delicate white, / And taper fingers catching at all things, / To bind them all about with tiny rings" (ll. 57–60).

Keats is, however, unable to sustain the synoptic vantage, precisely because it functions at odds with his deeply felt understanding of the workings of consumption. He cannot imagine a consummation in this scene of panoramic pleasures, and for several reasons. First, having everything precludes a focus on any one thing; there is an unavoidably serial quality to the description here that militates against attachment to a single object. Second, there is no room for desire to build in the synoptic aesthetic – since possession is already complete, there is no place for the tension of desire. But Keats's trouble with the synoptic goes deeper still, for ultimately he cannot believe in a scene of consumption that does not involve the loss or alteration of the thing being consumed. Thus violence intrudes upon this idyllic scene, appearing, it would seem, from nowhere:

> . . . a spring-head of clear waters
> Babbling so wildly of its lovely daughters
> The spreading blue bells: it may haply mourn
> That such fair clusters should be rudely torn
> From their fresh beds, and scattered thoughtlessly
> By infant hands, left on the path to die. (ll. 41–6)

Nature's doings might be, as the speaker insists, "gentle," but man's presence, his desire for possession, necessarily disturbs them. Little wonder that the minnows in the stream instantly disappear as a human hand approaches the water. Keats was to take up this theme again and more forcefully in "I had a dove, and the sweet dove died," written in 1819: possession destroys the thing possessed. Lovely things cannot be owned, and the true enjoyment of them can only be fleeting. The climax of the first half of "I stood tip-toe" is therefore an awkward and uncertain one:

> Were I in such a place, I sure should pray
> That nought less sweet might call my thoughts away,
> Than the soft rustle of a maiden's gown
> . . .
> O let me lead her gently o'er the brook,
> Watch her half-smiling lips, and downward look;
> O let me for one moment touch her wrist;
> Let me one moment to her breathing list;
> And as she leaves me may she often turn
> Her fair eyes looking through her locks auburne. (ll. 93–106)

Not only is this scene distanced by being described as a fiction within the fiction of the poem – "Were I in such a place, I sure should pray" – but it presents, at the moment when a consummation is expected, a disappearance. The watching, touching, and listening culminates not in a kiss or a promise but in the maiden's leaving. It is not enough to say, as critics often have, that such moments are simply a sign of Keats's adolescent inexperience. Inexperienced as he may be, he is also struggling with the constraints of the aesthetic in which he has chosen to work.

Over the course of his career, Keats was repeatedly drawn to the synoptic aesthetic and the promise it extended of offering a static world of complete satisfaction. In his later poems he, like Loudon, describes spaces that are even more bounded than the "little" hill: private bowers that despite their snugness are full of every sweet. But this optimistic synoptic aesthetic is increasingly brought into tension with an aesthetic of ephemerality, an aesthetic in which consummation means consumption and loss – the cake is eaten. "Ode on a Grecian Urn" (1820), for example, while it speaks to the universal theme of human mortality, does so in a way that reflects the peculiar exigencies of possession and loss in Keats's own era. It plays out its concerns in terms of an aesthetic rivalry, a rivalry not just between visual and verbal art but between an art of synopsis and an art of the ephemeral. The urn, in its circularity and comprehensiveness, not only offers a whole world in miniature but is itself an object possessed of traditional value, a value that can be enjoyed without being consumed. This synoptic virtue, it should be noted, while it is well-suited to visual art, is not unavailable to verbal art: the first lines of the poem especially are remarkable for their "exceptional compression."[44] But it is precisely the completeness and stasis of the urn that the poem will ultimately question. In an age when time seems to be passing ever more swiftly, the urn's sheer durability renders it both impressive and unnatural. When ruins, clouds, and ghosts are objects of fascination, it is little wonder that an intact ancient artifact, for all its authority, should be disturbing.

Critics have long known that the poem can be understood in the context of the controversies surrounding the arrival in England of the Elgin Marbles; *The Annals of the Fine Arts*, in which the poem made its public debut in 1820, was deeply involved in the evaluation of classical art as well as the contemporary debate over the relative value of poetry and

---

[44] Stuart Sperry, *Keats the Poet* (Princeton: Princeton University Press, 1973), 268.

painting.[45] I would argue, however, that Keats's interest in the latter debate
sprang not just from professional pride but also from the opportunity it
offered him to reflect on aesthetic tensions within the domain of poetry
itself – a rivalry between an aesthetic of intensified space and an aesthetic
of intensified temporality. After all, the concern with time and space that
was often mapped onto particular media clearly had ramifications *within*
those media as well, as Keats's representation of the landscape and the
lady in "I stood tip-toe" reveals. If, as Theresa Kelley argues, Keats's ode
is only ambivalently committed to *ekphrasis*, and if he tends to minimize
the narrative capacity of the urn – as if it were Etruscan rather than
Greek[46] – this is in part because he is concerned first and foremost with
the issue of temporality itself, and uses the debate over artistic media as a
forum in which to explore it. Thus he does not simply suggest, as many
of his contemporaries did, that verbal art is better suited to narrative
than visual art; he makes it appear that visual art has no narrative capacity
at all, when in fact the conventions of painting had long allowed for temporal development within the confines of an apparently static medium.
Whether the painter suggested a future inherent in the present by means
of legible signs or emblems, or a narrative dimension was implied by the
subject matter itself, as it generally was in history painting, the educated
viewer would have understood well enough that static images embodied
not only a present but also a past and a future. Furthermore, Romantic-
era painters were continually inventing new techniques to suggest dynamism and motion. Even if one argued, as Hazlitt did, that "painting gives
the event, poetry the progress of events,"[47] painting was at least granted
the power to represent one event in its completeness. One imagines that
Hazlitt would not, as Keats's speaker does, look at a painting of a man
and a woman about to kiss and assume that they would never touch.
Keats exaggerates the static qualities of the urn as part of his challenge to
the synoptic aesthetic as a whole, an aesthetic he associated not just with
visual art but with canonical art generally. In focusing on a classical artifact,
Keats is able to ponder the tenability of the traditional investment in a
notion of classical perfection and completeness. The urn's stasis arises not

[45] For a thorough account of the poem in relation to the *Annals*, see James O'Rourke, *Keats's Odes and Contemporary Criticism* (Gainesville: University Press of Florida, 1998), Chapter 2, "Antiquity, Romanticism, and Modernity: 'Ode on a Grecian Urn,'" 46–94.
[46] Theresa Kelley, "Keats, Ekphrasis, and History," in Nicholas Roe, ed., *Keats and History* (Cambridge: Cambridge University Press, 1995), 214, 227.
[47] Hazlitt, *Works*, V, 10.

only from its visual character but from its role as a sign of unchanging value and the cool certainties of elite culture. Keats thus hypostatizes visual stasis the more thoroughly to reveal the shortcomings of this culture, and opposes it to the homely pleasures that would, if only for a moment, satisfy the parching tongue or the lover's ardor.

Indeed, Keats goes further still, suggesting that this unnatural stasis cannot last. He challenges the ostensible durability of the urn – the fact that it can be enjoyed without being destroyed – by repeatedly linking it to things that are destroyed in the act of consumption. In the world of the poem, consummation is linked to violation and death. Throughout the poem, presumably innocent, pastoral love raises the specter of rape, as maidens loth try to evade pursuit. As many critics have remarked, the urn itself is immediately feminized, its idealized remoteness threatened by its status as a "still unravish'd bride": the urn might be broken, the bride violated, at any time.[48] The urn's similarity to the sacrificial heifer – with garlands that flank her sides like the leaf-fringed legend encircling the urn – is an even more dire prognostic. It is precisely because the poem can imagine no other options than the synoptic ideal – which is experienced as forbiddingly remote – and the heartbreakingly ephemeral, that the figures on the urn come to "hint of alienation and potential violence."[49]

It is this conflict of paradigms that accounts for that strange vacillation between cloying satisfaction and disappointed desire that characterizes almost all of Keats's major poetry. For if the synoptic purported to provide a fulfillment so complete as to put an end to narrative, the aesthetic of the ephemeral taught that because the objects most worth having were transient by their nature, desire could not in fact meet with any but a passing gratification. These competing ideologies gave rise to a peculiarly melancholy and ambivalent form of eroticism, one that sought to negotiate between the promise of complete satisfaction by means of the concentration of objects in space, and the dark suspicion that time, too, had been concentrated, making any satisfaction of desire a mere momentary affair.[50]

---

[48] Keats, *Complete Poems*, 372, l. 1. See Geraldine Friedman, "The Erotics of Interpretation in Keats's 'Ode on a Grecian Urn': Pursuing the Feminine," *Studies in Romanticism* 32 (1993), 225–43, and Daniel Watkins, "Historical Amnesia and Patriarchal Morality in Keats's 'Ode on a Grecian Urn,'" in G. A. Rosso and Daniel Watkins, eds., *Spirits of Fire: English Romantic Writers and Contemporary Historical Methods* (Rutherford, N. J.: Associated University Presses, 1990), 240–59.

[49] Kelley, "Keats, Ekphrasis, and History," 226.

[50] As Froma Zeitlin remarks of "Ode on a Grecian Urn," the poem creates in the male reader "a sexual excitement that is never quite discharged in a gratifying lyric conclusion" ("On Ravishing Urns: Keats in His Tradition," in Lynn A. Higgins and Brenda Silver, eds., *Rape and Representation* [New York: Columbia University Press, 1991], 279–80).

The pain inherent in the desire to experience the beauty of fleeting pleasures is most fully explored in another of Keats's major odes, the "Ode on Melancholy." Indeed, it is the poem's masochistic element that marks the distance between this account of melancholy and more traditional accounts of it. That the poem sets out to define melancholy in specifically modern terms is clear enough from its structure: the first of its three stanzas, as well as the original, canceled first stanza, prepares us for Keats's definition of melancholy by questioning the value of the traditional paraphernalia of melancholia. The modern accoutrements of melancholia are then described in detail in subsequent stanzas, as we will see in a moment. But the speaker also distinguishes his from earlier accounts of melancholy by speaking of it not as a disease in need of a cure but as an experience to be sought. In the standard version of the poem, it appears that the implied interlocutor is a melancholic already, and one who is considering various anodynes for his suffering. But the canceled first stanza recontextualizes what follows: the interlocutor is in fact trying to find melancholy, and in what was originally the second stanza he is simply making the mistake of confusing melancholy with the dull torpor and suicidal impulses with which it had sometimes been linked. The original first stanza is about actively seeking melancholy, building a ship to travel in search of it. Indeed, the island sought by this ship, a place "of Lethe dull" on which Melancholy can be found dreaming, recalls the island of the lotus-eaters, an allusion that underscores both the voluptuous aim of this search and the wrongheadedness of those who go about it in this way.[51] As we will see, melancholy is redefined here as not only desirable but as the source of the keenest pleasures man is capable of feeling. In his 1621 *Anatomy of Melancholy*, Robert Burton had already suggested, in the tradition of writers such as Ficino, that melancholics are often extraordinary men who are touched by genius; Keats goes even further, making melancholy not only a mark of exquisite taste but the necessary concomitant of all true pleasure.[52]

The poem's obsession with the paraphernalia of melancholy is a sign of the economic logic upon which the speaker's notion of melancholy is founded. Modern melancholy is desirable not only because it is a prerogative

---

[51] Keats, *Complete Poems*, from l. 10 of the cancelled first stanza.

[52] Burton informs his reader that an image of Angerona was set on an altar in the Temple of Volupia, but he does argue that anguish and pleasure are indissociable. Indeed, Robert Cummings argues that Burton "rather enforces a dissociation of anguish and pleasure by isolating from his source in Macrobius the observation that the augurs' annual sacrifice to Angerona was to the end 'she might expel all cares, anguish and vexation of the mind for the year following.' Keats on the other hand makes the point that contrary states of feeling may converge in a single sensation" ("Keats's Melancholy in the Temple of Delight," *Keats-Shelley Journal* 36 [1987], 50–1).

of leisure but also because it is the sign of pleasure in consumption. For while melancholy had been variously defined as a disease of physiological imbalance, idleness, astrological determination, and so on,[53] Keats definitively roots it in the act of consumption. The canceled first stanza teaches us that modern melancholy is not about fear, anguish, or even death. The true experience of melancholy is, on the contrary, nourishing, as we learn in the next stanza: "when the melancholy fit shall fall / Sudden from heaven like a weeping cloud, / That fosters the droop-headed flowers all, / And hides the green hill in an April shroud."[54] These lines are, of course, full of paradox, and it is precisely the paradox embodied in the simultaneity of "shrouding" and "fostering" that the poem will argue is constitutive of melancholy. To heighten these paradoxical effects, the reader is advised literally to luxuriate in the consumption of ephemeral beauties, to "glut" his sorrow on a rose or a rainbow, or on the "wealth" of peonies, or to "feed" upon his mistress's "rich" anger (l. 15, l. 17, l. 20, l. 18). As the speaker reminds us, the mistress dwells with a "Beauty that must die," but the melancholy here is less about mortality *per se* than about the fleeting nature of the finest pleasures. After all, while writers had long lamented the brevity of human life, rarely had the champions of pleasure represented enjoyment in as temporally condensed a form as we see here: "Turning to poison while the bee-mouth sips" (l. 24). The poem's finest image of this temporal intensity is one that recalls those edible, fleeting luxuries so often mentioned by Keats in his letters: "him whose strenuous tongue / Can burst Joy's grape against his palate fine" (ll. 27–8). The very act of tasting, an act of pleasure, is also one of "sadness" (l. 29), for the moment of consumption is simultaneously a moment of destruction and loss, of "bursting." We are reminded once again that you cannot have your cake and eat it, too. The pain of losing the object has become a constitutive part of the pleasure of having it, with the result that consummation itself takes on a new character. The anticipation of loss makes the very prospect of gratification suspenseful and even painful.

Although the speaker catalogues a number of different objects of desire in this poem, his attitude toward them makes clear that the serial approach of the picturesque is not available here. Joy's grape is a singular phenomenon – once burst, there is no sense that one can simply reach into the basket and find another. In this respect, Keatsian melancholy shares an important

---

[53] For an account of the history of conceptions of melancholy, see Juliana Schiesari, *The Gendering of Melancholia: Feminism, Psychoanalysis, and the Symbolics of Loss in Renaissance Literature* (Ithaca: Cornell University Press, 1992).

[54] Keats, *Complete Poems*, 374, ll. 11–14.

feature with the Freudian concept: the melancholic is defined by his incapacity for object substitution.

> An object-choice, an attachment of the libido to a particular person, had at one time existed; then, owing to a real slight or disappointment coming from this loved person, the object-relationship was shattered. The result was not the normal one of withdrawal of the libido from this object and a displacement of it on to a new one, but something different . . . The object-cathexis proved to have little power of resistance and was brought to an end. But the free libido was not displaced on to another object; it was withdrawn into the ego. There, however, it was not employed in any unspecified way, but served to establish an *identification* of the ego with the abandoned object. Thus the shadow of the object fell upon the ego.[55]

In Keats's ode the mere prospect of loss has the effect of reshaping subject / object relations. If attachment cannot, by its nature, be complete, if the moment of possession is also a moment of loss and identification with the lost object, then the subject himself – at least as he had been defined in the eighteenth century – must live always under a shadow. While the possession of land had made a man both grounded and free, the consumption of transient luxuries defined a subjectivity that seemed similarly ephemeral. This identification with loss makes the ego itself shadowlike. It also, as in Freud, gives rise to a curious solipsism: a state of mind has itself become an object of desire. Peter Sacks, in his account of the English elegy, describes the way the elegy can work to prevent "fixation on the part of the griever . . . Melancholia usually involves a lasting return to [a] kind of regressive narcissism . . . often including an identification between the ego and the dead such that the melancholic tends toward self-destruction."[56] The "Ode on Melancholy" effectually describes and enacts the melancholy counterpart to the elegy's work of mourning. In so doing it reveals the way changing conceptions of ownership can make what we might consider a pathological psychological state appear unavoidable, and even attractive, to an entire generation.

In Keats's poem this melancholy logic of consumption not only governs one's relations to both objects and persons but also renders them structurally equivalent to each other. Thus a man's mistress can be fed upon just like the grape and the rose. Because her beauties are represented as being

[55] Sigmund Freud, "Mourning and Melancholia," in *The Standard Edition of the Complete Psychological Works of Sigmund Freud*, 24 vols., vol. XIV, trans. and ed. James Strachey with Anna Freud (London: Hogarth Press, 1961), p. 248–9.
[56] Peter Sacks, *The English Elegy: Studies in the Genre from Spenser to Yeats* (Baltimore: Johns Hopkins University Press, 1985), 16–17.

as fleeting as theirs, one can ill-afford to waste time arguing with her. It is best simply to hold her hand and feed deeply upon her eyes, imagined in commercial terms as "peerless" (l. 20) rather than as the means of her own vision – they are "peer-less." Meanwhile, as love is commodified, the enjoyment of commodities is sexualized. The first stanza speaks of the consumption of medicines and poisons in terms of love relations: you should not let "the death-moth be / Your mournful Psyche," "Nor suffer thy pale forehead to be kiss'd / By nightshade, ruby grape of Proserpine" (ll. 6–7; ll. 3–4). In the canceled first stanza, one seeks melancholy in the manner of the hero of a quest romance, longing to find the lovely, dreamy goddess "Melancholy." The experience of melancholic consumption is rich in erotic pleasure.

The ephemeral nature of consumption renders pleasure not only melancholy but also antagonistic. As we saw in "I stood tip-toe," if consumption implies the destruction of its object, one cannot but have an antagonistic relation to that object – the bluebells mourn their gathering, and the fish wisely dart away at the approach of a hand. This antagonism becomes even more problematic when the object at stake is one's beloved. Keats's solution to this problem in "I stood tip-toe," having the maiden leave, is clearly not a very satisfying one. In many of his later poems, consummation takes the form of a struggle; it is fitting that the mistress described in "Melancholy" is angry, and that the speaker's attitude toward her shows an element of aggressive possessiveness as he "emprison[s]" (l. 19) her soft hand. This struggle, moreover, is not only intersubjective but also intrasubjective, because the lover himself would like to preserve the object of his desire. Keatsian lovers tend therefore to glorify their mistresses, to present them as powerful and independent, even as they represent their relations to them as embattled. Hence the first female figures we see in "Melancholy" are all immortals: Melancholy, like Circe, on her "isle of Lethe dull"; Psyche; and Proserpine, poised to give her kiss of death. After the interlude with the earthly mistress, the allegorical figure of Melancholy returns, fully deified and ready to make a trophy of the speaker, as he would gladly have her do. As in the work of Hazlitt and William Hogarth, the presence of allegorical figures is a sign that the ideal has become reified and even intimidating; in Bate's words, "allegorical images that Keats had once so warmly incorporated in narrative . . . now loom abstract and shadowlike" (*John Keats*, 524). The "shift in imagery from the sensory objects of the second stanza to the allegory of sensations in the third"[57] might appear, for those critics who

---

[57] O'Rourke, *Keats's Odes*, 133.

argue that Keats's virtue as a poet lies primarily in his willingness to accept the pains of reality, to mark a shortcoming, if not in terms of personal maturity then at least in terms of style. Indeed, the New Critics tended to find this ode a particularly unsavory and "decadent" one.[58] But efforts to rescue the poem by arguing that it simply aims for an open-eyed recognition of the hard truths of life risk mis- or underreading the poem's patently artificial modes of representation. The presence of allegory here signals both the power of melancholy and the speaker's erotic attraction to it.

The speaker's subjection to powerful women, whether in the form of an angry mistress, mythical goddess, or allegorical figure, serves two rather different functions at once. On the one hand, the mistress's distance serves to protect her from destruction, to hold the moment of consumption in abeyance. On the other hand, her unattainability serves in itself as an emblem of the painful insubstantiality of pleasure: the poem's primary conceit is that the enjoyment of ephemeral pleasures is like subjection to a cruel mistress. Possession *per se* is impossible, as is the manly subjectivity grounded in ownership. The highly refined and individualized subjectivity produced here is itself ephemeral and relatively powerless, a form of subjectivity that makes a man not merely a trophy but a "cloudy" one.

IV

For Keats, then, a petty-bourgeois suburbanite, the melancholy eroticism of transient pleasure-seeking seemed ultimately more feasible than synoptic pleasure. For although the synoptic aesthetic was devised precisely for men like Keats, its origins in gentlemanly property ownership could easily give it the appearance of mere illusory wish-fulfillment. Keats was not, however, the only canonical poet of his age to ruminate on the affective and erotic ramifications of the modern intensification of time and space. Although considered a "Lake Poet" and strongly associated with the rural cottages and bowers of his early poems, after 1810 Samuel Taylor Coleridge was in fact a man of the cities and suburbs. That he and Keats ran into each other in April 1819 as they were both on a neighborhood walk is more symbolically fitting than may at first appear.[59] In 1816 Coleridge moved into Moreton House in suburban Highgate, a place where the spirit of the

---

[58] See E. C. Pettet, *On the Poetry of Keats* (Cambridge: Cambridge University Press, 1957), 311; F. R. Leavis, *Revaluation: Tradition and Development in English Poetry* (New York: Norton, 1963), 260; and Douglas Bush, *John Keats: His Life and Writings* (New York: Macmillan, 1966), 148.

[59] Richard Holmes recounts the meeting in *Coleridge: Darker Reflections, 1804–1834* (New York: Pantheon, 1998), 496–7.

gardenesque could be fully experienced: "If Coleridge sometimes felt a captive in these early months at Moreton House, he loved the 'delicious' walks round Hampstead Heath and took much pleasure in the walled garden where many of his later poems sprouted."[60] Delicious walks notwithstanding, Coleridge was not unambivalent about the spatial condensation that lay at the heart of the suburban gardenesque. In a notebook entry of April 30, 1816 he offers

Reflections on my four gaudy Flower-pots, compared with the former Flower-poems – After a certain period, crowded with Poetry-counterfeiters, and illustrious with true Poets, there is formed for common use a vast *garden* of Language – all the shewy, and all the odorous Words, and Clusters of Words, are brought together . . . In such a state, any man of common practical reading, having a strong desire (to *be*? Oh no! but –) to be thought a Poet will present a Flower-Pot/ – gay and gaudy – but the *composition*! – That is wanting – [61]

The spirit of the gardenesque is not only gaudy but also makes improper use of space; it crowds beauties together without regard to composition. The result is a democratization of art that is also a vulgarization: "A Flower-Pot which would have inchanted [*sic*] us before Flower-gardens were common, for the very beauty of the component Flowers, will be rightly condemned as *common-place out of place*."[62]

If Coleridge was concerned by the condensation of space, he was even more dismayed by the condensation of time. In "The Delinquent Travellers," a poem of 1824, he sarcastically admonishes his countrymen to

> Keep moving! Steam, or Gas, or Stage,
> Hold, cabin, steerage, hencoop's cage –
> Tour, Journey, Voyage, Lounge, Ride, Walk,
> Skim, Sketch, Excursion, Travel-talk –
> For move you must! 'Tis now the rage,
> The law and fashion of the Age.[63]

Coleridge suggests that such rapid movement is no more than meaningless wheel-spinning at the same time that he acknowledges the impossibility of avoiding being drawn into its vortex: "Move, or be moved – there's no protection" (l. 36). Even the earth and atmosphere seem to be "whirring" (l. 39), but for Coleridge the hustle and bustle of modern life is anything

---

[60] *Ibid.*, 431.

[61] *The Notebooks of Samuel Taylor Coleridge*, 5 vols., vol. III, *1808–1819*, ed. Kathleen Coburn (Princeton: Princeton University Press, 1973), entry 4313.

[62] *Ibid.*

[63] *Coleridge: Poetical Works*, ed. Ernest Hartley Coleridge (Oxford: Oxford University Press, 1969), 444, ll. 16–21. Further references will be given parenthetically in the text.

but exhilarating. Indeed, as we shall see, many of Coleridge's late poems
rehearse his anxieties about living in a two-dimensional world of rapid
change. Moreover, they often express those anxieties – anxieties that are literally cosmic in scope – in erotic terms, in the form of melancholy, suspenseful, and self-abasing love poems.

While Coleridge's interest in time and space took on an emotional
urgency in his later life, the foundations of that interest were laid early
on. Michael Cooke, in a study of space in Coleridge's poetry, suggests
that "one of the products of the Romantic concern with nature and questioning the forms of society is . . . a heightened sense of space, not only in the
acknowledgment of its primary qualities, but also in the renewed awareness
of how these qualities, vacancy and formlessness, invade the very objects that
should be safeguards in relation to space."[64] Coleridge's understanding of
the categories of time and space was of course also inflected by his
reading of Immanuel Kant; unlike Keats, Coleridge made space and time
the objects of specifically philosophical rumination. Influenced by Kant's
notion that space and time are *a priori* intuitions, Coleridge believed that
these categories had a privileged role to play in subjectivity: "Kant's
merit consisted (mainly) in explaining the ground of the apodeixis in
Mathematics . . . and this he did by proving that Space and Time were 1.
neither general terms, 2. nor abstractions from Things, 3. nor Things themselves; but, 4. the pure a priori forms of the intuitive faculty."[65] Coleridge
believed further that the popular conception of space and time as fixed
external phenomena, things in the world, had the effect of limiting the intellectual, imaginative, and moral freedom of human beings. Thus he speaks of
Shakespeare's plays, in their lack of concern for the unities of time and
space, as superior to those of the ancients:

The stage, indeed, had nothing but curtains for its scenes, but this fact compelled
the actor, as well as the author, to appeal to the imaginations, and not the senses of
the audience: thus was obtained a power over space and time, which in an ancient
theatre would have been absurd, because it would have been contradictory. The
advantage is vastly in favour of our own early stage: the dramatic poet there
relies upon the imagination, upon the reason, and upon the noblest powers of
the human heart; he shakes off the iron bondage of space and time.[66]

[64] Michael Cooke, "The Manipulation of Space in Coleridge's Poetry," in Geoffrey Hartman, ed., *New Perspectives on Coleridge and Wordsworth* (New York: Columbia University Press, 1972), 166.
[65] *Collected Letters of Samuel Taylor Coleridge*, 6 vols., vol. IV, *1815–1819*, ed. Earl Leslie Griggs, (Oxford: Clarendon Press, 1959), 852.
[66] *The Collected Works of Samuel Taylor Coleridge*, 16 vols., vol. V, *Lectures 1808–1819 on Literature*, Part II, ed. R. A. Foakes (Princeton: Princeton University Press, 1987), 512 (from John Payne Collier's text of lecture 9 on Shakespeare).

Release from this bondage allows for an imaginative rather than a sensual engagement with the drama; it enables man to make use of his highest faculties.

But despite Coleridge's attraction to the idea of an imaginative freedom from time and space, he nevertheless argued that the experience of those structuring categories was essential to personal development. This is most obviously the case with respect to time. Coleridge followed Kant in believing that while space is "the form of all appearances of outer sense," time "is nothing other than the form of inner sense, i.e., of the intuition of our self and our inner state."[67] Time is therefore both a constraint upon the self and necessary for the production of self-consciousness:

I believe, that what we call *motion* is our consciousness of motion, arising from the interruption of motion = the acting of the Soul resisted./. Free unresisted action (the going forth of the Soul) Life without consciousness, properly infinite, i.e., unlimited – for whatever resists, limits, & vice versa / This is (psychologically speaking) SPACE. The sense of resistance or limitation TIME – & MOTION is a synthesis of the Two.[68]

The "going forth of the Soul," an experience of unrestricted space, is attractive for its freedom. But it is also a "Life without consciousness"; time functions as a valuable limit, prompting an awareness of self. Coleridge dramatized this conception of time in a poem of the 1810s, "Time, Real and Imaginary":

> Two lovely children run an endless race,
> A sister and a brother!
> This far outstripp'd the other;
> Yet ever runs she with reverted face,
> And looks and listens for the boy behind:
> For he, alas! is blind!
> O'er rough and smooth with even step he passed,
> And knows not whether he be first or last. (*Poetical Works*, 420)

The boy, embodying real time, is both dispassionate and unselfconscious. His sister, on the other hand, is aware not only of her own position but also of his. His slower, more regular progress limits her own; with her face reverted she, like Walter Benjamin's angel of history, is unable to be fully free in her pursuit of the future.[69] Time, as imagined, is different from real time but

---

[67] Immanuel Kant, *Critique of Pure Reason*, trans. and ed. Paul Guyer and Allen Wood (Cambridge: Cambridge University Press, 1998), 159, 163.

[68] *The Notebooks of Samuel Taylor Coleridge*, 5 vols., vol. I, *1794–1804*, ed. Kathleen Coburn (Princeton: Princeton University Press (1957), entry 1771.

[69] From "Theses on the Philosophy of History," in Walter Benjamin, *Illuminations*, ed. Hannah Arendt, trans. Harry Zohn (New York: Schocken, 1969), 257.

constrained by it nevertheless. The girl's superior awareness is absorbed in the task of monitoring the progress of regular time rather than her own progress. The children's pinions are "ostrich-like" because, though lovely, they will never fly. Here, the limitations of real time restrict the ideal freedom of the imagination. Such ideal freedom, moreover, has not only creative but also moral and spiritual implications. In one of his notebooks Coleridge defends the value of the measures of time in the book of Daniel by arguing for the spiritual significance of imaginary time. This "psychical Chronometry . . . May not be commensurable with ordinary Time, or abstract succession of infinite moments in parallel Lines equal to one line," but it is "a measurement of Time proper to the Soul in the state of inward Vision."[70] But as much as Coleridge values inward vision and imaginative freedom, he nevertheless recognizes that real time gives imaginary time its bearings. It is not simply that the girl, unlike her brother, can see; she knows herself and her place in the race precisely by "reverting" to her knowledge of her brother. The girl's concern slows her down but also humanizes her; the pathos of the poem arises from her sisterly solicitude.

Despite its apparently more mundane status, the three-dimensionality of space is similarly essential to self-consciousness. In his essay "On the Concept of 'Depth,'" Coleridge sets out to prove that depth is a concept developed less out of our sense of the external world than our experience of our own inwardness. He argues that our visual experiences are always experiences of "length and surface":

> Try to conceive depth otherwise [without reference to inwardness], and instead of depth you will only have an image of relative Length – that is, a perpendicular Line, which falling *on* an horizontal Line gives the exponent of Height –

$$\overline{\quad\quad\big|\quad\quad}$$

> turn the paper upside down, and you have the exponent of depth – but really, and in itself, it is in both cases only length.[71]

What we take to be indications of depth are, visually speaking, planar. It is only by exercising our intuitive faculties that we are able to conceive the

---

[70] *The Notebooks of Samuel Taylor Coleridge*, 5 vols., vol. IV, *1819–1826*, ed. Kathleen Coburn and Merton Christensen, (Princeton: Princeton University Press, 1990), entry 4912, July 1822.

[71] *The Collected Works of Samuel Taylor Coleridge*, 16 vols., vol. XI, *Shorter Works and Fragments*, Part I, ed. H. J. Jackson and J. R. de J. Jackson (Princeton: Princeton University Press, 1995), 452–3.

third dimension that is depth. He then goes on to argue that depth is not simply a physical property of things but a "Power":

Depth therefore must be that *by* not *with* which Space is filled – it must be that which causes it to be filled, and is therefore the true *sub*stance. – Depth therefore cannot be an *attribute* of Matter, which . . . is itself a mere abstraction, an ens rationis; but it must be a Power, the essence of which is *inwardness*, outwardness being its effect and mode of manifesting itself.[72]

Given their role in the production of self-consciousness, if space and time lose their character or their significance the result cannot but be a nightmare. It is exactly such a situation that Coleridge addresses in a poem of the 1810s or 1820s, "Limbo." The poem displays a wit and playfulness that Coleridge had learned from John Donne, but it also struggles with serious philosophical and theological questions. For Cooke, "Limbo" dramatizes Coleridge's "dread of the 'shrinking' and ultimately 'annihilating' power of limbo and its adumbrations in 'space'":[73]

> 'Tis a strange place, this Limbo! – not a Place,
> Yet name it so; – where Time and weary Space
> Fettered from flight, with night-mare sense of fleeing,
> Strive for their last crepuscular half-being; –
> Lank Space, and scytheless Time with branny hands
> Barren and soundless as the measuring sands,
> Not mark'd by flit of Shades, – unmeaning they
> As moonlight on the dial of the day! (*Poetical Works*, 430)

This is an airless place in which space and time appear to be obsolete, oldfashioned concepts. Denatured, lank and scytheless, space and time are so changed as to be meaningless. It is fitting that the major figure in the poem is a blind old man:

> . . . moonlight on the dial of the day!
> But that is lovely – looks like Human Time, –
> An Old Man with a steady look sublime,
> That stops his earthly task to watch the skies;
> But he is blind – a Statue hath such eyes . . . (430)

Even the "unmeaning" glow of moonlight on a sundial is too human an image to capture the horror of the loss of time as a category. After all, the deformation of *a priori* intuitions necessarily entails a deformation of the human. Thus the narrator decides that the analogy of the statue-like old man is too comforting to be appropriate: "No such sweet sights doth

[72] *Ibid.*, 453.   [73] Cooke, "Manipulation of Space," 178.

Limbo den immure, / Wall'd round, and made a spirit-jail secure, / By the mere horror of blank Naught-at-all, / Whose circumambience doth these ghosts enthrall" (430–1). Here, being surrounded is associated not with possession, as in the panorama or the gardenesque bower, but with a suffocating sensation of entrapment. Notwithstanding the "gardenesque" lesson of a poem like "This Lime-Tree Bower My Prison" (1797) – one can find everything one needs in a small space so long as it is "natural" – in his late poems Coleridge tends to respond claustrophobically to the snug bowers that so often charmed Keats. For Coleridge, the experience of space and time as stable, robust categories is essential to personal development and spiritual health; their distortion in "Limbo" is the stuff of nightmares.

While "Limbo" is unusual in its nightmarish vision of a state in which space and time are shrunk down to nothing, almost the whole body of Coleridge's late poetry struggles with a less extreme form of this problem: the objects of consciousness seem to have become both two-dimensional and fleeting. Poem after poem suggests a world after perspective, without depth or solidity. In such a world no amount of healthy self-consciousness can overcome the failure of the material to correspond to the spiritual. As Bate explains, "the organic or dynamic philosophy of nature – the conception of nature as a unifying process" (*John Keats*, 186) was fundamental to Coleridge's thought, and the experience of the depth and permanence of external objects was one sign of the effectiveness of this unification.

Over the course of his career, Coleridge used a variety of techniques to conceive of and figure the organic wholeness to which he was so attracted, the most important of which was the philosophical notion of dialectic. Unfortunately, dialectical synthesis often eluded him; Jerome Christensen argues that Coleridge therefore turned to the rhetorical figure of chiasmus as a substitute method for binding together extremes: "the chiasmus figures the promise of dialectic as merely the enabling presupposition of a rhetorical practice; its elegant mechanics render the concord of identity and opposite."[74] But while Christensen sees in a chiastic passage of the *Biographia Literaria* (1817) both "the first dialectical venture of English Romantic thought" and "the first, ineluctable lapse of dialectic,"[75] Coleridge never ceased to conceive of his ideal, unified world as one developed in terms of dialectical synthesis. In an effort, therefore, to provide an irrefutable logical basis for his synthesizing claims, Coleridge became increasingly fond of geometrical diagrams, especially

---

[74] Jerome Christensen, *Coleridge's Blessed Machine of Language* (Ithaca: Cornell University Press, 1981), 27.
[75] *Ibid.*, 172.

the triangle, which allowed him to contemplate "dynamically" the development of a third term out of two basic concepts. Thus in a notebook entry for 1822, he represents the "Genesis and ascending Scale of physical Powers, abstractly contemplated" in the form of triangular relationships.[76] Beginning with "Power, Sphere, Existence," he goes on to develop many other triads, including "Time, Space, Motion," and "Attraction, Repulsion, Extension."[77] As the original third term, "existence," suggests, in each case the third term embodies not just a synthesis of the first two but also an element of "coming into being." Hence the triads describe an ascending scale, as is clear in triad IX, "Vegetable, Insect, Animal," or "the completing and unifying" final triad, "Sense, Understanding, Conscious Self or Person." Coleridge does not represent these triads as I have done here, as one word following another, but uses lines to suggest their dynamic interrelation:

Each pair "points" to its synthesizing term, just as it points to the next triad on the page, which always appears under it. It is important that this diagramming is not only indicative of dynamism but also allows Coleridge to suggest depth in the two dimensions of the written page. For the horizontal line of ordinary text is here pulled into a shape, deepened. Of course, geometry, like perspectival painting, has its own more complicated techniques for suggesting three dimensions on the two dimensions of a piece of paper. But in the context of a manuscript, the mere act of adding another dimension to the line of the text is sufficient to produce what Coleridge calls "the exponent of depth." It is thus fitting that the fifth of Coleridge's triads is

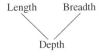

Depth is, for Coleridge, more than just another property of bodies and space. As a synthesizing category, it is allied with existence itself, with

[76] *Notebooks*, IV, entry 4928.
[77] It should be noted that the term "triad" is mine, not Coleridge's; he calls these sets "decads," presumably because there are ten of them.

force, motion, and human self-consciousness. Its presence is itself a sign of synthesis.

Given the moral and intellectual significance of depth in Coleridge's thinking, it comes as little surprise that he should regard even the aesthetic representation of it as valuable. In the same lecture in which he speaks of Shakespeare's superiority over the ancients in terms of shaking off "the iron bondage of space and time," he explains that the shortcomings of classical drama can be linked to the ancients' lack of knowledge of perspective: "In that mechanical branch of painting, perspective, it has been shown that the Romans were very deficient . . . Something of the same kind . . . was the case with the drama of the ancients . . . *All that is there represented seems to be, as it were, upon one flat surface.*"[78] Coleridge was to make the same complaint about medieval art; it is composed of "wiry outlines, surfaces imprisoned in the outlines without depth, without force," while one sees that in the paintings of the high Renaissance "the mighty spirit coming from within had succeeded in taming the intractable matter and in reducing the external form to a symbol of the inward and imaginable beauty."[79] An art characterized by depth does not simply provide a more lifelike image but gives one access to eternal truths. Indeed, as his account of the symbolic character of Renaissance painting suggests, for Coleridge perspectival painting has much in common with the privileged concept of the symbol, while outline is linked to allegory. Christensen explores the ramifications of this connection further: "the language of the imagination – the harmony of part and whole, the participation of all in God – is the language of the symbol."[80] Unfortunately, the "pervasive wish for a metaphysical continuity that is involved in [Coleridge's] promotion of the symbol is typically breached by a discourse that divulges the obdurate discontinuities of signification. Coleridge's metaphysical symbolism is transgressed by a discursive allegory."[81] Although Christensen sets out to show the inevitability of this transgression, for Coleridge it is not so much a problem endemic to human language as a social problem. He suggests that his is an era given to two-dimensional abstractions:

It is among the miseries of the present age that it recognizes no medium between *Literal* and *Metaphorical* . . . Now an Allegory is but a translation of abstract

---

[78] *Lectures 1808–1819 on Literature*, Part II, 511, emphasis mine.
[79] *The Philosophical Lectures of Samuel Taylor Coleridge*, ed. Kathleen Coburn (New York: Philosophical Library, 1949), 193.
[80] Jerome Christensen, "The Symbol's Errant Allegory: Coleridge and His Critics," *ELH* 45 (1978), 642.
[81] *Ibid.*, 644.

notions into a picture-language which is itself nothing but an abstraction from objects of the senses; the principal being more worthless even than its phantom proxy, both alike unsubstantial, and the former shapeless to boot. On the other hand a Symbol . . . is characterized by a translucence of the Special in the Individual or of the General in the Especial or of the Universal in the General. Above all by the translucence of the Eternal through and in the Temporal . . . The other are but empty echoes which the fancy arbitrarily associates with apparitions of matter.[82]

Coleridge remarked in a notebook entry of 1820 that "all outline is Abstraction": "So that $\frac{Space}{Time}$ { a Line, and the Figures in Flaxman's Homer, Eschylus & Dante may be regarded as gradual potenziations of Abstraction by the plastic Imagination?" John Flaxman's flat, neoclassical figures are at best only "gradual potenziations."[83] The great paintings of the Renaissance, on the other hand, express the inward beauty and force that give meaning to matter, just as the symbol does. The symbol thus functions like depth as Coleridge understands it, and depth functions like a symbol. Hovering between literal and metaphorical, depth is both a geometrical concept and a spiritual one.

For Coleridge, then, the experience of the world as two-dimensional and fleeting symptomatizes an illness that extends from the social to the spiritual, intellectual, and aesthetic. And because it represents a failure of unification, Coleridge increasingly dramatizes this illness in the form of melancholic love poems. These poems take as their premise the idea that genuine love is characterized precisely by the overcoming of two-dimensionality. This idea is explored in a short piece of 1812, "True Love, illustrated to the eye, geometrically." Here Coleridge uses a figure that is even more suggestive of perspectival drawing than his triads:

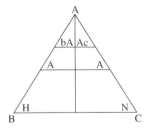

Let the Triangle AB and the Triangle AC form the Triangle ABC – representing *perfect Love* between B and C.

[82] *The Collected Works of Samuel Taylor Coleridge*, 16 vols., vol. VI, *Lay Sermons*, ed. R. J. White (Princeton: Princeton University Press, 1972), 30.
[83] *Notebooks*, IV, entry 4657.

The Basis or Line H.N. represents the common Basis of the human Nature.

The Line AA represents the characteristic qualities common to B and C, the basis of *their* particular Identity, the same in both and distinguishing both of them from other men & women.

The line b represents those qualities in B which are at once opposite yet correspondent to the line c or those qualities in C opposite & correspondent to b in B. – which two lines, bc, meet & become one at the point A.

– Then B.A.b added to Cac make BCAbc; but bc equals or is the same with A: therefore Bb & Cc being both equal to A, Bb equals Cc – They blend into one living Spirit: unity in duplicity.[84]

That Coleridge's "illustration" of true love actually takes the form of a mathematical proof of its existence is itself a sign of his pessimism regarding the possibility of achieving love in this world, an issue to which we will return. But what is perhaps most striking about this image is its suggestion of depth; indeed, this proof has much in common with the "perspective proof" – a type of mathematical diagram popular among Renaissance painters. These proofs, which in various ways aimed to reconcile optics, geometry, and pictorial values, often worked in precisely this way: a geometric diagram was accompanied by an explanation that included a verbal description and a recapitulation of the diagram by means of mathematical shorthand.[85] For painters in the Renaissance and beyond, the vanishing point had a profound metaphysical significance: it could represent heaven or death.[86] For Coleridge, too, this is the case. A, the point at which the pair become one, is an ideal point, a vanishing point toward which the lovers strive. Its "distance" is suggested by the fact that AB and AC are longer than BC. Of course, one could see in the figure a suggestion not of depth but of height, especially since A, the point of union, could be considered a "heavenly" goal. But the two intermediate points that lead to that goal are still emphatically mundane, representing individual qualities and then feminine and masculine ones. True love, it would seem, is characterized not only by unity but also by depth.

Unfortunately, imagining a smooth movement toward the vanishing point is no simple matter, even in high Renaissance painting. Indeed, Renaissance paintings often dramatize problems of perspective in order to

---

[84] Samuel Taylor Coleridge, "True Love, illustrated . . . geometrically," in *Shorter Works and Fragments*, ed. Jackson and Jackson, I, 287.

[85] In his longer version of this proof, which I did not reproduce here, Coleridge provides both a fuller "mathematical" account of the figure and a four-paragraph verbal account of its significance.

[86] For a discussion of perspective proofs and the spiritual significance of perspective, see James Elkins, *The Poetics of Perspective* (Ithaca: Cornell University Press, 1994), Chapter 3, "The Harmonious, the Compatible, the Equivalent," 81–116, and 16.

suggest spiritual concerns; James Elkins notes that the "obstruction of depth in paintings perspectival in nature produces a stifling, claustrophobic effect . . . In modern terms, we would say that an open perspective . . . expresses hope, and a closed one, despair."[87] Piranesi's *Carceri* are a later, Romantic manifestation of a similar phenomenon: in Piranesi's case incoherent perspective spaces elicit sensations of confusion and terror. At the same time, a too-ardent attachment to perspective could also be regarded as pathological. By the sixteenth century the discipline of perspective in painting was associated with obsessiveness and mathematical fastidiousness and therefore linked to melancholy. As Elkins wryly remarks, "it is not accidental that Durer put so much perspective into *Melencolia I*."[88] Coleridge's attachment to perspective sets him squarely within this meditative melancholy tradition. His very impulse to represent "true love" geometrically seems a sign of his distance from attaining it, and his mournful late poems dramatize the elusiveness of union, the failure of coherence, in both the metaphoric and the literal sense.

Coleridge had explored this elusiveness already in a poem of 1805, "Phantom":

> All look and likeness caught from earth
> All accident of kin and birth,
> Had pass'd away. There was no trace
> Of aught on that illumined face,
> Uprais'd beneath the rifted stone
> But of one spirit all her own; –
> She, she herself, and only she,
> Shone through her body visibly. (*Poetical Works*, 393)

The poem's single concrete image, of a face beneath a rifted stone, serves as an illustration of the epiphany that is the poem's subject: it is as though the stone that frames the face has cracked to allow its emergence from beneath. The face is "uprais'd" beneath the stone just as the woman's spirit shines through the materiality of her body. Here, as in Coleridge's account of the symbol, we see the translucence of the special in the individual, and the eternal in the temporal. The moment described is an ecstatic one, an experience of liberation and human communion. But although it describes a magical moment, the poem has an undeniably morbid quality – an unsurprising fact, given that Coleridge probably composed it en route to Malta after parting from Sara Hutchinson. A somber tone is established right away, when we read of the accidents of kin and birth having "passed away." The image of a shining spirit beneath a stone almost makes this seem a graveyard scene, in which a mournful lover only imagines that he sees his beloved again. This possibility is underscored by the poem's title, "Phantom." This moment of union, of the full symbolic revelation of the beloved, may after all be nothing more than a haunting, a scene not of "the translucence of the Eternal through and in the Temporal" but of the "phantom proxy" of allegory.

Indeed, after 1810 Coleridge's poems are not only increasingly populated with ghosts and apparitions but are also, time and again, presented as allegories. Morton Paley, author of the most thorough study of Coleridge's late poetry, notes that "Personification is seldom encountered in modern poetry, and even critics sympathetic to the later Coleridge have had difficulty with them. Yet prosopopoeia is the dominant trope of this part of Coleridge's poetic career."[89] Poem after poem openly proclaims itself to be an allegory, usually in its title or subtitle. The world described in these poems is one of failed connections and incongruities, one where the union that is love inevitably proves to be nothing more than a deceptive, fleeting apparition. "Phantom or Fact" (1834), for example, functions straightforwardly as an allegory of love lost. In this piece "a lovely form" sits beside the author's bed, shedding "a tender love so pure from earthly leaven" that it seems to him it was his "own spirit newly come from heaven, / Wooing its gentle way into my soul" (*Poetical Works*, 484–5). But "Alas! that change how fain would I forget! / That shrinking back, like one that had mistook!" Whether this idealized form is the author himself or his beloved, the critical fact is that the pure revelation of the spirit which is associated with love seems unsustainable. Within the poem itself this unsustainability is linked to a collapse into allegory. When the "author's" friend asks, "This riddling tale, to what does it belong? / Is't history? vision? or an idle song?" the author replies, "This tale's a fragment from the life of dreams; / But say, that years matur'd the silent strife, / And 'tis a record from the dream of life" (485). This story, which might have been a reliable history or an imaginative vision, is instead a dreamlike allegory. The moment that love fails is also the moment that pure spirit abandons its other self, disdaining the union that constitutes symbolism.

Not only do the characters within Coleridge's poems struggle with questions of interpretation and the lack of an organic correspondence between signifier and signified, but so must Coleridge's readers. Like the interlocutor of "Phantom or Fact?," we are constantly forced not only to decipher the meanings of Coleridge's allegories but also to wonder whether our very

---

[89] Morton Paley, *Coleridge's Later Poetry* (New York: Oxford University Press, 1996), 10–11.

framework for interpretation is appropriate. In "The Pang More Sharp than All" (1825), for instance, the reader is kept in suspense as to the significance of the allegorical characters until the very end of the poem. The reader is thus made to feel the anxiety experienced by the speaker within the poem. This anxiety-producing deferral of meaning is characteristic not only of Coleridge's late poetry but of his prose as well. Coleridge himself opposed his own circumlocutory prose style to a French Enlightenment style, with its "epigrammatic unconnected periods."[90] Christensen argues that Coleridge represents this French style as essentially masturbatory, characterized by "an erotic dynamics of rapid and total exchange." He goes on to explore Coleridge's claim that his own style was patterned on that of the English prose writers of the seventeenth century. This was a prose that was stately, difficult, and periodic, one that accustomed the reader to deferral; indeed, it taught the reader not only to expect but to "relish" continued deferral.[91] If the French style was masturbatory in character, Coleridge's was masochistic, characterized above all by self-imposed discipline and suspense.

The style itself of Coleridge's late work thus serves as the aesthetic, formal embodiment of nonunion, of unsatisfied desire. Anxious and painful as this unsatisfied desire can be, it does provide pleasures of its own, especially the painful pleasures of suspense and uncertainty. Angus Fletcher remarks that "Coleridge is the poet-critic of expectancy. Perhaps in order to intensify this method of response, he shifts, in later years, to a mode of poetry quite unlike that practiced in 'The Ancient Mariner' or 'Christabel.'" Fletcher finds a striking example of this expectancy in "Ne Plus Ultra," which he likens to George Herbert's "Prayer": "Verbless, the poem and its reader kneel down, waiting, devoted."[92] But in "Ne Plus Ultra" this devotional posture is maintained, not before God, but before "The Dragon foul and fell" (*Poetical Works*, 431). It would seem that the closest one can come to consummation with an absolute form of being lies in devotion, but Coleridge's pessimism of these years makes it hard for him to imagine devotion to any but a cruel master.

This masochistic response to the unintelligibility of the world is made even clearer in a poem of the 1830s, "Coeli Enarrant." In this poem the stars, like conspirators, leave all "blank on high, / No constellations alphabet the sky" (486). This illegibility is – fortunately? – replaced

---

[90] Christensen, *Blessed Machine*, 205.   [91] *Ibid.*, 206, 209.
[92] Angus Fletcher, "'Positive Negation': Threshold, Sequence, and Personification on Coleridge," in Hartman, ed., *New Perspectives on Coleridge and Wordsworth*, 133–64.

by a "positive negation," one that puts all mankind in the role of punished
child:

> The Heavens one large Black Letter only shew,
> And as a child beneath its master's blow
> Shrills out at once its task and its affright –
> The groaning world now learns to read aright,
> And with its Voice of Voices cries out, O! (486)

As E. H. Coleridge points out, the description of the schoolboy is reminiscent of a passage in Leigh Hunt's autobiography, in which he describes a
reading lesson by Boyer at Christ's Hospital. Boyer was a "notorious
flogging master" and Paley notes that "Although Coleridge claimed to
have been beaten by him only once and to have had one other narrow
escape, he must have witnessed other beatings: he remembered this aspect
of Boyer well, and referred to it a number of times in later years."[93] The
scene of punishment, poetically recapitulated on a cosmic scale, is simultaneously frightful and erotic. Although the world has now learned to
read aright, its final exclamation –"O!"– is strikingly ambiguous: is this a
cry of horror or pleasure? This ambiguity retroactively colors the reader's
sense of such words as "groaning." In the context of the notebook in
which it was written, this poem was preceded by one that was more straightforwardly about suspense and the link between pleasure and pain. Paley
describes it thus:

The Notebook entry begins with imagery of fire and the web of Time, a web which
at first provides support for the poet's vivid dream of happy infantile dependence . . .
Then something sinister happens. The web of time becomes not supportive but
entrapping, and the poet finds himself in a universe of perpetually deferred gratification: "What never is but only is to be / This is not Life – ."[94]

After another false start, Coleridge cancels these lines and writes the
poem we now know as "Coeli Ennerant." If the first poem moved
from an image of bliss to one of pain, the later one begins with pain and
discovers in it a perverse kind of bliss. Entrapment by a caregiver is
recast as punishment. Indeed, it is the suffering at the hands of the
father that marks the infant's nominal freedom, his ability to interpret
the world correctly as a place of entrapment. The experience of punishment
is at least a sign of being in the presence of the absolute, even if not in
communion with it. Consummation is to be had only in the form of
suffering, a release of tension that nevertheless leaves the suspense of the
scene intact.

[93] Paley, *Later Poetry*, 38.   [94] *Ibid.* Paley is quoting from NB 19 BL Add. MS. 47, 516 ff. 12v–13r.

The most ubiquitous of the cruel masters of the late poetry is, however, not God or "The Dragon foul and fell" but the allegorical feminine figure of Love. The desire for the communion embodied in love draws the speaker of poem after poem to recapitulate the painful experience of love's inevitable disappearance. This failure is dramatized with particular clarity in "Love's Apparition and Evanishment" (1833). Subtitled "An Allegoric Romance," the poem begins with an image, like the one from "Limbo," of an abandoned blind old man, presumably wise but helpless, who is simply waiting for his death. Unable to see or understand his surroundings, he has nothing to do but feel suspense. Given the associations we have seen between submissive eroticism and exoticism, it is also worth noting that this man is an Arab, surrounded by basking sand-asps. The description of the Arab prefaces our introduction to the speaker, who is likened to him: "Even thus, in vacant mood, one sultry hour, / Resting my eye upon a drooping plant, / With brow low-bent, within my garden-bower, / I sate upon the couch of camomile" (*Poetical Works*, 489). The account of the Arab determines our view of this scene: although snug within a garden bower like many a happy character in Keats's poetry, the speaker apparently feels as if he were abandoned in a desert. Unable to make meaning of the things around him, or even to reckon the passage of time, his thoughts ultimately turn inward.

> . . . whether 'twas a transient sleep, perchance,
> Flitted across the idle brain, the while
> I watch'd the sickly calm with aimless scope,
> In my own heart; or that, indeed a trance,
> Turn'd my eye inward – thee, O genial Hope,
> Love's elder sister! thee did I behold,
> Drest as a bridesmaid, but all pale and cold,
> With roseless cheek, all pale and cold and dim,
> Lie lifeless at my feet!
> And then came Love, a sylph in bridal trim,
> And stood beside my seat;
> She bent, and kiss'd her sister's lips,
> As she was wont to do; –
> Alas! 'twas but a chilling breath
> Woke just enough of life in death
> To make Hope die anew. (489)

The poem's temporal dynamics speed up, but only for the sake of intensifying the teasing suspense in which the speaker and the reader find themselves. The appearance of Hope seems at first to be a good thing – until we learn that she is essentially dead. Love's entrance onto the stage is even more cheering, until the final line of the poem. Love's apparition is just that: she is a vision, a ghost, an allegorical "phantom proxy," as insubstantial as the thing for which she stands. The speaker experiences his own emotional life as disjunctive, watching the two figures as if from a distance, even though they "represent" his own feelings. The "allegoric" romance, in which love is a visionary figure experienced from a distance, desirable but never attainable, is the only kind of romance that Coleridge wrote during his later life. Coleridge underscores the generic connection between his poem and the French *ballade* by closing the poem with "L'envoy," but the content of the "envoy" comments ironically on that connection: "In vain we supplicate the Powers above; / There is no resurrection for the Love / That, nursed in tenderest care, yet fades away / In the chill'd heart by gradual self-decay" (489).

This poem distinguishes itself from the traditional romance by its marked pessimism: there is nothing grand or heroic about this scene. The speaker suffers because of love, but not for it; he is not ennobled by his sufferings. Coleridge's late poems rehearse, again and again, the failure of love. It is as if the only pleasure available to him lies in the teasing repetition of the scene of his devastation at love's hands.

Perhaps because true love eludes them, the speakers of Coleridge's later poems increasingly idealize both that love and the woman who is its object. As Coleridge writes in his notebook around 1826:

Is there a man who has . . . truly and intensely loved a lovely and beautiful Woman, a Woman capable of gazing, in that inward . . . communion of Silence, on Vale, Lake, and Mountain Forest, in the richness of a rising or a setting Sun . . . she as she stands by his side smitten by the radiance, "herself a glory to behold, the Angel of the Vision."[95]

The moment the woman becomes, not a sharer in the beauty of the external scene, but herself the object of beauty, she is transformed into a powerful personification. This personification, moreover, confuses subject and object in a way that helps to account for the woman's ideal status: is she simply an angel within the vision, or does she actually enable the vision? Insofar as the beloved partakes of the character of love itself, she cannot but be ideal – in both senses of the word. She is idea incarnate, essence made manifest, as well as being deeply imbued with the value of union itself. But while the beloved comes to embody the very spirit of organic

---

[95] Cited in *ibid.*, from NB 26, BL Add. MS. 47524.

wholeness, the lover's failure to consummate his love for her puts her, and that wholeness, at an ever-greater remove. Paley argues that Coleridge's late love poetry "has much in common with the love-psychology encountered in early Italian poetry among the poets of the *dolce stil novo*," citing as evidence two Coleridge poems that can be confidently linked to Italian sources. In his words, "we may assume that Coleridge knew the love-psychology of stilno-vistic poems in which an image of the beloved woman crystallizes in the lover's heart and is worshipped there as in a shrine."[96] This notion of love suited Coleridge in part because of its emphasis on disjunction; the only possible union of lover and beloved is a literally ideal one.

We see in Coleridge, then, a peculiarly philosophical form of Romantic melancholy. Here, we find not so much a delight in pain as a pessimistic assurance that love as communion, as the experience of depth and perma-nence in the object world, is unavailable, so that there is nothing left but to worship the beloved as the unattainable incarnation of cosmic meaning. Coleridge's disappointment with Sara Hutchinson had prompted him, as early as the first decade of the century, to ruminate on the value of worshipful idealization, even to the point of self-deception, in "Constancy to an Ideal Object." As the years passed, Coleridge's desperation to maintain the ideal, the "yearning Thought" that was "The only constant in a world of change" (455), took on cosmic dimensions. The world as a whole seemed a place of ghosts, two-dimensionality, and painful evanishment. As he struggled to reconcile his emotional, philosophical, and theological convic-tions, it is impossible to say which had priority: his pessimism regarding the larger world in which he lived or his despair in the domain of romance. For Coleridge, each signified the other, and together they demanded a new aes-thetic, an aesthetic of riddles, surfaces, and allegories. So while Keats com-posed the most famous Romantic poem on melancholy, it was in Coleridge's poetry that the melancholy of late Romanticism took on its darkest hues.

---

[96] Paley, *Later Poetry*, 100.

Conclusion: *Languishing* femmes fatales

Edward Burne-Jones remarked of *The Wheel of Fortune* (1883; see book jacket) that "My Fortune's Wheel is a true image, and we take our turn at it, and are broken upon it."[1] At the end of the nineteenth century, the allegorical figure of Fortune, associated for the past two hundred years with painful pleasures, was more appealing than ever. Like William Hogarth's queen of the lottery, Burne-Jones's Fortune is a beautiful woman who reigns over men's lives, giving bodily form to the pleasures and pains of speculation. Unlike the medieval wheel of fortune, this modern form of torture is one that men seem almost to choose; they "take [their] turn at it" like the lottery or roulette wheel. In the "culture of abundance"[2] of late nineteenth-century England, the enjoyment of Fortune's vicissitudes had become a more highly refined affair than ever before. Burne-Jones admiringly remarked of Cardinal Newman that "In an age of sofas and cushions he taught me to be indifferent to comfort, and in an age of materialism he taught me to venture all on the unseen."[3] For Hogarth, working during the birth of finance capitalism, the speculative posture itself, the perception of oneself as "venturing all," already signaled one's distance from the spiritual, while for Burne-Jones speculation and spirituality have become one and the same. The sofas and cushions being already in place, speculation could now serve as a sign of one's indifference to worldly prosperity, one's willingness to take a turn at being "broken." In Burne-Jones's art the coexistence of luxury and an ascetic spirituality is registered both thematically and stylistically; in Henry James's words, Burne-Jones's was an "art of culture, of reflection, of intellectual luxury."[4]

[1] From an 1893 letter to Helen Mary Gaskell. Quoted in Penelope Fitzgerald, *Edward Burne-Jones: A Biography* (London: Michael Joseph, 1975), 245.
[2] Lawrence Birken, *Consuming Desire: Sexual Science and the Emergence of a Culture of Abundance, 1871–1914* (Ithaca: Cornell University Press, 1988).
[3] Quoted by Russell Ash in *Sir Edward Burne-Jones* (New York: Abrams, 1993), Introduction, 2.
[4] Quoted by John Christian in entry 155 of *The Pre-Raphaelites* (London: Tate Gallery, 1984), 237.

Fortune as she appears in Burne-Jones's painting breathes a rarefied air even as she presents her magnificently draped body for our admiration. The combination of renunciation and voluptuousness, pain and pleasure, the abstract and the sensual, appears here to be both inevitable and deeply attractive.

Fortune's costume, with highlights at the breasts and elaborately knotted drapery over the genitals, constructs a sexuality at once overt and off-limits. We have here – albeit in unusual form – a manifestation of two of Burne-Jones's favorite themes as described by a recent biographer: "the enchantment of the willing victim" and "love dominant and without pity."[5] Arguably, the painting is not really about *reversals* of fortune, despite the traditional iconography. The men on Fortune's wheel, whether king, poet, or slave, are all in the nude, their bodies contorted in similar attitudes – attitudes that could signify either voluptuous pleasure or bodily suffering. Although the men represent different levels in a hierarchy, these distinctions are signified only by the smallest of signs: chains on the slave's ankles, a crown and scepter for the king, and a laurel wreath for the poet. Aside from these emblems, the men look entirely alike: traditional social types have become essentially indistinguishable. It hardly matters who is on the top of the wheel and who is on the bottom – they all look, and appear to feel, the same. Their forms inspired by Michelangelo's massive male torsos, especially "The Dying Slave," they are all eroticized sufferers, and the viewer is encouraged to take pleasure in identifying both with their beauty and with their helplessness. The painting thus alludes to traditional notions of hierarchy only in order to suggest that subordination is man's common – and pleasurable – lot. All men are in fact equal – king and slave both enjoy a voluptuous submission to the "gigantic, passionless"[6] woman who governs their destiny.

Burne-Jones himself suffered for the painting's sake, working on "her" devotedly even through illness: "how hard I have worked on her in the middle of pain, or more correctly with pain in the middle of me."[7] This painting of suffering and pleasure, originally conceived as part of a tryptich with four allegorical figures, of which Fortune was only one, "came to have a significance for Burne-Jones out of proportion to all the rest, partly no doubt because he liked the composition . . . but also because it encapsulated

[5] Penelope Fitzgerald quoted by Russell Ash, in *Sir Edward Burne-Jones*, Introduction, 7.
[6] From Fortunée de Lisle's description of the painting, in *Burne-Jones* (London: Methuen, 1904), 125.
[7] Quoted from a letter to Lady Leighton by Georgiana Burne-Jones in *Memorials of Edward Burne-Jones* 2 vols., vol. II (New York: Macmillan, 1906), 128.

much of his personal philosophy."[8] The painting itself, like its principal figure, took on an exaggerated importance, and is believed to have been the painter's favorite among his finished oil paintings. Fittingly enough, the painting elicited similar sensations in its buyer. Arthur Balfour was a wealthy conservative who disagreed with Burne-Jones in political matters; he claimed, however, that in spite of their differences he could not help but patronize the artist, for upon first seeing his work he "instantly" became "a victim of [the artist's] mind and art."[9]

We critics of the twentieth and twenty-first centuries, not generally covetous of the status of "victim of . . . art," have sometimes let an embarrassment regarding images of pleasurable self-abasement hinder us from fully recognizing their ubiquity in and their significance to nineteenth-century art. This is particularly true within Romantic criticism, which has tended to treat representations of idealizing, submissive desire less as significant in themselves than as gestures to grander, more palatable themes – the brevity of pleasure, the human capacity for idealization, and so on – or as symptoms of larger social issues, such as the oppression of women. This book, too, has of course sought to read Romantic art in its historical context, to unravel the knot of causality that links Romantic art with Romantic-era politics and economics. As we have seen, Romantic art helps us to diagnose, and sometimes itself diagnoses, the peculiarly modern tension between high expectations for personal power and gratification and the fact of their frequent disappointment.

But the book has also sought to show that Romantic art not only takes such tension as its subject but makes art itself, and artistic form, central to its negotiation. That literature should serve as a privileged domain for exploring the nature of desire is perhaps unsurprising, but as we have seen, Romantic-era conceptions of desire were particularly well-fitted to being explored and consolidated in the aesthetic domain. This was true first of all because there were precedents for such conceptions in the art of the past, particularly in courtly love literature. The notion of idealizing, submissive desire found a natural home in literature, where it could serve as more or less familiar subject matter. But the mutual reliance that binds together Romantic conceptions of desire and Romantic art runs deeper still, since Romantic paradigms for desire made much of the faculty of imagination. That is, it is not simply that Romantic art takes desire as its subject but that it suggests that the experience of desire ought in some

---

[8] Christian, *The Pre-Raphaelites*, 236.
[9] Quoted in *ibid.*, 237.

ways to resemble the experience of Romantic art: it should be about losing oneself in an act of imaginative idealization. This mutual implication extended further still, because the principal features of Romantic desire – its interest in power relations and the regulation of gratification over time – lent themselves well to formal exposition. Thus, as we have seen, the exploration of the *shape* of desire in Romantic literature gives us new insight into the significance of certain common Romantic aesthetic modes: the picturesque, the sublime, the synoptic, the ephemeral – even the ostensibly un-Romantic mode of allegory. It also gives us new purchase on the nonteleological narrative structures that one so often comes upon in Romantic writing. We see, then, that the study of the Romantic conception of desire is not only enriched by an attendance to Romantic art but, to some extent, requires that attendance. At the same time, Romantic-era art cannot be fully understood apart from its task of aestheticizing one of the central facts of industrial-democratic culture, the deferral of the gratification of the promise of power and possession. And thus, although devised in a modern age devoted to the ideals of progressive change, Burne-Jones's wheel of Fortune, like Hogarth's lottery wheel, does not seem to be going anywhere in particular. Instead, it holds its sufferers – and its viewers – in a state of suspense, one for which they, and we, find ample recompense only in the monumental beauty of Fortune herself.

Bibliography

Adams, James Eli, *Dandies and Desert Saints: Styles of Victorian Manhood* (Ithaca: Cornell University Press, 1995).

Adburgham, Alison, *Shopping in Style: London from the Restoration to Edwardian Elegance* (Over Wallop: Thames and Hudson, 1979).

Addison, Joseph, *Selections from the Tatler and the Spectator*, ed. Angus Ross (London: Penguin, 1982).

Addison, Joseph, *The Spectator*, ed. Donald Bond, 5 vols. (Oxford: Clarendon Press, 1965).

Adorno, Theodor, *Negative Dialectics*, trans. E. B. Ashton (New York: Continuum, 1987).

Agnew, Jean-Christophe, *Worlds Apart: The Market and the Theater in Anglo-American Thought, 1550–1750* (Cambridge: Cambridge University Press, 1986).

Alexander, David, *Retailing in England during the Industrial Revolution* (London: Athlone Press, 1970).

Anon., *Exhibition of Female Flagellants*, vols. I and II of *Library Illustrative of Social Progress*, 7 vols., collected by Henry Thomas Buckle (London: Printed for G. Peacock, 186?).

Anon., *The London Tradesman* (London: Simpkin and Marshall, 1819).

Anon., *Madame Birchini's Dance*, 9th edn, vol. V of *Library Illustrative of Social Progress*, 7 vols., collected by Henry Thomas Buckle (London: Printed for G. Peacock, 186?).

Anon., "Original Anecdotes and Remarks of Eminent Persons: Napoleon Buonaparte," *The Monthly Magazine and British Register* 17: 3 (May 1797), 373–8.

Anon., *Purity of Heart* (New York: Oram and Mott, 1818).

Anon., *Reminiscences of an Old Draper*, ed. William H. Ablett (London: S. Low, Marston, Searle & Rivington, 1876).

Anon., Review of *Camilla*, by Frances Burney, *Analytical Review* 24 (August 1796), 142–248.

Anon., Review of *Camilla*, by Frances Burney, *British Critic* 8 (November 1796), 527–36.

Anon., Review of *Camilla*, by Frances Burney, *Monthly Review* 2: 21 (October 1796), 156–63.

Anon., Review of *Cecilia*, by Frances Burney, *Spectator* 55 (6 January 1883), 18–19.

Anon., Review of *Liber Amoris*, by William Hazlitt, *Examiner* (May 11, 1823), 313–15.

Anon., Review of *A Series of Plays*, by Joanna Baillie, *The Edinburgh Review* IV (July 1803), 269–86.

Appleby, Joyce, "Ideology and Theory: The Tension between Political and Economic Liberalism in Seventeenth-Century England," *The American Historical Review*, 81: 3 (June 1976), 499–515.

Arendt, Hannah, *On Revolution* (London: Penguin Books, 1990).

Armstrong, Nancy, *Desire and Domestic Fiction: A Political History of the Novel* (Oxford: Oxford University Press, 1987).

Ash, Russell, *Sir Edward Burne–Jones* (New York: Abrams, 1933).

Ashton, John, *The History of Gambling in England* (Chicago: Herbert Stone, 1899).

Atkins, John, *Sex in Literature*, 4 vols., vol. IV (New York: Riverrun Press, 1982).

Baillie, Joanna, *Dramas*, 3 vols. (London: Longman, 1836).

—, *The Dramatic and Poetical Works* (1851) (New York: Georg Olms Verlag, 1976).

—, *The Dramatic and Poetical Works of Joanna Baillie*, 2nd edn (London, 1853).

—, *A Series of Plays* (1798), (rpt. Oxford: Woodstock Books, 1990).

—, *A Series of Plays: in which it is attempted to delineate the stronger passions of the mind*, 3rd edn, 3 vols., vol. II (London: Longman, 1806).

Barker-Benfield, G. J., *The Culture of Sensibility* (Chicago: University of Chicago Press, 1992).

Batchen, Geoffrey, *Burning with Desire: The Conception of Photography* (London: MIT Press, 1997).

Bate, Walter Jackson, *Coleridge* (Cambridge, Mass.: Harvard University Press, 1987).

—, *John Keats* (Cambridge: Harvard University Press, 1963).

Bates, Catherine, *The Rhetoric of Courtship in Elizabethan Language and Literature* (Cambridge: Cambridge University Press, 1992).

Baudrillard, Jean, *Selected Writings*, ed. Mark Poster (Stanford: Stanford University Press, 1988).

Baynes, W., *Catalogue of Richardson's Collection of English Portraits . . . as described in Granger's Biographical History of England* (London: W. Baynes, 1792–9).

Benjamin, Walter, *Illuminations*, ed. Hannah Arendt, trans. Harry Zohn (New York: Schocken, 1969).

Bergler, Edmund, *The Psychology of Gambling* (New York: Hill and Wang, 1957).

Bermingham, Ann, *Landscape and Ideology: The English Rustic Tradition, 1740–1860* (Berkeley: University of California Press, 1986).

—, "The Picturesque and Ready-to-Wear Femininity," in Stephen Copley and Peter Garside, eds., *The Poetics of the Picturesque* (Cambridge: Cambridge University Press, 1994), 81–119.

Bersani, Leo, *The Freudian Body* (New York: Columbia University Press, 1986).

Birken, Lawrence, *Consuming Desire: Sexual Science and the Emergence of a Culture of Abundance 1871–1914* (Ithaca: Cornell University Press, 1988).

Blake, William, *The Marriage of Heaven and Hell* (Oxford: Oxford University Press, 1975).

Bockemühl, Michael, *J. M. W. Turner: The World of Light and Colour*, trans. Michael Claridge (Cologne: Taschen, 1993).

Borsay, Peter, *The English Urban Renaissance: Culture and Society in the Provincial Town, 1660–1770* (Oxford: Clarendon Press, 1989).

Bowlby, Rachel, *Just Looking: Consumer Culture in Dreiser, Gissing and Zola* (New York: Methuen, 1985).

Bowles, John, *Thoughts on the Late General Election. As Demonstrative of the Progress of Jacobinism*, 2nd edn (London: G. Woodfall, 1802).

Brenner, Reuven, and Gabrielle Brenner, *Gambling and Speculation* (Cambridge: Cambridge University Press, 1990).

Brewer, John, and Roy Porter, *Consumption and the World of Goods* (New York: Routledge, 1993).

Bromwich, David, *Hazlitt: The Mind of a Critic* (Oxford: Oxford University Press, 1983).

Brown, Laura, *Alexander Pope* (Oxford: Basil Blackwell, 1985).

—, *Ends of Empire: Women and Ideology in Early Eighteenth-Century English Literature* (Ithaca: Cornell University Press, 1993).

Burke, Edmund, "An Appeal from the New to the Old Whigs," in *The Works of Edmund Burke*, 6 vols., vol. V (London: Oxford University Press, 1906).

—, *A Philosophical Enquiry into the Origin of Our Ideas of the Sublime and Beautiful* (London: Rivington, 1812).

—, *Reflections on the Revolution in France* (New York: Anchor Books, 1973).

Burne-Jones, Georgiana, *Memorials of Edward Burne-Jones*, 2 vols. (New York: Macmillan, 1906).

Burney, Frances, *Camilla*, ed. Edward and Lillian Bloom (New York: Oxford University Press, 1983).

—, *Cecilia*, ed. Peter Sabor and Margaret Doody (Oxford: Oxford University Press, 1988).

—, *Evelina*, ed. Edward and Lillian Bloom (Oxford: Oxford University Press, 1968).

—, *The Wanderer*, ed. Margaret Doody, Robert Mack, and Peter Sabor (Oxford: Oxford University Press, 1991).

Burroughs, Catherine, "English Romantic Women Writers and Theatre Theory: Joanna Baillie's Prefaces to the *Plays on the Passions*," in Carol Shiner Wilson and Joel Haefner, eds., *Re-Visioning Romanticism: British Women Writers, 1776–1837* (Philadelphia: University of Pennsylvania Press, 1994), 274–96.

Bush, Douglas, *John Keats: His Life and Writings* (New York: Macmillan, 1966).

Butler, Judith, *The Psychic Life of Power: Theories in Subjection* (Stanford: Stanford University Press, 1997).

Butler, Marilyn, "Satire and the Images of Self in the Romantic Period: The Long Tradition of Hazlitt's *Liber Amoris*," in G. A. Rosso and Daniel P. Watkins, eds., *Spirits of Fire: English Romantic Writers and Contemporary Historical Methods* (Rutherford, N.J.: Associated University Presses, 1990), 153–69.

Campbell, Colin, *The Romantic Ethic and the Spirit of Modern Consumerism* (Oxford: Basil Blackwell, 1987).

Carhart, Margaret, *The Life and Work of Joanna Baillie* (New Haven: Yale University Press, 1923).

Carrier, James, *Gifts and Commodities: Exchange and Western Capitalism since 1700* (New York: Routledge, 1995).

Carswell, Donald, *Scott and His Circle* (New York: Doubleday, 1930).

Centlivre, Susannah, *The Basset-Table* (London: W. Feales, 1736).

Chandler, James, *England in 1819* (Chicago: University of Chicago Press, 1998).

Christensen, Jerome, *Coleridge's Blessed Machine of Language* (Ithaca: Cornell University Press, 1981).

—, *Lord Byron's Strength: Romantic Writing and Commercial Society* (Baltimore: Johns Hopkins University Press, 1993).

—, "The Symbol's Errant Allegory: Coleridge and His Critics," *ELH* 45 (1978), 640–59.

Christian, John, *The Pre-Raphaelites* (London: Tate Gallery, 1984).

Cleland, John, *Memoirs of a Woman of Pleasure*, ed. Peter Sabor (Oxford: Oxford University Press, 1986).

Cobbett, William, *Rural Rides*, ed. E. W. Martin (London: Macdonald, 1958).

Coleman, George (pseud.), *The Rodiad* (London: Cadell and Murray, 1810).

Coleridge, Samuel Taylor, *Coleridge: Poetical Works*, ed. Ernest Hartley Coleridge (Oxford: Oxford University Press, 1969).

—, *Collected Letters of Samuel Taylor Coleridge*, 6 vols., vol. IV, *1815–1819*, ed. Earl Leslie Griggs (Oxford: Clarendon Press, 1959).

—, *Lay Sermons*, in *The Collected Works of Samuel Taylor Coleridge*, 16 vols., vol. VI, ed. R. J. White (Princeton: Princeton University Press, 1972).

—, *Lectures 1808–1819 on Literature*, in *The Collected Works of Samuel Taylor Coleridge*, 16 vols., vol. V, Part II, ed. R. A. Foakes (Princeton: Princeton University Press, 1987).

—, *The Notebooks of Samuel Taylor Coleridge*, 5 vols., vol. I, *1794–1804*, ed. Kathleen Coburn (Princeton: Princeton University Press, 1957).

—, *The Notebooks of Samuel Taylor Coleridge*, 5 vols., vol. III, *1808–1819*, ed. Kathleen Coburn (Princeton: Princeton University Press, 1973).

—, *The Notebooks of Samuel Taylor Coleridge*, 5 vols., vol. IV, *1819–1826*, ed. Kathleen Coburn and Merton Christensen (Princeton: Princeton University Press, 1990).

—, *The Philosophical Lectures of Samuel Taylor Coleridge*, ed. Kathleen Coburn (New York: Philosophical Library, 1949).

—, *Shorter Works and Fragments*, in *The Collected Works of Samuel Taylor Coleridge*, 16 vols., vol. XI, part I, ed. H. J. Jackson and J. R. de J. Jackson (Princeton: Princeton University Press, 1995).

—, *Six Lectures on Revealed Religion*, in *The Collected Works of Samuel Taylor Coleridge*, 16 vols., vol. I, ed. Lewis Patton and Peter Mann (Princeton: Princeton University Press, 1971).

Colley, Linda, *Britons: Forging the Nation 1707–1837* (New Haven: Yale University Press, 1992).

Constable, John, *John Constable's Discourses*, ed. R. B. Beckett (Ipswich: Suffolk Records Society, 1970).

Copeland, Edward, *Women Writing about Money: Women's Fiction in England, 1790–1820* (Cambridge: Cambridge University Press, 1995).

Cooke, Michael, "The Manipulation of Space in Coleridge's Poetry," in Geoffrey Hartman, ed., *New Perspectives on Coleridge and Wordsworth* (New York: Columbia University Press, 1972), 165–94.

Cox, Jeffrey, *In the Shadows of Romance: Romantic Tragic Drama in Germany, England, and France* (Athens: Ohio University Press, 1987).

Crary, Jonathan, *Techniques of the Observer: On Vision and Modernity in the Nineteenth Century* (London: MIT Press, 1990).

Cummings, Robert, "Keats's Melancholy in the Temple of Delight," *Keats-Shelley Journal* 36 (1987), 50–62.

Curran, Stuart, "Romantic Poetry: The 'I' Altered," in Anne K. Mellor, ed., *Romanticism and Feminism* (Bloomington: Indiana University Press, 1988), 185–207.

Dabydeen, David, *Hogarth, Walpole, and Commercial Britain* (London: Hansib, 1987).

Daniels, Stephen, *Humphry Repton: Landscape Gardening and the Geography of Georgian England* (New Haven: Yale University Press, 1999).

—, "The Political Iconography of Woodland in Later Georgian England," in Denis Cosgrove and Stephen Daniels, eds., *The Iconography of Landscape* (Cambridge: Cambridge University Press, 1988), 43–82.

Davidoff, Leonore, *Worlds Between: Historical Perspectives on Gender and Class* (New York: Routledge, 1995).

Davidson, Arnold, "Sex and the Emergence of Sexuality," in Davidson, *The Emergence of Sexuality: Historical Epistemology and the Formation of Concepts* (Cambridge, Mass.: Harvard University Press, 2001), 30–65.

Davis, Dorothy, *Fairs, Shops, and Supermarkets: A History of English Shopping* (Toronto: University of Toronto Press, 1966).

Defoe, Daniel, *Defoe's Review*, ed. Arthur Wellesley Secord, 22 vols. (New York: Columbia University Press, 1938).

—, *Eleven Opinions of Mr. Harley* (May 14, 1711).

—, *Roxana* ed. David Blewett (London: Penguin, 1982).

Deleuze, Gilles, "Coldness and Cruelty," in Deleuze, *Masochism* (New York: Zone Books, 1989).

Doody, Margaret, *Frances Burney: The Life in the Works* (New Brunswick: Rutgers University Press, 1988).

Eagleton, Terry, *The Ideology of the Aesthetic* (Oxford: Basil Blackwell, 1990).

Elkins, James, *The Poetics of Perspective* (Ithaca: Cornell University Press, 1994).

Epstein, Julia, *The Iron Pen: Frances Burney and the Politics of Women's Writing* (Madison: University of Wisconsin Press, 1989).

Ferguson, Frances, *Solitude and the Sublime: Romanticism and the Aesthetics of Individuation* (New York: Routledge, 1992).

Fitzgerald, Penelope, *Edward Burne-Jones: A Biography* (London: Michael Joseph, 1975).

Fizer, Irene, "The Name of the Daughter: Identity and Incest in Evelina," in Patricia Yaeger and Beth Kowaleski-Wallace, eds., *Refiguring the Father: New Feminist Readings of Patriarchy* (Carbondale: Southern Illinois University Press, 1989), 78–107.

Fletcher, Angus, "Positive Negation: Threshold, Sequence, and Personification in Coleridge," in Geoffrey Hartman, ed., *New Perspectives on Coleridge and Wordsworth* (New York, Columbia University Press, 1972), 133–64.

Fordyce, David, *The Elements of Moral Philosophy* (London: Dodsley, 1754).

Foucault, Michel, *History of Sexuality*, 3 vols., vol. 1, trans. Robert Hurley (New York: Vintage Books, 1980).

—, *The Order of Things* (New York: Vintage, 1973).

Fox Talbot, William Henry, *The Pencil of Nature* (London: Longman, Brown, Green, and Longmans, 1844).

—, "Some Account of the Art of Photogenic Drawing," in Beaumont Newhall, ed., *Photography: Essays & Images* (New York: Museum of Modern Art, 1980), 23–31.

Freeman, Barbara Claire, *The Feminine Sublime: Gender and Excess in Women's Fiction* (Berkeley: University of California Press, 1995).

Freud, Sigmund, "Dostoevsky and Parricide," in *The Standard Edition of the Complete Psychological Works of Sigmund Freud*, 24 vols., vol. XXI, trans. and ed. James Strachey with Anna Freud (London: Hogarth Press, 1961), 177–94.

—, "The Economic Problem in Masochism," in Freud, *General Psychological Theory*, ed. Philip Rieff (New York: Macmillan, 1963).

—, "Mourning and Melancholia," in *The Standard Edition of the Complete Psychological Works of Sigmund Freud*, 24 vols., vol. XIV, trans. and ed. James Strachey with Anna Freud (London: Hogarth Press, 1957), 237–58.

Friedman, Geraldine, "The Erotics of Interpretation in Keats's 'Ode on a Grecian Urn': Pursuing the Feminine," *Studies in Romanticism* 32 (1993), 225–43.

Gallagher, Catherine, *Nobody's Story: The Vanishing Acts of Women Writers in the Marketplace, 1670–1820* (Berkeley: University of California Press, 1994).

Galperin, William, *The Return of the Visible in British Romanticism* (Baltimore: Johns Hopkins University Press, 1993).

Gilpin, William, *Essays on Picturesque Beauty* (London: R. Blamire, 1794).

Girouard, Mark, *Life in the English Country House* (New Haven: Yale University Press, 1978).

Gleckner, Robert, and Gerald Enscoe, eds., *Romanticism: Points of View*, 2nd edn (Detroit: Wayne State University Press, 1975).

Goodman, Dena, "Regendering the Republic of Letters: Private Association in the Public Sphere, 1780–1789," in Dario Castiglione and Lesley Sharpe, eds., *Shifting the Boundaries: Transformation of the Languages of Public and Private in the Eighteenth Century* (Exeter: University of Exeter Press, 1995), 22–40.

Gore, Alan, and Ann Gore, *The History of English Interiors* (Oxford: Phaidon, 1991).

Graham, Peter, *Don Juan and Regency England* (Charlottesville: University Press of Virginia, 1990).

Haydon, Benjamin Robert, *The Diary of Benjamin Robert Haydon*, 5 vols., vol. II, ed. Willard B. Pope (Cambridge, Mass.: Harvard University Press, 1960).

Hays, Mary, *The Memoirs of Emma Courtney*, ed. Eleanor Ty (Oxford: Oxford University Press, 1996).

Hazlitt, William, *The Complete Works of William Hazlitt*, 21 vols., ed. P. P. Howe, (London: J. M. Dent and Sons, 1930–4).

—, *Liber Amoris or The New Pygmalion*, intro. Michael Neve (London: Hogarth Press, 1985).

—, *Table-Talk*, ed. William Carew Hazlitt (London: George Bell & Sons, 1900).

—, *William Hazlitt: Selected Writings*, ed. Jon Cook (Oxford: Oxford University Press, 1991).

Hegel, G. W. F., *Phenomenology of Spirit*, trans. A. V. Miller, foreword J. N. Findlay (Oxford: Oxford University Press, 1977).

Hemans, Felicia, *Records of Woman, With Other Poems*, ed. Paula R. Feldman (Lexington: University Press of Kentucky, 1999).

Hertz, Neil, *The End of the Line: Essays on Psychoanalysis and the Sublime* (New York: Columbia University Press, 1985).

Herzog, Don, *Happy Slaves: A Critique of Consent Theory* (Chicago: University of Chicago Press, 1989).

Hinton, Laura, *The Perverse Gaze of Sympathy: Sadomasochistic Sentiments from "Clarissa" to "Rescue 911"* (Albany: SUNY Press, 1999).

Hirschman, Albert O., *The Passions and the Interests: Political Arguments for Capitalism before Its Triumph* (Princeton: Princeton University Press, 1977).

Holmes, Richard, *Coleridge: Darker Reflections, 1804–1834* (New York: Pantheon, 1998).

Hughes, Alan, "Art and Eighteenth-Century Acting Style, Part III: Passions," *Theatre Notebook* 41: 3 (1987), 128–39.

Hume, David, *An Inquiry Concerning the Principles of Morals* (New York: Macmillan, 1957).

Hunt, John Dixon, *The Figure in the Landscape: Poetry, Painting, and Gardening during the Eighteenth Century* (Baltimore: Johns Hopkins University Press, 1976).

Hunt, Lynn, *Politics, Culture, and Class in the French Revolution* (Berkeley: University of California Press, 1984).

Hyde, Ralph, *Panoramania!: The Art and Entertainment of the "All-Embracing" View* (London: Trefoil Publications in association with the Barbican Art Gallery, 1988).

Ingrassia, Catherine, *Authorship, Commerce, and Gender in Early Eighteenth-Century England* (Cambridge: Cambridge University Press, 1998).

Jenkins, Elizabeth, *Lady Caroline Lamb* (London: Victor Gollancz, 1932).

Johnson, Claudia, *Equivocal Beings: Politics, Gender, and Sentimentality in the 1790s* (Chicago: University of Chicago Press, 1995).

Jones, Elizabeth, "Keats in the Suburbs," *Keats-Shelley Journal* 45 (1996), 23–43.

Jones, Stanley, *Hazlitt: A Life* (Oxford: Oxford University Press, 1991).

Kant, Immanuel, *Critique of Pure Reason*, trans. and ed. Paul Guyer and Allen Wood (Cambridge: Cambridge University Press, 1998).

Kavanaugh, Thomas, *Enlightenment and the Shadows of Chance* (Baltimore: Johns Hopkins University Press, 1993).

Keach, William, *Arbitrary Power: Romanticism, Language, Politics* (Princeton: Princeton University Press, 2004).

Keats, John, *Complete Poems*, ed. Jack Stillinger (Cambridge, Mass.: Harvard University Press, 1978).

—, *Letters of John Keats*, ed. Robert Gittings (Oxford: Oxford University Press, 1970).

Kelley, Theresa, "Keats, Ekphrasis, and History," in Nicholas Roe, ed., *Keats and History* (Cambridge: Cambridge University Press, 1995), 212–37.

—, *Reinventing Allegory* (Cambridge: Cambridge University Press, 1997).

Kinnaird, John, *William Hazlitt: Critic of Power* (New York: Columbia University Press, 1978).

Klancher, John, *The Making of English Reading Audiences, 1790–1832* (Madison: University of Wisconsin Press, 1987).

Kojève, Alexandre, *Introduction to the Reading of Hegel: Lectures on the Phenomenology of Spirit*, assembled by Raymond Queneau, ed. Alan Bloom, trans. James Nichols, Jr. (Ithaca: Cornell University Press, 1969).

Kowaleski-Wallace, Elizabeth, *Consuming Subjects: Women, Shopping, and Business in the Eighteenth Century* (New York: Columbia University Press, 1997).

Krafft-Ebing, R. von, *Psychopathia Sexualis*, trans. F. J. Rebman, from the 12th German edn (New York: Physicians and Surgeons Book Company, 1926).

Lackington, James, *Memoirs of the First Forty-Five Years* (London: Whittaker, Treacher, and Arnot, 1830).

Lamb, Caroline, *Glenarvon*, ed. Frances Wilson (London: J. M. Dent, 1995).

Lamb, Charles, *Elia and the Last Essays of Elia*, ed. Jonathan Bate (Oxford: Oxford University Press, 1987).

—, ed., *Specimens of English Dramatic Poets Who Lived about the Time of Shakespeare* (London: Henry G. Bohn, 1854).

Landon, Letitia Elizabeth, *Selected Writings*, ed. Jerome McGann and Daniel Riess (Peterborough: Broadview Press, 1997).

Laplanche, Jean, *Life and Death in Psychoanalysis*, trans. Jeffrey Mehlman (Baltimore: Johns Hopkins University Press, 1976).

Lavater, Johann Casper, *Essays on Physiognomy*, trans. Henry Hunter (London: Printed for John Murray, 1789).

Leavis, F. R., *Revaluation: Tradition and Development in English Poetry* (New York: Norton, 1963).

Leslie, Doris, *This for Caroline* (London: Heinemann, 1964).

Levinson, Marjorie, *Keats's Life of Allegory: The Origins of a Style* (Oxford: Basil Blackwell, 1988).

Lickbarrow, Isabella, *Poetical Effusions* (London: J. Richardson, 1814).

Lisle, Fortunée de, *Burne-Jones* (London: Methuen, 1904).

Liu, Alan, *Wordsworth: The Sense of History* (Stanford: Stanford University Press, 1989).

Lonsdale, Roger, ed., *Eighteenth-Century Women Poets* (Oxford: Oxford University Press, 1990).

Loudon, John Claudius, *The Suburban Gardener, and Villa Companion* (London: Longman, Orme, Brown, Green and Longmans; Edinburgh: W. Black, 1832).

Lynch, Deidre, *The Economy of Character* (Chicago: University of Chicago Press, 1998).

Lyotard, Jean-François, *The Differend: Phrases in Dispute*, trans. Georges Van Den Abbeele (Minneapolis: University of Minnesota Press, 1988).

MacKendrick, Karmen, *Counterpleasures* (Albany: SUNY Press, 1999).

Mackie, Erin, *Market à la Mode: Fashion, Commodity, and Gender in "The Tatler" and "The Spectator"* (Baltimore: Johns Hopkins University Press, 1997).

Mann, Paul, *Masocriticism* (Albany: SUNY Press, 1999).

Marchand, Leslie A., ed., *Byron's Letters and Journals* (Cambridge, Mass.: Belknap Press, 1974).

Marcus, Stephen, *The Other Victorians* (New York: Basic Books, 1964).

Martineau, Jane, ed., *Victorian Fairy Painting* (London: Holberton, 1998).

Marx, Karl, *Capital*, 2 vols., vol. I, ed. Frederick Engels, trans. Samuel Moore and Edward Aveling (NewYork: International Publishers, 1987).

Mayr, Otto, *Authority, Liberty, and Automatic Machinery in Early Modern Europe* (Baltimore: Johns Hopkins University Press, 1986).

McClintock, Anne, *Imperial Leather: Race, Gender and Sexuality in the Imperial Contest* (New York: Routledge, 1995).

McCracken, Grant, *Culture and Consumption: New Approaches to the Symbolic Character of Consumer Goods and Activities* (Bloomington: Indiana University Press, 1988).

McGann, Jerome, ed., *Byron* (Oxford: Oxford University Press, 1986).

McKendrick, Neil, John Brewer, and J. H. Plumb, eds., *The Birth of a Consumer Society: The Commercialization of Eighteenth-Century England* (Bloomington: Indiana University Press, 1982).

McKeon, Michael, *The Origins of the English Novel 1600–1740* (Baltimore: Johns Hopkins University Press, 1987).

Meibom, Johann, *On the Use of Flogging in Venereal Affairs* (1639)(Chester: Import Publishing, 1961).

Meisel, Martin, *Realizations: Narrative, Pictorial, and Theatrical Arts in Nineteenth-Century England* (Princeton: Princeton University Press, 1983).

Mellor, Anne, *Mothers of the Nation: Women's Political Writing in England, 1780–1830* (Bloomington: Indiana University Press, 2000).

—, *Romanticism and Gender* (New York: Routledge, 1993).

Meyer, Donald, *Sex and Power: The Rise of Women in America, Russia, Sweden, and Italy* (Middletown, Conn.: Wesleyan University Press, 1987).

Michaels, Walter Benn, *The Gold Standard and the Logic of Naturalism* (Berkeley: University of California Press, 1987).

Millar, John, *The Origin of the Distinction of Ranks* (1771), in *John Millar of Glasgow*, ed. W. C. Lehmann (Cambridge: Cambridge University Press, 1960).

Miller, Mark, *Philosophical Chaucer: Love, Sex, and Agency in the Canterbury Tales* (Cambridge: Cambridge University Press, 2004).

Mui, Hoh-Cheung, and Lorna Mui, *Shops and Shopkeeping in Eighteenth-Century England* (London: Routledge, 1989).

Mukerji, Chandra, "Reading and Writing with Nature: A Materialist Approach to French Formal Gardens," in John Brewer and Roy Porter, eds., *Consumption and the World of Goods* (London: Routledge, 1993), 439–61.

Mulcaire, Terry, "Public Credit; Or, the Feminization of Virtue in the Marketplace," *PMLA* 114:5 (October 1999), 1029–42.

Noyes, John, *The Mastery of Submission: Inventions of Masochism* (Ithaca: Cornell University Press, 1997).

Oettermann, Stephen, *The Panorama: History of a Mass Medium* (New York: Zone Books, 1997).

O'Neill, John, "The Productive Body: An Essay on the Work of Consumption," *Queen's Quarterly* 85 (Summer 1978), 221–30.

O'Rourke, James, *Keats's Odes and Contemporary Criticism* (Gainesville: University Press of Florida, 1998).

Ovid, *The Metamorphoses of Ovid*, trans. Allen Mandelbaum (New York: Harcourt Brace, 1993).

Ozouf, Mona, *Festivals and the French Revolution*, trans. Alan Sheridan (Cambridge, Mass.: Harvard University Press, 1988).

Paley, Morton, *Coleridge's Later Poetry* (New York: Oxford University Press, 1996).

Pascoe, Judith, *Romantic Theatricality: Gender, Poetry, and Spectatorship* (Ithaca: Cornell University Press, 1997).

Pateman, Carole, *The Sexual Contract* (Stanford: Stanford University Press, 1988).

Paulson, Ronald, *Hogarth*, 3 vols. (New Brunswick: Rutgers University Press, 1991).

Payne Knight, Richard, *The Landscape, a Didactic Poem* (London: W. Bulmer & Co., 1794).

Pettet, E. C., *On the Poetry of Keats* (Cambridge: Cambridge University Press, 1957).

Pocock, J. G. A., *Virtue, Commerce, and History* (Cambridge: Cambridge University Press, 1985).

Pointon, Marcia, *Hanging the Head: Portraiture and Social Formation in Eighteenth-Century England* (New Haven: Yale University Press, 1993).

Pope, Alexander, *The Rape of the Lock, an Heroi-Comical Poem*, in *Pope: Poetical Works*, ed. Herbert Davis (Oxford: Oxford University Press, 1978), 86–109.

Porter, Roy, "Making Faces: Physiognomy and Fashion in Eighteenth-Century England," *Etudes Anglaises* 4 (October–December 1985), 385–96.

Praz, Mario, *The Romantic Agony*, 2nd edn, trans. Angus Davidson (Oxford: Oxford University Press, 1970).

Price, Uvedale, *Essays on the Picturesque*, 3 vols. (London: J. Mawman, 1810).

Qvist, George, *John Hunter 1728–1793* (London: William Heinemann, 1981).

Reik, Theodor, *Masochism in Modern Man*, trans. Margaret Beigel and Gertrud Kurth (New York: Farrar, Straus and Co., 1941).

Renwick, W. L., *English Literature 1789–1815* (Oxford: Clarendon, 1963).

Repton, Humphry, *Fragments on the Theory and Practice of Landscape Gardening* (London: T. Bensley and Son, 1816).

—, *A Letter to Uvedale Price, Esq.* (London: printed for G. Nicol, 1794).

Rey, Roselyne, *The History of Pain*, trans. Louise Elliott Wallace, J. A. Cadden, and S. W. Cadden (Cambridge, Mass.: Harvard University Press, 1998).

Richards, Thomas, *The Commodity Culture of Victorian England: Advertising and Spectacle, 1851–1914* (Stanford: Stanford University Press, 1990).

Roche, Sophie von la, *Sophie in London, 1786*, ed. Clare Williams (London: J. Cope, 1933).

Rolfe, W. D. Ian, "Breaking the Great Chain of Being," in W. F. Bynum and Roy Porter, eds., *William Hunter and the Eighteenth-Century Medical World* (Cambridge: Cambridge University Press, 1985), 297–319.

Rosenthal, Michael, *Constable: The Painter and His Landscape* (New Haven: Yale University Press, 1983).

de Rougemont, Denis, *Love in the Western World* (Princeton: Princeton University Press, 1983).

Rousseau, Jean-Jacques, *The Confessions of Jean-Jacques Rousseau* (1781), trans. and ed. J. M. Cohen (London: Penguin, 1953).

—, *The Social Contract*, trans. Maurice Cranston (New York: Penguin, 1968).

Sacks, Peter, *The English Elegy: Studies in the Genre from Spenser to Yeats* (Baltimore: Johns Hopkins University Press, 1985).

Saumarez Smith, Charles, *Eighteenth-Century Decoration: Design and the Domestic Interior in England* (New York: Abrams, 1993).

Scarry, Elaine, *The Body in Pain: The Making and Unmaking of the World* (New York: Oxford University Press, 1985).

Schaaf, Larry J., *The Photographic Art of William Henry Fox Talbot* (Princeton: Princeton University Press, 2000).

Schiesari, Juliana, "The Face of Domestication: Physiognomy, Gender Politics, and Humanism's Others," in Margo Hendricks and Patricia Parker, eds., *Women, "Race," and Writing in the Early Modern Period* (London: Routledge, 1994), 55–70.

—, *The Gendering of Melancholia: Feminism, Psychoanalysis, and the Symbolics of Loss in Renaissance Literature* (Ithaca: Cornell University Press, 1992).

Schivelbusch, Wolfgang, *Disenchanted Night: The Industrialization of Light in the Nineteenth Century*, trans. Angela Davies (Berkeley: University of California Press, 1988).

—, *The Railway Journey: The Industrialization of Time and Space in the Nineteenth Century* (Berkeley: University of California Press, 1986).

Schmiechen, James, and Kenneth Carls, *The British Market Hall: A Social and Architectural History* (New Haven: Yale University Press, 1999).

Scott, Walter, *The Miscellaneous Prose Works of Sir Walter Scott*, 28 vols., vol. VI, (Edinburgh: Robert Cadell, 1834).

Scrivener, Michael, *Poetry and Reform: Periodical Verse from the English Democratic Press 1792–1824* (Detroit: Wayne State University Press, 1992).

Shaftesbury, Anthony, Earl of, *Characteristics of Men, Manners, Opinions, Times*, 2 vols., ed. John Robertson (rpt. Indianapolis: Bobbs-Merrill, 1964).

Shammas, Carole, *The Pre-Industrial Consumer in England and America* (Oxford: Clarendon Press, 1990).

Shelley, Mary, *Frankenstein*, ed. Maurice Hindle (New York: Penguin, 1985).

Shelley, Percy Bysshe, *Shelley's Poetry and Prose*, ed. Donald Reiman and Sharon Powers (New York: Norton, 1977).

Sherman, Sandra, *Finance and Fictionality in the Early Eighteenth Century: Accounting for Defoe* (Cambridge: Cambridge University Press, 1996).

Silverman, Kaja, *Male Subjectivity at the Margins* (New York: Routledge, 1992).

Smith, Adam, *An Inquiry into the Nature and Causes of the Wealth of Nations*, 2 vols., ed. R. H. Campbell and A. S. Skinner (Oxford: Oxford University Press, 1976).

—, *The Theory of Moral Sentiments*, ed. A. L. Macfie and D. D. Raphael (Indianapolis: Liberty Classics, 1982).

Smith, Charlotte, *The Poems of Charlotte Smith*, ed. Stuart Curran (Oxford: Oxford University Press, 1993).

Soderholm, James, "Lady Caroline Lamb: Byron's Miniature Writ Large," *Keats-Shelley Journal* 40 (1991), 24–46.

Southey, Robert, *Letters from England* (London: The Cresset Press, 1951).

Sperry, Stuart, *Keats the Poet* (Princeton: Princeton University Press, 1973).

Straub, Kristina, *Divided Fictions: Fanny Burney and Feminine Strategy* (Lexington: University Press of Kentucky, 1987).

Summerson, John, *Architecture in Britain, 1530–1830*, 9th edn (New Haven: Yale University Press, 1993).

—, David Watkin, and G.-Tilman Mellinghoff, *John Soane* (London: Academy Editions, 1983).

—, *Sir John Soane* (London: Art and Technics, 1952).

Thompson, James, *Models of Value: Eighteenth-Century Political Economy and the Novel* (Durham: Duke University Press, 1996).

Traxler, Janina, "Courtly and Uncourtly Love in the *Prose Tristan*," in Donald Maddox and Sara Sturm-Maddox, eds., *Literary Aspects of Courtly Culture* (Cambridge: D. S. Brewer, 1994), 161–9.

Trilling, Lionel, *Freud and the Crisis of Our Culture* (Boston: Beacon Press, 1955).

Uglow, Jennifer, *Hogarth: A Life and a World* (London: Faber and Faber, 1997).

Van Sant, Ann Jessie, *Eighteenth-Century Sensibility and the Novel* (Cambridge: Cambridge University Press, 1993).

Vasari, Giorgio, *The Great Masters*, trans. Gaston de Vere, ed. Michael Sonino (New York: Park Lane, 1986).

Walker Bynum, Caroline, *Fragmentation and Redemption: Essays on Gender and the Human Body in Medieval Religion* (New York: Zone Books, 1992).

—, *Holy Feast and Holy Fast: The Religious Significance of Food to Medieval Women* (Berkeley: University of California Press, 1987).

Walpole, Horace, *The History of the Modern Taste in Gardening*, in *Horace Walpole: Gardenist*, ed. Isabel Chase (Princeton: Princeton University Press, 1943).

Watkins, Daniel, "Historical Amnesia and Patriarchal Morality in Keats's 'Ode on a Grecian Urn,'" in G. A. Rosso and Daniel Watkins, eds., *Spirits of Fire: English Romantic Writers and Contemporary Historical Methods* (Rutherford, N.J.: Associated University Presses, 1990), 240–59.

Watson, Nicola, *Revolution and the Form of the British Novel 1790–1825* (Oxford: Clarendon Press, 1994).

Weiskel, Thomas, *The Romantic Sublime* (Baltimore: Johns Hopkins University Press, 1976).

Williams, Linda, "Reading and Submission: Feminine Masochism and Feminist Criticism," *New Formations* 7 (1989), 9–19.

Wilson, Frances, "Caroline Lamb and Her Critics," in Wilson's edition of *Glenarvon* (London: Everyman, 1995).

—, "'An Exaggerated Woman': The Melodramas of Lady Caroline Lamb," in Wilson, ed., *Byromania: Portraits of the Artist in Nineteenth- and Twentieth-Century Culture* (Basingstoke: Macmillan, 1999), 195–220.

Wingrove, Elizabeth, *Rousseau's Republican Romance* (Princeton: Princeton University Press, 2000).

Wolin, Sheldon, *Tocqueville between Two Worlds* (Princeton: Princeton University Press, 2001).

Wollstonecraft, Mary, *Vindication of the Rights of Woman* (New York: Penguin, 1975).

Wordsworth, William, and S. T. Coleridge, *Lyrical Ballads*, ed. R. L. Brett and A. R. Jones (New York: Methuen, 1963).

—, *The Prelude: 1799, 1805, 1850*, ed. Jonathan Wordsworth, M. H. Abrams and Stephen Gill (New York: Norton, 1979).

Zeitlin, Froma, "On Ravishing Urns: Keats in His Tradition," in Lynn A. Higgins and Brenda Silver, eds., *Rape and Representation* (New York: Columbia University Press, 1991), 278–302.

Žižek, Slavoj, *Enjoy Your Symptom* (New York: Routledge, 1992).

Index

289

CAMBRIDGE STUDIES IN ROMANTICISM

FOUNDING EDITOR
MARILYN BUTLER, *University of Oxford*

GENERAL EDITOR
JAMES CHANDLER, *University of Chicago*

CPSIA information can be obtained at www.ICGtesting.com
Printed in the USA
LVOW01*2317071013

355884LV00003B/9/P